Ritual, Secrecy, and Civil Society

Also from Westphalia Press

westphaliapress.org

Ritual, Secrecy, and Civil Society

Volume 4, No. 2/ Volume 5, No. 1

Special Issue on Latin America

Guillermo de los Reyes, Special Issue Editor

WESTPHALIA PRESS
An imprint of Policy Studies Organization

Ritual, Secrecy, and Civil Society: Volume 4, No. 2/ Volume 5, No. 1
Special Issue on Latin America

Westphalia Press
An imprint of Policy Studies Organization
1527 New Hampshire Ave., NW
Washington, D.C. 20036
info@ipsonet.org

ISBN-13: 978-1-63391-628-9
ISBN-10: 1633916286

Cover design by Jeffrey Barnes:
jbarnes.design

Daniel Gutierrez-Sandoval, Executive Director
PSO and Westphalia Press

Updated material and comments on this edition
can be found at the Westphalia Press website:
www.westphaliapress.org

ABSTRACTS RITUAL JOURNAL:
SPECIAL ISSUE ON LATIN AMERICA
Special Editor: Guillermo de los Reyes

Table of Contents

Editorial Note, Special Issue on Freemasonry in Latin America

Guest Editor: Dr. Guillermo de los Reyes Heredia,
University of Houston

First of all, I would like to thank Pierre Mollier Editor in Chief of *Ritual, Secrecy, and Civil Society* for inviting me to put together a special issue on Freemasonry in Latin America. During the last decades, the study of Freemasonry in Latin America has evolved. A group of scholars for different parts of the Hispanic speaking world have explored the subject of Freemasonry from an academic perspective. It is important to mention that Professor José Antonio Ferrer Benimeli, who is the leading authority on Spanish Freemasonry and founder of the Center for Historical Research on Spanish Freemasonry (CEHME) at the University of Zaragoza, has been pivotal in this endeavor. The CEHME was created over three decades ago to promote the study and scientific development and dissemination of Masonic studies. Suich center has also created research groups, organize conferences and symposiums, and teach courses on Freemasonry in diverse Spanish and Latin American universities. Inspired and with the mentorship of the CEHME, a group of scholars (many of them who are contributors to this special issue) started a conference over a decade ago, dedicated to the study of Latin American and Caribbean Freemasonry. Furthermore, after this initiative, they created the first academic journal on Freemasonry studies in Latin America: *REHMLAC+. Revista de Estudios Históricos de la Masonería Latinoamericana y Caribeña* housed at the Universidad de Costa Rica. Some of the articles here were originally published in Spanish at *REHMLAC+* and translated into English with the purpose to make them available for a wider audience. So, I would like to thank the *REHMLAC+*'s team for their generosity.

The purpose of this special issue is to shed light on the much needed and much overlooked study of Latin American Freemasonry particularly outside Spain and Latin America. I hope that the various articles selected here advance research not only on the study of Latin American Freemasonry, but also on the region's intellectual cultural history and on the ongoing interdisciplinary debate on Freemasonry and its contributions throughout history. Most of the existing work outside Freemasonry studies does not consider the influence and the role that the various Masonic discourses have had in the formation of a national discourse, as well as, a literary cannon, and if these influences are mentioned it is only *en passant*. Part of the problem is that many scholars believe that there is not enough material available on Latin American Freemasonry. However, as you will witness here, the tremendous research done by these scholars fills that gap by spotlighting and using archival original research from Masonic and non-Masonic archives, exploring new evidence on Freemasonry in Latin America.

Seven articles were selected to be part of the special issue. The feature articles is "An Introduction to the Historiography of Latin American Freemasonry" by José Antonio Ferrer Benimeli, founder and honorary president of the CEHME. In his article Ferrer Benimeli studies the historiography of Latin American Masonic that is undergoing a methodological regeneration thus the author adds new research to the references outlined in previous publications. Ferrer Benimeli's article is divided into two parts. The first one discusses by Latin American country the principal works on the History of Freemasonry that have been published. The comment is based on both the works that offer a scientifically acceptable level (minority) and those without it (the majority). The second part is devoted to reporting the references. The author notes that his article is not a comprehensive study rather a point of reference on completing this historiography will continue in the future.

Eduardo Torres Cuevas in "Freemasonry in Cuba in the Nineteenth Century" analyzes the development of Cuban Freemasonry during the 19th century and its relations with the principal political, economic and cultural processes of the Island, in particular with those of emancipation and of the arrival of liberal, civic, lay and secular ideas. Torres Cuevas article also serves as state of question about what has been written in respect to this specific object of study. Another contribution entitled, "Notes on the "Symbolic Name" in Latin America" by Yvan Pozuelos inquires, why was the use of symbolic names exclusive of Spanish-American Freemasonry? Was the symbolic name a use originated by the Masons? When and why did this custom spread? So, in order to answer these questions Pozuelos studies the Asturian masonic community in Latin America (since it was one of the most important groups of Spanish immigrants), analyzing the Hispanic American symbolic names of Asturian Mason residents in Hispanic America.

Felipe Santiago del Solar "On the Origins of Freemasonry in Chile" analyzes the process of implantation of the Freemasonry in Chile with an emphasis on routes of entry of this kind of sociability and in the social contexts that have enhanced its institutionalization. Del Solar focuses on two periods: independence, where the Military Freemasonry had some presence but did not achieve its establishment, and the period of liberal revolts in the middle of 19th century where it produces its final institutionalization. In "Freemasonry as a Center of Political Action in Independent Mexico, 1821-1830", María Eugenia Vázquez Semadeni shows how some of the internal practices of Freemasonry, the masonic bodies, their channels of communication and the loyalties they generated were taken advantage of by the *Yorkinos* to establish a center of political action, that is to say, a space where agreements were reached and which enabled them to undertake initiatives to achieve, preserve, and exercise political power. I will show that this was in part possible due to the institutional structure arising from the establishment of the republican, representative and federal system, but also due to the fact that the *Yorkinos* created a discourse about the political system, themselves, and their opponents which for a time endowed their political actions with considerable legitimacy.

"Freemasonry, Civil Society, and the Public Sphere in Central America (1865–1876)" by Ricardo Martínez Esquivel argues that due to the specific characteristics of Latin American modernity, Freemasonry in Central America be regarded more as a process of socio-historical construction than as an analytical category. This article also addresses the nature of the relationships between modernity and the establishment and evolution of Freemasonry in Central America during the initial period of its active development (1865–1876). The last article of the collection, "Freemasonry, Control and Other Fraternal Loyalties: the Rescue of Porfirio Díaz by a Masonic Brother," by Guillermo de los Reyes Heredia explores the role that Porfirio Díaz played in Freemasonry and his relationship with such an institution, analyzing one of the stories that proves that Díaz benefited from his Masonic affiliation before he was president of Mexico. This story tells how Díaz managed to smuggle himself into Mexico with the help of a brother Mason in 1876, after his brief exile in New Orleans aboard the steamship, "City of Havana". In addition, De los Reyes Heredia studies how Díaz promoted the unification of the Scottish Rite lodges in an institution called The Symbolic Grand Diet. The primary reason why Díaz promoted such unification, as stated in this article was to carry out his plan of national reconciliation. Díaz knew he had to gain control of Freemasonry to avoid future confrontations and trouble. He didn't want anybody to interfere with his governmental policy of order and progress. Therefore, the dictator always made sure that neither masonry nor any other institution that had substantial influence in society were out of his control.

In summary, this special issue on Latin American Freemasonry shows that there is a robust number of works done on the topic from Latin America and Spain and that the field is very much alive and at its best. It is important, however, to promote a dialogue and build bridges with scholars from other parts of the world also working on the subject and related topics. Furthermore, it is also an invitation to learn more and continue expanding and studying the complex terrains of Freemasonry in Latin America.

Nota editorial, Edición especial acerca la Masonería en América Latina

Editor invitado: Dr. Guillermo de los Reyes Heredia,
Universidad de Houston

Primero que nada, me gustaría agradecer a Pierre Mollier, Editor de *Ritual, Secrecy, and Civil Sociey* por haberme invitado a elaborar una edición especial acerca de la Masonería en América Latina. Durante las últimas décadas, el estudio de la masonería en América Latina ha evolucionado. Un grupo de académicos de diferentes partes del mundo hispanohablante ha explorado a profundidad el tema de la masonería desde una perspectiva académica. Es importante mencionar que el Profesor José Antonio Ferrer Benimeli, que es la autoridad principal en la masonería española y fundador del Centro de Estudios Históricos de la Masonería en España (CEHME) en la Universidad de Zaragoza, ha sido figura clave en este esfuerzo. El CEHME fue creado hace tres décadas para promover el estudio y desarrollo científico y diseminación de los estudios de masonería. Este centro también ha creado grupos de investigación, organizado conferencias y simposios, y dado cursos acerca de la Masonería en varias universidades de España y América Latina. Inspirado y con la orientación del CEHME, un grupo de académicos (muchos de ellos contribuyeron a esta edición especial) empezaron una conferencia hace una década, dedicada al estudio de la Masonería en Latino América y el Caribe. Adicionalmente, después de esta iniciativa, crearon la primera revista académica sobre los estudios de la Masonería en América Latina: REHMLAC+ *Revista de Estudios Históricos de la Masonería Latinoamericana y Caribeña* con sede en la Universidad de Costa Rica. Algunos de los artículos fueron publicados originalmente en español en *REHMLAC+* y traducidos al inglés para que estén disponibles para una audiencia más amplia. Por ello, me gustaría agradecer profundamente al equipo de *REHMLAC+* por su generosidad.

El propósito de esta edición especial es resaltar el muy necesario e ignorado estudio de la Masonería latinoamericana particularmente fuera de España y América Latina. Espero que los varios artículos seleccionados aquí fomenten el avance de la investigación, no solamente del estudio de la Masonería latinoamericana, sino también de la historia cultural intelectual de la región y del debate interdisciplinario actual acerca de la masonería y sus contribuciones a través de la historia. La mayoría de la investigación existente fuera de los estudios de Masonería no considera la influencia y el papel que los discursos masónicos han tenido en la formación de un discurso nacional, así como de un canon literario, y si estas influencias se mencionan de manera superficial. Parte del problema es que muchos académicos creen que no hay suficiente material disponible acerca del tema de la

Masonería latinoamericana. Sin embargo, como ustedes podrán observar aquí, la gran investigación llevada a cabo por estos académicos llena ese vacío al resaltar y usar investigación original de archivos masónicos y no masónicos, explorando nueva evidencia en el tema de la Masonería en América Latina.

Se seleccionaron siete artículos para esta primera edición. El artículo central es "An Introduction to the Historiography of Latin American Freemasonry" de José Antonio Ferrer Benimeli, fundador y presidente honorario de la CEHME. En este artículo, Ferrer Benimeli estudia la historiografía de la Masonería latinoamericana que está viviendo una regeneración metodológica, de ahí que sea necesario añadir las nuevas investigaciones a las referencias bibliográficas apuntadas en anteriores publicaciones. Este trabajo se divide en dos partes. Una primera comenta por país del área iberoamericana las principales obras que sobre la Historia de la Masonería se han publicado hasta el momento. El comentario se basa tanto en las obras que ofrecen un nivel científico aceptable (minoría) como las que carecen de ello (mayoría). La segunda parte se dedica a informar de las referencias bibliográficas. El autor recalca que es un trabajo abierto cuya exhaustividad es tan compleja como grande la extensión geográfica abordada. Por lo tanto, el estudio sólo quiere ser un punto de referencia más sobre dicha historiografía que seguirá completándose en un futuro.

Eduardo Torres Cuevas, en "Freemasonry in Cuba in the Nineteenth Century," analiza el desarrollo de las Masonerías cubanas durante el siglo XIX y sus relaciones con los principales procesos políticos, económicos y sociales de la Isla, en especial con los de emancipación y de llegada de ideas liberales, civilistas, laicas y seculares. Asimismo, este trabajo funciona como un estado de cuestión sobre lo escrito con respecto al específico objeto de estudio. Otra contribución intitulada "Notes on the 'Symbolic Name' in Latin America" de Yvan Pozuelos investiga por qué el uso de nombres simbólicos fue exclusivo de las Masonerías hispanoamericanas. ¿Fue el uso del nombre simbólico original de los masones? ¿Cuándo y por qué se extendió la costumbre? El estudio de caso analizado fue la comunidad asturiana, ya que fue uno de los más importantes grupos de inmigrantes españoles en América. Con estas notas y el estudio regional se pretende contestar a estas interrogantes: ¿Fue el nombre simbólico un uso originado por los masones? ¿Fue exclusivo de la masonería? ¿Qué informaciones destacan de los nombres simbólicos hispanoamericanos de los masones de Asturias? ¿Qué datos revelan los nombres simbólicos Hispanoaméricanos de los masones asturianos residentes en Hispanoamérica?

Felipe Santiago Solar, en "On the Origins of Freemasonry in Chile," analiza el proceso de implantación de la Masonería en Chile poniendo énfasis en las vías de ingreso de este tipo de sociabilidad y en los contextos sociales que permitieron su institucionalización. Para ello, se centra en dos periodos: el de la independencia, donde la Masonería militar tuvo cierta presencia, pero no logró su establecimiento; y el periodo de las revueltas liberales a mediados del siglo XIX, donde se produce su institucionalización definitiva. En "Freemasonry as a Center of Political Action in Independent Mexico, 1821–1830," María Eugenia Vázquez Semadeni nos muestra cómo algunas prácticas internas de la masonería, los cuerpos masónicos, sus canales de comunicación y las lealtades que generaron fueron aprovechadas por los *Yorkinos* para establecer un centro de acción política. Es decir, un espacio donde se lograron acuerdos y que les permitió emprender iniciativas para lograr, preservar y ejercer el poder político. Vázquez Semadeni demuestra que esto fue en parte posible debido a la estructura institucional que surgió del establecimiento del sistema republicano, representativo y federal, pero también debido al hecho de que los *Yorkinos* crearon un discurso sobre el sistema político, ellos mismos y sus oponentes que por un tiempo le otorgó a sus acciones políticas una legitimidad considerable.

"Freemasonry, Civil Society, and the Public Sphere in Central America (1865-1876)" de Ricardo Martínez Esquivel argumenta que debido a las características específicas de la modernidad latinoamericana, la Masonería en América Central debe considerarse más como un proceso de construcción socio-histórica que como una categoría analítica. Este artículo también aborda la naturaleza de las relaciones entre la modernidad y el establecimiento y la evolución de la Masonería en Centroamérica durante el período inicial de su desarrollo activo (1865-1876). En el último artículo de la colección, "Freemasonry, Control and Other Fraternal Loyalties: the Rescue of Porfirio Díaz by a Masonic Brother," de Guillermo de los Reyes Heredia, se explora el papel que jugó Porfirio Díaz dentro de la Masonería y su relación con dicha institución. Se analiza una de las historias que comprueban que Díaz logró ciertos beneficios gracias a su afiliación masónica desde antes que fuera presidente de México. Esta historia narra la manera en que Díaz logró entrar de contrabando a México con la ayuda de un hermano masón en 1876, después de su breve exilio en Nueva Orleans a bordo del buque de vapor, "City of Havana". Asimismo, se describe cómo Díaz promovió la unificación de las logias del rito escocés en una institución que se llamó La Gran Dieta Simbólica. La razón principal por la cual Díaz promovió tal unificación, como se afirma en el artículo de De los Reyes, fue para llevar a cabo su plan de pacificación nacional. Díaz sabía que tenía que obtener el control de la Masonería para evitar que ésta le causara problemas para lograr el orden y progreso que caracterizó a su gobierno. Por tal motivo, el dictador siempre vigiló que ni la Masonería, ni cualquier otra institución que hubiera podido tener cierta influencia en la sociedad estuvieran fuera de su control.

Para resumir, esta edición especial acerca de la Masonería en Latinoamérica muestra que hay un número robusto de investigaciones acerca del tema llevadas a cabo en América Latina y España y que el campo está muy vivo y en su mejor momento. Es importante, sin embargo, promover un diálogo y entablar relaciones con académicos de otras partes del mundo que también están trabajando en el tema y otros temas relacionados. Adicionalmente, también es una invitación para aprender más y continuar expandiendo y estudiando los complejos terrenos de la Masonería en América Latina.

编者按，拉美共济会特刊

客座编辑：Guillermo de los Reyes Heredia博士

休斯顿大学

　　首先，我想感谢"仪式、秘密和公民社会"（*Ritual, Secrecy, and Civil Society*）期刊主编Pierre Mollier邀请我为拉美共济会撰写特刊。过去几十年里，关于拉美共济会的研究已不断发展。来自不同西语国家的学者已从学术的角度对共济会进行了探索。José Antonio Ferrer Benimeli教授是一位重要人物，他在对共济会的探索中发挥了至关重要的作用。他不仅是研究西班牙共济会的权威领导，还是萨拉戈萨大学（University of Zaragoza）西班牙共济会历史研究中心（Center for Historical Research on Spanish Freemasonry，简称CEHME）的创始人。CEHME于30年前建立，目的是为了推动共济会研究的传播和科学发展。该研究中心还创建了研究小组、组织了会议和研讨会，同时还在西班牙和拉美各大学教授共济会课程。受到CEHME的启发，加之是CEHME的成员，一群学者（其中大多数都是本期特刊的投稿者）于10年前开启了会议，专注研究了拉美和加勒比共济会。在此之后，他们还创建了首个研究拉美共济会的学术期刊：*REHMLAC+*，全称*Revista de Estudios Históricos de la Masonería Latinoamericana y Caribeña*。REHMLAC+设在哥斯达黎加大学（Universidad de Costa Rica）。本期特刊的部分文章最初以西语的方式在REHMLAC+上发表，之后被本刊翻译为英语，以便让更多的学者阅读。因此，我想对REHMLAC+的慷慨之情表示感谢。

　　本刊目的是阐明对拉美共济会的相关研究。虽然对拉美共济会进行研究是十分必要的，但这却经常被忽视，在西班牙和拉美地区之外的地方更是如此。我希望本刊选择的文章不仅能推动有关拉美共济会的研究，还能推动区域知识-文化历史和有关共济会的学科间辩论以及该辩论在历史上的贡献。共济会研究之外的大多数工作并未考虑共济会论述在形成国家话语和文化经典上产生的影响和扮演的角色，即便这些影响曾被提及，也仅仅是顺带而已。出现此问题的部分原因是因为许多学者认为可供研究的拉美共济会资料并不足够。然而，本刊中你会发现，作者所做的大量研究能填补这一空缺。通过使用共济会档案室和非共济会档案室中的原始研究，进而探索有关拉美共济会的新信息。

　　本期特刊共有七篇文章。其中专题文章"拉美共济会史学介绍"（An Introduction to the Historiography of Latin American Freemasonry）由CEHME创始人兼名誉主席José Antonio Ferrer Benimeli撰写。文章中，Ferrer Benimeli所研究的拉美共济会史学正在经历一次方法的更新（methodological regeneration），因此作者对以往出版物中所列的参考文献进行了新的研究。Ferrer Benimeli的文章由两部分组成。第一部分以拉美国家为例，讨论了以往有关共济会历史出版的主要作品。评论基于被科学所接受的作品和未被科学证实的作品，其中前者占少数，后者占多数。第二部分致力于报道参考文献。作者指出，其文章并不是一项全面性研究，仅仅是一项参考，因此，完成史学更新的工作还将在未来继续下去。

Eduardo Torres Cuevas 博士在文章"19世纪的古巴共济会"（Freemasonry in Cuba in the Nineteenth Century）中分析了19世纪期间古巴共济会的发展及其与古巴岛主要政治、经济和文化进程的关系，特别是和解放进程以及新观念（包括自由观念、公民观念、外行观念以及世俗观念）到来之间的关系。文章同时对有关该研究的文字记录提出了疑问。另一篇文章名为"拉美'象征名字'的注释"（Notes on the "Symbolic Name" in Latin America），作者是Yvan Pozuelos。这篇文章提出了如下问题：为何象征名的使用曾经并未出现在拉美共济会？象征名的使用是共济会成员发起的吗？这一习俗是在何时，出于何种原因得以传播？为回答这些问题，Pozuelos研究了拉美地区的阿斯图里亚（Asturian）共济会社区（因为该社区是最重要的西班牙移民团体之一），同时分析了拉美地区阿斯图利亚共济会居民的象征名。

作者Felipe Santiago del Solar在"论智利共济会的起源"（On the Origins of Freemasonry in Chile）中分析了共济会在智利的成立过程，重点强调了共济会社交性（sociability）在智利的进入途径，同时分析了多个社会情境下成立的共济会，这些社会情境都促进了共济会的制度化。Del Solar将焦点放在两个阶段：第一阶段描述军事共济会（Military Freemasonry）的独立，虽然其已经出现但并未正式成立。第二阶段描述19世纪中期的自由反抗（liberal revolts），在此期间共济会建立了最终的制度。

作者María Eugenia Vázquez Semadeni 在文章"1821-1830年间共济会作为墨西哥独立之后的政治行动中心"（Freemasonry as a Center of Political Action in Independent Mexico, 1821-1830）中展示了约克礼仪派（Yorkinos）如何利用共济会内部实践、共济会机构、机构间传播渠道和忠诚来建立政治行动中心。此中心用于达成协议，并能使协议主动实现、保存和行使政治权力。文章将展示上述观点成立的两点原因。首先有可能的是，制度结构从共和党、代表和联邦系统的成立中兴起。其次，事实证明，约克礼仪派创造了有关政治系统、自身和对手的话语，这在短时间内为其政治行动赋予了相当的合法性。

作者Ricardo Martínez Esquivel 撰写了"1865-1876年间中美洲的共济会、公民社会和公共领域"（Freemasonry, Civil Society, and the Public Sphere in Central America (1865–1876)）。文章认为，由于拉美现代性（modernity）的具体特点，其应该更多地被视为一种社会历史建构，而不属于分析范畴。文章还处理了现代性和中美洲共济会初期积极成立及发展（1865-1876年）之间的关系本质。

最后一篇文章"共济会、控制和兄弟般的忠诚：共济会兄弟对波费里奥·迪亚斯的营救"（Freemasonry, Control and Other Fraternal Loyalties: the Rescue of Porfirio Díaz by a Masonic Brother）由Guillermo de los Reyes Heredia博士撰写。文章探索了波费里奥·迪亚斯（Porfirio Díaz）在共济

会中扮演的角色以及他和共济会之间的关系，分析了一个能证明迪亚斯在被选为墨西哥总统之前受到共济会帮助的故事。这个故事讲述了迪亚斯在新奥尔良市"哈瓦那市"（City of Havana）轮船上度过短期流放后，如何于1876年受到共济会兄弟帮助而成功将自己偷运到墨西哥。此外，De los Reyes Heredia研究了迪亚斯如何在名为"The Symbolic Grand Diet"的机构中推动了苏格兰礼（Scottish Rite）共济会的统一。迪亚斯推动统一的主要原因是为了实施其民族和解（national reconciliation）计划。他知道自己不得不控制共济会才能避免未来的对抗和麻烦。他不想让任何人干预其政府的命令政策和进程。因此，这位独裁者总是确保任何对社会有实质性影响的共济会或其他机构都在其控制范围之内。

总而言之，本期拉美共济会特刊展示了许多来自拉美和西班牙的相关作品，并证明了该领域十分活跃，处于最佳状态。然而，与世界其他地区的相关学者建立友好关系、推动对话是极其重要的。此外，本文还邀请大家深入学习、继续扩大对拉美共济会复杂情况的研究。

An Introduction to the Historiography of Latin American Freemasonry[1]

José Antonio Ferrer Benimeli[2]

ABSTRACT

Masonic Latin American historiography is undergoing a methodological regeneration; therefore, it is necessary to add new research to the references outlined in previous publications. This paper is divided into two parts. The first one discusses the principal works on the History of Freemasonry that have been published in the various Latin American countries. The comment is based on both the works that offer a scientifically acceptable level (minority) and those without it (the majority). The second part is devoted to the bibliographical references. It must be emphasized that is an open proposal whose completeness is as complex as the large geographical area that encompasses Latin America. Therefore, it aims to be a point of reference on completing this historiography that will be expanded in the future.

Keywords: *Freemasonry, historiography, bibliography, Latin America*

RESUMEN

La historiografía masónica iberoamericana está viviendo una regeneración metodológica y de autores de ahí que sea necesario añadir las nuevas investigaciones a las referencias bibliográficas apuntadas en anteriores publicaciones. Este trabajo se divide en dos partes. Una primera comenta por país del área iberoamericano las principales obras que sobre la Historia de la Masonería se han publicado hasta el momento. El comentario se basa tanto en las obras que ofrecen un nivel científico aceptable (minoría) como las que carecen de ello (mayoría). La segunda

1 This article was previously published in the *REHMLAC* 1, No. 1 (May–November 2012). My thanks go to the editorial board of *REHMLAC* for authorizing the publication of this article in English. Works on Freemasonry are produced on a permanently ongoing basis, and so this study should be considered as an open-ended project. Information pertaining to it or subsequent supplementary contributions would be appreciated.

2 José Antonio Ferrer Benimeli. Spanish. Doctor of history (1972), emeritus associate professor of contemporary history, and founder and honorary president of the Center for Historical Studies of Spanish Freemasonry, University of Zaragoza, Spain. E-mail: bibliotecasalvadorzaragoza@gmail.com.

1

parte se dedica a informar de las referencias bibliográficas. Es preciso recalcar que es un trabajo abierto cuya exhaustividad es tan compleja como grande la extensión geográfica abordada. Por lo tanto, sólo quiere ser un punto de referencia más sobre dicha historiografía que seguirá completándose en un futuro.

Palabras clave: Masonería, historiografía, bibliografía, Latinoamérica

拉美共济会史学介绍

摘要

共济会拉美史学正经历着一次方法的更新，因此有必要对以往出版物的参考文献进行新的研究。本文分为两部分。第一部分以拉美国家为例，讨论了以往有关共济会历史出版的主要作品。评论基于被科学所接受的作品和未被科学证实的作品，其中前者占少数，后者占多数。第二部分致力于报道参考文献。需强调的是，这项工作是公开的，其完整性如同本文处理的大地理范围一样复杂。因此，完成史学更新的工作还将在未来继续下去。

关键词：共济会，史学，参考书目，拉美

Introduction

The bicentennial celebrations of independence in Latin American countries have allowed a process of historical revision led by universities, academies, research centers, and cultural centers, and they have brought about a host of meetings, conferences, seminars, and publications. In parallel, over recent decades a more critical and calmer outlook has set in among the majority of scholars and researchers of all tendencies owing to the advance of interdisciplinary approaches and a turning toward primary and newspaper documentary sources that were unknown or little used until a few years ago. The history of Freemasonry has not fallen outside of this revising and reelaborating, all the more so because of the prominence that nineteenth-century historiography of both a pro- and anti-Masonic nature granted to Freemasonry in relation to the years of the first insurgency and then with regard to independence.

Furthermore, the ignorance that in general exists regarding the history of Latin American and Caribbean Freemasonry is widely known. Based on a look at certain publishers' catalogs, whereas in Europe strictly historical and sociopolitical questions have been of greater interest, in Latin America essays of a philosophical, ritualistic, or mystical-esoteric kind have long been predominant.

Methodology and Sources

The methodology followed in the study of the history of Freemasonry in Europe and more specifically in Spain has been closely linked to universities and to the abundance and public availability of Masonic archives. Particularly in the Spanish and French cases, these archives have allowed historical studies to extend not only to mother-country Freemasonries but also to overseas counterparts, and in particular to those of Cuba, Puerto Rico, Santo Domingo, and the Philippines, which gained independence significantly later than that of the Latin American continental or mainland republics, where Freemasonry was introduced—with the rare exceptions of some lodges—precisely as a result of independence and after it was gained. As a consequence, in Spain's archives—including those on Freemasonry—there is hardly any Masonic documentation from the late eighteenth and early nineteenth centuries, with the exception of some denunciations made before the Inquisition. The value of these is very modest, since at best they relate to Freemasons who received their initiation in Europe, and in other cases they involve charges that were not even seen as credible by the Inquisition, as is pointed out in José Antonio Ferrer Benimeli, *Masonería e Inquisición en Latinoamérica*

durante el siglo XVIII (Caracas, 1971), José Martínez Millán, *Juan José Díaz de la Espada, obispo de La Habana ¿un prelado masón?* (Zaragoza, 1993), Henar Pizarro Llorente, *La represión de la masonería en el Tribunal del Santo Oficio de Cartagena de Indias a principio del siglo XIX* (Zaragoza, 1993), and, more recently, Rogelio Aragón Juárez, *Contra la Iglesia y el Estado: Masonería e Inquisición en Nueva España, 1760–1820*, an undergraduate thesis presented at the university of the Instituto Helénico in Mexico City in 2006 (*REHMLAC*, 2011). This question had previously been the focus of—among others—Nicolás Rangel, *Los precursores ideológicos de la guerra de Independencia: la masonería en México, siglo XVIII* (Mexico City, 1932) and Richard Greenleaf, *The Mexican Inquisition and the Masonic Movement: 1751–1820* (New Mexico, 1969).

Apart from the archives of the Inquisition, which have also been considered by José Martínez Millán in *Fuentes para el estudio de la masonería en la Sección de Inquisición del Archivo Histórico Nacional* (Zaragoza, 1985), equally indispensable for research on Latin American Freemasonry have been: those of the Grand Orient of France and the French National Library, which have been analyzed by Céline Sala in *Los archivos del desengaño: El mundo de las fuentes "ultra marinas"* (*REHMLAC*, 2011) and by Françoise Randouyer in *Fondos documentales de la masonería española en la Biblioteca Nacional de París* (Zaragoza, 1985); those of the Palace General Archive in Madrid, a very useful introduction to which is provided by Juan C. Gay Armenteros in *Fondos masónicos del Archivo General de Palacio* (Zaragoza, 1985); and those of the Salamanca archive, which has now changed its name once more and is known as the Documentation Center for Historical Memory rather than as the General Archive of the Spanish Civil War. The latter collection is described by its former director, María Teresa Díez de los Ríos, in *Fondos de la masonería en el Archivo Histórico Nacional: Sección Guerra Civil, de Salamanca* (1985), by Dionisio Piñuela García, Cristina Vicente López, and Mª Natividad Ortiz Albear in *Fuentes para el estudio de la masonería antillana conservadas en el Archivo Histórico Nacional. Sección "Guerra Civil"* (Zaragoza, 1995), and by Carmen Alonso Pascual and Blanca Desantes in *Orientaciones para la investigación de la masonería del siglo XX en el Archivo Histórico Nacional. Sección de fondos contemporáneos y archivo de Martínez Barrio* (Toledo, 1996).

But curiously—as happened in the Spain of the Cádiz Cortes—although there was no Freemasonry in insurgent Latin America, there did exist a powerful anti-Freemasonry that, taking advantage of the freedom of the press declared in Cádiz, created a strong and persistent popular anti-Masonic imagination, which marked not only the nineteenth-century historiography of Latin American Freemasonries but also the historiography of the leading figures of independence—hence the need for historical revision that the bicentennial celebrations of independence have emphasized, especially at universities in Mexico, Cuba, and Costa Rica. This historiographical revision has been hampered by the absence of good archives from Freemasonry itself, or by the obstacles placed before non-Masons who wish to work in them in the case of some archives. This is the reason why the history of the introduction of Freemasonry in the Caribbean has been produced using archival sources from Spain, France, England, and North America. In these places, there is no such research segregation that ultimately gives the impression that what is being attempted is to hide the nonexistence of Masonic archives or the chaotic state of disorganization that some of these are in. Fortunately, the same situation is not to be found in Europe.

In Spain, since the 1980s the driving force behind historical studies on Freemasonry has been the Center for Historical Studies of Spanish Freemasonry (CHSSM), as Yván Pozuelo Andrés points out in *La Historiografía masónica latinoamericanista actual. Presente y Futuro* (Santiago de Compostela, 2010). The following pages seek to be a continuation of and complement to Pozuelo Andrés's work.

Comprising more than one hundred faculty members from universities, secondary-education institutions, and research centers such as the CSIC (Consejo Superior de Investigaciones Científicas), the center has coordinated much of the work undertaken on Freemasonry over the last thirty years, including doctoral and undergraduate theses, congresses, seminars, courses, conferences, exhibitions, and scientific and popular publications of all kinds.

The methodology followed in general and described in different forums and journals can be found in José Antonio Ferrer Benimeli, *La historia ante la masonería. Reflexiones Metodológicas* (Oviedo, 1980) and *Método y experiencias en el estudio de la historia de la masonería española* (*REHMLAC*, 2010), and in Eric Saunier, *La prosopografía, una nueva vía para la historia de la masonería* (Bordeaux, 2006; *REHMLAC*, 2010).

From the methodological and bibliographic point of view, the twelve international symposia organized to date by the CHSSM have been especially important. The first three of these were devoted to the "methodology applied to the history of Freemasonry," and subsequent ones focused on the history of Spanish Freemasonry. They have always included studies on the Freemasonry of Hispanic America, and three thematic symposia were additionally devoted to this subject, the proceedings of which are contained in *Masonería española y América* (Cáceres, 1991), *La Masonería española entre Europa y América* (Zaragoza, 1993), and *La Masonería española y la crisis del 98* (Barcelona, 1997). A fourth thematic symposium (which was the thirteenth of the general symposia) took place in 2012, the proceedings of which are entitled *Gibraltar, Cádiz, América y la Masonería. Constitucionalismo y libertad de prensa, 1812–2012* (Gibraltar, 2012).

To keep track of some of the academic studies related to Ibero-American Freemasonries that have been produced in Europe, as a contribution to the construction of the history of Freemasonry in Latin America, there are three fundamental sources. First, there are the works and publications undertaken by and within the CHSSM (both standalone publications and the twenty-four volumes of proceedings of symposia organized by the center).[3] Second, there are works that have appeared in the *Revista de Estudios Históricos de la Masonería Latinoamericana y Caribeña* (*REHMLAC*),[4] edited by Ricardo Martínez Esquivel and Yván Pozuelo Andrés. This journal is part of the University of Costa Rica's Historical Studies on Freemasonry and Patriotic Societies in Central America Program. And thirdly, there is the *Bibliografía de la Masonería* (Madrid, 2004) by José Antonio Ferrer Benimeli and Susana Cuartero Escobés,[5] which was updated

---

3   See in particular volume 24, *Indices de Actas de los Simposios Internacionales de Historia de la Masonería española* (Zaragoza, Spain: Gobierno de Aragón, 2009), p. 892. For reasons of simplicity, in the text only the city and year are indicated; full bibliographic details can be found in the Appendix.

4   This digital journal began publication in May 2009 as a mouthpiece for the Center for Historical Studies of Latin American and Caribbean Freemasonry. There are also print editions of issues between May–November 2009 and May–November 2010, entitled *REHMLAC* (Paris: Publibook, 2011), p. 670. In the text, only *REHMLAC* and the year are cited. The rest of the bibliographic information appears in the Appendix. References are always to the digital version.

5   A first edition of the *Bibliografía* was published in 1974 by the Historical Research Institute of the Andrés Bello Catholic University in Caracas, which has 3,451 entries. A second edition consisting of 6,060 entries was published in 1978 by the Madrid-based Spanish University Foundation (SUF).

with the bulletins of the CHSSM from between 2004 and 2012. These bulletins are compilations of general information on the most significant publications from each year on the history of Free-masonry, both in Europe and in Latin America.[6]

The Introduction of Freemasonry in the Caribbean

One of the least studied issues has been the introduction of Freemasonry in the Caribbe-an and Latin America in general. An attempt at an introduction—subject to revisions and additions—is José Anto-nio Ferrer Benimeli, *Vías de penetración de la masonería en el Caribe* (*REHM-LAC*, 2009). This was presented for the first time at the University of Leiden in November 2004 under the title *La Franc-maçonnerie européenne: expan-sion en Amérique du Sud* (Brussels, 1992) and later in Havana in December 2007 at the First International Sympo-sium on the History of Latin American and Caribbean Freemasonry. A few years earlier, to mark the bicentennial of the French Revolution, the same au-thor presented a paper entitled *Révolu-tion Française et Littérature clandestine à Cuba. La Francmaçonnerie comme élément conspirateur* (Fort-de-France, 1988) at a congress held at the Univer-sity of the Antilles in Martinique on the revolutionary period in the Antilles.

French lodges in the Antilles have been considered in, among oth-ers, Guy Monduc, *Essai sur l'origine de l'histoire de la Franc-maçonnerie en Guadeloupe* (Paris, 1985), Elisabeth Es-calle and Marcel Gouyon-Guillaume, *Francs-Maçons des loges françaises "aux Amériques," 1770–1850. Contribution à l'étude de la Société créole* (Paris, 1993), André Combes, *La Franc-maçonnerie aux Antilles et en Guyane Française* (Fort-de-France, 1988) and *Las lo-gias del Grande Oriente de Francia en América Latina (1842–1870)* (Zarago-za, 1968), Charles Porset, *La Franc-ma-sonería en Santo Domingo (siglos XVIII y XIX)* (Zaragoza, 1993), Eric Saunier, *El espacio caribeño: un reto de poder para la francmasonería francesa* (*REHM-LAC*, 2009), and in Agnès Renault's two works *Los francmasones franceses de la jurisdicción de Cuba a principios del si-glo XIX* (*REHMLAC*, 2009) and *La in-fluencia de la masonería francesa en el Departamento Oriental de Cuba en los años veinte del siglo XIX. Los aportes de la prosopografía* (*REHMLAC*, 2009).

Juan Blázquez Miguel, *La ma-sonería en Haití. Esbozo histórico* (Zara-goza, 1993) takes an interest in the English origins of lodges in Haiti. The expert on Jamaica is Frederic W. Seal-Coon, who authored *La isla de Jamai-ca y su influencia masónica en la región* (Zaragoza, 1993), an English-language version of which was published in the London-based journal *Ars Quatuor Coronatorum* in 1991. It is an over-view of his classic work *An Histori-cal Account of Jamaican Freemasonry* (Kingston, 1976), which is essential

And a third edition containing 19,987 entries was published in 2004, again by the SUF.

6   To date, there have been twenty-six published issues between 1984 and 2011.

for understanding the introduction of Freemasonry into the Caribbean and Latin America. Cécile Revauger completes the Caribbean map with the small British Antillean islands in *Freemasonry in Barbados, Trinidad and Grenada: British or Homemade?* (Sheffield, 2010), which makes use of a rich and abundant bibliography. And Hubert A. Cabaña is finalizing a *History of Freemasonry in Curaçao*.

For the case of Mexico, and leaving aside general histories of Freemasonry, Lillian Estelle Fisher, in her era, focused squarely on *Early Masonry in Mexico, 1806–1828* (New Mexico, 1939), and, more recently, Carlos Francisco Martínez Moreno published *Logias masónicas en la Nueva España* (*REHMLAC*, 2011), which uses Masonic documentation to offer a history of the first lodges established in Mexico, specifically in Veracruz, Campeche, and Mérida, between 1816 and 1820. His Master's thesis *El establecimiento de las masonerías en México en el siglo XIX*, presented at the National Autonomous University of Mexico (UNAM) in the summer of 2011, also focused on this subject.

Ibero-American Independence

The most disputed and debated subject has been and continues to be the alleged prominent role played by Freemasonry in Ibero-American independence. In their respective eras, this question was addressed by, among many others, Nicolás Navar-ro in *La Masonería y la Independencia* (Caracas, 1928), Jorge Pacheco Quintero in *La Masonería en la emancipación de América* (Bogotá, 1943), Carlos Restrepo Canal in *Informe sobre la Masonería y la Independencia* (Bogotá, 1959), Américo Carnicelli in *La Masonería y la Independencia de América, 1810–1830* (Bogotá, 1970), José Antonio Ferrer Benimeli in *La masonería y la independencia de América española. Reflexiones metodológicas* (Seville, 1978), Julio Antonio Vaquero Iglesias in *Masonería e independencia americana según la historiografía decimonónica española* (Zaragoza, 1993), Morivalde Calvet Fagundes in *La masonería y la independencia de América Latina* (Zaragoza, 1993),[7] and José Luis Mora Mérida in *Ideario laicista-masónico e Iglesia católica en la formación de las nacionalidades hispanoamericanas* (Zaragoza, 1995). An updated overview of the question appears in Felipe Del Solar Guajardo's study *La Francmasonería y la Independencia de América: Un balance historiográfico* (Santiago, 2006).

From an alternative, Spanish-centric perspective, the issue is not emancipation or independence, but the loss of the colonies, which is dealt with in a general way by, among others, Manuel de Paz Sánchez in *Masonería española y emancipación colonial* (Barcelona, 2009). And from the point of view of commercial and strategic interests, England's stance is studied in Emilio Ocampo, *Inglaterra, la masonería y la independencia de América* (Buenos Aires, 2006).

---

7   I deal with these works and other related studies in the different editions of my *Bibliografía de la Masonería*.

The confusion that exists between Freemasonry, secret societies, and patriotic societies on the one hand and between Masonic lodges and Mirandista or Lautaro lodges on the other is due to the disparities in historical judgments on this issue. The so-called Lautaro, Rational Gentlemen, or Spanish Gathering lodges, derived from the London-focused and Mirandista American Grand Gathering, were not Masonic lodges. Rather, they were patriotic lodges with radically different objectives, and an abundance of contradictory studies exists on the subject, such as the works of Juan Canter, published between 1934 and 1941,[8] D. Duthu and Jaime Eyzaguirre, *La logia Lautarina y otros estudios sobre la independencia* (Santiago de Chile, 1973), Fabián Onsari, *San Martín, la logia Lautaro y la Franc-masonería* (Avellaneda, 1951), Raúl A. Ruiz y Ruiz, *La logia Lautaro y la Independencia de América* (Santa Fe, 1946), Mariano Paz Soldán, *La Logia Lautaro* (Lima, 1868), Antonio R. Zúñiga, *La logia Lautaro y la independencia de América* (Buenos Aires, 1922), Enrique Gandía, *La política secreta de la Gran Logia de Londres* (Buenos Aires, 1976), Benjamín Oviedo Martínez, *La logia Lautarina* (Santiago de Chile, 1929), Rómulo Avendaño, *La Sociedad Lautaro. Rectificaciones históricas* (Buenos Aires, 1870), Marcos Beltrán Ávila, *La pequeña Gran Logia que independizó a Bolivia, 1823–1825* (Cochambamba, 1948), José R. Guzmán, *Fray Servando Teresa de Mier y la sociedad Lautaro* (Mexico City, 1968), Willy Francisco Herrera Valdés, *Las sociedades secretas*

y la independencia política del cono sur americano: O'Higgins, San Martín y la logia Lautaro* (Madrid, 1985), Hipólito Guillermo Bolcatto, *La Logia Lautaro de Santa Fe* (Santa Fe, 2011), and many other studies of greatly varying value.

In view of these and many other publications, and with the aim of establishing boundaries and distinctions in relation to a still-relevant theme that continues to be the focal point for bitter disputes—which in many cases are the fruit of ignorance—I published some studies on the matter, first in Montevideo and then in different forums: José Antonio Ferrer Benimeli, *Aproximación a las llamadas logias Lautaro* (Montevideo, 1987; La Laguna, 1988), *Cádiz y las llamadas logias Lautaro o Caballeros Racionales* (Cádiz, 1988), and *Les Caballeros Racionales, les loges lotariens et les formes déviées de la franc-maçonnerie dans le monde hispanique* (Brussels, 1990; Paris, 1991).

Along these same lines of the distinction between Masonic and Mirandista lodges, and based on the departure point of Juan Canter, *Las sociedades secretas, políticas y literarias* (Buenos Aires, 1942) and del Alberto Gil Novales' renowned and definitive *Las sociedades patrióticas* (Madrid, 1975), fundamental studies in this area are María Eugenia Vázquez Semandeni, *La masonería en México entre las sociedades secretas y patrióticas, 1813–1830* (*REHMLAC*, 2011) and Frederic W. Seal-Coon, *La mítica masonería de Francisco de Miranda* (Zaragoza, 1995; Barcelona, 1997). From another per-

---

8   Titles are in the Appendix.

spective, equally illuminating are the academic Pedro Luis Barcia's *San Martín y la Masonería*, which is an introductory study in Ignacio Cuccoresse's work *San Martín* (Buenos Aires, 1993), and Pilar González Bernaldo de Quirós' *Producción de una nueva legitimidad: ejército y sociedades patrióticas en Buenos Aires entre 1810 y 1913* (Paris, 1990). To these must be added María Teresa Berruezo, *La propaganda independentista de la logia mirandina en Londres* (Zaragoza, 1993). In *La Francmasonería en la Independencia de Hispanoamérica* (Montevideo, 1988), Alfonso Fernández Cabrelli devotes a significant chapter to "Freemasonry, secret societies, and the Lautaro Lodge," a work of compilation and analysis that attempts to reach conclusions in an inclusive manner that is ultimately confusing owing to its excessive reconciling of antithetical theories.

Without departing from the subject of secret societies, an area in which Iris M. Zavala was a pioneer in the case of Spain with her *Masones, comuneros y carbonarios* (Madrid, 1971), a more or less convincing study of the birth of these secret societies, identified by the author as peninsular political organizations, the following works are of fundamental importance for the Mexican case: Professor Virginia Guedea's *Las sociedades secretas durante el movimiento de independencia* (Los Angeles, 1989) and *En torno a la Independencia y la Revolución* (Los Angeles, 1990), a prelude to her exemplary and illuminating classic *En busca de un gobierno alterno. Los guadalupes de México* (Mexico City, 1992), and to its follow-ups *Una forma de organización política: la sociedad secreta de Jalapa 1812* (Mexico City, 1993) and *De Conspiradores y sociedades secretas* (Mexico City, 2010).

These works that link the independence of Mexico with the Guadalupes broaden and further the path taken in their own eras by Wilbert H. Timmons in *Los Guadalupes: A Secret Society in the Mexican Revolution for Independence* (Pittsburgh, 1950) and by Ernesto de la Torre Villar in *Los Guadalupes y la independencia* (Mexico City, 1985). This latter work is considered by Virginia Guedea in *Comentario a la ponencia de Ernesto de la Torre sobre sociedades secretas en la guerra de Independencia* (Zamora, 1985).

At the other extreme, in the most conservative, clerical, and ahistorical tradition, are Félix Navarrete, *La masonería en la historia y en las leyes de México* (1957) and Patricio Maguirre, *La Masonería y la emancipación del Río de la Plata* (Buenos Aires, 1969), reissued by his followers (Buenos Aires, 2000). The latter is another manifestation of the work of an individual who dedicated many years of his life to an obsessive fight against the phantasm of Freemasonry through an eccentric journal that he wrote and published between 1981 and 1989, initially under the title of *Informaciones sobre la Masonería y otras sociedades secretas* and ultimately under the more sensationalist title of *Revelaciones sobre la Masonería*. Enrique Gandía also contributes to the question in *La independencia de América y las Sociedades Secretas* (Santa Fe, 1994) and in *Los orígenes probables de la logia Lautaro* (Buenos Aires, 1990), as does Emilio Corbière in *La masonería: política y sociedades secretas en Argentina* (Santa Fe, 1994).

Frederic W. Seal Coon's *Spanish-American Revolutionary Masonry: The Mythical Masonry of Francisco de Miranda* (London, 1981) is a more up-to-date and better-documented study, which was later made use of by León Zeldis for *Freemasonry's Contribution to South American Independence: A Factual Approach* (London, 1998) and its Spanish version, *La Francmasonería en la independencia de Chile y América* (Madrid, 1997). The works of Alfonso Freile and Antonio Egea on Miranda hardly add anything new to what had already been said by the Mirandista "classics," especially as in their brief biographies they do not call on the twenty volumes of Miranda's interesting and revealing diaries, which were published from 1938 by the General Miranda Archive and clearly demystify the question of Freemasonry.

Also related to secret societies and independence, this time those of the Cuba of Fernando VII, is José Leonardo Ruiz Sánchez's enlightening work *Independentismo y sociedades secretas en Cuba bajo el reinado de Fernando VII* (Zaragoza, 1993).

Carlos Francisco Martínez Moreno has produced a thought-provoking essay entitled ¿Es correcto hablar de sociedades patrióticas paramasónicas? (Mexico City, 2008). It serves as a counterpoint to A. H. Oliveira Marques, *Las Sociedades Patrióticas* (Zaragoza, 1995), which analyzes the connections between Masonic lodges and patriotic societies in the Azores, Portugal, and Brazil. This same issue is addressed from an alternative innovative perspective by Felipe Santiago Del Solar Guajardo in *José Miguel Carrera. Redes masónicas y sociedades secretas durante las guerras de la independencia en América del Sur* (Zaragoza, 2010). The protagonist of the work, José Miguel Carrera, is the only Chilean who we know with certainty was a Mason, since he joined the St. John No. 1 Lodge in New York in 1816, though after his initiation he never returned to Chile. Del Solar Guajardo returned to the same issue in *Secreto y Sociedades secretas en la crisis del Antiguo Régimen. Reflexiones para una historia interconectada con el mundo hispánico* (*REHMLAC*, 2011), a brilliant summary, though one that does not make sufficiently clear the distinction between Freemasonry on the one hand and Lautaro, Rational Gentlemen, or Oriental Lodges or the American Gathering and so forth on the other, which are radically different to Freemasonry. Along the same lines are the equally valuable works Mario Dotta, *Caudillos, doctores y masones. Protagonistas en la Gran Comarca Rioplatense, 1806–1865* (Montevideo, 2008) and Eugenia Molina, *Las modernas prácticas asociativas como ámbitos de defensa de lazos objetivos políticos durante el proceso revolucionario* (Talca, 2010).

Freemasonry and the Leading Figures of Independence

Intimately linked to this theme is the equally pertinent subject of the leaders of independence, who have entered the Masonic "sainthood" with a constancy and fidelity worthy of the best of causes. First among them is Francisco de Miranda. Following the interpretation of the aforementioned Seal-Coon and his *Mítica masonería de Francisco de Miranda* (Zaragoza, 1995) as well as that of Ferrer Benimeli in *Les "Caballeros Racionales," les loges Lautariennes et les formes déviées de la Francmaçonnerie dans le monde hispanique* (Bordeaux, 1991), in ¿Fué masón Miranda? (Maracaibo, 2008) Robert Arapé poses the question: Was Miranda a Mason? His answer is categorical: Miranda was never a Mason. José Pascual Mora García seems to accept this thesis, and he casts doubt on Miranda's affiliation with Freemasonry in his work *La Masonería. Su historia y su contribución en la construcción simbólica de la nación venezolana* (Morelia, 2011), doing so based on a series of writers who say nothing about the so-called Precursor's initiation into Freemasonry—authors such as Mariano Picón Salas, Alfredo Boulton, José Salcedo, Carmen Bohórquez, and Manuel Hernández.[9] Many more authors and works could have been added to this list—for example, William Spence Robertson, *La vida de Miranda* (Caracas, 2006), a work republished by Venezuela's National Academy of History, with the participation of seven universities[10] and the Fundación Polar, in the Bicentenario de la Independencia collection. This author states, in response to the theory that while in London Miranda founded "an association of Spanish American revolutionaries called the Lautaro Lodge," that an examination of his unpublished papers brings no evidence that he belonged to the Masonic Order or that he founded the Lautaro Lodge. Moreover, he adds, there are not even any traces of evidence that Miranda met San Martín.[11] The first edition of this now-classic biography of Miranda was published in 1929 by the University of North Carolina, Chapel Hill. William Spence Robertson's doctoral thesis, which he completed at Yale and which focused on *Francisco de Miranda and the Revolutionizing of Spanish América* (Washington, 1909), won him awards in 1903 and 1907, and it constitutes one of the most valuable and solid contributions for understanding the life and political activities of Francisco de Miranda.

The case of Bolívar, the only one of the "liberators" for whom there exists documentary evidence of a circumstantial affiliation with Freemasonry, was the subject of Frederic W. Seal Coon's masterful study *Simón Bolívar, Freemason* (London, 1977) and also of Edward

---

9   Titles are in the Appendix.

10   Universidad Central de Venezuela, Universidad Simón Bolívar, Universidad Católica Andrés Bello, Universidad Metropolitana, Universidad del Zulia, Universidad Cecilio Acosta, and Universidad de los Andes.

11   William Spence Robertson, *La vida de Miranda* (Caracas, Venezuela: Academia Nacional de la Historia, 2006).

Stolper, *More Light on Simon Bolívar, Freemason* (London, 1979). This subject had previously been dealt with by Manuel Pérez Vila in *La experiencia masónica de Bolívar en París* (Caracas, 1944) and then by Ferrer Benimeli in *Bolívar y la Masonería* (Porto Alegre and Madrid, 1983) and in ¿Bolívar masón? (Madrid, 1984), as well as by Ramón Díaz Sánchez in *Sí, Bolívar fue masón* (Caracas, 1956). However, José Luis Salcedo-Bastardo, *Simón Bolívar. La vita e il pensiero politico* (Rome, 1983), Laurence Tacon, *Simón Bolívar* (Paris, 1986), and Nelson Martínez, *Simón Bolívar* (Madrid, 1987), as is the case of many others, provide us with a view of Bolívar and his life that is more general and steers totally clear of Freemasonry. That said, this dimension is considered along traditional Masonic lines in Patricia Pasquali, *Bolívar, San Martín y la masonería en la independencia americana* (Buenos Aires, 2001) and in Fernández Cabrelli, *De Bolívar a Sandino. Hombres de la masonería en la prédica integradora* (Montevideo, 1989).

Of special interest is Eloy Reverón, *El fantasma de Bolívar en la Masonería Venezolana* (Caracas, 2001), which was published by the Venezuelan Institute for Masonic Studies. It is among the best and most thorough studies on Bolívar and his connections to Freemasonry to have been published in recent years.

Under this same heading there are a greater number of works that study San Martín and his alleged—although never proven—Masonic affiliation. Among the many that could be cited, besides those that I compiled and commented upon in my *Bibliografía de la Masonería* from 1978—for example, the study by Guillermo Furlong from the Argentine National Academy of History, *El General San Martín ¿masón-católico-deísta?* (Buenos Aires, 1956 and 1960) or Armando Tonelli, *El General San Martín y la masonería* (Buenos Aires, 1943)—are Enrique de Gandía, *San Martín masón* (Buenos Aires, 1990); Alcibíades Lappas' manipulated studies *San Martín y las logias* (Buenos Aires, 1978), *San Martín y su formación* (Buenos Aires, 1978), and *San Martín y su ideario liberal* (Buenos Aires, 1982); Fernando Nadra, *San Martín hoy* (Buenos Aires, 1974); and the previously cited posthumous work by Horacio Juan Cuccorese on *San Martín: catolicismo y masonería* (Buenos Aires, 1993), all of which are more well intentioned than they are correct in their attempts to clarify "the San Martín Masonic legend," a question that has continued to divide historians and Masonic scholars (though more the latter than the former). Another work that fits in here is the collective volume published upon the bicentennial of San Martín's birth, *Nuevos estudios sobre la vida y la obra del libertador general José de San Martín* (Buenos Aires, 1978). At the head of the work is Alcibíades Lappas, *San Martín y su formación*, which once again emphasizes commonplaces about "the Cádiz Lodges, the Rational Gentlemen, the Union of Patriots," and so forth.

This is a question that Ricardo Piccirelli dealt with in *San Martín y la política de los pueblos* (Buenos Aires, 1957). The third chapter of Piccirelli's excellent ideological and political bi-ography of San Martín focuses on the "Lautaro Lodge" until the political crisis of 1815, and it offers divergent opinions on the labeling of the Lautaro Lodge and similar subordinate ones as Masonic.

A similar critical line is taken in John Lynch, *San Martín, soldado argentino, héroe americano* (Barcelona, 2009), in which it is stated that the Lautaro Lodge was a political grouping rather than a Masonic one. Guadalupe Jiménez Codinach uses Lynch's succinct formulation as a starting point for *Auge de las sociedades secretas: la logia Lautaro y la independencia hispanoamericana* (Morelia, 2011). However, the text then becomes full of suppositions (San Martín's affiliation to the Lautaro Lodge No. 3 of Cádiz), contradictions (in relation to the Rational Gentlemen and Lautaro lodges), and unproven factual claims (Miranda's and San Martín's membership within Freemasonry).

Also worth highlighting is Emilio Ocampo's biography *Alvear en la Guerra con el Imperio del Brasil* (Buenos Aires, 2003), which, following the traditional historiography, identifies the Society of Oriental Gentlemen and Lautaro lodges with Masonic lodges, as a result of which it perpetuates the Masonic myth, though it does also reject and attack other accepted myths, such as Alvear's military incompetence.

As a counterpoint, the figure of José Martí, who came long after the other "liberators" and in the second wave of Latin American independence, has merited better studies, such as *Martí,*

España y la masonería (Santa Cruz de Tenerife, 2008), a serious and rigorous piece of research conducted from the University of La Laguna by Manuel de Paz Sánchez. He had previously focused especially on the story of Martí's death in a work published in Havana and Logroño, *La muerte de Martí, un debate historiográfico* (Havana, 1990; Logroño, 1991), and in collaboration with José Manuel Castellano he produced *Martí, masón y otras crónicas wangüermetianas* (Zaragoza, 1993). The former Grand Master of Cuban Freemasonry, Carlos Manuel Piñeiro y del Cueto, who died in exile in Puerto Rico, left us a personal testimony in *La ideología martiana frente a la doctrina comunista* (San Juan, 1979). Despite the proliferation of studies on Martí coinciding with the centennial of his death, however, he is scarcely linked to Freemasonry in studies that did not originate in Masonic circles, as is the case of Antonio Padilla Bolívar, *La lucha de José Martí* (Madrid, 1987) or of Carmen Almodóvar Muñoz, *Antología crítica de la historiografía cubana* (Havana, 1986). Meanwhile, Isidro Sepúlveda Muñoz in *Martí y Hostos* (Zaragoza, 1999) undertakes a comparative analysis of the Antillean turn-of-the-century nationalisms, while Samuel Sánchez Gálvez offers us definitive documentary evidence of Martí's Masonic membership in *Martí ciñó el mandil. Prueba documental de su filiación masónica* (Havana, 2007). One of the essays in Eduardo Torres Cuevas, *Historia de la masonería cubana. Seis ensayos* (Havana, 2004), namely *José Martí y la masonería española*, focuses on Martí and Spanish Freemasonry. It is a magnificent summary of the period of the Cuban-Spanish Masonic history that Martí experienced and that forged his thinking.

A few years earlier, Torres Cuevas produced a seminal work on Martí: *El alma visible de Cuba: José Martí y el partido revolucionario cubano* (Havana, 1984). Juan Blanco Rodríguez, *La actitud de Martí ante los españoles y la presencia de estos en el "Ejército Libertador" cubano* (Madrid, 1996) also provides illumination on the subject. In 2009, Ismael Acosta García published *José Martí, una vida por la libertad, la igualdad y la fraternidad* (Morelia, 2009), in which he devotes a long and comprehensive chapter to "Martí, Masón" that incorporates the most recent and decisive investigations into Martí's Masonic involvement in Madrid and ends a cycle begun many years before with, among others, Carlos Jinesta, *José Martí en Costa Rica* (San José, 1993) and continued by Manuel García Guatas in *La Zaragoza de José Martí* (Zaragoza, 1999), the city in which he obtained his doctorate.

Puerto Rico and Santo Domingo

Among the new studies on European Freemasonry and its relationship with Latin America, I wish to point out those produced by members of CHSSM or from within the center. In the case of Puerto Rico, worthy of note are the two volumes of José Antonio Ayala Pérez's *La masonería de obediencia española en Puerto Rico en los siglos XIX y XX* (Murcia, 1991–1993), a model for investigation and hitherto unknown findings. Ayala has also applied his characteristic rigor to Puerto Rican Freemasonry in other works—for example, *El contencioso masónico en Puerto Rico a finales del siglo XIX* (San Juan, 1989), *La masonería de obediencia española ante el conflicto colonial puertorriqueño* (Logroño, 1991; Zaragoza, 1993), *La conjunción masónica-librepensadora-protestante contra la Iglesia católica: el caso de Puerto Rico (1898–1925)* (Zaragoza, 1994), *La masonería de obediencia francesa en Puerto Rico de 1821 a 1841* (Madrid, 1991), and *Maçoneria, regionalisme i independencia al Puerto Rico de la fi del segle* (Barcelona, 1997).

Highly detailed complements to these works are Manuel de Paz Sánchez, *Españolismo versus separatismo en la masonería puertorriqueña: la logia Borinquen nº 81 de Mayagüez (1889–1897)* (Madrid, 1985) and Jesús Raúl Navarro García, *El desprestigio masónico en Puerto Rico durante la década ominosa* (Alicante, 1990). Paloma Vázquez Ibáñez, who defended her Master's dissertation *La Masonería y su influencia política en el Puerto Rico del siglo XIX y principios del XX* at the Pontifical Catholic University of Puerto Rico in 2004, later presented a glimpse of it at the Logroño symposium with *Puerto Rico, la carta autonómica de 1897 y su breve instauración* (Zaragoza, 2007). At the same symposium, Paul Estrade offered the biographical study *Betances, masón inconforme* (Zaragoza, 2007) on the man considered to be the father of the Puerto Rican homeland and the last of the Latin American nineteenth-century liberators, comparable to Benito Juárez and José Martí.

Previously, the Freemasonry of Puerto Rico had also been the focus of José Antonio Ferrer Benimeli's interest in *La masonería y la independencia de Puerto Rico. Análisis de un papel de 1823* (Logroño, 1993) and *Masones asturianos en la Cuba y Puerto Rico del siglo XIX* (Oviedo, 1993).

The focus on Masonic immigration between Asturias and Latin America found in the latter work received an expanded and more in-depth methodological treatment from Yván Pozuelo Andrés in *Las relaciones masónicas entre Asturias e Hispanoamérica en los siglos XIX y XX. Estado de la cuestión* (*REHMLAC*, 2009).

The subject of slavery in Puerto Rico is dealt with by Luis Antonio Otero González in *La masonería autóctona y española ante la esclavitud* (Zaragoza, 2010).

Finally in relation to Puerto Rico, one might also cite Otto Sievens Irizarry, *La masonería vista por autores puertorriqueños* (San Juan, 2010), Luis Antonio Otero González, *La Universidad Interamericana de Puerto Rico y su relación con la Masonería* (Santurce, Puerto Rico, 2008), and Miguel A. Pereira, *La modernidad en el periodismo masónico puertorriqueño del siglo XIX* (Santurce, Puerto Rico, 2009).

If we move from Puerto Rico to Santo Domingo, we find no major studies despite the interest that the archbishop/bishop of Higüey and founder of the Universidad Católica Madre y

Maestra, Mons. Hugo E. Polanco, had in the question during his time. To him we owe an introduction to the subject, *La Masonería en la República Dominicana* (Santo Domingo, 1985), an open, objective, and well-documented account produced out of an interest in historical matters and the author's pastoral concern with understanding rather than confrontation. Among other works, it draws on *Bibliografía masónica dominicana* (Santo Domingo, 1945) by Luis Florens, as well as the Masonic Constitution and the General Statutes for the Symbolic Order of the Dominican Republic, the *Reseña histórica del Supremo Consejo del Grado 33 y último del Rito Escocés Antiguo y Aceptado para la República Dominicana* (Santo Domingo, 1952) by the then-Sovereign Grand Commander Haim López Penha, and other bulletins, regulations, and internal documents from Dominican Freemasonry.

Equally important, despite its brevity, is the chapter that María Magdalena Guerrero Cano devotes to Freemasonry in her book *Disciplina y laxitud: La Iglesia dominicana en la época de la Anexión* (Cádiz, 1989), in which she addresses the formation of the Grand National Lodge of the Dominican Republic in 1858 and the problems that arose with Archbishop Monzón following the Spanish annexation, a question very ably explained in his time by José de la Gándara Navarro in *Anexión y guerra de Santo Domingo* (Madrid, 1884), from which Guerrero Cano takes her information.

As a necessary complement here,

Francisco Sánchez offers his *Historia sintética de la Masonería Dominicana* (Ciudad Trujillo, 1998).

Aware of the more recent historiographical vacuum, I would highlight two works. One focuses on French Santo Domingo: Jacques de Cauna, *Autour de la thèse du complot. Francmaçonnerie, Révolution et contre-Révolution à Saint-Domingue (1789–1791)*. And the other examines Hispanic Santo Domingo: José Antonio Ferrer Benimeli, *La logia dominicana Aurora nº 82 de San Pedro de Macorís (1889–1923)* (Caracas, 2005-*REHMLAC*, 2012).

The always-controversial issue of relations between the Catholic Church and Freemasonry, and more particularly during the Trujillo dictatorship, has been studied by Francisco Javier Alonso Vázquez, considered today to be the leading expert in this period of Dominican history, in *La pugna entre la Iglesia católica y la masonería en el ocaso de la dictadura de Trujillo* (Zaragoza, 2001), which analyzes Dominican Freemasonry's collaboration with the Trujillo dictatorship and the coercion suffered by the Catholic Church at the same time.

Cuba

In relation to Cuba it is noticeable that, compared to the rest of the Caribbean, there are more monographs on Freemasonry, published in and from the island as well as from outside of it. For this reason, it is not easy to make a rigorous critical selection of the Masonic-Cuban historiography from recent decades in the highly general style of

Carmen Almodóvar Muñoz, *Antología crítica de la historiografía cubana* (Havana, 1986).

Departing from Aurelio Miranda Álvarez's now-classic *Historia documentada de la masonería en Cuba* (La Habana, 1933), by way of an introduction it is worth citing Emilio Canciobello y Arango, *La masonería como factor decisivo en la formación y desarrollo de la Nacionalidad Cubana* (Havana, 1932) and Roger Fernández Callejas, *Historia moderna de la Francmasonería en Cuba. Su influencia en la independencia cubana* (Havana, 1985), as well as Fernández Callejas' previous works: *Historia de la Francmasonería en Cuba* (Havana, 1944), *Origen cubano de la masonería regular* (Havana, 1951), *A Report of Masonry in Cuba in 1969* (London, 1969), *Cien años de actividad masónica* (Havana, 1961), and *Primera manifestación pública masónica independiente* (Havana, 1949).

Of a certain complementary use are Francisco Ponte Domínguez, *El delito de francmasonería en Cuba: estudio histórico acerca de la alianza del altar y el trono, su persecución de la francmasonería en Cuba* (Mexico City, 1951) and *Historia de la Masonería del Rito Escocés en Cuba* (Mexico City, 1951). And to close this introduction, Orlando González González offers three works: *Valoración histórica del Gran Oriente de Cuba y las Antillas* (Havana, 1987), *La personalidad masónica literaria de Aramburu* (Havana, 1989), and *El periodismo masónico y la revista de la Gran Logia, en Miranda* (Havana, 1989). The latter comprises three lectures based on

Freemasonry that were given to mark the fiftieth anniversary of the death of the "Resp. Bro. Don Aurelio Miranda Álvarez."

Of special interest here owing to the date on which it was written and to its authorship is the *Mensaje Anual* by Grand Master Carlos M. Piñeiro y del Cueto, a realistic assessment of the work completed in his ten years of Masonic governance that was delivered in Havana on March 22, 1959, the centennial of the Grand Lodge of Cuba.

But in Cuba today, the reference point is the research team set up around University of Havana professor and president of the Cuban Academy of History Eduardo Torres Cuevas, the author of the crucial *Historia de Cuba (1868–1989)* (Havana, 1994–96), whose second volume on the "struggles for national independence and social transformations" features a brief section devoted to Freemasonry. More recently, in his *Historia de la masonería cubana* (Havana, 2004) he analyzes Cuban Freemasonry through six essays, five of which he had already presented in Spain at different symposiums organized by the CHSSM: *Los cuerpos masónicos cubanos durante el siglo XIX* (Zaragoza, 1993 and *REHMLAC*, 2012), *El 98, Cuba y la masonería cubana* (Zaragoza, 1999), *La masonería en Cuba durante la Primera República, 1902–1933)* (Zaragoza, 1991), *La masonería cubana en las décadas finales del siglo* (Zaragoza, 2001), *José Martí y la masonería española* (Zaragoza, 2004), and *El Gran Oriente de Cuba y las Antillas y la ruptura del 68*. The latter is the only one not previously presented through the CHSSM. Torres Cuevas subsequently offered *Sagasta, Cuba y las masonerías Cubana y Española* (Zaragoza, 2007), *Presencia republicana española en Cuba* (Zaragoza, 2010), and *Masonerías en Cuba durante el siglo XIX* (*REHMLAC*, 2012).

Professor Torres Cuevas' influence at the university level covers the universities of Havana and Cienfuegos. Some examples of it include Samuel Sánchez Gálvez's doctoral thesis *La logia masónica cienfueguera Fernandina de Jagua (1878–1902). Un estudio de caso*, which was defended at the University of Havana in 2010 and was published in brief overview form under the same title in *REHMLAC* in 2010. Previously, he had also published *Ciencia y cultura en Fernandina de Jagua* (*REHMLAC*, 2009), which he provided a glimpse of at the Third Ibero-American Congress of Thought, held in Holguín in 2006, under the title of *Masonería, Cultura y Ciencia. Apuntes para su estudio en Cienfuegos: 1878–1940*, and also at the First International Symposium on the History of Latin American and Caribbean Freemasonry in Havana in 2008, this time under the title of *Masonería, Ciencia y Cultura en la logia masónica cienfueguera Fernandina de Jagua, 1878–1902*. This same author also produced *Institucionalización de la masonería en Cienfuegos* (*REHMLAC*, 2009), *Legados perdurables: masonería en Cienfuegos (1878–1902)* (Cienfuegos, 2010), and *Los nombres simbólicos en la logia masónica cienfueguera Fernandina de Jagua: expresiones de pensamiento* (Cienfuegos, 2007).

In turn, Dr. Samuel Sánchez Gálvez supervised Aimara Olga Amador Alonso's thesis *Significación sociocultural de los símbolos empleados en las logias masónicas de la ciudad de Cienfuegos* (Cienfuegos, 2011); Haens Beltrán Alonso's Master's thesis in historical and anthropological studies, entitled *Aproximación al funcionamiento de la Gran Logia de la isla de Cuba desde la revista "La Gran Logia" (1929–1933)* (Cienfuegos, 2011); and Yuniel Fonseca Pozo's Doctoral thesis currently in preparation, *La Gran Logia Oriental de Cuba: un caso de cisma masónico.*

Haens Beltrán Alonso and Jency Mendoza Otero, professors at the Carlos Rafael Rodríguez University of Cienfuegos, offered a preview of Beltrán Alonso's thesis *La masonería cubana y el proceso revolucionario de los años 30: Aproximación desde la revista La Gran Logia, 1931–1933*, which was published in *REHMLAC.*

In *Españoles y Cubanos en la Masonería. Manuel Curros Enríquez* (REHMLAC, 2010) Janet Iglesias Cruz and Javiher Gutiérrez of the University of Havana demonstrate through a case study how the contradictory ideologies of Spaniards and Cubans coexisted in Freemasonry. And in *La simbología masónica en el Cementerio de Colón* (REHMLAC, 2010), the same authors study the presence of lodges and Masonic symbols in the monumental Colón cemetery in Havana.

Chee Kung Tong ¿Vínculos masónicos? (REHMLAC, 2009) by María Teresa Montes de Oca Choy and Yasmín Ydoy Ortiz, who are also affiliated with the University of Havana, offers a series of thought-provoking reflections on the use of Masonic symbols by a Chinese society established in Cuba in the nineteenth century.

Cuban Freemasonry has also been considered from France by Dominique Soucy, who in 1999 published *La diffusion des concepts maçonniques dans la société cubaine du XIXème siècle* (Paris, 1999). She is the author of a doctoral thesis that was defended in December 2003 at the Université de Paris VIII-Saint-Denis and published three years later under the title *Masonería y nación. Redes masónicas y políticas en la construcción identitaria cubana (1811–1902)* (Santa Cruz de Tenerife, 2006). This work is a critical interpretation of and reflection upon the basic role of the ideas of Cuban Freemasonry in the formation of the national state and consciousness, something pointed out by her thesis supervisor Paul Estrade, who has driven forward studies on Cuban Freemasonry from Paris. Dominique Soucy has subsequently presented other works, such as *Intervención del Grande Oriente de Francia en la historia de la masonería cubana* (Zaragoza, 2007), *Hacia una mediología de la masonería cubana* (Zaragoza, 2001), *El Palenque literario: Un testimonio de la realidad masónica de Cuba (1876–1883)* (Zaragoza, 2004), *Vicente Antonio de Castro y la opción reformista: desde "La Cartera Cubana" hasta Yara* (Zaragoza, 2010), and, in collaboration with Delphine Sappez, *Autonomismo y masonería en Cuba* (REHMLAC, 2009).

In terms of biographies, in a

similar vein to Roger Fernández Callejas, *Vicente Antonio de Castro. Masón y patriota, precursor del 68* (La Habana, 1946) and Orlando González González, *La personalidad masónica literaria de Aramburu* (La Habana, 1989) in their respective eras, María Dolores Domingo Acebrón has put forward via the Spanish National Research Council in Madrid a series of interesting studies: *Francisco Arredondo y Miranda: masón y mambí* (Zaragoza, 1993), *Víctor Patricio Landaluze, un pintor español masón y anti-independentista en Cuba en la primera mitad del siglo XIX* (Zaragoza, 1995), *Rafael María de Labra y su relación con la masonería en Madrid y en Cuba (1880–1918)* (Zaragoza, 2004), *Independencia en el Caribe, Cuba: José de Armas y Céspedes: masón* (Zaragoza, 2010), and *Antonio Govín y Torres. El papel del autonomismo y su relación con la masonería en Cuba 1878–1898* (Zaragoza, 2001). The subject of autonomism and the figure of Govín y Torres are also considered by Delphine Sappez in *Antonio Govín y Torres, nexo entre masonería y autonomismo en Cuba* (Zaragoza, 2010).

To these studies one must add Manuel Hernández González, *Liberalismo y masonería en la América de las guerras de la Independencia: Cabral de Noroña y sus reflexiones sobre la masonería* (Alicante, 1990), Francisco López Casimiro, *Ramón Blanco Erenas, capitán general de Cuba y la masonería* (Badajoz, 2009), and Paul Estrade, *Un masón audaz y conformista, paradigmático del Gran Oriente de Francia: el franco-cubano Severiano de Heredia (1836–1901)* (Zaragoza, 2010). The lat-ter work was subsequently turned into a book: *Severiano de Heredia, ce mulâtre cubain que Paris fit "maire" et la République ministre* (Paris, 2011). Estrade's subject, Severiano de Heredia, moved to France and later became president of the Council of Paris and minister of public works, and he dedicated his life to politics, Freemasonry, and relations with Cuba and Latin America. And purely symbolically, on the basis of having been born in Cuba in 1877, there is Julio Mangada Rosenörn, who is studied by Carlos Navajas Zubeldia in *Biografía masónica y militar de Julio Mangada Rosenörn* (Zaragoza, 1993). Mangada Rosenörn's military career led him to Puerto Rico and the Spain of the Second Republic and the civil war, and he went into exile with the Masons in Mexico, where he was made a member of the Supreme Council.

Manuel de Paz Sánchez, meanwhile, focuses his studies and accounts on Luis Felipe Gómez Wangüemert: *Luis Felipe Gómez Wangüemert y la masonería palmera y cubana de la década de 1930. Notas para un estudio* (Santa Cruz de Tenerife, 1981 and 2010), *Wangüemert y Cuba* (La Laguna, 1991), *Masones y anticlericalismo en Luis F. Gómez Wangüemert* (Zaragoza, 1995; Las Palmas, 2010), and *Crónica y semblanza wangüemertiana de Mercedes Pinto: una feminista canaria en Cuba (1935–1936)* (Las Palmas, 1980 and 2010). In another work, the same author extends his study to other military figures: *El enigma Sandoval y otros "enigmas" militares españoles: Bayo Giroud, Rodríguez Lozano ...* (Zaragoza, 2007).

Ferrer Benimeli provides detailed information in *1817, un año clave para la masonería tinerfeña y cubana* (Santa Cruz de Tenerife, 1984), in *Implantación de logias y distribución geográfico-histórica de la masonería española* (Zaragoza, 1987), and in the overview study *Apuntes históricos de la masonería cubano-española del siglo XIX* (Zaragoza, 1993), in which he notes that in Cuba during the nineteenth century, the Grand Orient of Spain alone founded eighty-six lodges, while the Grand National Orient of Spain founded forty-two, the Spanish Grand Orient forty-four, and the Spanish Grand Lodge of Memphis and Mizraim seventeen, to name only the most important Obediences of the time.

These lodges, which are referred to by Pere Sánchez Ferré in *Masonería y colonialismo español* (Madrid, 1989), were studied by José Manuel Castellano Gil in his doctoral thesis *La masonería de Obediencia española en Cuba durante el siglo XIX*, which was defended at the University of La Laguna in December 1992 and subsequently published under the title *La Masonería española en Cuba* (Santa Cruz de Tenerife, 1996). This work is a model for the conducting of research and the presenting of revealing and little-known findings—for example, the high participation of Creoles in lodges of Spanish origin and the fact that out of the approximately eight thousand Freemasons calculated to have been on the island in the nineteenth century, around five thousand (70% of the total) were members of Spanish Obediences established in Cuba.

While the majority of studies produced in Cuba and France about Cuban Freemasonry focus on the so-called native and autonomist Freemasonry that some identify as the only authentic form owing to its involvement in the ideological and political struggles for independence, in Spain, based on the documents preserved in the Salamanca archive, the focus of study has been the more than two hundred lodges created on the island and recognized by various Spanish Obediences.

Beforehand, professor Manuel de Paz Sánchez published *Aspectos generales y principales características de la implantación sistemática de la francmasonería en la Gran Antilla durante el último tercio del siglo XIX* (Seville, 1979) and *Hipótesis en torno a un desarrollo paralelo de la masonería canaria y cubana durante el primer tercio del presente siglo. Acotaciones para un estudio* (Las Palmas, 1982), which he followed up a few years later with *España, Cuba y Marruecos. Masonería, identidades y construcción nacional* (Las Palmas, 2009 and 2010). Manuel Hernández González, meanwhile, published *Masonería, liberalismo y cuestión nacional en la Cuba del trienio liberal* (Zaragoza, 1995).

With the material preserved in what is now called the Documentation Center for Historical Memory in Salamanca, other works have been produced. These include those of José Miguel Delgado Idarreta and Abilio Jorge Torres on Cuban lodges that had the distinctive title of "Zaragoza," and their socioprofessional composition and mentality (Zaragoza, 1993 and 1995); that of Carmen Mellado and Concha Ponce on Valencian Freemasonry before the Cuban-Spanish war of 1895–96 (Zaragoza, 1993); Manuel Júlbez Campos, *Modelos de masonería española identificada con América* (Zaragoza, 1993); and Pere Sánchez Ferré's study of Catalan Freemasonry and the Cuban colonial conflict (Barcelona, 1984–85).

The questions of revolution and independence were studied in his time by (among others) Martín Landa Bacallado in *La Masonería y la revolución cubana. Semejanzas e idearios* (Havana, 1964). The same aspects have since also been addressed in José Manuel Castellano, *La masonería en Cuba y el conflicto colonial* (Barcelona, 1997), Luis Martín, *La masonería española y la independencia de Cuba* (Nantes, 1992), Eduardo Enríquez del Árbol, *Masonería y patriotismo ante el desastre: la defensa de la institución en Cuba por los Grandes Orientes españoles (1895–1898)* (Granada, 1998), Manuel de Paz Sánchez, *La masonería y la pérdida de las colonias: impresiones sobre el caso cubano* (Zaragoza, 1993), and Pedro Pascual Martínez, *La prensa masónica de España y Cuba (1868–1898)* (Zaragoza, 1999).

María Dolores Domingo Acebrón has examined certain aspects of the Cuban wars in *La masonería durante la guerra de los diez años. Cuba (1868–1878)* (Alicante, 1990) and *Integrismo y masonería. Los cuerpos de voluntarios en Cuba (1868–1898)* (Zaragoza, 1999). And while studying Cuba, Jean-Pierre Bastian once again pursued the subject of Protestantism through a work that underwent slight variations in its title during its publication first in Spain, then in Colombia, and finally in Cuba: *Las redes francmasonas y protestantes en el movimiento independentista cubano, 1868–1898* (Zaragoza, 1999), *Sociedades protestantes y logias en la lucha independentista cubana, 1868–1898* (Medellín, 2001), and *Francmasones y protestantes en el movimiento revolucionario de la independencia cubana, 1868–1898* (Havana, 2012). It is interesting to observe how the title used in Spain speaks in terms of "independence movements," in Cuba in terms of "revolutionary movement," and in Colombia in terms of "Protestant societies," rather than in terms of networks.

The emigration to and exile in Cuba on the part of Spanish Freemasons has been studied by Alberto Valín Fernández in *Galicia y su emigración en la masonería cubana* (Zaragoza, 1993-Barcelona 1997; Santiago de Compostela, 2001), by Manuel de Paz Sánchez in *Los residentes españoles en Cuba y la masonería después de la independencia* (Madrid, 1986), and by Antonio Morales Benítez and Fernando Sigler Silvera in *La masonería gaditana de obediencia cubana: la logia Tolerancia y Fraternidad* (Zaragoza, 1993)—in this case the focus is on the establishment of a lodge of Cuban Obedience in Spain—as well as by José Ignacio Cruz Orozco in *La masonería valenciana y América* (Valencia, 1993) and in *Solidaridad y exilio. La masonería española en América, (1939-1977)* (Zaragoza, 1993), by José Antonio Ferrer Benimeli in *Masones asturianos en la Cuba y Puerto*

Rico del siglo XIX (Oviedo, 1993), and by Juan José Morales Ruiz in *Masones menorquines en América latina durante el siglo XIX* (Zaragoza, 1993). Cuban immigration to North America is analyzed through a very detailed case study by Manuel Hernández González in *La orden cubana de los Caballeros de la Luz en el exilio norteamericano* (Zaragoza, 1993).

Complementing this latter work is Jorge L. Romeu Beltrán, *Estudio estadístico del auge y declive de la Gran Logia de Cuba (1945–2012)* (*REHM-LAC*, 2012), a work conducted not as a historical study but rather through the clinical techniques of statistics and new analytical tools.

The peculiar and interesting question of symbolic names began to be studied by Françoise Randouyer in *Les noms symboliques des Maçons espagnols* (Paris, 1982) and in *Ideología masónica a través de los nombres simbólicos* (Salamanca, 1987), and although this issue occupies a prominent place in each and every local and regional historical account of Freemasonry, as the main focus of study and in relation in particular to Cuba it has only been studied in Pilar Amador, *Mensajes de mentalidad expresados a través de los nombres simbólicos de los masones de América: Cuba* (Zaragoza, 1993) and in Yván Pozuelo Andrés, *Notas sobre el "nombre simbólico" en Hispanoamérica* (*REHMLAC*, 2012), the most complete and in-depth study out of those conducted on the question of symbolic names.

Intimately linked to the foregoing is the joint work by Luis Martín and Françoise Randouyer, *Título distintivo e ideología en las logias de las Antillas* (Zaragoza, 1993), as well as that by María Elena Muñoz Echeverría and María Jesús Ocaña Vázquez, *Elementos indígenas y de ultramar en los sellos de las logias de Cuba y Filipinas* (Zaragoza, 1993), which involves a research focus used with increasing frequency that combines art and ideology. And in *La crisis del 98 en la filatelia masónica* (Zaragoza, 1999), Joan Sabater i Pie focuses his attention on the independence movements of Cuba and the Philippines through the wealth of postage stamps dedicated to national heroes who fought for the independence of their respective countries.[12]

A new research avenue is offered by Fernando Redondo Díaz in his brief study *La prensa militar y el papel de la masonería en ultramar* (Zaragoza, 1999), in which he considers military opinion journalism and how it viewed the overseas emancipation and independence movements and their connection with Freemasonry, especially native Cuban Freemasonry. Still on the subject of the press—in this case its Masonic version—Yván Pozuelo Andrés presented a model work at the Tenth Central American History Congress that was organized in Managua (July 12–16, 2010) by the National Autonomous University of Nicaragua. His paper was entitled *Relaciones y opiniones oficiales de las masonerías españolas sobre Iberoamérica durante la II República*

---

12   Today, Joan Sabater i Pie's rich philatelic collection is held at the Biblioteca Pública Arús in Barcelona, where it can be consulted.

(1931–1935) *(REHMLAC*, 2011). In it, he first offers some incisive thoughts on the way in which the history of Freemasonry is written and then analyzes the reports on Spanish America found in the bulletins and official journals of the Spanish Grand Orient and the Spanish Grand Lodge, the only two Obediences in existence during the Spanish Second Republic (1930–1936). The reports are grouped both by topic and by journals and bulletins. Its final charts and appendices are fundamental and a reflection of a well-executed work.

The same could be said of Yordanka Jiménez Pabón, who focuses on the always-controversial role of women in Cuban Freemasonry in *La masonería femenina en Cuba: entre la aceptación y el veto* (Zaragoza, 2010), and also of Julio de la Cueva Merino, who in *El lugar de la masonería en la recepción eclesiástica de las guerras coloniales y el desastre de 1898* (Zaragoza, 1999) deals with his characteristic insight with ecclesiastic thinking on the Cuban and Philippine insurrections that contributed to the ideological justification of repression and a "just war" against not only enemies of the fatherland, but also, and above all those, of the Church.

Closely linked to this issue is the question of anti-Freemasonry, in relation to which José Antonio Ferrer Benimeli in *La antimasonería en España y América Latina* (Zaragoza, 1995) attempts a summary to help later studies on the issue to go into greater depth. In this more general context—applicable to all of Latin America—it is necessary to cite Yván Pozuelo Andrés' revealing work *Masonería en los periódicos digitales hispanoamericanos (2006–2007)* (*REHMLAC*, 2009), or the more specific and commemorative works by José Antonio Ferrer Benimeli, namely *La masonería española y el IV Centenario del descubrimiento de América* (Zaragoza, 1993) and *La Francmaçonnerie en Espagne et Amérique Latine* (Paris, 1990 and 1996), or André Jansen, *La masonería en la literatura hispanoamericana* (Zaragoza, 1993), which in fact confines itself to Masonic references in Cuban writer Alejo Carpentier's *Explosion in a Cathedral.*

A different focus and geographic context are to be found in Steven C. Bullock's study *Revolutionary Brotherhood: Freemasonry and the Transformation of the American Social Order, 1730–1840* (North Carolina, 1996) and in Francisco López Casimiro's *La masonería y el conflicto colonial en la prensa de la baja Extremadura* (Zaragoza, 1993), in which there are some references to Cuba, though the principal consideration of the work is the conflict in the Philippines.

From another perspective, it is also important to include Aldo A. Mola, *Las logias italianas en Latinoamérica (1860–1940)* (Zaragoza, 1993), Luigi Polo Friz, *Albert A. Goodall, un enviado especial del Supremo Consejo de Boston al mundo masónico sudamericano y europeo en la segunda mitad del siglo XIX* (Zaragoza, 1993), and Marco Novarino, *La masonería italiana y la independencia de Cuba* (Zaragoza, 1993).

Argentina

If we move on to analyze some of the works dedicated to Argentina, there is one name that stands out: Pilar González Bernaldo de Quirós. She produced her doctoral thesis, *Civilité et politique aux origines de la nation argentine. Ses sociabilités à Buenos Aires, 1829–1862* (Paris, 1999) at the Sorbonne under the supervision of Professor François-Xavier Guerra. This study analyzes the links and forms of sociability at the moment of the birth of modern politics and the establishment of the nation. And among the different "sociabilities," Masonic lodges appear beside reading rooms; literary, philanthropic, and mutual societies; fraternities; electoral clubs; African societies; hobby groups; and so forth. But Freemasonry is described as a society for reflection and a club for recreation. Prior to this work, she published an interesting summary as part of one of the symposia organized by the Center for Historical Studies of Spanish Freemasonry: *Masonería y política: el supuesto origen masónico de la organización nacional (Análisis de un Banco de datos sobre la pertenencia masónica de la clase política porteña durante la formación del Estado-Nación (1852–1862)* (Zaragoza, 1993). Pilar Gonzalez Bernaldo de Quirós expresses surprise that—despite the importance of Freemasonry in Argentina from 1854—there are no reliable studies on this institution from the country. The abundant literature that can be found relates to the ethical and religious controversies between defenders and detractors. And in all cas-

es, she adds, the arguments used tend to confuse the actual historical analysis. She concludes by noting that Latin American university historians have shown a total disregard for this issue, which, judging by their attitude, has yet to acquire the status of historical subject. For a critical analysis of Argentine Masonic historiography, see first of all Pilar González Bernaldo de Quirós, *Masonería y Nación: la construcción masónica de una memoria histórica nacional* (Chile, 1990), as well as *Masonería y revolución de Independencia en el Río de la Plata: 130 años de historiografía* (Alicante, 1990), and *La Revolución Francesa y la emergencia de nuevas prácticas de la política: la irrupción de la sociabilidad política en el Río de la Plata revolucionario* (Santiago, 1991). Supplementary analysis is available through a prior work by Ana Mª Larrègle, *Consideraciones sobre la masonería en Argentina (1900–1920)* (Zaragoza, 1989). As a curious side note, a revealing special issue of the journal *Todo es Historia* was devoted specifically to Argentine Freemasonry (Buenos Aires, April 2001). Its articles include Abel Alexander, *La construcción virtual de la Argentina. Fotógrafos masones del siglo XIX*, Carlos Arechaga, *Masones en la Historia argentina. La abjuración de Mitre*, and Gregorio Caro Figueroa, *De secretos a discretos*.

The editor-in-chief of *Todo es Historia*, the late journalist Emilio J. Corbière, a man interested in historical and political themes, devoted two important books to Argentine Freemasonry: *La Masonería. Política y sociedades secretas en Argentina* (Buenos Aires,

1998) and its follow-up *La Masonería. II Tradición y revolución* (Buenos Aires, 2001). In both, in response to the traditional mythic-heroic history, he offers an interpretation of Freemasonry in general and the Argentine strand of it in particular, which is more linked to the history of ideas.

The Freemasonry of the Río de la Plata is considered in José Eduardo de Cara, *A Maçonaria no Rio de Prata* (Rio de Janeiro, 1983), a work that, in reality, is a study and classification of Argentine Masonic medals. An emblematic and controversial figure in Argentine Masonic historiography is Alcibíades Lappas, who, in addition to the aforementioned writings dedicated to San Martín and his controversial and manipulated book *La Masonería argentina a través de sus hombres*, also left us *La masonería en la ocupación del desierto* (Buenos Aires, 1981).

It is worth highlighting two Master's-level theses defended by Dévrig Mollès at the Université Haute Bretagne-Rennes II in France. The first, presented in the year 2000, is entitled *La franc-maçonnerie espagnole en Argentine: les origines du Grand Orient Fédéral Argentino (1925–1935)*, and the second, defended in 2001, is *La franc-maçonnerie espagnole exilée entre Europe et Amérique. Le Triangle latin. Le pôle argentin (1920–1945)*. The subjects covered in the thesis are also developed in *Un puente transatlántico: la Gran Logia Filial Hispano-Argentina del Grande Oriente Español en la circunstancia Euro-americana de Entreguerras* (Zaragoza, 2007) and in *Exilia-dos, emigrados y modernizadores: el crisol masónico euro-argentino. Europa-Río de la Plata, 1840–1880* (Zaragoza, 2010).

The exile of Spaniards in Argentina is also brilliantly considered by María Elena Rodríguez Lettieri in *El exilio español en la Primera República y la Masonería argentina* (Zaragoza, 2010), who had previously undertaken the interesting study *La masonería española en la República Argentina* (Zaragoza, 2007). The subject of Spanish exile in Argentina has also been addressed by Jorge Ferro in *Noticias sobre la masonería española originadas en el Río de la Plata (1892–1910)* (Zaragoza, 2004) and by Eduardo Callaey in *Masonería y republicanos: el exilio republicano en Argentina* (Zaragoza, 2007). This latter author has turned to producing books devoted to medieval Freemasonry, the monastic origins of Freemasonry, the Knights Templar and Freemasonry, and the Christian origins of Freemasonry. These are beyond the scope of this part of the bibliographic review's remit of the history of Freemasonry in Argentina rather than what Argentines have written about Freemasonry in general. The same remark can be made of Jorge Francisco Ferro and his recent publications about operative Masonry, secret societies, the Templars, knighthoods' hermetic secrets, and so forth, as well as of others with similar interests such as Teófilo Martines del Duero, who also considers traditional operative Masonry; Jorge E. Sanguinetti, who writes about spirituality and Freemasonry; Pablo Mateo Tesija, who discusses art and Freemasonry; Federico González, who considers hermeticism and Freemasonry,[13] and so many other publications from Buenos Aires-based publishing house Kier that have nothing to do with the history of the Argentine Freemasonry.

Although its title suggests that it should go at the start of this bibliographic review, it is necessary to cite the reflections of Jorge Francisco Ferro in *Objeto, métodos y perspectivas de la masonología científica* (Zaragoza, 2001). Although these are somewhat generic and do not refer to Argentina in particular, his extensive appendix does, and it brings together a panorama of Argentine Freemasonry around the third millennium, and it also lists and describes the various Masonic Obediences that existed in Argentina from the formation of the first grand lodge in 1857. More specific and perhaps less well known is the work by the same author entitled *El linaje masónico de la familia Cambacérès en la Argentina (1801–1888)* (Zaragoza, 2007).

And to study Argentine Freemasonry based on the Masonic documentation in the Salamanca archive, of fundamental importance is María Blanca Desantes and María José Portela Santamaría, *Orientaciones para la investigación de la masonería en Argentina* (Zaragoza, 1993), which provides a detailed description of the source collections relating to around a hundred lodges, chambers, chapters, federal and provincial grand lodges, Argentine supreme councils, and so forth.

Fortunately, now long behind us are the multiple editions of works such

as Aníbal A. Rotjer's *La Masonería en la Argentina y en el mundo* (Buenos Aires, 1973) and those of Patricio José Maguirre, archetypes of Masonic conspiratorial paranoia.

Finally, in *Homenaje a Mitre* (Buenos Aires, 2004), the academic José Eduardo Cara offers a brilliant summary of Bartolomé Mitre, leader-general, president of the nation, Grand Master of Argentine Freemasonry, and founder of the National Academy of History, on the occasion of the 183rd anniversary of the birth of the great debunker of the Lautaro lodges.

Uruguay and Paraguay

Closely linked to the issue of Argentine Freemasonry is Uruguayan Freemasonry, because the first Argentine lodge was introduced in the mid-nineteenth century from Montevideo. Once again, Pilar González Bernaldo de Quirós, in her aforementioned doctoral thesis *Civilité et politique aux origines de la nation argentine* (Paris, 1999) devotes a revealing chapter to "the introduction of Freemasonry in the Río de la Plata basin," in which she produces a masterly summary of the origins of both Uruguayan and Argentine Freemasonry. To do so, she made use of, in addition to the archives of the Grand Lodge of Freemasonry of Uruguay, Daoiz Pérez Fontana's unpublished *La Masonería y los Masones en la organización de la República. Apuntes para la historia* (Montevideo, n.d.) as well as of the many publications of

---

13 Titles are in the Appendix.

Alfonso Fernández Cabrelli, namely *Masonería y sociedades secretas en las luchas emancipadoras de la Patria Grande* (Montevideo, 1975), *Masonería, Morenismo, artiguismo* (Montevideo, 1982), *Presencia masónica en la Cisplatina* (Montevideo, 1987), *Masones y artiguistas en la Banda Oriental* (Montevideo, 1986), and *Iglesia ultramontana y masonería en la transformación de la sociedad oriental* (Montevideo, 1990). A collaborator of the CHSSM, Fernández Cabrelli presented an interesting and curious paper entitled *El exilio rioplatense de una logia catalana dependiente del Gran Oriente del Uruguay* (Zaragoza, 1993) at a symposium on Spanish Freemasonry and the Americas. And although he died prematurely and prior to the Toledo symposium of 1995, the work that he had submitted was published posthumously: *La múltiple actividad del masón español Adolfo Vázquez-Gómez en el Río de la Plata* (Toledo, 1996). Previously, at the Cáceres symposium in 1991, Alfonso Esponera presented the study *Mariano Soler y la Masonería en el Uruguay de 1884* (Zaragoza, 1993). A year earlier came Alcibíades Lappas's *La logia masónica "Jorge Washington" de Concepción del Uruguay. Entre Ríos (1822-1922)* (Buenos Aires, 1970).

Enrique Dussel, an author and editor of several books on the history of the Church, produced the short study *Tensiones en el espacio religioso: masones, liberales y protestantes en la obra de Mariano Soler* (Mexico City, 1990), dedicated to the first archbishop of Montevideo and his *La masonería y el Catolicismo* (Montevideo, 1884). This work, published in the same year as the *Humanum genus*, reveals a bishop who was called progressive but who was at the same time an ultramontanist and deeply "Romanized." Dussel seems to handle the nineteenth century better than he does the eighteenth, as his work on the latter century is based on the very outdated Eduardo Mendoza, *La historia de la masonería en Perú* (Lima, 1966). Consequently, he seems to be unaware of what has been researched and published over the decades in relation in particular to the Freemasons and Jesuits, as a result of which he falls victim to errors and key nineteenth-century commonplaces by making the enlightened Spaniards the agents of expulsion of the Jesuits owing to Masonic ties that they never had. The same could be said of his ignorance regarding the Lautaro lodges.

The research work by Professor Mario Dotta Ostria of the University of the Republic in Montevideo, entitled *La Masonería en el proceso histórico del Uruguay* (Montevideo, n.d.) represents an attempt to integrate into the Uruguayan and Río de la Plata historiography the role played by Freemasonry in the shaping of Uruguay. But its first part, which spans from the eighteenth century to independence, and which is based principally on the *Diccionario Enciclopédico de la Masonería* (Mexico City, 1977) by Frau and Arús[14] and on the aforementioned Alcibíades Lappas, *La Masonería Argentina a través de sus*

---

14 On the different editions of the *Diccionario Enciclopédico de la Masonería* by Lorenzo Frau Abrines and Rosendo Arús y Arderiu (Havana, 1883, Mexico City, 1955, Buenos Aires, 1962, and Mexico

hombres (Buenos Aires, 2000), is full of errors and historical commonplaces that the historiography overcame many decades ago.

Mario Dotta Ostria has also produced the following works, among others: *Italianos, Masonería e Iglesia durante el Gobierno de Santos* (Montevideo, n.d.), *Inmigrantes, curas y masones en tiempos del General Máximo Santos* (Montevideo, 2005), *Caudillos, doctores y masones. Protagonistas en la gran comarca rioplatense, 1806–1864* (Montevideo, 2007), *Oligarquías, militares y masones. La guerra contra el Paraguay y la consolidación de las asimetrías regionales* (Montevideo, 2011)—in which nineteenth-century Freemasonry, which the author knows very well, takes center stage—and *El artiguismo y las vertientes universales* (Montevideo, 2008), though this work does not consider the question of Freemasonry.

However, the journalist Gustavo E. Villa does do so in *Artigas, las instrucciones del año XIII y la masonería* (Montevideo, 2010), a work on José Gervasio Artigas that won an award at the essay contest of the Grand Lodge of Freemasonry of Uruguay in 2010. Its references to possible Freemasons and friends and enemies of Artigas are taken from Humberto Scardino and Luis Pérez Martela, *Biografías Masónicas* (Montevideo, 1991).

Of more interest are the two volumes by Julio Fernández Techera of *Jesuitas, masones y universidad en el Uruguay* (Montevideo, 2007 and 2010), which correspond to a doctoral thesis defended at Complutense University of

Madrid in 2003 and encompass the periods of 1680 to 1859 and 1860 to 1903 respectively. The second volume specifically focuses on the difficulties of the founding of the Seminary College, the name given to the Jesuit college in Montevideo. Both volumes critically analyze the historiographical interpretations of the processes through which Jesuits and Masons were involved—especially with regard to the topic of education—with an in-depth review of Arturo Ardao's "classical" and repeated thesis on the traditional ideological confrontation between Jesuits and Masons over the nineteenth century, which is set out in several of his works, and especially in *Racionalismo y liberalismo en el Uruguay* (Montevideo, 1962) and in *Espiritualismo y Positivismo en el Uruguay* (Montevideo, 1968).

Before this, Susana Monreal had already published her impeccable doctoral thesis *Krausismo en el Uruguay. Algunos fundamentos del Estado tutor* (Montevideo, 1993), which, in discussing Krausism's relations with liberal and Catholic circles, addresses the question of "Krausism and Freemasonry" and their anthropological convergences.

On the real origins of Freemasonry in Uruguay, the book that makes greatest use of the sources and that is of the greatest value is Miguel Salsamendi, *Crónicas del levantamiento de Columnas de las logias nacidas bajo la jurisdicción masónica uruguaya y datos biográficos de sus fundadores, des el 21 de enero de 1830 al 30 de junio de 2000* (Montevideo, 2001), a text that is

City, 1977), as well as on the aforementioned *Bibliografía de la Masonería*.

the result of many years of patient and fruitful work. It is based on Masonic proceedings, files, and documents from over 170 years of Masonic history. It is considered as a documentary treasure trove written for internal use, and it was released in a limited run of 350 copies.

The link between Freemasonry and Protestantism has been studied by Mirtha E. Coitinho of the Methodist Church Commission and Archive in Uruguay, who published *Testigos de un silencio, Metodismo y masonería en el Uruguay del siglo XIX* (Montevideo, 2009). This work is an attempt to broach this subject in which esotericism and symbolic interpretations of the places of worship of the Uruguayan Methodist Episcopal Church and of some lodge rituals play an important role.

Books that have recently achieved greater publication success include Fernando Amado's *En penumbras. La Masonería uruguaya (1973–2008)* (Montevideo, 2008) and *La masonería uruguaya. El fin de la discreción* (Montevideo, 2011). These works deal with recent pressing issues in Uruguay's history such as the 1973 coup, as well as with Freemasonry and politics, the Catholic Church and Freemasonry, military lodges, the prominent figures of the Grand Lodge of Uruguay, and the internal situation of Freemasonry during a difficult period.

Daniel Pelúas subsequently published *El ojo que todo lo ve* (Montevideo, 2012), the subtitle of which is: *Ritos, símbolos y lenguajes de la masonería / Para entender a las logias uruguayas.* In addition to containing a carefully produced graphic part, the work offers interesting information alongside other more debatable—if not erroneous—material, such as that relating to Lautaro lodges.

The stay of a Spanish Freemason in Uruguay is the subject of Juan Félix Larrea López's paper *El olvidado modernista Viriato Díaz-Pérez en Paraguay* (Zaragoza, 1993). Although it is completely unrelated to the history of Freemasonry in Paraguay, it is worth mentioning Paraguayan journalist Christian Gadea Saguier's work *El misterio de los masones. Viaje al interior de sus secretos* (Asunción, 2006) as an archetype of what is the central preoccupation of so many writers and readers interested in Freemasonry.

Chile, Peru, and Ecuador

From Chile, a few years ago, Fernando Pinto Lagarrigue left us a sociopolitical essay entitled *La masonería, su influencia en Chile* (Santiago, 1966), which was reissued in 1973. In its time, it filled in the gaps of Benjamín Oviedo, *La masonería en Chile. Bosquejo histórico. La colonia, la independencia, la república* (Santiago, 1929), a work that was then considered to be a "classic" and that was based principally on the bulletins of the Grand Lodge of Chile. Oviedo's work was also the object of Manuel Romo, *La masonería en Chile de Benjamín Oviedo* (Santiago, 2000). After Benjamín Oviedo, the Publications Department of the Grand Lodge of Chile proposed to continue its efforts to increase popular knowledge of Freemasonry and its history. In this regard, René García

Valenzuela—who was Grand Master of the Grand Lodge of Chile on two occasions and who had already published two books on the subject: *El origen aparente de la Francmasonería en Chile y la Respetable Logia Simbólica "Filantropía Chilena* (Santiago, 1949) and *Contribución al estudio de la Historia del Supremo Consejo de Chile* (Santiago, 1969)—offered what could be considered his fundamental work: *Introducción a la historia de la Francmasonería en Chile* (Santiago, 1992).

Both this work by García Valenzuela and that by Benjamín Oviedo are critically analyzed by Felipe Santiago del Solar Guajardo in *Masonología chilena. O la porfiada memoria institucional de una élite decimonónica* (*REHMLAC*, 2011).

It is also necessary to highlight the five volumes of Manuel Sepúlveda Chavarría, *Crónicas de la Masonería Chilena (1750–1944)* (Santiago, 1994), which is also divided chronologically according to the respective terms of the Grand Masters. The meticulous work and the contribution of abundant documentation suffer, however, as in the case of Américo Carnicelli in relation to Colombia, from the absence of the mandatory and scientific critical apparatus that methodologically justify and accredit what has been said. In any case, it is a light and enjoyable read, and it is finished off by some very useful analytical and onomastic indices. It is to be hoped that the follow-up work that has been announced serves to provide a culmination of what is an obligatory reference work for everything that

might be considered about the history of Chilean Freemasonry.

A new and brief attempt to consider Chilean Freemasonry is Felipe Santiago del Solar Guajardo's *La Francmasonería en Chile. De sus orígenes hasta su institucionalización* (*REHMLAC*, 2010). The most useful part of this study is its second part, which corresponds to the second half of the nineteenth century, the period when Freemasonry in Chile became institutionalized and when the Grand Lodge of Chile was created. The first part suffers from a certain lack of clarity and historical critique in relation to the Lautaro lodges, which produces the impression that these have been confused or identified with Masonic lodges. It makes very worthwhile use of the unpublished Manuel Romo, *Concepción y sus primeras logias, 1856–1860*.

More specific in terms of their focus are Günter Böhm *Manuel de Lima, fundador de la masonería chilena* (Santiago, 1979); Manuel Romo, *El masón Ventura Blanco Encalada (1782–1856)* (Santiago, 2011); Christian Gazmuri, *El "48" chileno. Igualitarios, reformistas, radicales, masones y bomberos* (Santiago, 1998); the joint Pereira, Kramp, and Carvajal work on the La República Masonic university in Santiago, entitled *Universidad La República* (Santiago, 1996); and the subsequent book by Jorge Carvajal Muñoz, *Libertad, Igualdad, Fraternidad. Regresando al futuro* (Santiago, 1997), a general sociological essay with a brief reference to Freemasonry linked to the two fundamental concepts of secularism and rationalism in education, according to the particular take of the author, who was then rector of the Universidad La República, president of the Secular Institute of Contemporary Studies, and president of the Council of Rectors of Secular Colleges of Chile. This is a subject that he would expand upon in another work, this time written in his capacity as Grand Master of the Grand Lodge of Chile: *Masonería y temas de la sociedad actual* (Santiago, 2002) which is billed in its subtitle as "public speeches by the Grand Master of the Grand Lodge of Chile."

To these works it is important to add Carmen Castellano Acuña's brief *La Masonería en Chile* (Rome, 2001), as well as Penélope Ramírez Benito's two biographical accounts of Antonio de Lezama's Republican exile in Chile: *La masonería postsagastina: el caso de Antonio de Lezama (1882–1971)* (Zaragoza, 2007) and *El exilio republicano en Chile. Antonio de Lezama, escritor, periodista y masón* (Zaragoza, 2010). Also worth mentioning is Sady Delgado Chabouty, *Investigación sobre el masón Alberto Bachelet Martínez en la R.L. "La Cantera" 130 del Valle de Las Condes* (Santiago, 2003), which serves as an introduction to the controversial question of Salvador Allende's involvement in Freemasonry.

Among those who have addressed this matter, it is worth citing: Marshall S. Loke, *Presidente de Chile marxista y masón* (New York, 1998), Raúl Carmona Soto, *Allende, pensamiento masónico* (Caracas, 1983), Jorge Ibáñez Vergara, *Allende y la Masonería* (Santiago, 1998), and, especially, journalist Juan Gonzalo

Racha's *Allende Masón. La visión de un profano* (Santiago, 2008), which is supplemented by a facsimile copy of Salvador Allende's Masonic testament from the "Progreso" No. 4 Lodge of Valparaíso, dated November 16, 1935, as well as by two CDs of his Masonic speeches.

The other side of the coin can be seen in Hernán Vidal's *La Gran Logia de Chile (1973–1990). Su comportamiento ante el fin de la democracia y las violaciones de los derechos humanos* (Santiago, 2006). This work is critically analyzed by Felipe del Solar Guajardo in *La Gran Logia de Chile (1973–1990). Análisis crítico al libro de Hernán Vidal referente al tema de la participación de la Francmasonería durante la dictadura militar* (Santiago, 2008).

This subject of the activities of Chilean Freemasonry during the difficult and turbulent years of the military dictatorship, as well as during the preceding and following ones, is bravely analyzed in a way that does not shy away from stark reality by Sebastián Jans P., a prominent member of the Grand Lodge of Chile, in *Los grandes desafíos enfrentados por la masonería chilena en los últimos cincuenta años* (Santiago, 2012), which recounts the history of Chilean Freemasonry through the activities of the Grand Masters.

The latest new work to point out is Felipe Santiago del Solar Guajardo's book *Las logias de ultramar. En torno a los orígenes de la masonería en Chile, 1850–1862* (Santiago, 2012), whose publication marked the 150th anniversary of the founding of the Grand Lodge of Chile.

There is scarcely a worthwhile recent historical account of Peruvian Freemasonry, or at least one subsequent to Eduardo Silva, *Historia de la masonería en el Perú* (Lima, 1966). However, there are many other types of books of a more general nature, such as the many editions and book translations of Serge Raynaud de la Ferrerie, and, in particular, *El libro negro de la Francmasonería* (Lima, 1981), of which there had been eleven printings by 1981. Of greater interest is Rosa del Carmen Bruno Jofre's *La introducción del sistema lancasteriano en Perú: liberalismo, masonería y libertad religiosa* (Mexico City, 1990), which analyzes the first attempt to set up public education under the direction of James Thomson during the era of Bolívar and San Martín. This involved the monitorial model (the use of students who assist in teaching), the use of the Bible as a text book, strict discipline, memorization, and Christian teaching. The only reference made to Freemasonry in the work comes through a discussion of the leaders of independence, which repeats the usual commonplaces about the Lautaro lodge, the American Grand Gathering, and so forth. According to the author (an education professor at the University of Manitoba) here, most of the leaders received "the Masonic light." The interpretation made of Freemasonry and the process of secularization, and especially of its links to the leaders of independence, is strikingly poor, a logical consequence of the only two sources—one of which is from 1949—that are cited: Algdu [sic], *Liminar de los Anales Masónicos de la Resp. Log. Simb. Concordia Universal num. 14: apuntes sipnóticos [sic] al conmemorar cien años de su fundación* (Callao, 1949) and, from 1976, the previously discussed Ramón Martínez Zaldúa, *Historia de la Masonería en Hispano-América* (Mexico City, 1967). Manuel Moreno Alonso, *La "Santa Trinidad" de la democracia en Lima en el I Centenario de la revolución Francesa* (Zaragoza, 1993) combines some of the commemorative speeches from Lima's "Honor y Progreso nº 5" Lodge with standard false commonplaces on the alleged role of Freemasonry in the French Revolution.[15]

The same comments could be about Ecuador, a country in relation to which there exists a work by Washington Padilla, research coordinator on Protestantism in the Andean region: *La actividad de las Sociedades Bíblicas en Ecuador durante el primer liberalismo* (Mexico City, 1990). This study forms part of a book edited by Jean-Pierre Bastian, *Protestantes, liberales y francmasones*, whose title is simply a cover for disseminating the history of Protestantism in Latin America. The least studied element of the title—although it may be the term that has the greatest selling power, hence its inclusion—is the "Freemasons" part. Padilla's study serves as an example. The single mention of Freemasonry is the following: "The Masonic Lodge [sic] was also an active force from the beginning of the

---

15   On this issue, see José Antonio Ferrer Benimeli, "La masonería española y el primer centenario de la revolución francesa," in *Masonería, revolución y reacción* (Alicante, Spain: Instituto de Cultura Juan Gil Albert, 1990), 1:13–28.

Republic. Vice President Santander and his minister José María Castillo were its first presidents. The first secret society was founded in Quito in 1824 (or 1825). It had the backing of General Juan José Flores, commander general of the Department of Ecuador at that time." This remark is not accompanied by any archival or bibliographic reference.

In a different context, it is worth pointing out the pertinence of *Preguntas y comentarios sobre la masonería* (Quito, 1997). The questions and comments referred to in the title are actually some of the many put in writing to José Antonio Ferrer Benimeli at the Catholic Pontifical University of Ecuador in Quito as part of the series of lectures given there at the end of October 1996, not all of which could be answered owing to the number of them and the limited time available. They nevertheless attest to the interest that Freemasonry continues to prompt in certain forums, particularly at this particular university, where the lectures represented the first time that the subject of Freemasonry had been raised there. These questions were also compiled for this reason by Jorge Moreno Egas in the university's *Revista del Instituto de Historia Eclesiástica Ecuatoriana*. The occasion was capitalized upon by Dr. Jorge Villalba through his publishing in the same issue of the journal a paper entitled *La masonería en tierras americanas* (Quito, 1997), which in reality is nothing more than a few tendentious and unfortunate comments about Freemasonry, the Jesuits, independence of the Americas, Bolívar, and so forth, extrapolated from Américo Carnicelli, *La Masonería en*

la Independencia de Bogotá (Bogotá, 1970) and Marcelino Menéndez Pelayo, *Historia de los Heterodoxos españoles* (Madrid, 1992).

Brazil

Brazil represents an important facet of Latin America, both because it is the country with the greatest Masonic presence over the course of its history and because of its bibliographic output, though that which refers to the history of Freemasonry continues to be a minority current compared to other thematic areas such as ritualism, symbolism, philosophy, and spiritualism.

In Brazil, the one particular name that stands out is Morivalde Calvet Fagundes, who in the last decades of the twentieth century drove forward studies on Freemasonry in his capacity as founder of the Brazilian Masonic Academy of Letters, headquartered in Rio de Janeiro and as organizer of the International Historical and Geographical Congresses [of Freemasonry]. The first of these congresses took place in Rio between March 19 and 21 in 1981, and attendees came from Brazil, Argentina, Uruguay, Portugal, Spain, Italy, and Belgium. The proceedings were published shortly after in four volumes. The first is entitled *Formação Histórica da Maçonaria* (Río de Janeiro, 1983), and if we are to confine ourselves solely to the works relating to the history of Freemasonry in Brazil, it is important to highlight Alcibíades Lappas, *Algumas revelações sobre os inícios da Maçõnaria no Brasil*. This study is, in reality, limited to the implementation of certain French and English lodges in the eighteenth and early nineteenth centuries, and it uses as its principal sources Manoel Joaquim de Menezes, *Exposição Histórica da Maçonaria no Brasil* (Rio de Janeiro, 1872), Isa Ch'an, *Achegas para a história da Maçonaria no Brasil* (Sao Paulo, 1968), and two works by Kurt Prober: *Cadastro geral das Lojas Maçônicas do Brasil* (Sao Vicente, 1975) and *História do Supremo Conselho do Rito Escocés Antigo e Aceito no Brasil* (Sao Vicente, 1979).

Rizzardo da Camino's contribution in the same volume of proceedings, *Os primordios da maçonaria brasileira*, is a very superficial one that lacks any great value—even on an informational level—although it is enriched by the opinion of the moderator, Antonio Carlos Tavares Barbosa, who is much more extensive and profound than the object of his criticism.

From the second volume of the congress's proceedings, entitled *Formação Social da Maçonaria* (Río de Janeiro, 1983), worthy of note is Carlos Dienstbach's *A maçonaria e a colonização alemã no Rio Grande do Sul*, an introduction to the history of Freemasonry in the Valle de Sinos, where the German colonization of Rio Grande do Sul began, and to the influence of Freemasonry within it, which revolved around Jorge Antonio Von Schaeffer.

In *A vinculações diretas e indiretas de Almeida Júnior a Maçonaria*, Jorge Luis Antonio considers a very specific and biographical issue, namely the painter Almeida Júnior–a renowned figure in Brazil—and the exaltation of Freemasonry through his art. The text uses a good methodology that is enriched by the sources consulted.

The third volume of proceedings, *Panorama atual da Maçonaria no mundo* (Rio de Janeiro, 1982), is dedicated in its entirety to Masonic general themes. Some of these, such as women and Freemasonry, are of great contemporary relevance, but none of them relates to any specific aspect of the history of Freemasonry in Brazil. However, the fourth volume, *História Política da Maçonaria* (Río de Janeiro, 1983), contains, in addition to studies on general issues, some works that are of particular interest in relation to the history of Brazilian Freemasonry. For example, in *A Maçonaria na formação da Nacionalidade Brasileira*, Luiz Luna recounts a series of Brazilian historical developments before arriving at the conclusion that, from start to finish, Freemasonry influenced the formation of Brazilian nationality through the actions of individuals or lodges, sometimes directly and at other times indirectly. Methodologically, it makes several mistakes by attributing things to Freemasonry that are unproven and on some occasions false.

José Castellani, meanwhile, offers a contribution on the emblematic figure of Pedro I in *D. Pedro I and Maçonaria*. The conclusion reached by the author is that Emperor Pedro was a fundamental and essential part of both Freemasonry and the emancipation or independence movement, even if ulterior interests can be detected in both cases.

Another interesting paper, because of the issue it addresses, is Renato de Alencar, *A Questão religiosa e a Maçonaria Brasileira* (Río de Janeiro, 1982). However, it handles its subject matter in a strikingly poor way in terms of methodology and the sources used in view of this being one of the most frequently and most effectively studied areas. It is appropriate to recall here two fundamental works by Nilo Pereira, *Conflitos entre a igreja e o estado no Brasil* (Recife, 1970) and *Dom Vital e a questão religiosa no Brasil* (Recife, 1966), both of which were published by the Federal University of Pernambuco, as well as Ramón de Oliveira's preceding work *O conflito maçônico-religioso de 1872* (Petropolis, 1945). The same issue—among others—was later dealt with in Marcelo Linhares, *A Maçonaria e a questão religiosa do segundo Imperio (Apontamentos)* (Brasilia, 1988) and in José Castellani, *Os Maçons e a Questão Religiosa do Século XIX* (Londrina, 1996). However, undoubtedly the most comprehensive study is that of Brasilia University professor David Gueiros Vieira, a figure considered by the Protestant historiography to be one of the leading specialists on the Religious Question in Brazil. His *O protestantismo, A Maçonaria e A Questão Religiosa no Brasil* (Brasilia, 1980) seeks to investigate whether Protestantism was present alongside Freemasonry in the events that took place in Brazil during the quarter of a century that culminated in the so-called Religious Question. A model of critical and methodological rigor, this work is an example of the output of what was at the time a new generation of researchers. Ten years lat-

er, and as part of the symposium held in São Leopoldo in 1986 on "Protestantism, liberalism, and Freemasonry in nineteenth-century Latin America," coordinated by Professor Jean-Pierre Bastian of the Faculty of Protestant Theology in Strasbourg, he produced *Liberalismo, masonería y protestantismo en Brasil, siglo XIX* (Mexico City, 1990), in which he offers a brief summary of the origins of Freemasonry in general and of the history of Freemasonry in nineteenth-century Brazil in particular. For this author, the idea of "progress" was the element that united liberalism, Freemasonry, and Protestantism in Brazil during the nineteenth century. Through positivism, the idea of progress was later associated with the idea of power and order. The Republic would put an end to the liberalism-Freemasonry-Protestantism connection, and this was the point when Protestantism gave up on the idea of conquering the Brazilian elite and concentrated its efforts on evangelizing the poorer sectors of society.

Pursuing this same ideological line, Antonio Gouvea Mendonça, a history professor at the Methodist Institute of Higher Education in São Bernardo do Campo (São Paulo), deals with the Religious Question in *La cuestión religiosa y la incursión del protestantismo en Brasil durante el siglo XIX: reflexiones e hipótesis* (Mexico City, 1990). Its analysis of the Religious Question focuses on the struggle between the Catholic Church and the liberal world, which was aggravated when the Bishop of Olinda (Don Vital) forbade masses celebrated at the behest of Freemasonry and forced Masonic priests to renounce it. It was at this moment that Protestant missions gave their backing to a new form of education as a path to liberalism and progress.

And Hans-Jürgen Prien, professor of Church history at the Faculty of Protestant Theology of the University of Marburg, Germany, in his brief study *Protestantismo, liberalismo y francmasonería en América Latina durante el siglo XIX: problemas de investigación (Mexico City, 1990)* focuses above all on liberalism and Protestantism, the first two terms of the work's title, and especially on Protestantism, both in terms of missions of an Anglo-Saxon origin and in terms of the Protestantism of immigrants or Europeans, in particular those of German origin, which was characterized by strong ideological infiltration, especially in the South of Brazil, where German colonization was very significant. The section on Freemasonry is very poor and disappointing for the historian, though it is significant, owing to the express recognition made by the author, that Protestant missions (for example, Presbyterian, Methodist, and Baptist ones) sought the help of Masons and Freemasonry to penetrate Brazilian and Latin American society, as a result of which he concludes that Freemasonry had a decisive role in spreading Protestantism in Latin America.

These latter works are to be found in Jean-Pierre Bastian's *Protestantes, liberales y francmasones* (Mexico City, 1990), the proceedings of the aforementioned San Leopoldo symposium. Its texts are preceded by a significant introduction from Professor Bastian himself, which provides a better understanding of his ideology and historical concern with Protestantism rather than with Freemasonry, which is relegated to the mere role of fellow methodological and commercial travel companion.

A useful complement here that comes from a radically different perspective is Sister Mary Crescentia Thornton's *The Church and Freemasonry in Brazil, 1872–1875: A Study in Regalism* (Washington, 1948). Among the most recent works to study the Religious Question and its link to Freemasonry are Thiago Werneck Gonçalves, *O hábito e o avental: a Igreja católica e a maçonaria na Questão Religiosa (1872–1875)* (Río de Janeiro, 2010), a paper that was presented at the Fifth Political History Week held at Rio de Janeiro State University, and Luiz Mário Ferreira Costa, *A consolidação e a transformação do mito da "conspiração maçônica em terras brasileiras (REHMLAC,* 2011), which shows how, as a result of the Religious Question, an anti-Masonic narrative took hold in Brazil, partly motivated by Rome and its condemnation of Freemasonry. In response to the conflict, something that seemed impossible occurred: the union of the two existing Grand Orients then in Brazil. The final part deals with the impact of Léo Taxil and of "The Protocols of the Elders of Zion" as outstanding examples of the Brazilian anti-Masonic narrative. Along this same line, it is necessary to cite Luis Eugênio Vescio's work *O Crime do Padre Sorio: Maçonaria e Igreja Católica no Rio Grande do Sul (1893–1928)* (Porto Alegre, 2001), which shifts the conflict to another scenario and a chronological period subsequent to the Religious Question in Recife, and Kim Richardson's *Anti-Masonic Speech, "Quebra-Quilos," and the Empire of Brazil* (London, 2010).

The general problem of the Church and Freemasonry and, in particular, the developments that shaped their relations in 1982 are addressed from different perspectives by Boaventura Kloppenburg in *A Maçonaria no Brasil. Orientação para católicos* (Petropolis, 1961) and in *Igreja e Maçonaria* (Petrópolis, 1984), as well as by Morivalde Calvet Fagundes in *Dialogos com a Igreja* (Caxias do Sul, 1987), this latter work having been presented at the Third International Historical and Geographical Congress, which took places in Caxias do Sul in late March 1986. Brazil is also Valerio Alberton's focus in the Brazilian version of José Antonio Ferrer Benimeli and Giovanni Caprile's *Massoneria e Chiesa Cattolica, ieri, oggi e domani* (Rome, 1979 and 1982). Alberton is a coauthor who contributes to all matters related to Brazil in the Brazilian edition, *Maçonaria e Igreja católica ontem, hoje e amanha* (São Paulo, 1981), of which there are at least six editions and in which an extensive bibliography for Brazil related to the theme under study is provided.

Important from a bibliographic standpoint is Morivalde Calvet Fagundes, *Subsidio para a História da Literatura Maçônica Brasileira (século XIX)* (Caxias do Sul, 1989), which offers a detailed biographical and bibliographic journey through Brazilian authors who have focused on Freemasonry. The first part of the study does this by dividing the authors into common groups: historians, symbolists and ritualists, orators, journalists, artists and scientists, scholars, poets, biographers, teachers, apologists, and defenders and opponents. In the second part, he produces biographies of figures that he refers to as "symbolic men," starting with Pedro I of Brazil and IV of Portugal. And in the third and last part, he deals with the "exponents of an ideal," namely: abolitionists, revolutionaries, federalists, administrators, pioneers, soldiers, and so forth.

A complement to this work is José Castellani, *Os maçons que fizeram a história do Brasil* (Sao Paulo, 1991), the writing of which was prompted by the 150th anniversary of Brazil's independence. Morivalde Calvet Fagundes subsequently published *Os maçones: vida e obra* (Rio de Janeiro, 1991). More than offering a collection of thirty-four short biographies of notable Masons, the author produces a mosaic of Freemasonry's presence in Brazil's history. The political dimension is addressed by the same author in *A Maçonaria na formação da nacionalidade brasileira* (Río de Janeiro, 1983). Prior to this work, the Brazilian Masonic Academy of Letters published under his editorship *Antología Poética Nacional Maçônica* (Rio de Janeiro, 1980) whose first volume provides fifty-four biographies of the many Masonic poets. The aim of the project was to reach one hundred such biographies. Meanwhile, in the second part of *Revelações históricas da Maçonaria* (Santa María, 1985) José

Luiz Silveira contributes the biographies of eighteen Masons, all of whom are Brazilian except for Miranda, Bolívar, and Allan Kardec.

If one leaves to one side Calvet Fagundes' other works—for example, *Uma visão dialética da maçonaria brasileira* (Rio de Janeiro, 1985), *Maçonaria: Espíritu e Realidade* (Río de Janeiro, 1982), *Peregrinando pelo Río Grande* (Porto Alegre, 1995), and *Rocha Negra a legendaria* (Londrina, 1989)—and one focuses on *Revelações da Historia da Maçonaria Gaúcha* (Rio de Janeiro, 1987), we can appreciate that gaucho life was a very dear theme to him, and one that he knew well, since he was very proud of his gaucho birth and calling. In this paper, presented in the first volume of the proceedings of the Third International Historical and Geographical Congress, *Episodios da História antiga e moderna da maçonaria* (Caxias do Sul, 1986), a very useful addition to the historical part is a chronological listing of the 195 lodges founded in Río Grande do Sul between 1831 and 1975, with an indication of each lodge's locality, year, obedience, and rite provided. Another individual who takes an interest in gaucho Freemasonry is Eliane Lucia Colussi in *A Maçonaria Gaúcha no século XIX* (Passo Fundo, 1998).

But within the field of gaucho history, General Calvet Fagundes' most important work is *História da Revolução farroupilha* (Caxias do Sul, 1984). The "Farrapos" revolution is studied as a human phenomenon and with a military and professional interpretation delivered by a specialist. One chapter,

Uma viagem maçônica, is devoted to the Freemasonry. It expands upon what had previously been broached in one of his previous works, *A Maçonaria e as Forças Secretas da Revolução* (Rio de Janeiro, 1976 and 1980), which is divided into three parts devoted to the secret forces in the world, in Brazil, and in the "farroupilha" revolution. This book exhibits a deep knowledge of history and bravely confronts a fair few past commonplaces. In its time, it was described as an "iconoclastic work that debunks myths and reforms concepts."

The Pernambuco revolutions have also been linked to a greater or lesser extent to certain Masonic activities, as is highlighted in A. Tenorio D'Albuquerque, *Maçonaria e as revoluções pernambucanas* (Río de Janeiro, n.d.), Raimundo Nonato Da Silva, *O Areópago de Itambé e as Revoluções Pernambucanas* (Río de Janeiro, n.d.), and Eufran de Oliveira Souza-Paulo Viana Nunes, *O Areópago de Itambé e a revolução de 1817* (Natal, 1997). The same could be said of the Inconfidência Mineira, studied by A. Tenorio D'Albuquerque in *A Maçonaria e a Inconfidencia mineira* (Río de Janeiro, n.d.) and in a counteroffer by José Castellani and Guilherme Costa, *A Conjuração Mineira e a Maçonaria que não Houve* (Sao Paulo, 1992).

Closely linked with the question of revolution are books that focus on Freemasonry and Brazilian independence, such as Manoel R. Ferreira and Tito Livio Ferreira's *A Maçonaria na Independencia Brasileira* (São Paulo, 1972) and A. Tenorio D'Albuquerque's

A Maçonaria e a Independencia do Brasil (Río de Janeiro, n.d.). Like all of Albuquerque's works, the latter study is overly apologetic, as all of Brazil's important historical events are interpreted as movements of a Masonic nature that were promoted by Masons.

In *A Bucha, a Maçonaria e o espírito liberal* (Sao Paulo, 1982), Brasil Bandecchi studies the involvement of Freemasonry in the independence process and its presence in São Paulo in the fight for the Republic and abolition. José Castellani does the same in several of his works, including in *A Maçonaria e o Movimento Republicano Brasileiro* (São Paulo, 1989), *A longa luta da Maçonaria para o advento da República* (Londrina, 1990), and his histories of the two Grand Orients: *História do Grande Oriente do Brasil* (Brasilia, 1993) and *História do Grande Oriente de São Paulo. A Maçonaria Paulista na História do Brasil* (Brasilia, 1994). These historical accounts are complemented by two other works by the same author: *O Grande Oriente de São Paulo, 75 Anos* (São Paulo, 1996) and *A Cisão de 1927 no Grande Oriente do Brasil* (Rio de Janeiro, 1995).

More specific, but no less interesting, are Avila Junior and Celso Jaloto, *A maçonaria baiana e sua história* (Salvador, 2000) and Berenice Abreu de Castro Neves, *Intrépidos romeiros do progresso: os maçons cearenses do impeiro* (Fortaleza, 2002), whose title is sufficiently expressive and forms part of the collective work *Intelectuais*, edited by Federico de Castro Neves and Simone de Souza.

Another equally key issue in the Brazilian Masonic historiography is the abolition of slavery in 1888, which is the focus of a very broad and uneven body of literature. The aforementioned A. Tenorio D'Albuquerque produced *A Maçonaria e a Libertação dos Escravos* (Rio de Janeiro, 1970) with his usual style. The work's two subtitles are sufficiently expressive: "A abolição da escravatura, uma grandiosa vitória da Maçonaria" and "Todas as leis beneficiadoras dos escravizados foram de iniciativa de maçons."

The polar opposite of the previous work and an academic contrast in terms of how to handle the issue is the book by Margaret Marchiori Bakos, *RS: Escravismo e abolição* (Porto Alegre, 1982), which discusses the abolition of slavery based on the socioeconomic context of the Second Empire and on the role of political parties and positivist Republicans, without forgetting the role of the press. Curiously, Freemasonry is not even mentioned.

However, the body of literature by Masonic authors who emphasize the prominence of Freemasonry in abolition is large. Coinciding with the hundredth anniversary of abolition, Luigi Gonzaga Bittencourt's *Cem Anos da Abolição* (Londrina, 1988) offered a reminder of the events from a century before. José Castellani does likewise in four short works from the perspective of the role of Freemasonry: *Os maçons e o Movimento Abolicionista da Escravatura* (Londrina, 1988), *A lutta pela abolição da Escratura* (São Paulo, 1988), *Os maçons e o Movimento Abolicionista da Escravatura* (São Paulo, 1988), and *Os Maçons e o Movimento Abolicionista Brasileiro* (Londrina, 1989). Morival-de Calvet Fagundes also addresses this issue in two of his works, namely *A abolição foi lenta e gradual* (Londrina, 1988) and *Os Abolicionistas* (Caxias do Sul, 1990), and it is additionally considered in João Nepomuceno Silva's *Em torno de abolição* (Londrina, 1988) and in Asdrúbal da Silva Mendes's *A abolição* (Londrina, 1988). Later, it would be Francisco das Chagas Carvalho Neves's turn in *La abolición de la esclavitud y la masonería brasileña* (Zaragoza, 1993) and Santiago Marcos Enrique de Almeida's in *La masonería y la abolición de la esclavitud en Brasil* (Zaragoza, 1993). Both took advantage of the Cáceres Memorial Symposium on "Spanish Freemasonry and the Americas" organized by the CHSSM to present two studies of a matter that was not well known in Spain.

More consistency and dedication can be found in the 234 pages of Abrahim Baze, *Escravidão. O Amazonas e a Maçonaria edificaram a História* (Manaus, 2000). Although the number of authors interested in Freemasonry and the abolition of slavery in Brazil could be extended further, based on its intriguing nature I will conclude with Orestes Lima Cipolatti and Laura Pereira de Alcântara, *O Mogorim. A escravidão no Rio de Janeiro* (Rio de Janeiro, 1990), a "television romance" and a work of fiction, but one with a historical basis that pays homage to Castro Alves, considered the poet of slavery par excellence.

William Almeida de Carvalho recently took a new interest in this question in *Maçonaria, Tráfico de Escravos e o Banco do Brasil* (São Paulo, 2010), which examines, in particular, the 1870s, the decade that preceded abolition. But Almeida de Carvalho is particularly interested in the initiatives carried out by Masons and non-Masons following the pioneering attitude of the Riograndense Republic—a result of the "Farroupilha" revolution—which was led by two Masons who granted freedom to slaves. The next step was to extinguish slave trafficking from 1850, which also occurred under the initiative of another Freemason, until the key date of May 13, 1888 arrived following the end of the war with Paraguay. In addition to this date's marking the end of the fight for abolition, it was the trigger for the military uprising of 1889, the end of the Empire, and the proclamation of the Republic on November 15, 1889.

Within this same period, but with a more general view of the history of Freemasonry, is José Castellani, *A Maçonaria Brasileira na Década da Abolição e da República* (Londrina, 2001).

William Almeida de Carvalho subsequently published a *Pequena História no Brasil* (*REHMLAC*, 2010), an overview of Brazilian Masonic history, though one conducted via the Grand Orient of Brazil rather than the grand lodges. For this reason, the Appendix offers a list of the Grand Masters of the Grand Orient of Brazil only. In reality, it is a brief summary of José Castellani's classic book *História do Grande Oriente do Brasil* (Brasilia, 1993), which was recently reissued by William Almeida de Carvalho under the same title, to which the subtitle of *Maçonaria na História do Brasil* (Sao Paulo, 2009) was added. This subtitle corresponds to a second part written by Almeida de Carvalho, which is confined to the recent history of the Grand Orient of Brazil. And because the two authors are members of the Grand Orient, the work has become its "official history."

In *Os maçons brasileiros e sua história* (*REHMLAC*, 2010), Michel Goulart da Silva reviews the work by Castellani, a doctor and historian who died in 2004, and the review is accompanied by a hard-hitting methodological critique, especially in relation to the contribution of Almeida de Carvalho, who is accused of overt bias. Goulart da Silva describes in passing his concept of history, which is very different from that of Castellani and above all from that of Almeida Carvalho, in relation to whom an absence of references to historiographical developments from recent decades is noted.

Spiritism and theosophy are studied in detail by Marcelo Freitas Gil in *Trabalhadores, Maçonaria e Espiritismo em Pelotas: 1877–1937* (*REHMLAC*, 2011). The author conducts a bibliographic analysis of the role played by both Freemasonry and spiritism in relation to the urban workers of Pelotas, a city in Río Grande do Sul, during the period prior to the installation of the Estado Novo, or dictatorship, of Getúlio Vargas. It was an era during which spiritism and Freemasonry, which were identified in a sense with Communists and enemies of the regime, came under suspicion. Freitas' work indirectly illustrates Pelotas's history and socioeconomic situation, as well as the history of Freemasonry in that city from its arrival there in 1841.

Theosophy in Brazil is also dealt with very briefly by Spain's top specialist in the subject, Professor Esteban Cortijo Parralejo, in *Masonería y teosofía en Iberoamérica: Argentina, México y Brasil* (Zaragoza, 1995), a work that uses correspondence with Roso de Luna from Spanish theosophists who were present in Argentina, Mexico, and Brazil and involved in initiatives aimed at an "Ibero-American Confederation."

Journalism has been studied in, among others, Thiago Werneck Gonçalves, *O periodismo maçônico oitocentista da Corte imperial brasileira: notas de pesquisa* (*REHMLAC*, 2011), a report on a graduate research project in history undertaken at Fluminense Federal University and entitled *Periodismo maçônico, política e opinião pública na Corte imperial brasileira (1870–1875)* (Río de Janeiro, 2011). Both works deal with the role played by the press disseminated in the Imperial Court during the period between 1870 and 1875 in the formation of public opinion and in the construction of public spaces. Werneck Gonçalves first offers a brief historical account of the introduction of journalism into Brazil from 1808, and, in particular, its subsequent Masonic form, and he uses a rich and essential bibliography to do so. One point of interest that is noted is the confrontation with the Catholic Church through the bulletins of the Grand Orient and Supreme Council of Brazil.

In 1999, Alexandre Mansur Barata, a history professor at the Federal University of Juiz de Fora, published *Luzes e sombras: a ação da maçonaria brasileira, 1870–1910* (Campinas, 1999) through the University of Campinas, and, in 2006, he focused on a chronological spectrum from almost a century prior in *Maçonaria, sociabilidade ilustrada e independencia do Brasil (1790–1822)* (São Paulo, 2006). More recently, he has revisited this second work with a brief summary with the suggestive title of *"E é certo que os homens se convencem mais pela experiencia do que pela teoria": Cultura política e sociabilidade maçônica (1790–1822)* (*REHMLAC*, 2011), which makes use of a phrase used by Hipólito José Da Costa in *Cartas sobre a Framaçonaria* (London, 1802) and analyzes Masonic sociability in Portuguese America, especially in the city of Rio de Janeiro during the passage from the eighteenth century to the nineteenth, a period when some national Masonic Obediences, in spite of divisions, intrigues, and conflicts, adopted constitutional texts—in the modern sense—that would organize the Masonic powers at a time when Brazil was striving to find a new social and political order.

As an example of the multiple approaches that can be taken in studying Freemasonry, I refer to Marco Morel and Françoise Oliveira Souza, *O poder da Maçonaria: a história de uma sociedade secreta no Brasil* (Río de Janeiro, 2008). Within the issue of anti-Freemasonry, which is generally of little value and made up of an abundant conspiracy-obsessed literature, it is gratifying to find works such as that of Oliveira Souza and that of Jefferson William Gohl, *O real e o imaginario. A experiência da Maçonaria na Loja União III em Porto União da Vitória. 1936 a 1950* (Curitiba, 2003) a Master's history thesis from the Federal University of Paraná. The author tries to capture the nature of the imagined Masonic plotting through a particular lodge in southern Pará, coming at a time when the world was in the grip of immense fears due to the emergence of dictatorships and the Second World War, etc. During this period, Judaism was a prominent issue among extremist groups and in totalitarian states, and Brazil shut down secret societies in 1937.

Whereas in Europe Masonic philately has generated more interest in terms of the commemoration of historical events or of celebrated Masons, in Brazil, and more particularly in the case of Kurt Prober, the focus is on Masonic medals (commemorative or otherwise). Prober examines these in *Catálogo das Duas Maiores Coleções de Medalhas Maçônicas Brasileiras: Coleção Eureka e Coleção Gonçalves Ledo* (Río de Janeiro, 1988), which was soon followed up with an expanded second edition entitled *Catálogo das Medalhas Maçônicas-Brasileiras* (Rio de Janeiro, 1989).

Colombia

Colombia was once home to one of the best-known, most cited, and most prestigious historians of Freemasonry in Latin America: the American Américo Carnicelli (from Richmond, Virginia), who spent more than forty years in Colombia studying and researching Masonic activity in South America. The four volumes of his *La Masonería en la Independencia de América* (Bogotá, 1970) and *Historia de la Masonería Colombiana, 1833–1940* (Bogotá, 1975) are essential and now considered classics. Carnicelli's work is meticulous, though its contribution of an exhaustive volume of sources suffers from a lack of the required scientific critical apparatus to accredit and explain the location of the information and documents put forward.

Nowadays, Colombia does not have any particularly striking or internationally recognized works. However, there are some references that are worthy of note—for example, Jaime Montoya, *Masonería íntima* (Bogotá, 1988); Amparo Ibáñez's thesis *Entre dioses y demonios. Masones y jesuitas en Colombia en el siglo XIX* (Santa Fe de Bogotá, 1990), the stance of which was corroborated at the National Library in Bogotá based on the amount of controversial pamphlets and books preserved there, which proliferated throughout the nineteenth century and especially in its first third, in a similar manner to the case of Mexico; and the degree project conducted jointly by Adriana Cuberos and Alberto Cuberos at the District University of Bogotá, *La Masonería y la Constitución de 1863* (Santa Fe de Bogotá, 1991).

In a similar vein, Enrique Santos Molano's biography *Antonio Mariño, filósofo revolucionario* (Bogotá, 1999) briefly refers to Freemasonry, as does Gilberto Loaiza Cano's valuable and well-documented *Manuel Ancízar y su época, (1811–1882). Biografía de un político hispanoamericano del siglo XIX* (Medellín, 2004). One of the chapters of this work addresses diplomacy and Freemasonry in South America, over which Poinsett's shadow hangs, though this chapter is not the work's best. Some years later, the same author, who acknowledges the university-produced historiography's lack of interest in studies on Freemasonry, addressed the subject once again in a work entitled *La masonería y las facciones del liberalismo colombiano durante el siglo XIX. El caso de la masonería en la Costa Atlántica* (Medellín, 2007), where the author examines the links between Freemasonry and the formation of regional groups, in particular the curious and strange case of the alliance on the Atlantic coast of liberal Freemasonry with Catholicism. The work uses Masonic documents, but, as with Carnicelli, from whom the author takes these, it does not indicate where they are located.

One very particular aspect of Freemasonry is addressed by José Antonio Ferrer Benimeli in *Fiesta-Masonería-Nación* (Bogotá, 1999).

One of the latest works devoted to Freemasonry in Colombia is Mario Aranco Jaramillo's *Libertad y tolerancia. La Masonería colombiana en los inicios de la República, (1810–1860)* (Bogotá, 2008).

Straddling Colombia and Venezuela, Daniel Lahoud of the Andrés Bello Catholic University in Caracas published a brief work entitled *Masonería en Venezuela y Nueva Granada (Colombia) en los primeros años del siglo XIX* (Caracas, 2006). In spite of the errors that it contains, it contributes new ideas and information.

Venezuela

The literature on Freemasonry in Venezuela is richer than that for neighboring countries, and there are some works which are worthy of attention. There is, for example, the anonymous *Sucinta relación de la masonería en Venezuela* (Caracas, 1852), dating back to the nineteenth century, while from the early twentieth century there is José Austria, *Exposición legal al cumplir diez años de existencia de la masonería (1918–1928), Puerto Cabello, Venezuela* (Valencia, 1928) and Acislio Valdivieso Montaño's *Introducción a la masonería venezolana* (Caracas, 1928) and *Un capítulo de historia masónica venezolana* (Caracas, 1930). Celestino Romero's *Raíz histórica de la masonería en Venezuela* (Caracas, 1957) then followed these. From many years later there is an interesting and full report by the Grand Lodge of the Republic of Venezuela entitled *La situación masónica en Venezuela* (Caracas, 1980). Hello Castellón, meanwhile, offers us *Guía histórica de la Masonería Venezolana* (Caracas, 1985), a very useful and complete work that includes a brief account

of the historical roots of Venezuelan Freemasonry between 1793 and 1984, which is followed by the usual Masonic biographies of the leading figures of independence, starting with Miranda and Bolívar, whose profiles alternate between history and legend. There then follows, among other information, a list of the 107 "regular lodges of Venezuela" of the time, the timeline of Venezuelan Freemasonry and biographies of all active Freemasons in 1985.

Hello Castellón is also the author of *Así es la Masonería* (Caracas, 1990) and *La Revolución de Francia obra de la Masonería* (Caracas, 1989), the title of which sufficiently expresses the falsity of its content.

Studies that offer more of an overview are José Antonio Ferrer Benimeli's entry for *Masonería* in the *Diccionario de Historia de Venezuela* (Caracas, 1988) and Carlos Rodríguez Jiménez's *La Francmasonería en Venezuela* (Caracas, 1990), a chapter from the autobiography of its author, who was the first consul general in Japan between 1931 and 1951 and then ambassador from 1951 to 1965. It is a double autobiography, a diplomatic one and a Masonic one, and it was written at the suggestion of a mutual friend, José Antonio Bello López, whom I cordially thank for his brotherly and sincere friendship and for everything that he has taught me in recent years through his example and generosity. Carmen Gómez Liendo focuses on the recurrent theme of emancipation in *La masonería en Venezuela. Influencia en la emancipación* (Caracas, 1990), as do Francisco

Franco, *Masonería, librepensamiento y catolicismo en la Mérida de finales del siglo XIX* (Mérida, 1998), and Edgar Perramón, *Breve Historia de la Masonería en Venezuela* (Caracas, 1997). A concise history of Freemasonry in Venezuela can also be found in Luis E. Capecchi, *Desarrollo histórico de la Masonería venezolana* (Antimano, 2006). Additionally of interest and use is *Listado de las logias que han existido en Venezuela, desde su origen en el país, hasta 2000*, an unpublished work by Justo F. Fernández—author of *La Masonería organizada* (Los Teques, 1998)—that was produced especially for Efraín Subero's *La Masonería en Venezuela* (Caracas, 2000).

The work was the most important and ambitious project undertaken by the Grand Lodge of the Republic of Venezuela, as it was supposed to contain fourteen volumes, of which only the first two saw the light in 2000, as scholar and man of letters Efraín Subero died in 2007 without having published any other volume. The volumes actually published are a miscellany that begins with a lecture entitled *La Masonería como origen de la Independencia de Venezuela*, which is followed by three Masonic bibliographies. The first encompasses the printed matter described by the National Library. The second consists of the Masonic entries contained in Angel Raúl Villasana, *Repertorio Bibliográfico de Venezuela 1808–1950*. And the third comprises a scattered set of bibliographic works and periodicals. This third part is the core of the project and is of great importance, since it brings together almost every-thing published in and about Venezuela, with the inclusion of chapters and parts of works that he considered worthy of interest.

One of the most prolific Venezuelan authors in recent years has been Eloy Reverón García, who started out by publishing *Influjos masónicos en la Instauración del Matrimonio Civil y Registros Civiles para Nacimientos, Matrimonios y defunciones* (Caracas, 1988) with Venezuela's National Academy of History. The work was then reissued with the title *Influjos masónicos en la instauración del Matrimonio Civil* (Caracas, 1990). These were followed up with *Masonería en Venezuela (Siglo XIX)* (Caracas, 1992) and other titles such as *Masonería Desnuda* (Caracas, 1994), *Crisis de la Masonería Venezolana (Siglo XX), Mito y realidad en la Historiografía masónica* (Sartenejas, 1995), *Memoria Masónica de Venezuela* (Caracas, 1996), and the aforementioned *El Fantasma de Bolívar en la Masonería Venezolana* (Caracas, 1997). These works were published by the National Academy of History, Simón Bolívar University, the Central University of Venezuela, the Institute for Advanced Diplomatic Studies, and the Venezuelan Institute of Masonic Studies.

As is the case of Andres Bello Catholic University, which published out of Caracas the first edition of *Bibliografía de la Masonería* by José Antonio Ferrer Benimeli back in 1974, today several universities are starting to take an interest in Freemasonry as an object of study. In this regard, it is necessary to note Lisandro Alvarado Central

Western University in Barquisimeto and the Master's dissertation presented by Yasmina Mejía, *História Social de la masonería en el Estado Lara: Respetable Logia "Estrella de Occidente" n° 50 (1856–1960)* (Barquisimeto, 2005).

At the Seventh International Seminar organized by Dr. Moisés Guzmán Pérez on "Liberalism, Freemasonry and independence in Latin America," which took place in 2011 at the Michoacán University of Saint Nicholas of Hidalgo in Morelia, José Pascual Mora García, a professor at the University of the Andes in Venezuela, presented an important work entitled *La Masonería, su historia y su contribución en la construcción simbólica de la nación venezolana (siglo XIX)*, in which the author considers a history silenced by the official historiography, on the basis that the subject of Freemasonry has not experienced the same fate as that of independence.

Central America

In the case of Central America, one of the countries for which we have the most literature related to Freemasonry is Costa Rica. Leaving aside H. Caucois, *Nociones de masonería simbólica* (San José, 1871), a curious work—translated by Spes, a member of the "Caridad" Lodge—which has no more value than a purely anecdotal one linked to the date of its publication, the first source to take into account is Ar-thur George Malin Gillot, *Documentos Históricos referentes a la Masonería en Costa Rica* (San José, 1926). Ten years after the publication of this work, Federico Góngora expanded the geographical scope with *Documentos históricos de la Masonería Centroamericana (Antigua y Aceptada) desde el año 1824 a 1933* (San José, 1937), which would later be complemented with *Mis últimos Documentos de la Masonería Centroamericana* (San José, 1942).

At the same time as being considered the father of Costa Rican Masonic historiography and its main point of reference, the versatile Rafael Obregón Loría,[16] former director of the History School of the University of Costa Rica and founder of the San José Masonic Museum, also studied the origins and establishment of Freemasonry in Costa Rica. He offered *Antecedentes Históricos de la Masonería en Costa Rica* (San José, n.d.), but his main work, divided into four periods and written with the collaboration of George Bowden, is *La Masonería en Costa Rica*. The first two periods were published in San José in 1938, while the third and fourth periods were published in 1940 and 1950 respectively. Obregón had access to the Masonic archives, and his books make for obligatory reading. He also devoted a couple of books to Dr. Francisco Calvo, a priest, the founder of Costa Rican Freemasonry, and a key individual who shaped its path and nature in the country: *Presbítero Doctor Francisco Calvo*

---

16   Obregón Loría also deals in his publications with political and military developments in Costa Rica, the rectors of the Saint Thomas University, anti-Spanish movements in Central America, Costa Rica's international relations, the war against the filibusters, independence and national history, the legislature, and so forth.

(Ganganelli) organizador de la masonería en Costa Rica (San José, 1961). The work was republished in 1965, and that same year he produced *Actividades masónicas en Centro América antes de 1865* (San José, 1965). Required complementary material is the reports and proceedings of the Grand Lodge of Costa Rica, which have been preserved for the 1901–1940 period and are also available in English as the *Proceedings of the Grand Lodge of Costa Rica*.

Today, Costa Rica is, along with Cuba and Mexico, the third source of impetus of the history of Freemasonry in the Caribbean and in Latin America in general. The driving force behind the studies being undertaken is University of Costa Rica professor Miguel Guzmán Stein, who in February 2005 defended at the Universidad de Zaragoza (Spain)—where he completed his studies in history—a monumental and still-unpublished five-volume doctoral thesis of almost two thousand pages entitled *Liberalismo, educación, iglesia y masonería. El proceso de formación y secularización del estado nacional a través de las relaciones institucionales en Costa Rica en el siglo XIX*. In reality, the work is four theses rolled into one on many different though interconnected issues, namely liberalism, education, the Church, and Freemasonry. It is in relation to the latter that he produced his history of Freemasonry in Costa Rica from its establishment in 1865 until 1899, through which he also makes a detailed contribution of different tables with Masonic and profane information relating to all members of the lodges identified in the period in question.

Prior to this, Miguel Guzmán Stein, a loyal participant in CHSSM's symposia, having started attending at the Cáceres symposium in 1991, which was devoted to "Spanish Freemasonry and America," had presented, with his characteristic trustworthiness, knowledge of the material, and exhaustive depth, works as diverse as: *Masones españoles en Costa Rica: el Krausismo y la Institución Libre de Enseñanza en la formación y desarrollo de la democracia liberal costarricense* (Zaragoza, 1993), a subject very dear to the author, as is anything related to teaching, in particular in its university form; *Masones y liberales y cubanos: Intervención y aporte al desarrollo social, político y cultural de Costa Rica en el siglo XIX* (Zaragoza, 1995), in which he analyzes the three social, political, and cultural strands of the Costa Rican national state, with a special focus on Cuban and Spanish immigration, which benefited from Freemasonry's associational spirit; and *Costa Rica, España y Cuba: Antecedentes, desarrollo e impacto del movimiento de independencia cubano en la sociedad costarricense finisecular y la masonería* (Zaragoza, 1999), a work that reveals that Costa Rica was especially sensitive to the Cuban cause, which was encouraged by the presence of so many Cuban immigrants in Costa Rica, and, in particular, intellectuals dedicated to teaching.

Of special interest is the informational and above all methodological analysis that Guzmán Stein offers in *Base de datos para la historia de la masonería en Costa Rica en el siglo XIX* (Zaragoza, 2004). In it, he adds genealogies—a form that he is accustomed to—as well as sociabilities and power networks to the traditional records. Especially curious is the detailed genealogy of the founder of Freemasonry in Costa Rica, the canon penitentiary of the cathedral, Dr. Francisco Calvo.

Within the realm of Masonic biography, it is important to highlight an interesting study with the significant title of *Dr. José Mª Castro Madriz, Presidente de la República, Presidente del Congreso, diputado, Magistrado, Embajador, Rector y masón grado 33* (Zaragoza, 2007) as well as the no less interesting, curious, or disconcerting case related to the dictator Francisco Franco, *De cómo el Generalísimo Franco Bahamonde, Jefe del Estado Español, otorgó la Orden de Caballero de Isabel la Católica a un masón gallego que fue dos veces Gran Maestre de la Gran Logia de Costa Rica*, the subtitle of which is *Masonería y guerra civil española en Costa Rica* (Zaragoza, 2004). In fact, this is a well-documented—bibliographically and archivally—biographical dictionary of around thirty Spaniards who emigrated to Costa Rica and who gained a social and political foothold through Freemasonry. Of these, five rose to the position of Grand Master of the Grand Lodge of Costa Rica.

Still in the biographical genre, Guzmán Stein has also addressed a figure whom he knows very well and spent years researching: *Andrés Cassard y su vida en Nueva York. Tres nuevas facetas de un masón polifacético*, the follow-up to which he announced in *La literatura masónica y la carrera editorial de An-* *drés Cassard. Primer inventario de su obra (1855–1875)* (*REHMLAC*, 2012). Guzmán Stein's interest in Cassard was, in fact, clear to see at the First International Symposium on the History of Latin American and Caribbean Freemasonry, which took place in Havana between December 5 and 8 in 2007. At the symposium, Guzmán Stein presented a hotly debated paper with the title *Andrés Cassard y las masonerías cubana y colombiana en la fundación de la masonería centroamericana. Relación de un protagonismo personal en tres jurisdicciones (1865–1877)*.

Another area that Guzmán Stein knows well and has worked on is that of relations between the Catholic Church and Freemasonry in Costa Rica. It was a central element of his doctoral thesis, and he put forward for consideration a vital aspect of it at the Third Central American History Congress in 1996 in *Masonería, Iglesia y Estado: la tolerancia y los mecanismos de represión asociativa y religiosa en Costa Rica (1865–1880)* (San José, 1996). He returned to it again in *Masonería, Iglesia y Estado: Las relaciones entre el Poder Civil y el Poder Eclesiástico y las formas asociativas en Costa Rica (1865–1875)* at the Fourth Central American History Congress (*REHMLAC*, 2009) and expanded upon it in *La "Cuestión Confirma" y la represión ideológica: el debate entre el clero reaccionario, el clero liberal y masón y la autoridad vaticana en Costa Rica (1878–1880)*, which was presented at the First International Symposium on Latin American and Caribbean Freemasonry (Havana, 2007).

Guzmán Stein has also produced a study that relates to the theme of repression: *Legislación antimasónica española. Siglos XVIII–XIX* (San José, 1981). This work was presented at the Hispano-American Symposium on the Laws of the Indies, which was organized by the Costa Rican Institute of Hispanic Culture.

Another of the aspects that Guzmán Stein has paid special attention to is gravestones, which he covered in *La lapidaria fúnebre-masónica en Costa Rica como fuente de investigación de una comunidad inédita* (*REHMLAC*, 2010), a study that considers Costa Rica's Sephardic Jewish community and its links with Freemasonry. The gravestones are located in particular in the Foreigners' Cemetery in San José, which is a socio-cultural and historical center of great value that reveals how Sephardic family networks in the case of Costa Rica involved bonds and inheritances connected with Freemasonry.

Freemasonry, social networks, and political power have also been of interest to Guzmán Stein in another branch of his multifaceted research. He has considered these matters in at least three works: *Masonería y redes sociales en Costa Rica en el siglo XIX*, a paper at the 2005 Research Workshops organized by the University of Costa Rica's Center for Central American Historical Research; *El Paisaje de la Nación: Liberalismo, masonería y redes sociales en la reorganización del uso del poder en el Estado, Costa Rica 1870–1882*, which was presented at the Fourth International Congress of the Association of European Historians of Latin America, held in Castellón, Spain, in 2005; and *Masonería, civilismo y autoritarismo. Las logias y el poder político en Costa Rica 1870–1877*.

To round off Guzmán Stein's works, it is worth mentioning his study entitled *La fundación del Supremo Consejo Centroamericano y la revolución de 1870 en la construcción de un Estado Liberal democrático en Costa Rica*, which was presented at the First International Symposium on Latin American and Caribbean Freemasonry in 2007. And as a complementary epilogue, Luis Alvarenga conducted a long and in-depth interview with Guzmán Stein for "La Hora de Sofía" on the subject of Freemasonry's presence and influence in Central America, a truly forensic account of why and how he became interested in a subject in relation to which he has come to be the fundamental point of reference in Hispanic America.

A more recent entrant into the study field of Freemasonry in the Caribbean, and in Costa Rica, in particular, is Ricardo Martínez Esquivel, who considered the organization of Freemasonry in Costa Rica in *Consolidación de la masonería en Costa Rica (1865–1899)*, a paper presented at the Historical Research Workshops organized by the University of Costa Rica in December 2006. He is also the author of various other works, including *Actividades masónicas en la ciudad de Puntarenas 1870–1876* (San José, 2007), which was published in *InterSedes*, the digital journal of the campuses of the University of Costa Rica; *Unión fraternal: el desarrollo de una logia masónica y la promulgación del Código Civil en Costa Rica (1882-1888)*, which was presented at the Second International Symposium on the History of Latin American and Caribbean Freemasonry and Patriotic Societies, held in Havana in December 2008; and *Documentos y discursos antimasónicos católicos en Costa Rica (1865-1899)*, perhaps Martínez Esquivel's fullest study on Costa Rican Freemasonry. The opening year of its chosen chronological focus of 1865 to 1899 coincides with the organization of Costa Rican Freemasonry, while the closing year marks the organization of the Grand Lodge of Costa Rica. The work centers on the reaction of the Church and its official discourse on Freemasonry as a result of liberal reforms that sought to secularize society. Of interest here is the analysis conducted on the discourse of papal documents within what certain schools—such as the Protestant school of Strasbourg–have called modernity.

In turn, in *La identificación del desarticulador del mundo católico: el liberalismo, la masonería y el protestantismo en la prensa católica en Costa Rica (1880-1900) (REHMLAC, 2011)* Esteban Sánchez Solano analyzes the key role that the Catholic press had at the end of the nineteenth century in the construction of a kind of catechism in which liberalism, Freemasonry, and Protestantism were included as enemies of Catholicism. Jaime Valverde's *Las sectas en Costa Rica. Pentecostalismo y conflictividad social* (San José, 1990) and Pedro Carrasco's *El problema de las sectas: criterios para una aproximación*

analítica (Santiago de Chile, 2005) provide a useful expansion of the study of denominations in Costa Rica.

Jean-Pierre Bastian has produced two fundamental studies on this matter: *Modernidad e Independencia. Ensayo sobre las revoluciones hispanas* (Mexico City, 1993) and *Modernidad religiosa. Europa Latina y América Latina en perspectiva comparada* (Mexico City, 2004). And Arturo Piedra Solano offers *Notas sobre la relación entre liberalismo, francmasonería y penetración protestante en Centroamérica* (Mexico City, 1990). He concludes—in what is perhaps a transposition of his own ideology—that Freemasonry and liberalism sought to develop relations with Protestantism in search of a religious ideology that could compete with and limit the Catholic Church. This interpretation and conclusion seem to ignore the spirituality and religious origin of Freemasonry itself and to overlook the fact that Freemasonry's purpose is not to fight against the Catholic Church. Another subject studied by Martínez Esquivel is social representations in relation to Freemasonry. At the aforementioned Hispano-American Symposium on the Laws of the Indies, he presented a paper with the title of *Representaciones sociales sobre la masonería en Costa Rica*. He also delivered this study a few years later in 2007 at the previously described First Symposium on the History of Freemasonry in Havana, and it is complemented by *Conspiradores políticos y sectas misteriosas. Imaginarios sociales sobre la masonería en Costa Rica (1865-1899)* (San José, 2009).

More directly tied to the implantation and characteristics of Freemasonry in Costa Rica are his *Masones y su participación política en Costa Rica (1865–1889)* (San José, 2008) and *Composición socio-ocupacional de los masones del siglo XIX* (San José, 2008), both of which were published in *Diálogos*, a digital journal from the University of Costa Rica. Along the same lines, it is necessary to include *Redes masónicas y reforma jurídica en Costa Rica (1865–1888)*, a paper presented at the Historical Research Workshops organized by the Center for Central American Historical Research in March 2009, and *La Constitución de la Orden Francmasónica de la República de Costa Rica*, published over a century beforehand by the Central American Supreme Council (San José, 1871).

Two other works by Martínez Esquivel that are to a greater or lesser extent linked to Freemasonry must also be cited: *Sociedades de ideas en Puerto Limón durante la década de 1890*, a paper presented at the Second Study Seminar for Research on the Costa Rican Caribbean, organized by the University of Costa Rica and held at its Puerto Limón campus in February 2009; and *Masonería y el establecimiento de la Sociedad Teosófica en Costa Rica (1904–1910)* (Zaragoza, 2010), in which he offers an interesting table of differences and similarities in relation to Masonic and theosophic sociabilities, as well as their compatibilities or instances of double affiliation, such as that of Antonio Quesada Castro, who was Grand Master of the Grand Lodge of Costa Rica in 1906 and at the same time a member of the Virya theosophical lodge.

Also related to theosophy in Costa Rica is Esteban Rodríguez Dobles, *Conflicto en torno a las representaciones sociales del alma y los milagros. La confrontación entre la Iglesia católica y la Sociedad Teosófica en Costa Rica (1904–1917)* (*REHMLAC*, 2011). An essential complement here is Marta Elena Casaus Arzu's recent study *El vitalismo teosófico como discurso alternativo de las élites intelectuales centroamericanas en las décadas de 1920 y 1930. Principales difusores: Porfirio Barba Jacob, Carlos Wyld Ospina y Alberto Masferrer* (*REHMLAC*, 2011), in which she provides an authoritative description of theosophical vitalism as an alternative philosophical doctrine to positivism and as an alternative political doctrine to Marxism. In contrast to Europe's regenerationism, in Latin America—and in particular in Central America—vitalism and theosophy appeared as complementary doctrines and were at the origin of nationalist spiritualism or theosophical vitalism.

Ricardo Martínez Esquivel's review of the two international symposia of the history of Latin American and Caribbean Freemasonry held in Havana in December 2007 and 2008 reproduces the objectives of the debate as well as the detailed programs of both, and it will be of great use for those who were unable to attend the symposia.

The importance of the first symposium lies in the fact that it was where the Center for Historical Studies of Latin American and Caribbean Freemasonry was founded, with its headquarters in the University of Havana's Casa de Altos Estudios Don Fernando Ortiz, with Professor Eduardo Torres Cuevas as its chair. The second symposium was no less important because, in addition to its quality and sessions, it entailed the creation of the journal *Revista de Estudios Históricos de la Masonería Latinoamericana y Caribeña* (*REHMLAC*), which is part of the Freemasonry and Patriotic Societies in Central America Study Program, overseen by Professor Miguel Guzmán Stein, of the University of Costa Rica's General Studies School. This digital, multidisciplinary, and semiannual academic publication is under the direction of Ricardo Martínez Esquivel and edited by Yván Pozuelo Andrés. It has been in regular publication, with seven digital editions now having been published. There is also a print edition of the first three volumes entitled *REHMLAC*, which covers the period between May 2009 till today. It is now undoubtedly the main outlet for disseminating studies on the history of Freemasonry in Latin America.

Finally, Martínez Esquivel has produced an important study that serves as a bridge to other Central American countries: *Un estudio comparado del establecimiento de logias en Costa Rica y Guatemala (1865–1903)* (San José, 2008). Guatemala is where the Association for the Promotion of Historical Studies in Central America is based. It has started to publish works on the history of Central American Freemasonry online.

There are a couple of works by Annie Lemistre on Nicaragua, which were published in the Grand Orient of France's journal *Chroniques d'Histoire Maçonnique*. The first is *De la Francmaçonnerie en Amérique Centrale (Origine et développement)* (Paris, 1986), a brief overview of the origins of Freemasonry in this region based, above all, on the previously mentioned works by Rafael Obregón Loría. And the second is *Les Maçons de Nicaragua: Episodes d'une lutte pour la démocratie* (Paris, 1986), which only references three "known" Freemasons—and no documentary proof is even given here—and which displays a certain chauvinism in its desire to link the history of Nicaragua with a French ideological-revolutionary influence.

From Panama, there is José Oller's old *del Supremo Consejo Nacional de Panamá* (Panama City, 1934). The founder of Freemasonry in Guatemala is studied by Rafael Obregón Loría—who has also studied its founder in Costa Rica—in *José Quirce Filguera. Fundador de la Masonería en la República de Guatemala* (San José, 1951). And the same author also addresses the issue of the Central American Supreme Council's move to Guatemala in ¿Por qué se trasladó a Guatemala el Supremo Consejo Centroamericano? (San José, 1952).

Nor are there many recent studies on Freemasonry in El Salvador, a country focused on during his day by Francisco J. Ponte Domínguez in *Historia de la Masonería en el Salvador* (El Salvador, 1960). The exception here is Roberto Armando Valdés Valle's doctoral thesis, entitled *Masones, Liberales y Ultramontanos salvadoreños. Debate político y constitucional en algunas publicaciones impresas durante la etapa final del proceso de secularización del Estado Salvadoreño 1885–1886* and defended in November 2009 at the José Simeón Cañas Central American University in El Salvador. A brief summary of the thesis was published in *REHMLAC* in 2010, in which the author explains the reasons behind the study and the sources used in it, as well as the difficulties that he encountered. He had previously published a few more specific studies—for example, *La Masonería en el Gobierno de Rafael Zaldívar (1876–1885)* (El Salvador, 2008)—and presented a paper at the second international symposium in Havana that was entitled *Relevancia política de los masones salvadoreños durante el año 1885* (Havana, 2008).

But the official origins of Freemasonry in El Salvador during the final third of the nineteenth century, including its members and the role it played at the social, historical, and political levels, as well as the clergy's subsequent reaction to it, are examined in Roberto Armando Valdés Valle, *Origen, miembros y primeras acciones de la masonería en El Salvador (1871–1872)* (*REHMLAC,* 2009). This study, which is enriched through the sources it makes use of, in particular, the "Masonic Record of the Central American Supreme Council," complements Rafael Obregón Loría's classic works. Valdés Valle has also produced a study entitled *Elementos para la discusión sobre masonería, política y secularización en la Centroamérica del siglo XIX* (*REHMLAC,* 2011), which

contributes to our understanding of the reasons behind press debates on the political activities of Central American Freemasons in the nineteenth century, and above all on the conflict that set the Catholic church against Freemasonry.

A final work by the same author, in which he also considers anti-Freemasonry and the press, is the paper that he presented at the Eleventh International Symposium on the History of Spanish Freemasonry, which was held in Almería in October 2009: *Antimasonismo en las páginas del periódico salvadoreño "El Católico" durante el año 1885* (Zaragoza, 2010). The paper offers, above all, an analysis of the ideology of the *El Católico* newspaper through the anti-Masonic texts that it published.

Also in relation to El Salvador, in *Antimasonismo y antiliberalismo en el pensamiento de Oscar Arnulfo Romero, 1962–1965* (*REHMLAC,* 2011) René Antonio Chanta Martínez once again deals with the conflict between the Salvadoran Catholic Church and Freemasonry, though in relation to the twentieth century, and, more specifically, with regard to the emblematic figure of Monsignor Romero between 1962 and 1965, when he was episcopal vicar for the San Miguel diocese. He does so through articles published in the Catholic newspaper *El Chaparrastique*, of which Monsignor Romero was the editor. The abundant bibliography used enriches a little-known aspect of the murder of the Salvadoran archbishop, in whose writings a link between Freemasonry and Communism appears with a disconcerting frequency.

A new article by Chanta Martínez, *Francmasonería, Iglesia y publicaciones impresas: La Discusión, 1881* (Guatemala, 2008) was published in the *Boletín de la Asociación para el fomento de Estudios Históricos en Centroamérica.*

There is a similar lack of works on Freemasonry in Honduras. Accordingly, citations here must be limited to Rafael Jerez Alvarado, *Bodas de plata de la Respetable Logia Francisco Morazán nº 11* (Tegucigalpa, 1987) and José Mª Díaz Castellanos, *Morazán, Benemérito de la masonería hondureña* (Tegucigalpa, 2009).

Mexico

An interest among universities in Freemasonry and secret societies of a political nature is awakening in Mexico, an understandable development in a country in which Freemasonry marked the period of history immediately surrounding independence. Luis Ramos' *Bibliografía masónica* is very revealing in this regard. In 1990, Ramos produced out of the Faculty of Philosophy and Literature of UNAM a set of "teaching support notebooks," in which he compiled a bibliography of works on Freemasonry contained in his city's libraries. There are 502 entries in total, some of which correspond to the wealth of pro- and anti-Masonic pamphlets from the early nineteenth century. These studies are enriched by *Historiografía de la masonería en México* (Durango, 1991) by Rebeca Treviño Montemayor, and by the insights of Gaspar Hernández

Arnulfo's doctoral thesis *La francmasonería en el siglo XVIII: el proceso de transformación de la masonería operativa o antigua a la masonería especulativa o moderna* (Mexico City, 1999). Hernández Arnulfo located an interesting collection of intriguing papers related to early-nineteenth-century Mexican Freemasonry in the National Library.

Another necessary complement is the very useful *Diccionario de Impresores y editores de la Independencia de México 1808–1821* (Mexico City, 2010) by Professor Moisés Guzmán Pérez, which relates to a period when press freedom allowed a proliferation of publications of all kinds whose ideologies often polarized toward publishers or printers with shared affinities. Also worth noting are Miguel Angel Castro and Guadalupe Curiel, *Publicaciones periódicas mexicanas del siglo XIX: 1822–1825* (Mexico City, 2000), Pedro Pascual, *Ausencia de periódicos y libros masónicos en la Independencia de América* (Mexico, 1995), and the complementary J. M. Miquel I. Verges, *La independencia mexicana y la prensa insurgente* (Mexico City, 1985). Its counterpart from the other side of the Atlantic is Beatriz Sánchez Hita's annotated catalog *Los periódicos del Cádiz de la Guerra de la Independencia (1808–1814)* (Cádiz, 2008)

Jean-Pierre Bastian has also produced a critical overview analysis of the historiography of Mexican Freemasonry in *La francmasonería en la historiografía mexicanista* (Zaragoza, 1995), which was also published under the title *Una ausencia notoria: la francmasonería en la historiografía mexicanista* (Mexico City, 1995). During his time as a professor at the University of the Americas Puebla, Paul Rich also dealt with the problems related to Masonic-Mexican historiography, in the form of two publications that are available online: *Problems in the Historiography of Mexican Freemasonry, Part I* and *Towards a Revisionist View of Poinsett: Problems in the Historiography of Mexican Freemasonry, Part II* (1997). He also coauthored two works with Guillermo de los Reyes Heredia and Antonio Lara: *Smuggling Masonic Books to Mexico* (New York, 2003) and *Continuing Adventures in Masonic Bibliography* (Washington, 2000).

María Eugenia Vázquez Semadeni has produced an updated and accurate summary with the title *Historiografía sobre la Masonería en México. Breve revisión* (REHMLAC, 2010), in which she masterfully establishes the current status of the Masonic bibliography in and on Mexico. She divides the literature into two major sections: nonacademic historiography, which in general entails works by Masons and anti-Masonic individuals; and academic historiography, which in turn is divided into traditional and recent history, with the latter adapted to specific historical periods. To avoid repetitions, I refer readers to her for works on which I do not provide any commentary, given the overlap in critical criteria.

Leaving aside authors who, in their own periods, focused on Freemasonry and the Inquisition in Mexi-co—for example, Nicolás Rangel, José Toribio Medina, Eduardo Mendoza Silva, and M. L. Pérez-Marchand, who are studied by José Antonio Ferrer Benimeli in *Masonería e Inquisición en Latinoamérica durante el siglo XVIII* (Caracas, 1973), and to whom it is necessary to add some more recent studies such as Gabriel Torres Puga, *Centinela mexicano contra Francmasones. Un enredo detectivesco del licenciado Borunda en las causas judiciales contra franceses de 1794* (Mexico, 2005)—the history of Freemasonry in Mexico was of particular interest to Ramón Martínez Zaldúa, who, in 1965, produced a thesis on the role of Freemasonry in the Mexican Revolution that is unsustainable today: *La Masonería en Hispanoamérica. Su influencia decisiva en la Revolución Mexicana* (Mexico City, 1965). He has also produced other works that follow the same ideological line. These include *Historia de la masonería en México y en el mundo* (Mexico City, 1977), *¿Qué es la masonería? Pasado, presente y futuro* (Mexico City, 1980), *Masonería es ...* (Mexico City, 1999), and an expanded second edition of his first work that has been presented with variations to its title and subtitle: *Historia de la Masonería en Hispanoamérica. ¿Es o no religión la Masonería?* (Mexico City, n.d.). The latter features a prologue by Juan Simeón Vidarte, a parliamentarian and a secretary of the Spanish Socialist Workers' Party during the Spanish Second Republic.

However, there are essentially three authors who are considered to have produced "classics" and who are viewed as the progenitors of the history of Freemasonry in Mexico: José María Mateos, Luis Zalce y Rodríguez, and Richard E. Chism. The first of this trio, the founder of the Mexican National Rite and Worshipful Master of the Fortaleza No. 6 Lodge, published the first edition of his *Historia de la Masonería en México desde 1806 hasta 1884* (Mexico City, 1884) in *La Tolerancia,* the official newspaper of the Grand Orient of the same Rite. A facsimile edition of this work was published in 1994. There is a republished, two-volume version of Luis Zalce y Rodríguez's *Apuntes para la historia de la masonería en México* (Mexico City, 1950) from 1987. The subtitle from the first edition, "my readings and memories," clearly establishes the difference between the two parts. The author dedicated the work to the Confederation of Regular Grand Lodges of the United Mexican States and to the Supreme Council of the Ancient and Accepted Scottish Rite for the Mexican Jurisdiction. Finally, Richard E. Chism authored *Una contribución a la Historia Masónica de México* (Mexico City, 1899), which was likewise republished in Mexico in 1993.

The value of these three authors lies in their personal accounts of the particularities of the Freemasonry that they experienced as privileged participants. However, in terms of the origins of Freemasonry in Mexico, insurgency, and independence, they suffer from an absence of documentary evidence, and they lack historical value due to the fact that they limit themselves to repeating what has now become the mythology of Mexican Freemasonry, hence Zalce's drawing of a distinction between his readings and his memories.

To these works it is necessary to add a study that is considered by some to be a classic, namely Thomas B. Davies' *Aspects of Freemasonry in Modern Mexico: An Example of Social Cleavage* (New York, 1976), a book that is an example of methodological rigor. Similarly worthy of mention are two of the least known or cited works, in spite of their great historiographical value, especially if one takes into account the dates when they were written and published in the prestigious London-based research journal *Ars Quatuor Coronatorum*: Robert Freke Gould, *Freemasonry in Mexico* (London, 1893–1895) and F. E. Young, *Mexican Masonry in 1909* (London, 1909).

These last authors are from the Masonic world, and they stand in contrast to the other extreme of the most polemical works—for example, Carlos M. Bustamante, *Diario Histórico de México 1822–1848* (Mexico City, 1980), Lorenzo de Zavala, *Ensayo histórico de las revoluciones de México desde 1808 hasta 1830* (Paris, 1831–1832), Lucas Alamán, *Historia de Méjico desde los primeros movimientos que prepararon su independencia en el año 1808 hasta la época presente* (Mexico City, 1986), and José María Mora, *México y sus revoluciones* (Mexico City, 1986). The Ernesto de la Torre Villar Library, which holds a rich collection of books on Freemasonry, is hosted at the research institute named for José María Mora. These authors, to a large extent, help us to configure the myths that persist in relation to Mexican Freemasonry and its alleged leading role in the country's independence and subsequent national history.

Of a more specific nature are the following studies: Marcos E. Folange, *History of Masonry in Mexico 1791–1950* (Mexico City, 1975), Antonio Salazar Páez, *Historia de la G.L. Unida Mexicana* (Barcelona, 1997), Rosa Mª Martínez Codes, *El impacto de la masonería en la legislación reformista de la primera generación de liberales en México* (Zaragoza, 1993), Tomás Lork Frutos, *Breves apuntes históricos sobre la masonería en Zacatecas* (Zacatecas, 1990), James L. D'Acosta, *Notes on the History of Yoltee Lodge*, Peter Ingram, *La Francmasonería Mexicana temprana. Un capítulo confuso de nuestra Historia* (Barcelona, 1997)—a good summary of the works of Gould and Young—and the many offerings that relate to an individual who was of crucial importance not only in the history of Mexican Freemasonry but also in Latin American history as a whole, namely Joel Poinsett. I will only refer readers by way of example to León Zeldis and his brief Masonic diplomatic biography *Joel Poinsett. Masón, diplomático y revolucionario* (Zaragoza, 2004), which provides a bibliographic summary on this multifaceted and debated personality, and also to José Fuentes Mares, *Poinsett: Historia de una gran intriga* (Mexico City, 1951), which focuses more on ills brought upon Mexico by Poinsett and Freemasonry.

The influence of Spain's Cádiz Cortes and Constitution of 1812 and the repercussions of these in Mexico are the subject of José Antonio Ferrer Benimeli's studies *Las Cortes de Cádiz, América y la Masonería* (Tlaxcala, 2010; Madrid, 2011) and *Utopía y realidad del liberalismo masónico. De las Cortes de Cádiz a la independencia de México* (Morelia, 2012).

Jean-Pierre Bastian of the Faculty of Protestant Theology of Marc Bloch University in Strasbourg has devoted hundreds of monothematic works to Protestantism in both Europe and Hispanic America, in which it is difficult to establish a boundary between chauvinist narcissism and colonizing missionary proselytism. Some of these works consider the pairing of Protestants and Freemasons in Mexico, and they always do so in relation to a series of highly recurrent ideas such as revolution, liberalism, modernity, and the now-eclipsed "societies of ideas" or "sociétés de pensée" that at one time were fashionable in the French historiography: *Itinerario de un intelectual popular protestante, liberal y francmasón, José Rumbia Guzmán* (Mexico City, 1987; Tlaxcala, 1989), *El paradigma de 1789. Sociedades de ideas y revolución mexicana* (Mexico City, 1988), *Los disidentes, sociedades protestantes y revolución en México, 1872–1911* (Mexico City, 1989), *Jacobinismo y ruptura revolucionaria durante el porfiriato* (Mexico City, 1990), *La francmasonería dividida y el poder liberal en México, 1872–1911* (Zaragoza, 1993), and *Las sociedades protestantes y la oposición a Porfirio Díaz en México, 1877–1911* (Mexico City, 1990 and 1993), a chapter in the miscellaneous work that he compiled and edited, the title of which is *Protestantes, liberales y francmasones. Sociedades de ideas y modernidad en América Latina, siglo XIX* (Mexico City, 1990).

Some years later, Bastian would offer a new variant by replacing the liberals with the spiritists in his classic ideological triumvirate: *Protestants, Freemasons and Spiritists in the Mexican revolution, 1910–1920* (New York, 2007 and 2011).

In his undergraduate thesis *Perspectivas internacionales de la masonería y su influencia en la política mexicana* (Universidad de las Américas-Puebla, 1994), Guillermo de los Reyes Heredia focused on the relationship between the international dimensions of Freemasonry and Mexican politics, before then examining *Freemasonry and Folklore in Mexican Presidentialism* (Ohio, 1997), as well as many other contribituons to the topic. The works that he coauthored with Paul Rich include *Civil Society and Freemasonry: The Cardenista Rite and Mexico* (Houston, 2002), *Mexican Freemasonry. The Devil's Government* (New York, 1994), *Mexican Freemasonry and Porfirism* (New York, 1995), *Mexican Grand Masters and Presidents* (New York, 1995), and *Reappraising Scottish Rite Freemasonry in Latin America* (Washington, 1995). In turn, Paul Rich published, in coauthorship with Antonio Lara, *Continuing Adventures in Masonic Bibliography* (Washington, 2000). De los Reyes Heredia's book *Masonería, política y sociedad en México* (Puebla, 2009), is where he presents a journey through the history of Mexican Freemasonry, providing exhaustive analysis of the subject as he does so.

José Enciso Contreras, whose first work was the unpublished *Masones en la revolución mexicana, el caso de Zacatecas, etapa precursora, 1900–1901* (Mexico City, 1989), published *Orígenes y primeras actividades de la masonería en Zacatecas* (Zacatecas, 1985), a work very much influenced by Isabel Olmos Sánchez, *La sociedad mexicana en vísperas de la independencia (1787–1821)* and by Richard Greenleaf, *The Mexican Inquisition and the Masonic Movement, 1751–1820* (New Mexico, 1969). The issue of Freemasonry in the process of Mexican independence is also addressed by Héctor Díaz Zermeño, who follows the now-eclipsed French trend of focusing on "societies of ideas or thought," in *La masonería como sociedad de ideas contrapunteada en el proceso de la independencia de Hispanoamérica y México, 1782–1833* (Mexico City, 2009). Díaz Zermeño also continues the nineteenth-century tradition of turning all liberals into Masons, though without providing documentary evidence. In turn, Michael Costeloe's study of political parties in postindependence Mexico, *La primera república federal de México (1824–1835)* (Mexico City, 1975), once again presents adherents to the Scottish and York Rites as leading figures in the fight for independence. Although it incorporates the press as an important source of information, it lacks a truly critical historical approach that goes beyond the mere compiling of information from newspapers.

Of interest are Rogelio Aragón's study *La Masonería en las revoluciones decimonónicas de México* (Madrid, 2008), which turns to the now-traditional literature of Mateos, Chism,

Zalce, Costeloe, and Alamán, and María Eugenia Claps Arenas, *Vínculos del primer liberalismo hispánico. Comuneros españoles y yorkinos mexicanos*, which was presented at the Colegio de México's Mexico-Spain (Nineteenth and Twentieth Centuries) Permanent Seminar. The same author had previously devoted her attention to the journalistic activities related to Hispanic America undertaken by Spanish exiles in London in her Master's thesis in history, entitled *La producción hemerográfica que los españoles exiliados en Londres dedicaron a Hispanoamérica. El caso de México (1824–1827)* (Mexico City, 1999), and she also completed a doctoral thesis: *La formación del liberalismo en México. Ramón Ceruti y la prensa yorkina (1825–1830)* (Alcalá de Henares, 2007).

In *La cruz y el compás: compromiso y conflicto* (Mexico City, 1992), Sara A. Frahm puts forward the reasons behind the presence of so many Catholic priests within Freemasonry, some of whom were important political leaders, even though Freemasonry was forbidden by the Catholic Church.

By way of contrast, Rodolfo Téllez-Cuevas in *El papel de la masonería en la política y la administración mexicana* (Toluca, 2009) and in particular in *La masonería en el proceso de formación del estado laico mexicano* (Mexico City, 2011) considers the importance attributed to Freemasonry over the course of more than two hundred years of Mexican history in relation to the development of secularism and the secular state. Following the same line of secularism, though based on greatly superior argumentation in methodological and bibliographical terms, are Carlos Francisco Martínez Moreno's *Dos perspectivas sobre los esfuerzos de la secularización en la Masonería simbólica en México durante los siglos XIX y XX* (Mexico City, 2009) and Guillermo de los Reyes Heredia's *El impacto de la masonería en los orígenes del discurso secular, laico y anticlerical en México* (Mexico City, 2010).

Educational reform in Mexico, an area through which Freemasons and freethinkers were involved in anticlericalism, is the subject of Cecilia Adriana Bautista García's *Maestros y Masones: la contienda por la reforma educativa en México 1930–1940* (Mexico City, 2005).

For Lila Lorenzo and Sergio García Guzmán, meanwhile, the issue under study in *La masonería femenina mexicana* (Oviedo, 2010) is women's involvement in Freemasonry in Mexico, a relatively late development in view of the fact that, until the 1930s, Mexican women's interest in Freemasonry had not awoken. The authors display great knowledge of the subject. Cecilia Adriana Bautista García also takes an interest in educational reform in *Maestros y Masones: La contienda por la Reforma Educativa en México, 1930–1940* (Mexico City, 2005). The revolutionary and postrevolutionary periods have been studied in Mario Aldana Rendón, *Masonería y revolución en Jalisco* (Mexico City, 2004) and in Beatriz Urias Horcasitas, *De moral y regeneración: el programa de "ingerencia social" postrevolucionario visto a través de las vis-*

tas masónicas mexicanas, 1930–1945 (Mexico City, 2004). The research quality and the methodology deployed are what make these works worthy of being taken into account.

Very uneven in its approach, development, and use of sources is Alejandro Gutiérrez Hernández, *El ciudadano desde el hermetismo. El caso de la Masonería*, which is part of a book edited by María Teresa Ayllón Trujillo, María Rosa Nuño Gutiérrez, and Wanderleia E. Brinckmann entitled *Familia, Identidad y Territorio. Actores y agentes en la construcción de la ciudadanía democrática* (Granada, 2010). Based on very general and generic considerations, this volume addresses in particular Mexican Freemasonry, its origins, and its characteristics, as well as Freemasonry in San Luis Potosí and societies of ideas in Latin America during the nineteenth century.

In 2011, Salvador Alejandro Lira Saucedo defended an undergraduate thesis at the University of Zacatecas entitled *Del templo a la palabra. Hermenéutica y mitocrítica en la liturgia masónica*, in which he considers a very difficult and original subject, and one that is uncommon within university studies, namely Masonic liturgies. He has also produced a summary based on the thesis with the title *Del templo a la palabra. Rescate filológico y estudio mitocrítico de cinco liturgias Francmasónicas* (*REHMLAC*, 2012).

Carlos Francisco Martínez Moreno's *Estado Nación laico y secularización masónica en México* (REHMLAC, 2012) is a thought-provoking work, in which the author addresses the Mexican National Rite in the context of the secularizing change of Mexico's Masonic-political orientation.

Marco Antonio Flores Zavala's book *El grupo masón en la política zacatecana, 1880–1914* (Zacatecas, 2002) offers an interesting, methodologically focused, and promising insight into the change that Mexico's new Masonic historiography must follow in relation to its regional history as a prior step toward a demythologized national historical account in the future. His works along these lines that are worth highlighting include *Los ciclos de la masonería mexicana. Siglos XVIII–XIX* (Zaragoza, 2004), *La masonería en la República Federal. Apuntes sobre las logias mexicanas (1821–1840)* (Zacatecas, 2005), *Masonería, masones y prensa en Zacatecas, 1870–1908* (Chiapas, 2007), *La Masonería y las fiestas cívicas en torno a Benito Juárez* (Mexico City, 2007), *La masonería y el Estado laico: escribir y leer en la masonería. Prácticas seculares de los masones* (Mexico City, 2009), *Periódicos francmasónicos mexicanos. Apuntes para la construcción de un corpus hemerográfico masónico* (Zaragoza, 2010); *Entre amigos y masones o las nuevas formas de asociación en Zacatecas (1813–1829)* (*REHMLAC*, 2012)—in which he sets out the traits common to the lodges of Zacatecas and the Society of Friends of the Country—and the biography *Tomás Lorck Ávila, un masón mexicano del siglo XIX* (Zaragoza, 2007).

José Luis Trueba Lara's *Masones en México. Historia del poder oculto*

(Mexico City, 2007) and Wenceslao Vargas Márquez's *La Masonería en la Presidencia de México* (Mexico City, 2010) contribute new informational focal points, though they do not manage to produce an objective history of Freemasonry, as they are excessively preoccupied with the traditional issue of its political participation alongside power-holding groups, a notion that is not always consistent with the historical truth.

Of fundamental importance is the undergraduate thesis defended at the Autonomous University of Yucatán by Yuri Hulkin Balam Ramos, entitled *Etnografía de la masonería en Yucatán. El caso de la Gran Logia Unida "La Oriental"* (Mérida-Yucatán, 1987), as is his subsequent Master's thesis in anthropology, presented at the Colegio de Michoacán under the title *El papel político de la masonería en Zamora, Michoacán (1913–1990)* (Zamora, 1992).

Two more works of interest are Moisés González Navarro's *Masones y cristeros en Jalisco* (Mexico City, 2000) and *Presencia de la masonería alemana en México: Carlos de Gager (1853–1885)* (REHMLAC, 2011), by Martha Celis de la Cruz, who sadly left us prematurely.

It is worth highlighting Carlos Francisco Martínez Moreno's previously described Master's thesis that was presented at UNAM in 2011 and entitled *El establecimiento de las masonerías en México en el siglo XIX*, a study that offers novel and demystifying positions, as well as a preliminary descriptive overview of the grand lodges of nineteenth-century Mexican Freemasonry.

Martínez Moreno's thesis is supplemented by his innovative work—also described previously—*Logias masónicas en la Nueva España* (REHMLAC, 2011).

Prior to this work, he had devoted his attention in particular to Benito Juárez and his much-debated Masonic affiliation in *Benito Juárez: ¿más que un Aprendiz de Masón?* (Mexico City, 2008), to Spaniards' exile in Mexico in *La Masonería española en el exilio de México* (Zaragoza, 2010), to Freemasonry and the Mexican Constitution in *Masones en defensa de la República y de la Constitución mexicana* (Mexico City, 2010), and to York Rite federalists in *La Sociedad de los Yorkinos Federalistas* (REHMLAC, 2009), a hermeneutic offering on this group's general regulations and statutes in the context of Masonic history. The conclusion that he reaches is that the group was a para-Masonic society with clear political goals.

The York Rite is also focused on by Ana Oropesa Alfaro in her undergraduate thesis *El proyecto político yorkino: la política popular en la campaña presidencial de Vicente Guerrero* (Mexico City, 2010).

The theme of Benito Juárez is additionally addressed by—among many others—Carmen Vázquez Mantecón in *Muerte y vida eterna de Benito Juárez* (Mexico City, 2006), which focuses, in particular, on the construction of a myth around Juárez by Freemasons that was faithfully maintained through tributes and public activities. This theme is also one that María Eugenia Vázquez

Semadeni knows well, and she studies it with her characteristic skill in *Juárez y la masonería* (Mexico City, 2006) and in *La masonería durante el período juarista* (Mexico City, 2007).

Among the most recent publications on Mexican Freemasonry, it is important to note Guillermo De los Reyes Heredia, *Herencias secretas. Masonería, política y sociedad en México* (Puebla, 2009), in which the author analyzes the impact of Freemasonry in liberal and secular nationalist discourse in Mexico. The work rounds off his previous studies *The Cross and the Compass: The Influence of the Catholic Religion and Masonry in the Formation of the Mexican Political Thought* (Cambridge, 2007), *Translating Smuggling and Recovering Books in Nineteenth Century Mexico: Thomas Smith Webb's El Monitor de los Masones Libres o Ilustraciones sobre la Masonería* (Houston, 2006), and *Freemasonry's Educational Role* (1997), co-authored with Paul Rich and available online and many other publications by this scholar.

Secularización del Estado y la sociedad (Mexico City, 2010), a volume edited by Patricia Galeana and published by Mexico's Senate to mark the 150th anniversary of the country's reform laws, contains two contributions on Freemasonry and liberalism. The first is Guillermo De los Reyes, *El impacto de la Masonería en los orígenes del discurso secular, laico y anticlerical en México*, and the second is Carlos Francisco Martínez Moreno, *Masones en defensa de la República y de la Constitución mexicana. Dos sociedades patrióticas paramasónicas en el siglo XIX*. These study, with the two authors' characteristic trustworthiness, the influence of Freemasonry and the importance of secularism in cementing fundamental freedoms.

Meanwhile, María Eugenia Vázquez Semadeni, who had previously published an interesting and essential work entitled *La Gran Legión del Águila Negra* (Zamora, 2007), in which she provides documents on the titular lodge's founding, statutes, and objectives, and who had offered equally fundamental documents on York Rite Obediences in *Las Obediencias masónicas del rito de York como centro de acción política. México 1825–1830* (Chiapas, 2009), *Masonería, Papeles públicos y cultura política* (Mexico City, 2009), has also contributed an important and decisive work with the title *La formación de una cultura política republicana. El debate público sobre la masonería. México 1821–1830* (Mexico City, 2010). This latter study focuses on so-called political culture and is based on her doctoral thesis *La interacción entre el debate público sobre la masonería y la cultura política, 1761–1830*, which she defended at the Colegio de Michoacán in 2008. Prior to its defense, she had presented a snapshot of it at the Eleventh International Symposium on the History of Spanish Freemasonry, held in Logroño in July 2006. Under the title of *La masonería mexicana en el debate público 1808–1830* (Zaragoza, 2007), this paper demonstrates the importance of public debate as a new way of doing politics and creating a popular imagining of Freemasonry. And at the twelfth symposium in Almería she presented *Criminal seguida a Luis Zuluaga por infiel al Rito de York* (Zaragoza, 2010), an intriguing and interesting study on a Masonic judge in the city of Chihuahua in which she addresses once more the confusion that existed in 1827 between Masonic activities and politics and between adherents to the York and Scottish Rites.

In the winter of 2011, and now at UCLA, in *La imagen pública de la masonería en Nueva España, 1761–1821* (Zamora, 2011) this same author went into greater depth, revising and correcting her work and expanding its bibliography, on a subject that she knows perfectly owing to its having been part of her doctoral thesis. Based on an analysis of political language, her interest is not the history of Freemasonry but rather how during the second half of the eighteenth century and the first decades of the nineteenth a popular imagining of Freemasonry came to be configured.

Linked to the issue of repression, though this time that of a political nature, Francisco Sánchez Montoya has studied the case of an exiled Spanish parliamentary deputy in *La represión al catedrático Manuel Martínez Pedroso, masón, diputado por Ceuta y miembro de las Cortes en el exilio mexicano* (Zaragoza, 2010).

With regard to this same episode of the exile of Spaniards in Mexico, and in particular that of Lucio Martínez Gil, Grand Master of the Spanish Grand Orient, as well as the internal conflicts that he lived through there and the ups and downs of the Luis Companys Lodge—an institution that still exists in the Valley of Mexico—it is worth noting Pere Sánchez Ferré's paper *Del exilio a la resistencia. Las logias Luis Companys* (Zaragoza, 2010). The exile of another key figure in the history of the Spanish Grand Orient is considered by Amparo Guerra Gómez in *Diego Martínez Barrio y el Gran Oriente Español: República y exilio americano* (Zaragoza, 1993). Finally, Ignacio Cruz Orozco has also addressed Spanish republican exile in Mexico, a subject that he knows well and has spent years working on, in ¡Hermanos del mundo! *Ayudadnos a libertar España. Nuevas aportaciones sobre la masonería española en el exilio republicano de México* (Zaragoza, 2010).

In addition to the previously mentioned universities—for example, the Autonomous University of Zacatecas, the Autonomous University of Puebla, the Autonomous University of Yucatán, the UNAM's Institute of Historical Research, and the Colegio de Michoacán—the Autonomous University of Tlaxcala has also joined in with the study of Freemasonry. In September 2009, it organized a course, in collaboration with other institutions, called *La Masonería como problema político-religioso. Reflexiones históricas*, which was delivered by Dr. José Antonio Ferrer Benimeli and which then became the subject of a publication (Tlaxcala, 2010). The course was subsequently delivered once more in August 2010 at the Ibero-American University in Mexico City, this time led by Dr. Cristina Torales Pacheco. In October 2010, it was the turn of UNAM's Faculty of Political and Social Sciences when it delivered the course *Geopolítica de la Masonería*, which was organized by Dr. Leopoldo González Aguayo, coordinator and leader of the project Geopolitical Schools and the Formation of a Mexican Geopolitical Design. In turn, at the Michoacán University of Saint Nicholas of Hidalgo in Morelia, Dr. Moisés Guzmán Pérez organized an international seminar series over the course of 2011 (March 14 to November 24) that focused on liberalism, Freemasonry, and independence in Hispanic America. Of these, at least eight deal directly with Freemasonry, with seven focusing on it in Mexico and one on it in Venezuela. These works are: José Antonio Ferrer Benimeli, *Utopía y realidad del liberalismo masónico. De las Cortes de Cádiz a la Independencia de México*, Guadalupe Jiménez Codinach, *Auge de las sociedades secretas: la logia Lautaro y la independencia Hispanoamericana*, Jaime Olveda, *Las logias en los primeros años republicanos, 1822–1828*, Eduardo Adolfo Oropesa Villavicencio, *Masones en la Nueva España. Libros prohibidos y liberalismo*, José Pascual Mora García, *La masonería. Su historia y su contribución en la construcción simbólica de la nación venezolana. Siglo XIX*, Ramón Alonso Pérez Escutia, *Los orígenes de la masonería en Michoacán, 1821–1834*, and María Eugenia Vázquez Semadeni, *Del mar a la política. Masonería en Nueva España. México, 1816–1823*.

Finally, and as an extension of Mexican universities' involvement in the history of Freemasonry, it is worth mentioning the International Conference on American and Latin American Freemasonry: A New Past and A New Future, which was held on December 5, 2011, at the UCLA History Department and organized by its chair, Dr. Margaret Jacob, and by Dr. María Eugenia Vázquez Semadeni. The Grand Lodge of California and the Institute for Masonic Studies also contributed to the event. The event included the following papers: Margaret C. Jacob, *Where We Now Are in Masonic Studies*; José Antonio Ferrer Benimeli, *Utopia and Reality of Masonic Liberalism: From the Courts of Cadiz to Mexican Independence*; Eduardo Torres Cuevas, *Origins and Development of Freemasonry in* Cuba; Jorge Luis Romeu, *Challenges and Characteristics of Cuban Freemasons in the 20ᵗʰ Century: A Demographic Approach*; Miguel Guzmán Stein, *The Relation Among Freemasonry, State, and Catholic Church in Central America: Formation of the Secular States in Latin America*; Ricardo Martínez Esquivel, *Mystical Sociability: Freemasons and Theosophists in the Organization of Co-Freemasonry and the Liberal Catholic Church in Costa Rica during the 1920's*; María Eugenia Vázquez Semadeni, *American Origins of Mexican Freemasonry*; and Guillermo de los Reyes Heredia, *The Relation Between Mexican and American Freemasonry, Late 19ᵗʰ and Early 20ᵗʰ Centuries*.

The new revisionist approach that is taking shape in Mexico with regard to the historiography of Freemasonry responds to the sound criteria set out at other levels, with great skill, in Rafael Rojas, *La escritura de la independencia. El surgimiento de la opinión pública en México* (Mexico City, 2003), Alfredo Ávila, *En nombre de la nación. La formación del Gobierno representati-*

vo en México, 1808–1824 (Mexico City, 2002) and *Para la libertad. Los republicanos en tiempos del Imperio, 1821–1823* (Mexico City, 2004), Elías Palti, *La invención de una legitimidad. Razón y retórica en el pensamiento mexicano del siglo XIX (un estudio sobre las formas del discurso político)* (Mexico City, 2005), and, in particular, the edited volume by Alfredo Ávila and Virginia Guedea, *La independencia de México. Temas e interpretaciones recientes* (Mexico City, 2007). It is difficult to choose from among the different themes skillfully addressed in the latter work by the nine authors' contributions, especially when it comes to those which analyze recent, traditional, and general interpretations from the historiography: Alfredo Ávila, *Interpretaciones recientes en la historia del pensamiento de la emancipación*, Roberto Breña, *El peso de las interpretaciones tradicionales en la historiografía peninsular actual sobre el primer liberalismo español y los procesos emancipadores americanos (una interpretación alternativa)*, and Jaime E. Rodríguez O., *Interpretaciones generales de las independencias.*

And with that, I bring to an end this quick and incomplete bibliographic journey through Latin America that started in the islands of the Caribbean and, after a short trip through South America, returned to the continental Caribbean and Mexico.

Bibliographic Appendix

Acereda, Alberto. "Dos caras desconocidas de Rubén Darío: El poeta masón y el poeta inédito." *Hispania* 88, no. 3 (2005): 423–444.

Acosta García, Ismael. *José Martí. Una vida por la libertad, la igualdad y la fraternidad, Morelia.* Mexico City: Sociedad Cultural Miguel Hidalgo, 2009.

Agramonte, Manuel Alejandro, and Leiner Méndez Ruiz. "Concepciones históricas y simbólicas de la masonería en dos obras cubanas de la historiografía del siglo XIX." Paper presented at the II Simposio Internacional de Historia de la Masonería y Sociedades Patrióticas Latinoamericanas y Caribeñas, Cátedra Transdisciplinaria de Estudios Históricos de la Masonería Cubana Vicente Antonio de Castro (CTEHMAC), Casa de Altos Estudios Don Fernando Ortiz, Universidad de La Habana, Oficina del Historiador de la Ciudad de La Habana, Gran Logia de Cuba de A.L y A.M, and Centro de Estudios Históricos de la Masonería Española (CEHME) of the Universidad de Zaragoza, Havana, Cuba, December 2–6, 2008.

Alaman, Luis. *Historia de Méjico desde los primeros movimientos que prepararon su independencia en el año 1808 hasta la época presente.* Mexico City: Libros del Bachiller Sansón Carrasco, 1986.

Aldana Rendon, Mario. *Masonería y revolución en Jalisco*. Jalisco: n.p, 2004.

Albuquerque, A. Tenorio. *A Maçonaria e a inconfidencia mineira*. Rio de Janeiro: Ed. Espiritualista, n.d.

_____. *A maçonaria e a Independencia do Brasil*. Rio de Janeiro: Ed. Aurora, n.d.

_____. *A Maçonaria e a Libertação dos Escravos*. Rio de Janeiro: Ed. Aurora, 1970.

_____. *A Maçonaria e as revoluções pernambucanas*. Rio de Janeiro: Ed. Aurora, n.d..

Alencar, Renato. "A Questão religiosa e a Maçonaria brasileira." *História Politica da Maçonaria* 4 (1991): 173–198.

Alexander, Abel. "La construcción virtual de la Argentina. Fotógrafos masones del siglo XIX." *Todo Es Historia* 405 (2001): 74–76.

Algdu. *Liminar de los Anales Masónicos de la Resp. Log. Simb. Concordia Universal: apuntes sinópticos al conmemorar cien años de su fundación*. Callao, Peru: Talleres Gráficos Quirós, 1949.

Almeida de Carvalho, William. *Maçonaria, Tráfico de Escravos e o Banco do Brasil*. Sao Paulo: Madrás, 2010.

_____. "Pequena História da Maçonaria no Brasil." *REHMLAC* 2, no. 1 (May–November 2010): 30–58. https://revistas.ucr.ac.cr/index.php/rehmlac/article/view/6609/6298

Almodóvar Muñoz, Carmen. *Antología crítica de la historiografía cubana*. Havana: Ed. Pueblo y Educación, 1986.

Alonso Pascual, Carmen, and Blanca, Desantes. "Orientación para la investigación de la masonería del siglo XX en el Archivo Histórico Nacional, Sección de fondos contemporáneos y archivos de Martínez Barrio." In *La masonería en la España del siglo XX*, edited by José Antonio Ferrer Benimeli, 2:1109–18. Toledo, Spain: Universidad de Toledo, 1996.

Alonso Vázquez, Francisco Javier. "La pugna entre la Iglesia católica y la masonería en el ocaso de la dictadura de Trujillo." In *La masonería española en el 2000. Una revisión histórica*, edited by José Antonio Ferrer Benimeli, 2:783-804. Zaragoza, Spain: Gobierno de Aragón, 2001.

Alvarenga, Luis. "*La Hora de Sofía*. Entrevista al Dr. Miguel Guzmán-Stein: La masonería, su persecución y su influencia en Centroamérica." *REHMLAC* 2, no. 2 (December 2010–April 2011): 172–189. https://revistas.ucr.ac.cr/index.php/rehmlac/article/view/6603/6294

Amaral, Giana Lange do. *O Gymnasio Pelotense e a Maçonaria: uma face da história da educação em Pelotas*. Pelotas, Brazil: Seiva Publicações, 1999.

Amado, Fernando. *En penumbras. La Masonería uruguaya (1973–2008)*. Montevideo: Fin de Siglo, 2008.

_____. *La masonería uruguaya. El fin de la discreción*. Montevideo: Sudamericana, 2011.

Amador Alonso, Aimara Olga. "Significación sociocultural de los símbolos empleados en las logias masónicas de la ciudad de Cienfuegos." Undergraduate dissertation, Universidad de Cienfuegos, Cuba, 2011.

Amador Carretero, Pilar. "Mensajes de mentalidad expresados a través de los nombres simbólicos de los masones de América y Cuba." In *Masonería Española y América*, edited by José Antonio Ferrer Benimeli, 2:967–981. Zaragoza, Spain: CEHME, 1993.

Anónimo, Sucinta. *Relación de la masonería en Venezuela*. Caracas: Valentín Espinel, 1852.

Antonio, Jorge Luis. "As vinculações diretas e indiretas de Almeida Junior a Maçonaria." In *Formação social da Maçonaria*, 2:99–116. São Paulo: Academia Brasileira Maçônica de Artes Ciências E Letras, 1981.

Aragón Juárez, Rogelio. "Contra la Iglesia y el Estado: Masonería e Inquisición en Nueva España, 1760–1820." Undergraduate dissertation, Universidad del Instituto Helénico, Mexico City, 2006.

_____. "Contra la Iglesia y el Estado: Masonería e Inquisición en Nueva España, 1760-1820." *REHMLAC* 3, no. 1 (May–November 2011): 197–202. https://revistas.ucr.ac.cr/index.php/rehmlac/article/view/22480/22719

_____. "La masonería en las revoluciones decimonónicas de México." *HISPANIA NOVA. Revista de Historia Contemporánea* 8 (2008): 251–266. hispanianova.rediris.es/8/dossier/8d005.pdf.

Arango Jaramillo, Mario. *Libertad y tolerancia. La masonería colombiana en los inicios de la República 1810–1860*. Bogotá: n.p., 2008.

Arapé, Robert. "¿Fue masón Miranda?" In *Miranda. El Visionario*, edited by Luis Cañón. Maracaibo, Venezuela: Panorama, 2008.

Ardao, Arturo. *Espiritualismo y Positivismo en el Uruguay*. Montevideo: n.p., 1968.

_____. *Racionalismo y liberalismo en el Uruguay*. Montevideo: n.p., 1962.

Arechaga, Carlos A. "Masones en la Historia argentina. La abjuración de Mitre." *Todo Es Historia* 405 (2001): 26–31.

Austria, José. *Exposición legal al cumplir diez años de existencia de la masonería (1918–1928)*. Puerto Cabello, Venezuela: Valencia, Impr. y Lit. Branger, 1928.

Avendaño, Rómulo. "La Sociedad Lautaro. Rectificaciones históricas." *La Revista de Buenos Aires* 19 (1869): 439–445; 20 (1870): 129–141.

Ávila, Alfredo. *En nombre de la nación. La formación del Gobierno representativo en México, 1808–1824*. Mexico City: Taurus, 2002.

_____. *Para la libertad. Los republicanos en tiempos del Imperio, 1821–1823.* Mexico City: UNAM, 2004.

Ávila, Alfredo, and Virginia Guedea., eds. *La independencia de México. Temas e interpretaciones recientes.* Mexico City: UNAM, 2007.

Ávila, Júnior, and Celso Jaloto. *A Maçonaria baiana e sua história.* Salvador, Brazil: p y A Ed., 2000.

Ayala Pérez, José Antonio. "La conjunción masónico-librepensadora-protestante contra la Iglesia católica. El caso de Puerto Rico (1898–1925)." In *La Masonería Española entre Europa y América*, edited by José Antonio Ferrer Benimeli, 1:417–438. Zaragoza, Spain: CEHME, 1995.

_____. "El contencioso masónico en Puerto Rico a finales del siglo XIX (1871–1899)." *Revista del Centro de Estudios Avanzados de Puerto Rico y el Caribe* 8 (January–June 1989): 98–117.

_____. "Maçoneria, regionalisme i independencia al Puerto Rico de la fi del segle." *L'Avenç* 218 (1997): 52–54.

_____. "La masonería de obediencia española ante el conflicto colonial puertorriqueño." *Cuadernos de Investigación Histórica. Brocar* 17 (1991): 21–37. Also in *Masonería Española y América*, edited by José Antonio Ferrer Benimeli, 2:1127–1143. Zaragoza, Spain: CEHME, 1993.

_____. *La Masonería de obediencia española en Puerto Rico en los siglos XIX y XX.* Murcia, Spain: Universidad de Murcia, 1991–1993.

_____. "La masonería de obediencia francesa en Puerto Rico de 1821 a 1841." *Cuadernos Hispanoamericanos* 491 (1991): 65–82.

Azevedo, Célia Marinho. "Maçonaria: história e historiografía." *Revista da USP* 32 (1996–1997).

Balam Ramos, Yuri Hulkin. "Etnografía de la masonería en Yucatán: el caso de la G.L. Unida 'La Oriental Peninsular.'" Undergraduate dissertation, Universidad Autónoma de Yucatán, Mexico, 1987.

_____. *El papel político de la masonería en Zamora, Michoacán (1913–1990).* Zamora, Mexico: n.p., 1992.

Bandecchi, Brasil. *A Bucha, a Maçonaria e o Espírito liberal.* Sao Paulo, Brazil: Ed. Parna, 1982.

Barcia, Pedro Luis. "San Martín y la Masonería." In *San Martín, Catolicismo y masonería*, edited by Ignacio-Juan Cuccorese, 9–17. Buenos Aires: Instituto Nacional Sanmartiniano, 1993.

_____. *Luzes e Sombras. A ação da maçonaria brasileira (1870–1910).* Campinas, Brazil: Editora da Unicamp, Centro Memórias-Unicamp, 1999.

Bastian, Jean Pierre. "Una ausencia notoria: la francmasonería en la historiografía mexicanista." *Historia mexi-*

cana 44, no. 175 (January–March 1995): 439–461.

_____. *Los disidentes. Sociedades protestantes y revolución en México 1872–1911*. Mexico City: Colegio de México, 1989.

_____. "Emancipación política de 1898 e influencia del protestantismo en Cuba y Puerto Rico." *Anuario de Historia de la Iglesia* 7 (1998): 145–161. dialnet.unirioja.es/servlet/articulo?codigo=236837.

_____. "La francmasonería dividida y el poder liberal en México, 1872–1911." In *Masonería Española y América*, edited by José Antonio Ferrer Benimeli, 1:415–436. Zaragoza, Spain: CEHME, 1993.

_____. "La francmasonería en la historiografía mexicanista." In *La Masonería Española entre Europa y América*, edited by José Antonio Ferrer Benimeli, 2:869–888. Zaragoza, Spain: CEHME, 1995.

_____. "Francmasones y protestantes en el movimiento revolucionario de la independencia cubana, 1868–1898." In *Protestantismo en Cuba. Recuento histórico y perspectiva desde sus orígenes hasta principios del siglo XXI*, vol. 2, edited by. R. Molina. Havana: Ed. Caminos, 2012.

_____. "Itinerario de un intelectual popular protestante, liberal y francmasón, José Rumbia Guzmán 1866–1913." *Cristianismo y Sociedad* 25, no. 92 (1987): 91–108.

_____. "Jacobinismo y ruptura revolucionaria durante el porfiriato." *Signos, Anuario de Humanidades* 2 (1990). Also in *Journal of Mexican Studies / Estudios Mexicanos* 7 (1991).

_____. *Modernidad e independencia. Ensayo sobre las revoluciones hispanas.* Mexico City: Fondo de Cultura Económica, 1993.

_____. *La modernidad religiosa: Europa latina y América Latina en perspectiva comparada.* Mexico City: Fondo de Cultura Económica, 2004.

_____. "El paradigma de 1789. Sociedades de ideas y revolución mexicana." *Historia Mexicana* 38 (1988).

_____. *Protestantes, liberales y francmasones. Sociedades de ideas y modernidad en América Latina, siglo XIX.* Mexico City: Fondo de Cultura Económica, 1990.

_____. *Protestantismo y modernidad latinoamericana. Historia de unas minorías religiosas activas en América Latina.* Mexico City: Fondo de Cultura Económica, 1994.

_____. "Protestants, Francmaçons et spirites : pluralité religieuse et mouvement révolutionnaire. Mexique 1911–1920." *Social Sciences and Missions* 24 (2011): 7–38.

_____. "Protestants, Freemasons and Spiritits in the Mexican Revolution."

In *Faith and Impiety in Revolutionary Mexico*, edited by Matthew Butler. New York: Palgrave Macmillas, 2007.

———. "Las redes francmasonas y protestantes en el movimiento independentista cubano 1869–1898." In *La Masonería Española y la crisis colonial del 98*, edited by José Antonio Ferrer Benimeli, 2:947–961. Zaragoza, Spain: CEHME, 1999.

———. "Sociedades protestantes y logias en la lucha independentista cubana." *Revista de Historia* (2001).

Bautista García, Cecilia Adriana. "Maestros y Masones: La contienda por la reforma educativa en México, 1930–1940." *Relaciones, Revista del Colegio de Michoacan* 26, no. 104 (2005).

Baze, Abraham. *Escravidão. O Amazonas e a Maçonaria edificaron a História*. Manaus, Brazil: Travessia, 2000.

Beltrán Alonso, Haens. "Aproximación al funcionamiento de la Gran Logia de la isla de Cuba desde la revista 'La Gran Logia' (1929–1933)." Master's dissertation, Universidad de Cienfuegos, Cuba, 2011.

Beltrán Alonso, Haens, and Jency Mendoza Otero. "La masonería cubana y el proceso revolucionario de los años 30. Aproximación desde la revista 'La Gran Logia' 1931–1933." *REHMLAC* 4, no. 1 (May–November 2012): 189–206. https://revistas.ucr.ac.cr/index.php/rehmlac/article/view/12148/11423

Beltrán Ávila, Marcos. *La pequeña Gran Logia que independizó a Bolivia, 1823–1825*. Cochabamba, Bolivia: n.p., 1948.

Berruezo León, María Teresa. "La propaganda independentista de la logia mirandista en Londres." In *Masonería Española y América*, edited by José Antonio Ferrer Benimeli, 1:95–114. Zaragoza, Spain: CEHME, 1993.

Bianchi, Vittoria. *La Massoneria in America Latina*. Rome, Italy: Ed. Erasmo, 2008.

Bittencourt, Luigi Gonzaga. "Cem Anos da Abolição." *A Trolha* 18, no. 35 (May–June 1988): 51–55.

Blanco Rodríguez, Juan Andrés. "La actitud de Martí ante los españoles y la presencia de estos en el 'Ejército Libertador' cubano." In *Antes del desastre: Orígenes y antecedentes de la crisis del 98*, edited by Juan Pablo Fusi and Antonio Niño, 1:163–174. Madrid: Universidad Complutense, 1996.

Blázquez Miguel, Juan. "La Masonería en Haití. Estudio histórico." In *Masonería Española y América*, edited by José Antonio Ferrer Benimeli, 1:163–174. Zaragoza, Spain: CEHME, 1993.

Böhm, Günter. *Manuel de Lima, fundador de la masonería chilena*. Santiago, Chile: Universidad de Chile, 1979.

Bohórquez, Carmen. *Francisco de Miranda. Precursor de las independencias de la América Latina*. Caracas: Universidad Católica Andrés Bello, 2002.

Bolcatto, Hipólito Guillermo. *La Logia Lautaro de Santa Fe*. Santa Fe: n.p., 2011.

Boulton, Alfredo. *Miranda, Bolívar y Sucre. Tres estudios iconográficos*. Caracas: Italgráfica, 1959.

Bruno Jofre, Rosa del Carmen. "La introducción del sistema lancasteriano en Perú: liberalismo, masonería y libertad religiosa." In *Protestantes, liberales y francmasones. Sociedades de ideas y modernidad en América Latina, siglo XIX*, edited by Jean Pierre Bastian, 84–96. Mexico City: Fondo de Cultura Económica, 1990.

Bullock, Steven C. *Revolutionary Brotherhood: Freemasonry and the Transformation of the American Social Order, 1730–1840*. Chapel Hill, NC: University of North Carolina Press, 1996.

Bustamante, Carlos María. *Diario Histórico de México, 1822–1848*. Mexico City: Ed. Josefina Zoraida Vázquez, 2002.

Cabañas, Hubert A. *History of Freemasonry in Curaçao*. Curaçao: n.p., 2012.

Cálix Suazo, Miguel. "¿Realmente fue masón José Francisco Morazán Quesada?" *REHMLAC* 2, no. 2 (December 2010–April 2011): 160–171. https://revistas.ucr.ac.cr/index.php/rehmlac/article/view/6602/6293

Callaey, Eduardo R. *De Templo Salomonis Liber y otros textos de Masonería Medieval*. Madrid: Manakel, 2010.

_____. *La masonería y sus orígenes cristianos: Ordo laicorum ab monacorum ordine. El esoterismo masónico en los antiguos documentos benedictinos*. Buenos Aires: Kier, 2006.

_____. "Masones y republicanos españoles: el exilio republicano en Argentina." In *La masonería española en la época de Sagasta (1825–1903)*, edited by José Antonio Ferrer Benimeli, 1:775–808. Zaragoza, Spain: CEHME, 2006.

_____. *Monjes y canteros. Una aproximación a los orígenes de la Francmasonería*. Buenos Aires: Ed. Dunken, 2001.

_____. *Ordo Laicorum ab Monacorum Ordine. Los orígenes monásticos de la Francmasonería*. Buenos Aires: Academia de Estuios Masónicos, 2004.

_____. *El otro Imperio Cristiano. De la Orden del Temple a la Francmasonería*. Buenos Aires: Nowtilus, 2005.

Calvet Fagundes, Morivalde. "A abolição foi lenta e gradual." *A Trolha* 34 (March–April 1988): 66–68.

_____. "Os abolicionistas." In *Subsidios para a História da Literatura Maçônica Brasileira (século XIX)*, 163–170. Caxias do Sul, Brazil: Educus, 1989.

_____. *Antología Poética Nacional Maçônica*. Rio de Janeiro: Academia Maçônica de Letras, 1980.

_____. "Dialogos com a Igreja." In *Episodios da História Antiga e Moderna da*

Maçonaria, 1:129–152. São Paulo: Academia Brasileira Maçônica de Artes Ciências E Letras.

_____. "Episodios da História Antiga e Moderna da Maçonaria." (Caxias do Sul, Brazil, 1986; Rio de Janeiro, 1987).

_____. *Formação Histórica da Maçonaria*. Rio de Janeiro: Ed. Esperanto, 1983.

_____. *Formação Social da Maçonaria*. Rio de Janeiro: Ed. Aurora, 1983.

_____. *História da revolução farroupilha*. Caxias do Sul, Brazil: Ed. da Universidade do Caxias do Sul, 1984.

_____. "História Política da Maçonaria." In *Anais do I Congresso Internacional de História e Geografia da Maçonaria*. Rio de Janeiro: Ed. Aurora, 1982.

_____. *A Maçonaria e as forças secretas da revolução*. Rio de Janeiro: Ed. Maçônica, 1976.

_____. *Maçonaria: Espirito e Realidade*. Rio de Janeiro: Ed. Aurora, 1982.

_____. "A Maçonaria na formação da nacionalidade brasileira." In *História Política da Maçonaria*. Rio de Janeiro: Academia Brasileira Maçônica de Letras, 1982.

_____. *Os Maçons: vida e obra*. Rio de Janeiro, Brazil: Ed. Aurora, 1991.

_____. "La masonería y la independencia de América Latina." In *Masonería Española y América*, edited by José Antonio Ferrer Benimeli, 2:1069–1082. Zaragoza, Spain: CEHME, 1993.

_____. *Panorama atual da Maçonaria no mundo*. Rio de Janeiro: Ed. Aurora, 1982.

_____. "Revelações da História Gaúcha." In *Episodios da História Antiga e Moderna*, 1:153–183. Caxias do Sul, Brazil: n.p., 1987.

_____. "Rocha Negra" a legendaria. Londrina, Brazil: Ed. Maçonica A Trolha, 1989.

_____. *Uma visão dialetica da Maçonaria brasileira*. Rio de Janeiro: Ed. Aurora, 1985.

Campos, Pedro Moacyr de, and Júlio do Carmo Hildebrand. *O Grande Oriente do Brasil em Santa Catarina: de Jerónimo Coelho até nossos días*. Florianópolis, Brazil: GOB/SC, 2008.

Cancio-Bello y Arango, Emilio. "La Masonería como factor decisivo en la formación y desarrollo de la Nacionalidad cubana." *Boletín Oficial del Supremo Consejo del Grado 33 para la República de Cuba* 27 (1932): 750–753 and 769–771.

Canter, Juan. "La Logia Lautaro y la revolución de octubre de 1812." *La Nación* (Buenos Aires), October 3, 1934.

_____. "La Logia Lautaro y la independencia de América según Antonio R. Zúñiga." *Crítica Histórica* (1933): 1–14.

_____. "La Logia Lautaro y Mendoza." *Revista de la Junta Provincial de Estudios Históricos* 2 (1936): 78–90.

_____. "La Logia Lautaro y su evolución." *La Nación* (Buenos Aires), October 12, 1934.

_____. "La Sociedad Patriótica y la Logia Lautaro. Resumen de la conferencia pronunciada en el Ateneo Ibero-Americano." *La Nación* (Buenos Aires), October 10, 1934.

_____. "Las Sociedades secretas y literarias." In *Historia de la Nación Argentina, Buenos Aires, Academia Nacional de la Historia, 1936–1940*, 5:189–305. Buenos Aires: n.p., 1941.

Capecchi Gómez, Luis Eduardo. *Desarrollo Histórico de la Masonería en Venezuela*. Venezuela: Antimano, 2011.

Cara, José Eduardo de. "Homenaje a Mitre Símbolo." *Revista de Cultura y opinión* 4, no. 81 (July–August 2004): 27–31.

_____. "A Maçonaria no Rio da Prata. Subsidios para o estudio e classificação dal medallas maçonicas argentinas." In *Formação Social da Maçonaria*, 1:21–52. Rio de Janeiro, Brazil: Academia Brasileira Maçônica de Letras, 1983.

Caro Figueroa, Gregorio A. "De secretos a discretos." *Todo Es Historia* 405 (2001): 4–5.

Carmona Soto, Raúl. "Allende, pensamiento masónico." *Lautaro* (August–October 1983).

Carnicelli, Américo. *Historia de la Masonería Colombiana, 1833–1940*. 2 vols. Bogotá: n.p., 1975.

_____. *La Masonería en la Independencia de América, 1810–1830. Secretos de la Historia*. 2 vols. Bogotá: n.p., 1970.

Carvajal Muñoz, Jorge. *Libertad, Igualdad, Fraternidad. Regresando al futuro*. Santiago, Chile: LOM Ed., 2007.

_____. *Masonería y temas de la sociedad actual. Intervenciones públicas del Gran Maestro de la Gran Logia de Chile*. Santiago, Chile: LOM Ed., 2002.

Carvalho Neves, Francisco das Chagas. "La abolición de la esclavitud y la masonería brasileña." In *Masonería Española y América*, edited by José Antonio Ferrer Benimeli, 1:73–80. Zaragoza, Spain: CEHME, 1993.

Casaus Arzú, Marta Elena. "El abordaje del 'problema del indio' en las corrientes espiritualistas y teosóficas." Paper presented at the XIV Encuentro de Latinoamericanistas Españoles, Universidad de Santiago de Compostela, Santiago de Compostela, Spain, September 15–18, 2010.

_____. "La creación de nuevos espacios públicos en Centroamérica a principios del siglo XX: La influencia de las redes teosóficas en la opinión pública centroamericana." *Revista de Historia* 46 (July–December 2002): 11–59. articlearchives.com/latin-america/guatemala/1076885-1.html.

_____. "La influencia de la teosofía en la emancipación de las mujeres guatemaltecas: La Sociedad Gabriela Mistral." *Anuario de Estudios Centroamericanos* 27, no. 1(2001): 31–58.

_____. "El vitalismo teosófico como discurso alternativo de las élites intelectuales centroamericanas en las décadas de 1920 y 1930. Principales difusores: Porfirio Barba Jacob, Carlos Wyld Ospina y Alberto Masferrer." *REHMLAC* 3, no. 1 (May–November 2011): 81–120. https://revistas.ucr.ac.cr/index.php/rehmlac/article/view/6588/6279

Castellani, José. *A Cição de 1927 no Grande Oriente do Brasil*. Rio de Janeiro: Supremo Conselho, 1995.

_____. *A conjuração Mineira e a Maçonaria que nao houve*. São Paulo: Ed. Gazeta Maçônica, 1992.

_____. *O Grande Oriente de Sao Paulo. 75 Anos*. São Paulo: Ed. do Grande Oriente de São Paulo, 1996.

_____. *História do Grande Oriente do Brasil*. Brasilia: Ed. do Grande Oriente do Brasil, 1993.

_____. *História do Grande Oriente de São Paulo*. Brasilia: Ed. do Grande Oriente do Brasil, 1994.

_____. "A longa luta da Maçonaria para o advento da Republica." *Caderno de Pesquisas Maçônicas* 2 (1990).

_____. "A luta da Maçonaria pela abolição da Escravatura." In *A Verdade*, 16–23. São Paulo: n.p., 1988.

_____. *A Maçonaria Brasileira na decada da Abolição e da Republica*. Londrina, Brazil: Ed. A Trolha, 2001.

_____. *A Maçonaria e o Movimento Republicano Brasileiro*. São Paulo: Ed. Traço, 1989.

_____. *A Maçonaria Paulista na História do Brasil*. Brasilia, Brazil: Ed. do Grande Oriente do Brasil, 1994.

_____. *Os maçons e a Questão Religiosa do seculo XIX*. Londrina, Brazil: Ed. A Trolha, 1996.

_____. "Os Maçons e o Movimento Abolicionista Brasileiro." *Caderno de Pesquisas Maçônicas* (1989).

_____. "Os maçons e o Movimento Abolicionista da Escravatura." *A Trolha* 18, no. 34 (March–April 1988): 59–63.

_____. *Os maçons na Independencia do Brasil*. Londrina, Brazil: Ed. A Trolha, 1993.

_____. "Os maçons que fizeram a história do Brasil." *A Gazeta Maçônica* (1991).

Castellani, José, and William Carvalho. *História do Grande Oriente do Brasil. A Maçonaria na História do Brasil*. São Paulo: Madrás Ed., 2009.

Castellano Acuna, Carmen. *La Massoneria in Chile*. Rome: n.p., 2001.

Castellano Gil, José Manuel. "Estudio

crítico de la Historiografía masónica cubana." In *La Masonería Española entre Europa y América*, edited by José Antonio Ferrer Benimeli, 1:3–20. Zaragoza: CEHME, 1995.

_____. "La Masonería de Obediencia española en Cuba durante el siglo XIX." Doctoral dissertation, Universidad de La Laguna, Spain, 1992.

_____. *La masonería española en Cuba, Santa Cruz de Tenerife*. Tenerife, Spain: Centro de la Cultura Popular Canaria, 1996.

Castellano Gil, José Manuel, and Manuel de Paz Sánchez. "Martí masón y otras crónicas wangüermetianas." In *La Masonería Española entre Europa y América*, edited by, José Antonio Ferrer Benimeli, 2:671–688. Zaragoza: CEHME, 1995.

Castellón, Hell. *Así es la Masonería*. Caracas: n.p., 1990.

_____. *Guía Histórica de la masonería venezolana*. Caracas: Lito-Jet, 1995.

_____. *La Revolución de Francia obra de la Masonería*. Caracas: n.p., 1989.

Castro Neves, Berenice Abreu de. "Intrépidos romeiros do progresso: os maçons cearenses do Império." In *Intelectuais*, edited by, Frederico de Castro Neves and Simone de Souza. Fortaleza, Brazil: Ed. Demócrito Rocha, 2002.

Castro, Miguel Angel, and Guadalupe Curiel. *Publicaciones periódicas mexicanas del siglo XIX: 1822–1825*. Mexico City: UNAM, 2000.

Caucois, H. *Nociones de Masonería Simbólica, traducidas por el H. Spes, miembro activo de la Resp. Log. Caridad. Segundo Cuaderno, Grado Aprendiz*. San José, Costa Rica: Impr. de la Paz, 1871.

Cauna, Jacques. "Autour de la thèse du complot. Francmaçonnerie, Révolution et contre-Révolution à Saint-Domingue (1789–1791)."

Celis de la Cruz, Martha. "Presencia de la masonería alemana en México: Carlos de Gager (1853–1855)." *REHMLAC* 2, no. 2 (December 2010–April 2011): 151–159. https://revistas.ucr.ac.cr/index.php/rehmlac/article/view/6601/6292

Claps Arenas, María Eugenia. "La formación del liberalismo en México. Ramón Ceruti y la prensa yorkina (1825–1830)." Doctoral dissertation, Universidad de Alcalá de Henares, Spain, 2007.

_____. "La producción hemerográfica que los españoles exiliados en Londres dedicaron a Hispanoamérica. El caso de México, 1824–1827." Master's dissertation, Universidad de Alcalá de Henares, Spain.

_____. "Vínculos del primer liberalismo hispánico. Comuneros españoles y yorkinos mexicanos." *Seminario Permanente México-España*. Mexico City: El Colegio de México, n.d.

Colusi, Eliane Lucia. *A Maçonaria Gaúcha no século XIX*. Passo Fundo, Brazil: n.p., 1998.

Combes, André. In *La période révolutionnaire aux Antilles dans la littérature française (1750-1850) et dans les littératures caribéennes francophone, anglophone et hispanophone*, edited by Roger Toumson and Charles Porset, 155–180. Fort-de-France, Martinique: Université des Antilles, 1988.

———. "Las logias del Grande Oriente de Francia en América Latina (1842–1870)." In *Masonería Española y América*, edited by José Antonio Ferrer Benimeli, 1:175–199. Zaragoza, Spain: CEHME, 1993.

Corbière, Emilio. *La masonería: política y sociedades secretas en Argentina*. Santa Fe, Argentina: n.p., 1994.

Cortijo Parralejo, Esteban. "Masonería y teosofía en Iberoamérica: Argentina, México y Brasil." In *La Masonería Española entre Europa y América*, edited by José Antonio Ferrer Benimeli, 1:379–401. Zaragoza, Spain: CEHME, 1995.

Costa, Frederico Guilherme. *A maçonaria na emancipação do Escravo*. Londrina, Brazil: A Trolha, 1999.

Costeloe, Machael P. *La primera república federal de México (1824–1835). Un estudio de los partidos políticos en el México independiente*. Mexico City: Fondo Cultura Económica, 1975.

Couyoumdjan, Ricardo. "Masonería de habla inglesa en Chile. Algunas noticias." *Boletín de la Academia Chilena de la Historia* 42, no. 105 (1995).

Cuberos, Adriana, and Albert Cuberos. *La Masonería y la Constitución de 1863*. Santa Fe de Bogotá, Colombia: n.p., 1991.

Cuccoresse, Horacio Juan. *San Martín. Catolicismo y masonería*. Buenos Aires: Instituto Nacional Sanmartiniano, 1993.

Cueva Merino, Julio de la. "El lugar de la masonería en la recepción eclesiástica de las guerras coloniales y el desastre de 1898." In *La Masonería Española y la crisis colonial del 98*, edited by José Antonio Ferrer Benimeli, 2:527–541. Zaragoza, Spain: CEHME, 1999.

Cruz Orozco, José Ignacio. "¡Hermanos del mundo! Ayudadnos a libertar España. Nuevas aportaciones sobre la masonería española en el exilio republicano de México." In *La Masonería Española: Represión y Exilios. XII Symposium Internacional de Historia de la Masonería Española*, edited by José Antonio Ferrer Benimeli, 1:199–210. Zaragoza, Spain: CEHME, 2010.

———. "La masonería valenciana y América." In *Los valencianos en América. Jornadas sobre la emigración*, 99–106. Valencia, Spain: Generalitat Valenciana, 1993.

———. "Solidaridad y exilio. La masonería española en América (1939–

1977)." In *Masonería Española y América*, edited by José Antonio Ferrer Benimeli, 1:533–550. Zaragoza: CEHME, 1993.

Ch'An, Isa. *Achegas para a história da Maçonaria no Brasil*. São Paulo: n.p., 1968.

Chanta Martínez, René Antonio. "Antimasonería y antiliberalismo en el pensamiento de Oscar Arnulfo Romero 1962–1965." *REHMLAC* 3, no. 1 (May–November 2011): 121–141. https://revistas.ucr.ac.cr/index.php/rehmlac/article/view/6589/6280

_____. "Francmasonería, Iglesia y publicaciones impresas en el Salvador: La discusión, 1881." *AFEHC* entry no. 2003, August 11, 2008. afehc-historia-centroamericana.org/index.php?action=fi_aff&id=2003

Chaverri, Milton, and Luis Calvo. *Ciento Veinte Aniversario Respetable Logia Regeneración Nº 1*. San José: Logia Regeneración Nº 1, 2008.

Chism, Richard E. *Una contribución a la Historia de la Masonería de México*. Mexico City: Impr. de El Minero Mexicano, 1899; Mexico City: Ed. Herbasa, 1993.

Chocano, Magdalena. "Lima masónica: las logias simbólicas y su progreso en el medio urbano a fines del siglo XIX." *Revista de Indias* 70, no. 249 (2010).

D'Acosta, James L. "Notes on the History of Yoltee." In *Proceedings of the M.W.* York Grand Lodge of Mexico F. and M, 55–71. Mexico City: n.p., 1983.

Davies, Thomas B. *Aspects of Freemasonry in Modern Mexico: An Example of Social Cleavage*. New York: Vantage Press, 1976.

_____. "The 'Sad Night' of Mexican Masonry." *Revista de Historia de América* 91 (January–May 1981): 83–111.

De la Cruz de Lemos, Vladimir. "R H Rafael Obregón Loría, Benemérito de la Masonería Costarricense, en el centenario de su natalicio." *Reflexiones* 90, no. 2 (2011): 179–185. latindex.ucr.ac.cr/reflexiones-90-2/rfx-90-2-13.pdf

De los Reyes Heredia, Guillermo. "The Cross and the Compass: The Influence of the Catholic Religion and Masonry in the Formation of the Mexican Political Thought." In *Hispanic Religious Thought*, Nicolas Kanellos, ed., 3:8–24 Cambridge: Cambridge Scholars Press, 2007.

_____. "Freemasonry and folklore in Mexican Presidentialism." In *Journal of American Culture* 20 (summer 1997).

_____. "Freemasonry, Folklore, and Cultural Production in A Social Literary Context: The Impact of Literature and Folklore in Mexican and American Masonry." Paper presented at the International Conference of the History of Freemasonry, Centre interdisciplinaire bordelais d'étude des lumières-Lumières Nature Société, Université de Bordeaux III Centre d'étude de la Littérature Françaises des XVIIe et XVIIIe Siècles

(CELLF), Sorbonne IV. Paris Chair of Freemasonry, Faculty of Religious Studies, University of Leiden Centre de la Méditerrannée Moderne et Contemporaine, Université de Nice Sophia-Antipolis, The Interdisciplinary Research Group Freemasonry, Free University of Brussels, The George Washington Masonic Memorial, Alexandria, VA, May 26–30, 2011.

_____. "El impacto de la masonería en los orígenes del discurso secular, laico y anticlerical en México." In *Secularización del Estado y la sociedad*, edited by Patricia Galdeana. Mexico City: Senado de la República, LXI Legislatura, Siglo XXI Ed., 2010.

_____. *Herencias secretas: Masonería, política y sociedad en México*. Puebla, Mexico: Benemérita Universidad Autónoma de Puebla, 2009.

_____. "Perspectivas internacionales de la masonería y su influencia en la política mexicana." Undergraduate dissertation, Universidad de las Américas, Santa Catarina, Mexico, 1994.

_____. "The Relation Between Mexican and American Freemasonry, Late 19th and Early 20th Centuries." Paper presented at the International Conference on American and Latin American Freemasonry: A New Past and a New Future, Freemasonry and Civil Society Program of the History Department of the University of California at Los Angeles (UCLA), The Grand Lodge of California, California's Institute for Masonic Studies, Los Angeles, December 3, 2011.

_____. "Translating, Smuggling, and Recovering Books in Nineteenth Century Mexico: Thomas Smith Webb's *El Monitor de los Masones Libres*: ó, Illustraciones sobre la Masonería." In *The Critical Importance of Region: Recovering the U.S. Hispanic Literary Heritage Project Vol. VI.*, edited by Antonia Castañeda and Gabriel Meléndez. Houston: Arte Público Press, 2006.

De los Reyes Heredia, Guillermo, and Paul Rich. "Policy Making and the Control of the Nongovernmental Sector: Porfirio Díaz and the Grand Diet." *Review of Policy Research* 22, no. 5 (September 2005): 721–725.

Del Solar Guajardo, Felipe Santiago. "La Francmasonería en Chile: De sus orígenes hasta su institucionalización." *REHMLAC* 2, no. 1 (May–November 2010): 1–15. https://revistas.ucr.ac.cr/index.php/rehmlac/article/view/6607/6296

_____. "La Francmasonería y la Independencia de América. Un balance historiográfico." In *Primeras Jornadas de Estudios Históricos de la Francmasonería chilena*, 229–240. Santiago, Chile: n.p., 2006.

_____. "La Gran Logia de Chile (1973–1990). Análisis crítico al libro de Hernán Vidal referente al tema de la participación de la Francmasonería durante la dictadura militar." In *Terceras Jornadas de Estudios Históricos de la Francmasonería Chilena*, 85–97. Santiago, Chile: n.p., 2007.

———. *Las logias de ultramar. En torno a los orígenes de la masonería en Chile, 1850–1862*. Santiago, Chile: Gran Logia de Chile, 2012.

———. "José Miguel Carrera: redes masónicas durante las guerras de la independencia en América del Sur." In *La Masonería Española: Represión y Exilios. XII Symposium Internacional de Historia de la Masonería Española*, edited by José Antonio Ferrer Benimeli, 1:475–496. Zaragoza, Spain: CEHME, Gobierno de Aragón, Departamento de Educación, Cultura y Deporte, 2011.

———. "Masones y Sociedades Secretas: redes militares durante las guerras de independencia en América del Sur." *Amérique Latine Histoire et Mémoire. Les Cahiers ALHIM* 19 (2010). alhim.revues.org/index3475.html

———. "Masonología chilena. O la porfiada memoria institucional de una élite decimonónica." *REHMLAC* 3, no. 1 (May–November 2011): 183–196. https://revistas.ucr.ac.cr/index.php/rehmlac/article/view/6592/6283

———. "Secreto y Sociedades Secretas en la crisis del Antiguo Régimen. Reflexiones para una historia interconectada con el mundo hispánico." *REHMLAC* 3, no. 2 (December 2011–April 2012): 132–156. https://revistas.ucr.ac.cr/index.php/rehmlac/article/view/6578/6269

Delgado Chabouti, Sady. *Investigación sobre el masón Alberto Bachelet Martínez en la R. L. 'La Cantera' n. 130 del Valle de Las Condes*. Santiago, Chile: n.p., 2003.

Delgado Idarreta, José Miguel. "Las Logias 'Zaragoza' cubanas: mentalidad." In *La Masonería Española entre Europa y América*, edited by José Antonio Ferrer Benimeli, 1:21–29. Zaragoza, Spain: CEHME, 1995.

———. "Logias 'Zaragoza' en Cuba." In *Masonería Española y América*, edited by José Antonio Ferrer Benimeli, 1:299–311. Zaragoza, Spain: CEHME, 1993.

Desantes, María Blanca, and María José Portela Santamaría. "Orientaciones para la investigación de la masonería en Argentina." In *Masonería Española y América*, edited by José Antonio Ferrer Benimeli, 2:899–966. Zaragoza, Spain: CEHME, 1993.

Díaz Castellanos, José Mª. *Morazán. Benemérito de la masonería hondureña*. Tegucigalpa: n.p., 2009.

Díaz Sánchez, Ramón. "Sí, Bolívar fue masón." *Élite*, July 28, 1956.

Díaz Zermeño, Héctor. *La masonería como sociedad de ideas contrapunteada en el proceso de la independencia de Hispanoamérica y México, 1782–1833*. Madrid: n.p., 2009.

Dienstbach, Carlos. "A maçonaria e a colonização alemã no Rio Grande do Sul." In *Formação social da Maçonaria. Anais do I Congresso Internacional de História y Geografía*, 2:73–90. Rio de Janeiro: Ed. Aurora, 1982.

Díez de los Ríos, María Teresa. "Fondos de la masonería en el Archivo Histórico Nacional: Sección Guerra Civil, de Salamanca." In *La Masonería en la Historia de España, Zaragoza*, edited by José Antonio Ferrer Benimeli, 333–348. Zaragoza: Gobierno de Aragón, 1985.

Domingo Acebrón, María Dolores. "Francisco Arredondo y Miranda: masón y mambí." In *Masonería Española y América*, edited by José Antonio Ferrer Benimeli, 2:629–636. Zaragoza: CEHME, 1993.

_____. "Independencia en el Caribe, Cuba: José de Armas y Céspedes, masón." In *La Masonería Española: Represión y Exilios*, edited by José Antonio Ferrer Benimeli, 1:573–580. Zaragoza, Spain: CEHME, 2010.

_____. "Integrismo y masonería. Los cuerpos de voluntarios en Cuba (1868–1898)." In *La Masonería Española y la crisis colonial del 98*, edited by José Antonio Ferrer Benimeli, 1:267–275. Zaragoza: CEHME, 1999.

_____. "La masonería durante la guerra de los diez años. Cuba (1868–1878)." In *Masonería, revolución y reacción*, edited by José Antonio Ferrer Benimeli, 2:977–987. Alicante: Institución Cultural "Juan Gil Albert," 1990.

_____. "El papel del autonomismo y su relación con la masonería en Cuba, 1878–1898. Antonio Govin y Torres." In *La Masonería española en el 2000. Una revisión histórica*, edited by José Antonio Ferrer Benimeli, 1:459–468.

Zaragoza, Spain: Gobierno de Aragón, Departamento de Educación, Cultura y Deporte, 2001.

_____. "Rafael Mª de Labra y su relación con la masonería en Madrid y en Cuba (1880–1918)." In *La Masonería en Madrid y en España del siglo XVIII al XXI*, edited by José Antonio Ferrer Benimeli, 2:833–842. Zaragoza: CEHME, 2004.

_____. "Víctor Patricio Landaluze: un pintor español masón y anti-independentista en Cuba en la primera mitad del siglo XIX." In *La Masonería Española entre Europa y América*, edited by José Antonio Ferrer Benimeli, 1:31-40. Zaragoza: CEHME, 1995.

Domingo Cuadriello, Jorge. "La actividad masónica de los exiliados españoles en Cuba." In *La Masonería en Madrid y en España del siglo XVIII al XXI*, edited by José Antonio Ferrer Benimeli, 1:569–578. Zaragoza: CEHME, 2004.

Dotta Ostria, Mario. *El artiguismo y las vertientes universales*. Montevideo: Ed. de la Plaza, 2008.

_____. *Caudillos, doctores y masones. Protagonistas en la gran comarca rioplatense*. Montevideo: Ed. de la Plaza, 2007.

_____. *Inmigrantes, curas y masones en tiempos del General Máximo Santos*. Montevideo: Ed. de la Plaza, 2005.

_____. *Italianos, Masonería e Iglesia durante el Gobierno de Santos*. Montevideo: Ed. de la Plaza, 2000.

_____. "La Masonería y el proceso histórico del Uruguay" [online].

_____. *Oligarcas, militares y masones. La guerra contra el Paraguay y la consolidación de las asimetrías regionales.* Montevideo: Ed. de la Plaza, 2011.

Dussel, Enrique. "Tensiones en el espacio religioso: masones, liberales y protestantes en la obra de Mariano Soler (1884–1902)." In *Protestantes, liberales y francmasones. Sociedades de ideas y modernidad en América Latina, siglo XIX*, edited by Jean Pierre Bastian, 24–38. Mexico City: Fondo de Cultura Económica, 1990.

Egea López, Antonio. *Francisco Miranda*. Madrid: Historia 16, 1987.

_____. *El pensamiento filosófico y político de Francisco de Miranda*. Caracas: n.p., 1983.

Enciso Contreras, José. *Masones en la revolución mexicana, el caso de Zacatecas: etapa precursora, 1900–1901.* Zacatecas, Mexico: Inédito, 1989.

_____. "Orígenes y primeras actividades de la masonería en Zacatecas." *Investigaciones científicas* 8 (1995).

Enrique de Almeida, Santiago Marcos. "La masonería y la abolición de la esclavitud en Brasil." In *Masonería Española y América*, edited by José Antonio Ferrer Benimeli 1:81–93. Zaragoza: CEHME, 1993.

Enríquez del Árbol, Eduardo. "Masonería y patriotismo ante el desastre: la defensa de la institución en Cuba por los Grandes Orientes españoles (1895–1898)." In *Homenaje a Tomás Quesada Quesada*, 897–920. Granada, Spain: Universidad de Granada, 1998.

Escalle, Elisabeth, and Marcel Gouyon-Guillaume. *Francs-maçons des loges françaises "aux Amériques" 1770–1850. Contribution à l'étude de la Société créole.* Paris: 1993.

Esponera, Alfonso. "Mariano Soler y la Masonería en el Uruguay de 1884." In *Masonería Española y América*, edited by José Antonio Ferrer Benimeli, 2:689–706. Zaragoza: CEHME, 1993.

Estrade, Paul. "Betances, masón inconforme." In *La masonería española en la época de Sagasta (1825–1903)*, edited by José Antonio Ferrer Benimeli, 1:559–570. Zaragoza: CEHME, 2006.

_____. "Un masón audaz y conformista, paradigmático del Gran Oriente de Francia: el franco-cubano Severiano de Heredia (1836–1901)." In *La Masonería Española: Represión y Exilios*, edited by José Antonio Ferrer Benimeli, 1:545–558. Zaragoza: CEHME, 2010.

_____. *Severiano de Heredia, ce mulâtre cubain que Paris fit "maire" et la République ministre.* Paris: Ed. Les Indes Savantes, 2011.

Eyzaguirre, Jaime. *La Logia Lautarina*. Santiago, Chile: Editorial Francisco de Aguirre, 1973.

Fallas Barrantes, Marco Antonio. "El liberalismo, el cultivo del café y la masonería en Costa Rica." In *Las instituciones costarricenses en el siglo XX*, edited by Carmen Lila Gómez U, 53–81. San José, Costa Rica: EUCR, 1987.

Fernández Cabrelli, Alfonso.

_____. *De Bolívar a Sandino. Hombres de la masonería en la prédica integradora*. Montevideo: Ed. América Una, 1989.

_____. "El exilio rioplatense de una logia catalana dependiente del Gran Oriente de Uruguay." In *Masonería Española y América*, edited by José Antonio Ferrer Benimeli, 1:437–448.

_____. *La Francmasonería en la independencia de Hispanoamérica*. Montevideo: Ed. América Una, 1988.

_____. *Iglesia ultramontana y masonería en la transformación de la sociedad oriental*. Montevideo: Ed. América Una, 1990.

_____. *Masones y artiguistas en la Banda Oriental*. Montevideo: Ed. América Una, 1986.

_____. *Masonería, morenismo, artiguismo: masonería e influencia de la francmasonería en los movimientos independentistas del Río de la Plata*. Montevideo: Ed. America Una, 1982.

_____. *Masonería y sociedades secretas en las luchas emancipadoras de la Patria Grande*. Montevideo: Ed. America Una, 1975.

_____. "La múltiple actividad del masón español Adolfo Vázquez-Gómez en el Río de la Plata." In *La masonería en la España del siglo XX*, edited by José Antonio Ferrer Benimeli, 1: 257–270. Toledo, Spain: Universidad de Castilla-La Mancha, 1996.

_____. *Presencia masónica en la Cisplatina*. Montevideo: Ed. América Una, 1987.

Fernández Callejas, Roger. *Historia de la Francmasonería en Cuba*. Havana: Ed. Orientación Masónica, 1944.

_____. *Historia moderna de la Francmasonería en Cuba. Su influencia en la independencia de Cuba*. Havana: Academia Cubana de Estudios Masónicos, 1985.

_____. *Primera manifestación pública masónica de carácter independiente*. Havana: n.p., 1949.

_____. *Origen cubano de la masonería regular*. Havana: n.p., 1951.

_____. "A report on masonry in Cuba in 1969." *Ars Quatuor Coronatorum* 101 (1969): 101–103.

_____. *Vicente Antonio de Castro. Masón y patriota, precursor del 68*. Havana: Ed. Acacia, 1946.

Fernández, Justo F. "Listado de las logias que han existido en Venezuela, desde su origen en el país, hasta 2000." In

La Masonería en Venezuela, edited by Frain Subero, 2: 340–349. Caracas: Biblioteca Masónica de Venezuela, 2000.

———. *La masonería organizada*. Los Teques, Venezuela: E. Miranda, 1998.

Fernández Techera, Julio. *Jesuitas, masones y universidad en el Uruguay*. Montevideo: Plaza, 2007–2010.

Ferreira Costa, Luiz Mário. "A consolidação e transformação do mito da 'conspiração maçônica' em terras brasileiras." *REHMLAC* 3, no. 1 May–November 2011: 45–61. https://revistas.ucr.ac.cr/index.php/rehmlac/article/view/6586/6277

———. "A historia das narrativas antimaçônicas." *Revista História Catarina* 22 (2010): 62–66.

———. *Maçonaria e antimaçonaria: uma análise da História secreta do Brasil de Gustavo Barroso*. Juiz de Fora, Brazil: Universidade Federal de Juiz de Fora, 2009.

Ferreira, Manoel Rodrigues and Tito Livio Ferreira. *A maçonaria na independência brasileira*. São Paulo: Gráficas Bíblicas, 1962.

Ferrer Benimeli, José Antonio. "1817, un año clave para la masonería tinerfeña y cubana." In *Jornadas de Estudios Canarias-América*, 1:61–90. Santa Cruz de Tenerife, Spain: Caja General de Ahorros de Canarias, 1984.

———. "L'antimaçonnisme en Espagne et en Amérique latine." In *Les courants antimaçonniques hier et aujourd'hui*, edited by Alain Dierkens, 77–86. Brussels: Éditions de l'Université de Bruxelles, 1993.

———. "Aproximación a la historiografía de la masonería latinoamericana." *REHMLAC* 4, no. 1 (May–November 2012): 2–121. https://revistas.ucr.ac.cr/index.php/rehmlac/article/view/12144/11419

———. "Aproximación a las llamadas logias Lautaro." *Hoy es Historia* 4, no. 23 (September–October 1987): 48–58. Also in: *Serta gratulatoria in honorem Juan Regulo*, 3:389–401. La Laguna, Spain: Universidad La Laguna, 1988. And in: *Los canarios en el estuario del Río de la Plata*, 175–194. Santa Cruz de Tenerife, Spain: Caja General de Ahorros, 1990.

———. "Bibliografía de la masonería." In *La masonería en la historia de España: actas del I Symposium de Metodología Aplicada a la Historia de la Masonería Española: Zaragoza, 20-22 de junio de 1983*, edited by José Antonio Ferrer Benimeli, 371–377. Zaragoza, Spain: CEHME, 1989.

———. "¿Bolívar masón?" *Historia 16* 9, no. 96 (1984): 109–118.

———. "Bolívar y la Masonería." *Estudios Ibero-Americanos* 9, no. 1–2 (July–December 1983): 1–51. Also in: *Revista de Indias* 43, no. 172 (July–December 1983): 631–687.

_____. *Bibliografía de la Masonería, Introducción Histórico-crítica.* Caracas: Universidad Católica Andrés Bello, 1974.

_____. "Les Caballeros Racionales, les loges lautariennes et les formes déviées de la Franc-maçonnerie dans le monde hispanique." In *Les révolutions ibériques et Ibéro-Américaines à l'aube du XIXe siècle, Actes du colloque de Bordeaux 2-4 juillet 1989,* 191–203. Paris: Editions CNRS, 1991.

_____. "Cádiz y las llamadas 'Logias' Lautaro o Caballeros Racionales." In *De la Ilustración al Romanticismo. Ideas y movimientos clandestinos,* 149–176. Cádiz, Spain: Universidad de Cádiz, 1988.

_____. "Las Cortes de Cádiz, América y la Masonería." *Cuadernos Hispano-Americanos* 460 (1988): 7–34. Also in: *La Guerra de las conciencias. Monarquía e independencias en el mundo hispano y lusitano,* edited by Cristina Torales. Tlascala, Mexico: Instituto Tlaxalteca de Cultura, 2010, 201–244. And in: *Cortes y Constitución de Cádiz. 200 años,* edited by José Antonio Escudero, 2:69–97. Madrid: Espasa, 2011.

_____. "Fiesta-Masonería-Nación." *Revista Memoria. Archivo General de la Nación* (1999): 8–29.

_____. "La Francmaçonnerie en Espagne et Amérique Latine." *Rev. Notre Histoire* 66 (1990): 84–89. Also in: *La Franc-maçonnerie,* 152–160. Paris: Desclée de Brouwer, 1996.

_____. "La Francmaçonnerie européenne : expansion en Amérique du Sud." *La Pensée et les hommes* 19 (1992) : 91–107.

_____. "La Historia ante la Masonería, reflexiones metodológicas." *El Basilisco* 9 (January–April 1980): 31–40.

_____. "Implantación de logias y distribución geográfico histórica de la masonería española." In *La Masonería en la España del siglo XIX,* 1:57–216. Valladolid, Spain: Junta de Castilla y León, 1987.

_____. Índices de actas de los Symposia Internacionales de Historia de la Masonería Española. Zaragoza: CEHME, 2009.

_____. "La logia dominicana 'Aurora n. 82' de San Pedro de Macoris (1889–1923)." In *Libro homenaje al P. José del Rey Fajardo,* edited by Allan R. Brewer, 1:575–605. Caracas: Ed. Jurídica Venezolana, 2005. Also in: *REHMLAC* 3, no. 2 (December 2011–April 2012): 1–41. rehmlac.com/recursos/vols/v3/n2 /rehmlac.vol3.n2-jferrer.pdf

_____. *La masonería.* Zaragoza, Spain: Alianza Editorial, 2001.

_____. "Masonería." In *Diccionario de Historia de Venezuela,* 2:849–852. Caracas: Fundación Polar, 1981.

_____. *La masonería como problema político religioso. Reflexiones históricas.* Tlaxcala, Mexico: Universidad Autónoma de Tlaxcala-Fideicomiso Colegio

Historia de Tlaxcala, 2010.

_____. *Masonería e Inquisición en Latinoamérica durante el siglo XVIII*. Caracas: Universidad Andrés Bello, 1973.

_____. "Masonería e Inquisición en Latinoamérica durante el siglo XVIII." In *La Masonería en Venezuela de Efrain Subero*, 352–418. Caracas: Gran Logia República de Venezuela, 2000.

_____, ed. *La Masonería Española entre Europa y América*. Zaragoza, Spain: CEHME, 1995.

_____, ed. *Masonería Española y América*. Zaragoza, Spain: CEHME, 1993.

_____, ed. *La Masonería Española: Represión y Exilios*. Zaragoza, Spain: CEHME, Gobierno de Aragón, Departamento de Educación, Cultura y Deporte, 2011.

_____. "La masonería española y el IV Centenario del descubrimiento de América." In *Masonería Española y América*, 1:3–24. Zaragoza, Spain: CEHME, 1993.

_____, ed. *La Masonería Española y la crisis colonial del 98*. Zaragoza, Spain: CEHME, 1999.

_____. *Masonería, Iglesia e Ilustración. Un conflicto ideológico-político-religioso. I: Las bases del conflicto (1700–1739)*. Madrid: Fundación Española Universitaria, 1976.

_____. *Masonería, Iglesia e Ilustración. Un conflicto ideológico-político-religioso. II: Inquisición: Procesos históricos (1739–1749)*. Madrid: Fundación Española Universitaria, 1976.

_____. *Masonería, Iglesia e Ilustración. Un conflicto ideológico-político-religioso. III: Institucionalización del conflicto (1750–1800)*. Madrid: Fundación Española Universitaria, 1977.

_____. *Masonería, Iglesia e Ilustración. Un conflicto ideológico-político-religioso. IV: La otra cara del conflicto. Conclusión y Bibliografía*. Madrid: Fundación Española Universitaria, 1977.

_____. "La masonería y la independencia de América española (Reflexiones metodológicas)." *Anuario de Estudios Americanos* 35 (1981): 159–177.

_____. "La masonería y la independencia de Puerto Rico: Análisis de un papel de 1823." In *Brocar. Cuadernos de Investigación Histórica* 17 (1991): 37–53.

_____. "Masones asturianos en la Cuba y Puerto Rico del siglo XIX." *Ástura. Nuevos cartafueyos d'Asturies* 9 (1993) : 61–69.

_____. "Métodos y experiencias en el estudio de la historia de la masonería española." *REHMLAC* 1, no. 2 (December 2009–April 2010): 44–62. https://revistas.ucr.ac.cr/index.php/rehmlac/article/view/6617/6306

_____. "Révolution Française et littérature clandestine à Cuba. La Francmaçonnerie comme élément conspirateur." In *La période révolutionnaire aux Antilles dans la littérature française (1750-1850) et dans les littératures caribéennes francophone, anglophone et hispanophone*, edited by Roger Toumson and Charles Porset, 29–48. Fort-de-France: Université des Antilles, 1988.

_____. "Utopia and Reality of Masonic Liberalism: From the Courts of Cadiz to Mexican Independence." Paper presented at the International Conference on American and Latin American Freemasonry: A New Past and a New Future, Freemasonry and Civil Society Program of the History Department of the University of California at Los Angeles (UCLA), The Grand Lodge of California, California's Institute for Masonic Studies, Los Angeles, December 3, 2011.

_____. "Vías de penetración de la masonería en el Caribe." *REHMLAC* 1, no. 1 (May–November 2009): 2–19. https://revistas.ucr.ac.cr/index.php/rehmlac/article/view/6853/6540

Ferrer Benimeli, José Antonio, Giovanni Caprile, and Valerio Alberton. *Maçonaria e Igreja católica, ontem hoje e amanhã*. São Paulo: Ed. Paulinas, 1981–2010.

Ferrer Benimeli, José Antonio, and Susana Cuartero. *Bibliografía de la Masonería*. Madrid: Fundación Universitaria Española, 2004.

Ferro, Jorge Francisco. *La Iglesia Célti-ca. Monjes Culdeos y Masones operativos*. Buenos Aires: Lumen, 2008.

_____. "El linaje masónico de la familia Cambacérès en la Argentina." In *La masonería española en la época de Sagasta (1825–1903)*, edited by José Antonio Ferrer Benimeli, 1:589–594. Zaragoza, Spain: CEHME and the Fundación Práxedes Mateo-Sagasta, 2006.

_____. *La Masonería operativa*. Buenos Aires: Kier, 2008.

_____. "Noticias sobre la masonería española originadas en el Río de la Plata (1892–1910)." In *La Masonería en Madrid y en España del siglo XVIII al XXI*, edited by José Antonio Ferrer Benimeli, 1:503–508. Zaragoza, Spain: Gobierno de Aragón, 2004.

_____. "Objeto, métodos y perspectivas de la masonología científica." In *La Masonería española en el 2000. Una revisión histórica*, 2:981–991. Zaragoza, Spain: Gobierno de Aragón, Departamento de Cultura y Turismo, 2001.

_____. *Secretos Herméticos de la Caballería*. Buenos Aires: Lumen, 2006.

_____. *Las Sociedades secretas*. Buenos Aires: Lumen, 2008.

_____. *Los Templarios y el Grial. Leyenda y realidad*. Buenos Aires: Lumen, 2005.

Figueiredo, Joaquim Gervásio de. *Dicionário de termos maçónicos*. São Paulo: Pensamento, 2000.

Fisher, Lillian Estelle. "Early Masonry in Mexico, 1806–1828." *Southwestern Historical Quaterly* 42 (1939): 198–214.

Florens, Luis. "Bibliografía masónica dominicana." *Revista Juventud Universitaria* 15 (1945): 18–20.

Flores Zavala, Marco Antonio. "Los ciclos de la masonería mexicana. Siglos XVIII–XIX." In *La Masonería en Madrid y en España del siglo XVIII al XXI*, edited by José Antonio Ferrer Benimeli, 1:489–501. Zaragoza: Gobierno de Aragón, 2004.

———. *El grupo masón en la política zacatecana, 1880–1914*. Zacatecas, Mexico: Asociación de Investigaciones Filosóficas "Francisco García Sabina," 2002.

———. "La masonería en la República Federal. Apuntes sobre las logias mexicanas (1825–1840)." In *Raíces del federalismo mexicano*, edited by Manuel Miño Grijalva, 125–136. Zacatecas, Mexico: Universidad Autónoma de Zacatecas, 2005.

———. "Masonería, masones y prensa en Zacatecas, 1870–1908." Paper presented at the IV Encuentro Internacional de Historiadores de la Prensa en Iberoamerica, Universidad de Costa Rica, San José, Costa Rica, 2007.

———. "La Masonería y las fiestas cívicas en torno a Benito Juárez." In *Juárez, la masonería y el Liberalismo político*. Mexico City: n.p., 2007.

———. "La masonería y el Estado laico: escribir y leer en la masonería. Prácticas seculares de los masones." In *El Estado laico y los Derechos Humanos en México, 1810–2010*. Mexico City: UNAM, 2010.

———. "Periódicos francmasones mexicanos. Apuntes para la construcción de un corpus hemerográfico masónico." In en *La Masonería Española: Represión y Exilios*, edited by José Antonio Ferrer Benimeli, 2:1153–1168. Zaragoza, Spain: CEHME, 2010.

———. "Tomás Lorck Avila, un masón mexicano del siglo XIX." In *La masonería española en la época de Sagasta (1825–1903)*, edited by José Antonio Ferrer Benimeli, 2:977–1001. Zaragoza, Spain: CEHME and the Fundación Práxedes Mateo-Sagasta, 2006.

Flores Zavala, Marco Antonio, and José Saúl Castorena Hernández. "Entre amigos y masones o las nuevas formas de asociación en Zacatecas (1813–1820)." *REHMLAC* 3, no. 2 (December 2011–April 2012): 105–130. https://revistas.ucr.ac.cr/index.php/rehmlac/article/view/6577/6268

Folange, Marcos E. "History of Masonry in Mexico 1791–1950." *Proceedings of the M.W. York Grande Lodge of Mexico P. and A.M.* [Mexico] (1981): 44–62.

Fonseca Pozo, Yuniel. "La Gran Logia Oriental de Cuba: un curso de cisma masónico" Doctoral dissertation, Universidad de Cienfuegos, Cuba.

Frahm, Sara A. *La cruz y el compás: compromiso y conflicto*. Mexico City: n.p., 1992.

Franco, Francisco. "Masonería, librepensamiento y catolicismo en la Mérida de finales del siglo XIX." In *Presente y pasado. Revista de Historia* 3, no. 5 (January–June 1998): 23–55.

Frau Abrines, Lorenzo, and Rosendo Arús y Arderiu. *Diccionario enciclopédico de la Masonería*. Havana: n.p., 1883 / Barcelona: n.p., 1891 / Mexico City: n.p., 1955 / Buenos Aires: n.p., 1962 / Mexico City: n.p., 1977.

Freile, Alfonso J. "Francisco de Miranda e la massoneria." *Rivista massonica* 64–8, no. 5 (1975): 301–305.

_____. *Miranda y sus relaciones con la Masonería*. Caracas: R.L. Gandhi nº 114, 1969.

Freitas Gil, Marcelo. "Trabalhadores, Maçonaria e Espiritismo em Pelotas: 1877–1937." *REHMLAC* 3, no. 1 (May–November 2011): 62–80.

Freitas Gil, Marcelo. "A cidade de Pelotas e a maçonaria." *Revista História Catarina* 22 (2010): 72–75.

_____. "Trabalhadores, Maçonaria e Espiritismo em Pelotas: 1877–1937." *REHMLAC* 3, no. 1 (May–November 2011): 62–80. https://revistas.ucr.ac.cr/index.php/rehmlac/article/view/6587/6278

Fuentes Mares, José. *Poinsett: historia de una gran intriga*. Mexico City: n.p., 1951.

Furlong, Guillermo. *El general San Martín ¿Masón-católico-deista?* Buenos Aires: Club del Libro, 1950 / Ed. Theoria, 1963.

Gadea Saguier, Christian. *El misterio de los masones. Viaje al interior de sus secretos*. Asunción: Ediciones y Arte, 2006.

Galeana, Patricia, ed. *Secularización del Estado y la sociedad. 150 Aniversario de las Leyes de Reforma*. Mexico City: Siglo XXI Ed., 2010.

Gándara Navarro, José de la. *Anexión y guerra de Santo Domingo*. Madrid: Impr. del "Correo Militar," 1884.

Gandía, Enrique de. *La Independencia de América y las Sociedades Secretas*. Santa Fe: Ed. Sudamericana, 1994.

_____. *Los orígenes probables de la logia Lautaro*. Buenos Aires: n.p., 1990.

_____. *La política secreta de la Gran Logia de Londres*. Buenos Aires: n.p., 1976.

_____. "San Martín masón." *Historia* 39 (1990): 3–33.

García, Elvira. "Historia de la masonería en Colombia (1833–1940)." *Cuadernos de Administración* 12 (n.d.): 69–76.

García Guatas, Manuel. *La Zaragoza de José Martí*. Zaragoza: Institución Fernando el Católico, 1999.

García Giráldez, Teresa. "El espiritualismo en el antiimperialismo centroamericano, 1890–1945." Paper presented at the XIV Encuentro de Latinoamericanistas Españoles, Universidad de Santiago de Compostela, Santiago de Compostela, Spain, September 15–18, 2010.

García Valenzuela, René. *Contribución al estudio de la Historia del Supremo Consejo de Chile*. Santiago, Chile: n.p., 1869.

_____. *Introducción a la historia de la Francmasonería en Chile*. Santiago, Chile: Ediciones de la G.L. de Chile, 1992.

_____. *El origen aparente de la Francmasonería en Chile y la Respetable Logia Simbólica "Filantropía Chilena."* Santiago, Chile: Impr. Universal, 1949.

Gastego Acuña, Carmen. "La Massoneria in Chile." *Officinae* 13, no. 3 (2001): 23–24.

Gay Armenteros, Juan Carlos. "Fondos masónicos del Archivo General de Palacio." In *La Masonería en la Historia de España*, edited by José Antonio Ferrer Benimeli, 365–370. Zaragoza, Spain: Gobierno de Aragón, 1985.

Gazmuri, Cristina. *El 48 chileno. Igualitarios, reformistas, radicales, masones y bomberos*. Santiago, Chile: Ed. Universitaria, 1993.

Gil Novales, Alberto. *Las Sociedades Patrióticas*. Madrid: Tecnos, 1975.

Gillot, Arthur George Malin. *Documentos Históricos referentes a la Masonería en Costa Rica*. San José, Costa Rica: Impr. Alsina, 1926.

Gohl, Jefferson William. "O real e o Imaginario: A Experiência da Maçonaria na Loja União III em Porto União da Vitória 1936 a 1950." Master's dissertation, Universidade Federal do Paraná, Curitiba, Brazil, 2003.

Gómez Liendo, Carmen. "La masonería en Venezuela. Influencia en la emancipación." *Anuario de Estudios Bolivarianos* 1, no. 1 (1990): 45–107.

Góngora Herrera, Federico. *Documentos de la Masonería Centroamericana (Antigua y Aceptada). Desde el año 1824–1933*. San José, Costa Rica: Imprenta Española, 1937.

_____. *Mis últimos documentos de la Masonería Centroamericana Antigua y Aceptada. Años 1809–1939*. San José, Costa Rica: Gran Logia de Costa Rica, 1940.

González Bernaldo de Quirós, Pilar. *Civilidad y política en los orígenes de la nación argentina. Las sociabilidades en Buenos Aires, 1829–1862*. Buenos Aires: Fondo de Cultura Económica, 2008.

_____. *Civilité et politique aux origines de la nation argentine. Les sociabilités à Buenos Aires 1829–1862*. Paris : Publications de la Sorbonne, 1999.

_____. "Masonería y Nación: la construcción masónica de una memoria histórica nacional." *Historia* (Santiago, Chile) 25 (1990): 81–101.

_____. "Masonería y política: el supuesto origen masónico de la organización nacional. Análisis de un banco de datos sobre la pertenencia masónica de la clase política porteña durante la formación del Estado-Nación (1852–1862)." In *Masonería Española y América*, edited by José Antonio Ferrer Benimeli, 1:271–287. Zaragoza, Spain: CEHME, 1993.

_____. "Masonería y Revolución de Independencia en el Río de la Plata: 130 años de historiografía." In *Masonería, Revolución y Reacción*, edited by José Antonio Ferrer Benimeli, 2:1035–1054. Alicante, Spain: Instituto Alicantino Juan Gil-Albert/CEHME, 1990.

_____. "Producción de una nueva legitimidad: ejército y sociedades patrióticas en Buenos Aires entre 1810–1813." *Cahiers des Amériques Latines* 10 (1990): 177–195.

_____. "La Revolución Francesa y la emergencia de nuevas prácticas de la política: la irrupción de la sociabilidad en el Río de la Plata revolucionario (1810–1815)." In *La Revolución Francesa y Chile*, edited by Ricardo Krebs and Cristian Gazmuri, 111–135. Santiago, Chile: Ed. Universitaria, 1990.

González García, Yamileth. "El presidente Castro, el clero y la masonería." In "La segunda administración del Dr. José María Castro Madriz (1866–1868)." Undergraduate dissertation, Universi-

dad de Costa Rica, Costa Rica, 1971.

González González, Orlando R. *El periodismo masónico y la revista de la Gran Logia, en Miranda. Tres conferencias en el cincuentenario del fallecimiento del Resp. Hno. Don Aurelio Miranda Alvarez*. Havana: Academia Cubana Estudios Masónicos, 1989.

_____. *La personalidad masónica literaria de Aramburu*. Havana: Academia Cubana Estudios Masónicos, 1989.

_____. *Valoración histórica del Gran Oriente de Cuba y las Antillas*. Havana: Academia Cubana Estudios Masónicos, 1987.

González Navarro, Moisés. *Masones y cristeros en Jalisco*. Mexico City: Ed. Colegio de México, 2000.

Gonzalo Racha, Juan. *Allende masón. La visión de un profano*. Santiago, Chile: Ed. PAX-Chile, 2008.

Goulart Da Silva, Michel. "Os maçons brasileiros e sua história." *REHMLAC* 2, no. 1 (May–November 2010): 93–98. https://revistas.ucr.ac.cr/index.php/rehmlac/article/view/22479/22641 *Revista História Catarina* 22 (2010): 67–71.

Gould, Robert Freke. "Freemasonry in Mexico." In *Ars Quatuor Coronatorum* 6 (1893): 113–117; 7 (1894): 72–76; 8 (1895): 219–222; 10 (1897): 66–69.

Gouvea Mendonça, Antonio. "La cuestión religiosa y la incursión del protestantismo en Brasil durante el siglo XIX: reflexiones e hipótesis." In *Protestantes, liberales y francmasones. Sociedades de ideas y modernidad en América Latina, siglo XIX*, edited by Jean Pierre Bastian, 67–83. Mexico City: Fondo de Cultura Económica, 1990.

Gran Logia de la República de Venezuela, *La situación masónica en Venezuela*. Caracas: n.p., 1989.

Greenleaf, Richard. "The Mexican Inquisition and the Masonic Movement: 1751–1820." *New Mexico Historical Review* 44, no. 2 (1969): 92–117.

Guedea, Virginia. "Comentario a la ponencia de Ernesto de la Torre sobre sociedades secretas en la guerra de Independencia." In *Repaso de la Independencia*, edited by Carlos Herrejón Peredo. Zamora, Mexico: El Colegio de Michoacan, 1985.

_____. "De conspiradores y sociedades secretas." *Rev. Retratos e Historias en México* 25 (2010).

_____. *En busca de un gobierno alterno: Los Guadalupes de México*. Mexico City: UNAM, 1992.

_____. "En torno a la Independencia y la Revolución." In *The revolutionary process in Mexico. Essay on political and social change 1880–1940*, edited by Jaime Rodríguez. Los Angeles: UCLA Press, 1990.

_____. "Una nueva forma de organización política: la sociedad secreta de

Jalapa 1812." In *Un hombre entre Europa y América. Homenaje a Juan Antonio Ortega y Medina*, edited by Amaya Garritz, 185–208. Mexico City: UNAM, 1993.

_____. "Las sociedades secretas durante el movimiento de Independencia." In *The Independence of Mexico and the Creation of the New Nation*, edited by Jaime Rodríguez, 45–62. Los Angeles: UCLA Press, 1989.

Gueiros Vieira, David. "Liberalismo, masonería y protestantismo en Brasil, siglo XIX." In *Protestantes, liberales y francmasones. Sociedades de ideas y modernidad en América Latina, siglo XIX*, edited by Jean Pierre Bastian, 39–66. Mexico City: Fondo de Cultura Económica, 1990.

_____. *O protestantismo a maçonaria e a questão Religiosa no Brasil*. Brasilia: Editora Universidade de Brasilia, 1980.

Guerra Gómez, Amparo. "Diego Martínez Barrio y el Gran Oriente Español: República y exilio americano." In *Masonería Española y América*, edited by José Antonio Ferrer Benimeli, 2:775–786. Zaragoza, Spain: CEHME, 1993.

Guerra, François-Xavier. *Modernidad e independencias. Ensayos sobre las revoluciones hispánicas*. Mexico City: Fondo de Cultura Económica, 2008.

Guerrero Cano, María Magdalena. "La Francmasonería." In *Disciplina y laxitud: la Iglesia dominicana en la época de la Anexión*, 236–243. Cádiz, Spain: Universidad de Cádiz, 1989.

Guillén, Julio. "Correo insurgente de Londres capturado por un corsario puertorriqueño, 1811." *Boletín de la Academia Chilena de la Historia* 27, no. 63 (1960): 125-155.

Gutiérrez Hernández, Alejandro. "El ciudadano desde el hermetismo. El caso de la Masonería." In *Familia, Identidad y Territorio. Actores y agentes en la construcción de la ciudadanía democrática*. Granada, Spain: Universidad de Granada, 2010.

Guzmán, José R. "Fray Servando Teresa de Mier y la sociedad Lautaro." *Anales del Instituto Nacional de Antropología e Historia* (1967–1968): 257–288.

Guzmán Pérez, Moisés. *Diccionario de Impresos y editores de la Independencia de México*. Mexico City: Ed. Porrúa, 2010.

_____, ed. *Liberalismo, masonería e Independencias en Hispanoamérica*. Morelia, Mexico, in press.

Guzmán-Stein, Miguel. "Andres Cassard and the Relationship between Freemasonry in the United States and Latin America (1856–73)." Paper presented at the International Conference of the History of Freemasonry, Centre interdisciplinaire bordelais d'étude des lumières-Lumières Nature Société, Université de Bordeaux III Centre d'étude de la Littérature Françaises des XVIIe et XVIIIe Siècles (CELLF), Sorbonne IV. Paris Chair of Freemassonary, Fac-

ulty of Religious Studies, University of Leiden Centre de la Méditerrannée Moderne et Contemporaine, Université de Nice Sophia-Antipolis The Interdisciplinary Research Group Freemasonary, Free University of Brussels, The George Washington Masonic Memorial, Alexandria, VA, May 26–30, 2011.

_____. "Andrés Cassard y las masonerías cubana y colombiana en la fundación de la masonería centroamericana: relación de un protagonismo personal en tres jurisdicciones." Paper presented at the I Simposio Internacional de Historia de la Masonería Latinoamericana y Caribeña, Cátedra Transdisciplinaria de Estudios Históricos de la Masonería Cubana Vicente Antonio de Castro (CTEHMAC), Casa de Altos Estudios Don Fernando Ortiz, Universidad de La Habana, Oficina del Historiador de la Ciudad de La Habana, Gran Logia de Cuba de A.L y A.M, and the Centro de Estudios Históricos de la Masonería Española (CEHME) of the Universidad de Zaragoza, Havana, Cuba, December 5–8 2007.

_____. "Andrés Cassard y su vida en Nueva York. Tres nuevas facetas de un masón polifacético." In *La Masonería Española: Represión y Exilios*, edited by José Antonio Ferrer Benimeli, 1:509–544. Zaragoza, Spain: CEHME, 2010.

_____. "Base de datos para la historia de la masonería en Costa Rica en el siglo XIX." In *La Masonería en Madrid y en España del siglo XVIII al XXI*, edited by José Antonio Ferrer Benimeli. Zaragoza: CEHME, 2004.

_____. "Costa Rica, España y Cuba: Antecedentes, desarrollo e impacto del movimiento de independencia en la sociedad costarricense finisecular y la masonería." In: *La Masonería Española y la crisis colonial del 98*, edited by José Antonio Ferrer Benimeli, 2:1041–1087. Zaragoza, Spain: CEHME, 1999.

_____. "La 'Cuestión Confirma' y la represión ideológica: El debate entre el clero reaccionario, el clero liberal y masón y la autoridad vaticana en Costa Rica (1870–1880)." Paper presented at the I Simposio Internacional de Historia de la Masonería Latinoamericana y Caribeña, Cátedra Transdisciplinaria de Estudios Históricos de la Masonería Cubana Vicente Antonio de Castro (CTEHMAC), Casa de Altos Estudios Don Fernando Ortiz, Universidad de La Habana, Oficina del Historiador de la Ciudad de La Habana, Gran Logia de Cuba de A.L y A.M, and the Centro de Estudios Históricos de la Masonería Española (CEHME) of the Universidad de Zaragoza, Havana, Cuba, December 5–8 2007.

_____. "La "Cuestión Confirma" y la represión ideológica: El debate entre el clero reaccionario, el clero liberal y masón y la autoridad vaticana en Costa Rica (1870–1880)." Paper presented at the I Encuentro de Historia Eclesial de Costa Rica, Instituto de Investigación Histórica y Patrimonial de la Arquidiócesis de San José and Universidad Católica Anselmo Llorente y Lafuente, San José, April 14–16, 2010.

_____. "De cómo el Generalísimo Francisco Franco Bahamonde, jefe del estado español, otorgó la Orden de Caballero de Isabel la Católica a un masón gallego que fue dos veces Gran Maestro de la Gran Logia de Costa Rica." In *La Masonería en Madrid y en España del siglo XVIII al XXI*, edited by José Antonio Ferrer Benimeli. Zaragoza: CEHME, 2004.

_____. "Dr. José María Castro Madriz: Masón y liberal, diputado, embajador, ministro, Presidente de la República, Presidente del Congreso, Presidente de la Corte Suprema de Justicia." In *La masonería española en la época de Sagasta (1825–1903)*, edited by José Antoni Ferrer Benimeli. Zaragoza, Spain: CEHME and the Fundación Práxedes Mateo-Sagasta, 2006.

_____. "La fundación del Supremo Consejo Centroamericano y la revolución de 1870 en la construcción de un Estado Liberal democrático en Costa Rica." Paper presented at the I Simposio Internacional de Historia de la Masonería Latinoamericana y Caribeña, Cátedra Transdisciplinaria de Estudios Históricos de la Masonería Cubana Vicente Antonio de Castro (CTEHMAC), Casa de Altos Estudios Don Fernando Ortiz, Universidad de La Habana, Oficina del Historiador de la Ciudad de La Habana, Gran Logia de Cuba de A.L y A.M, and the Centro de Estudios Históricos de la Masonería Española (CEHME) of the Universidad de Zaragoza, Havana, Cuba, December 5–8 2007.

_____. "La lapidaria fúnebre-masónica en Costa Rica como fuente de investigación de una comunidad inédita." *REHMLAC* 1, no. 2 (December 2009–April 2010): 88–120. https://revistas.ucr.ac.cr/index.php/rehmlac/article/view/6619/6308

_____. "Legislación Antimasónica Española. Siglos XVIII y XIX." *Simposio Hispanoamericano sobre las Leyes de Indias, Instituto Costarricense de Cultura Hispánica*. San José: Instituto de Cooperación Iberoamericana (I.C.I), Ministerio de Cultura, Juventud y Deportes, 1981.

_____. "Liberalismo, Educación, Iglesia y Masonería: el proceso de formación y secularización del Estado Nacional a través de las relaciones institucionales en Costa Rica en el siglo XIX." Doctoral dissertation, Universidad de Zaragoza, 2005).

_____. "La literatura masónica y la carrera editorial de Andrés Cassard. Primer inventario de su obra (1855–1875)." Paper presented at the III Symposium de historia las masonerías y las sociedades patrióticas latinoamericanas y caribeñas: Masonería, Independencia, Revolución y Secularización, Universidad Nacional Autónoma de México, Museo Nacional de Arte, Recinto de homenaje a don Benito Juárez del Palacio Nacional, Centro de Estudios Históricos de la Masonería Latinoamericana y Caribeña, Grupo México, Mexico City, December 2–4, 2010.

_____. "Las Logias de Mecánicos de Limón (C.R.): Destrucción y Reconstrucción del Espíritu Asociativo de la Población Negra Caribeña." Paper presented at the II Congreso Centroamericano de Historia, Universidad de San Carlos, Ciudad de Guatemala, 1993.

_____. "Masonería, civilismo y autoritarismo. Las logias y el uso del poder en Costa Rica 1870–1877." In *La masonería española en la época de Sagasta (1825–1903)*, edited by José Antoni Ferrer Benimeli. Zaragoza: CEHME and the Fundación Práxedes Mateo-Sagasta, 2006.

_____. "Masonería en Costa Rica en el siglo XIX." Undergraduate dissertation, Universidad de Zaragoza, 1993).

_____. "Masonería, Iglesia y Estado: Las relaciones entre el Poder Civil y el Poder Eclesiástico y las formas Asociativas en Costa Rica (1865–1875)." *REHMLAC* 1, no. 1 (May–November 2009): 100–134. https://revistas.ucr.ac.cr/index.php/rehmlac/article/view/6859/6546

_____. "Masones españoles en Costa Rica: el Krausismo y la Institución Libre de Enseñanza en la formación y desarrollo de la Democracia Liberal Costarricense." In *Masonería Española y América*, edited by José Antonio Ferrer Benimeli, 1:449–470. Zaragoza: CEHME, 1993.

_____. "Masones y liberales, españoles y cubanos: Intervención y aporte al desarrollo social, político y cultural de Costa Rica en el siglo XIX." In *La Ma-*

sonería Española entre Europa y América*, edited by José Antonio Ferrer Benimeli, 1:41–50. Zaragoza: CEHME, 1995.

_____. "Mujer, Masonería y libertad de conciencia en las logias de Costa Rica (1865–1877)." Paper presented at the XII Symposium Internacional de Historia de la Masonería Española. La Masonería Española: Represión y Exilios, Universidad de Almería, Universidad de Zaragoza, Grupo de Investigación Sur Clio, Centro de Estudios Históricos de la Masonería Española (CEHME), Junta de Andalucía, Gobierno de Aragón, Diputación de Almería, Ayuntamiento de Almería, Instituto de Estudios Almerienses and Fundación Unicaja, Almería, Spain, October 7–10, 2009.

_____. "El paisaje de la Nación: Liberalismo, masonería y redes sociales en la reorganización del uso del poder en el Estado. Costa Rica 1870–1882." Paper presented at the XIV Congreso Internacional de la Asociación de Historiadores Latinoamericanos Europeos, Castellón, Spain, 2005.

_____. "The Relation Among Freemasonry, State, and Catholic Church in Central America; Formation of the Secular States in Latin America." Paper presented at the International Conference on American and Latin American Freemasonry: A New Past and a New Future, Freemasonry and Civil Society Program of the History Department of the University of California at Los Angeles (UCLA), The Grand Lodge of California, California's Institute for Masonic Studies, Los Angeles, December 3, 2011

Hernández Arnulfo, Gaspar. "La francmasonería en el siglo XVIII: el proceso de transición de la masonería operativa o antigua a la masonería especulativa o moderna." Doctoral dissertation, 1999.

Hernández González, Manuel. *Francisco de Miranda y Canarias*. Santa Cruz de Tenerife, Spain: Idea, 2005.

_____. "Liberalismo y masonería en la América de las guerras de la Independencia: Cabral de Noroña y sus reflexiones sobre la masonería." In *Masonería, revolución y reacción*, edited by José Antonio Ferrer Benimeli, 2:829–826. Alicante, Spain: Institución Cultural "Juan Gil Albert," 1990.

_____. "Masonería, liberalismo y cuestión nacional en la Cuba del trienio liberal." In *La Masonería Española entre Europa y América*, edited by José Antonio Ferrer Benimeli, 1:51–64. Zaragoza: CEHME, 1995.

_____. "La orden cubana de los Caballeros de la Luz en el exilio norteamericano." In *Masonería Española y América*, edited by José Antonio Ferrer Benimeli, 1:401–414. Zaragoza, Spain: CEHME, 1993.

Herrera, Sajid Alfredo. "De las antiguas a las nuevas formas de sociabilidad, El Salvador: 1824–1850." Paper presented at the Masonería Sociedades Patrióticas panel of the X Congreso Centroamericano de Historia, Universidad Nacional Autónoma de Nicaragua, Managua, July 12–16, 2010.

Herrera Valdés, Willy Francisco. "Las sociedades secretas y la independencia política del cono sur americano: O'Higgins, San Martín y la logia Lautaro." Doctoral dissertation, Universidad Complutense de Madrid, 1985.

Ibáñez Fonseca, Amparo. *Entre dioses y demonios. Masones y jesuitas en Colombia en el siglo XIX*. Santa Fe de Bogotá, Colombia: Universidad Distrital, 1990.

Ibáñez Vergara, Jorge. "Allende y la Masonería." *Revista de la logia Hiram nº 65* 70 (1998).

Iglesias Cruz, Janet, and Javier Gutiérrez Forte. "Las elecciones de 1908: los masones y sus logias en la política de los primeros años de la República Cubana." In *200 años de Iberoamérica (1810–2010). Congreso Internacional. Actas del XIV Encuentro de Latinoamericanistas Españoles*, edited by Eduardo Rey Tristán and Patricia Calvo González, 225–235. Santiago de Compostela: Universidad de Santiago de Compostela, 2010. halshs.archives-ouvertes.fr/docs/00/52/92/78/PDF/AT4_Gutierrez-Iglesias.pdf.

_____. "Españoles y Cubanos en la Masonería/Manuel Curros Enriquez." *REHMLAC* 1, no. 2 (December 2009–April 2010): 121–129. https://revistas.ucr.ac.cr/index.php/rehmlac/article/view/6620/6309

_____. "La Simbología masónica en el Cementerio de Colón." *REHMLAC* 2, no. 1 (May–November 2010): 59–73. https://revistas.ucr.ac.cr/index.php/rehmlac/article/view/6610/6299

Ingram, Peter. "La Francmasonería mexicana temprana. Un capítulo confuso en nuestra historia." In *Logia de Estudios e Investigaciones Duque de Wharton* (1996–1997): 269–288.

Jacob, Margaret. "Where We Now Are in Masonic Studies." Paper presented at the International Conference on American and Latin American Freemasonry: A New Past and a New Future, Freemasonry and Civil Society Program of the History Department of the University of California at Los Angeles (UCLA), The Grand Lodge of California, California's Institute for Masonic Studies, Los Angeles, December 3, 2011.

Jans P., Sebastian. *Los grandes desafíos enfrentados por la masonería chilena en los últimos cincuenta años*. Santiago, Chile: G.L. Chile, 2012.

Jansen, André. "La masonería en la literatura hispanoamericana." In *La Masonería Española entre Europa y América*, edited by José Antonio Ferrer Benimeli, 1:27–45. Zaragoza: CEHME, 1995.

Jerez Alvarado, Rafael. *Bodas de plata de la Resp. Logia Francisco Morazán nº 11*. Tegucigalpa: CETTNA, 1987.

Jiménez Codinach, Guadalupe. "Auge de las sociedades secretas: la logia Lautaro y la independencia hispanoamericana." In *Liberalismo, masonería e Independencias en Hispanoamérica*, edited by Moisés Guzmán Pérez (in press).

Jiménez Pabón, Yordanka. "La masonería femenina en Cuba: entre la aceptación y el veto." In *La Masonería Española: Represión y Exilios*, edited by José Antonio Ferrer Benimeli, 2:1359–1372. Zaragoza, Spain: CEHME, 2010.

Jiménez Rodríguez, Carlos. "La Francmasonería en Venezuela." In *Vida y acción en varios mundos*, 63–110. Caracas: Gráficas Aeca, 1990.

Jinestra, Carlos. *José Martí en Costa Rica*. San José, Costa Rica: Librería Alsina, 1933.

Jocelyn-Holt, Alfredo. *La independencia de Chile, tradición, modernización y mito*. Santiago, Chile: Planeta-Ariel, 2001.

Jorge Torres, Abilio. "Composición socio-profesional en la Masonería riojana." In *Masonería, Política y Sociedad*, edited by José Antonio Ferrer Benimeli, 1:145–162. Zaragoza: CEHME, 1989.

Júlbez Campos, Manuel Mª. "Modelos de Masonería española identificada con América." In *Masonería Española y América*, edited by José Antonio Ferrer Benimeli, 1:289–298. Zaragoza, Spain: CEHME, 1993.

Kloppenbourg, Boaventura. "Igreja e Maçonaria." *Pregunte e responderemos* 275 (1984): 303–314.

_____. *A maçonaria no Brasil. Orientação para católicos*. Petrópolis, Brazil: Ed. Vozes, 1961.

Lahoud, Daniel. "La Masonería en Venezuela y Nueva Granada (Colombia) en los primeros años del Siglo XIX." *Tierra Firme* 24, no. 96 (2006).

Landa Bacallado, Martín A. *La masonería y la revolución cubana. Semejanzas de idearios*. Havana: n.p., 1964.

Lappas, Alcibíades. "Algumas revelações sobre os inícios da maçonaria no Brasil." In *Formação. Historia da Maçonaria*, 63–80. Rio de Janeiro: Ed. Esperanto, 1983.

_____. "La logia masónica Jorge Washington de Concepción del Uruguay. Entre Ríos (1822–1923)." *Revista de Historia Enterriana* 4–5 (1970): 354–389.

_____. *La masonería argentina a través de sus hombres*. Buenos Aires: Sucesores de A. Lappas, 2000.

_____. *La masonería en la ocupación del desierto*. Buenos Aires: Instituto Histórico Organización Nacional, 1981.

_____. *Nuevos estudios sobre la vida y la obra del Libertador General José de San Martín*. Buenos Aires: Junta de Estudios Históricos de San José de Flores, 1978.

_____. *San Martín y su formación*. Buenos Aires: Junta de Estudios Históricos de San José, 1978.

————. "San Martín y las logias." *La Nación* (Buenos Aires), February 25, 1978.

————. *San Martín y su ideario liberal.* Buenos Aires: Símbolo, 1982.

Larrain, Jorge. *Modernidad, razón e identidad en América Latina.* Santiago, Chile: Ed. Andrés Bello, 1996.

Larrègle, Ana María. "Consideraciones sobre la masonería en la Argentina (1900–1920). In *Masonería, política y sociedad*, edited by José Antonio Ferrer Benimeli, 2:1111–1120. Zaragoza, Spain: CEHME, 1989.

Larreta López, Juan Félix. "El olvidado modernista Viriato Díaz-Pérez en Paraguay." In *Masonería Española y América*, edited by José Antonio Ferrer Benimeli, 2:749–756. Zaragoza, Spain: CEHME, 1993.

Lemistre, Annie. "De la Francmaçonnerie en Amérique Centrale (Origine et développement)" *Chroniques d'Histoire Maçonnique* 36 (1986) : 59–65.

————. "Les Maçons du Nicaragua : Episodes d'une lutte pour la démocratie." *Chroniques d'Histoire Maçonnique* 37 (1986) : 53–57.

Linhares, Marcelo. *A Maçonaria e a questão religiosa do segundo Imperio (Apontamentos).* Brasilia: Senado Federal, 1988.

Lira Saucedo, Alejandro. "Del templo a la palabra. Hermenéutica y mitocrítica en la liturgia masónica." Undergraduate disseration, Universidad de Zacatecas, Mexico, 2011.

————. "Del templo a la palabra. Rescate filológico y estudio mitocrítico de cinco liturgias Francmasónicas." *REHMLAC* 3, no. 2 (December 2011–April 2012): 185–205. https://revistas.ucr.ac.cr/index.php/rehmlac/article/view/6580/6271

Loaiza Cano, Gilberto. "Cultura política popular y espiritismo (Colombia, siglo XIX)." *Historia y Espacio* 32 (January–June 2009): 1–21. historiayespacio.com/rev32/pdf/Rev%2032%20Cultura%20politica%20popular%20y%20espiritismo.pdf

————. "Hombres de sociedades (Masonería y sociabilidad político-intelectual en Colombia e Hispanoamérica durante la segunda mitad del siglo XIX)." *Revista Historia y Espacio* 17 (2001): 93–131.

————. *Manuel Ancízar (1811–1882) y su época. Biografía de un político hispanoamericano del siglo XIX.* Medellín: Universidad Nacional de Colombia, 2004.

————. "La masonería y las facciones del liberalismo colombiano durante el siglo XIX. El caso de la masonería de la Costa Atlántica." *Historia y Sociedad* 13 (2007). bibliotecavirtual.clacso.org.ar/ar/libros/colombia/fche/4.pdf

————. *Sociabilidad, política y religión en la definición de la nación (Colombia,*

1820–1886). Bogotá, Colombia: Universidad Externado de Colombia, 2011.

Loke, Marshall S. "Presidente de Chile, marxista y masón." In *The Royal Arch Mason*. New York: n.p., 1972.

López Bernal, Carlos Gregorio. "Alberto Masferrer y Augusto César Sandino: Espiritualismo y utopía en los años veinte." *Revista Humanidades* 4, no. 2 (January–February–March 2003).

López Casimiro, Francisco. "La masonería y el conflicto colonial en la prensa de la baja Extremadura." In *Masonería Española y América*, edited by José Antonio Ferrer Benimeli, 2:789–810. Zaragoza, Spain: CEHME, 1993.

———. "Ramón Blanco Erenas, capitán general de Cuba y la masonería." *Boletín de la Real Academia de Extremadura de Letras y las Artes* 17 (2009): 109–122.

López Penha, Haim. *Reseña histórica del Supremo Consejo del Grado 33 y último del Rito Escocés Antiguo y Aceptado para la República Dominicana*. Santo Domingo, Dominican Republic: Ed. Montalvo, 1952.

Lorenzo, Lila, and Sergio García Guzmán. "La masonería femenina mexicana." *Cultura Masónica* 2, no. 5 (October 2010): 92–102.

Lork Frutos, Tomás. "Breves apuntes históricos sobre la masonería en Zacatecas." *Revista Alarife* 1, no. 3 (1990): 20–22.

Luna, Luiz. "A Maçonaria na formação da Nacionalidade Brasileira." In *História Política da Maçonaria. Anais do I Congresso Internacional de História e Geografía*, 4:131–150. Rio de Janeiro: n.p., 1981.

Lynch, John. *San Martín, soldado argentino, héroe americano*. Barcelona: n.p., 2009.

Maguirre, José Patricio. *La Masonería y la emancipación del Río de la Plata*. Buenos Aires: n.p., 1969 / Buenos Aires: Ed. Santiago Apóstol, 2000.

Mansur Barata, Alexandre. "E é certo que os homêns se convencem mais pela experiência do que pela teoria: cultura política e sociabilidade maçônica no mundo luso-brasileiro (1790–1822)." *REHMLAC* 3, no. 1 (May–November 2011): 1–19. https://revistas.ucr.ac.cr/index.php/rehmlac/article/view/6583/6274

———. *Luzes e sombras: a ação da maçonaria brasileira 1870–1910*. Campinas, Brazil: Ed. de UNICAMP, 1999.

———. *Maçonaria, sociabilidades ilustradas e independencia do Brasil (1790–1822)*. São Paulo: Annablume, 2006.

Marchiori Bakos, Margaret. *RS: Escravição e abolição*. Porto Alegre: Mercado Aberto, 1982.

Martín Martínez, Luis P. "La Franc-Maçonnerie espagnole et l'indépendance de Cuba." In *Mélanges offerts à Paul Roche. Acta Hispanica*, 169–179. Nantes,

France: Université de Nantes, 1992.

Martín Martínez, Luis P., and Fran-çoise Randouyer. "Título distintivo e ideología en las logias de las Antillas." In *Masonería Española y América*, edited by José Antonio Ferrer Benimeli, 1:115–127. Zaragoza, Spain: CEHME, 1993.

Martínez de Codes, Rosa Mª. "El impacto de la masonería en la legislación reformista de la primera generación de liberales en México." In *Masonería Española y América*, edited by José Antonio Ferrer Benimeli, 1:129–145. Zaragoza, Spain: CEHME, 1993.

Martínez Díaz, Nelson. *Simón Bolívar*. Madrid: Historia 16, 1987.

Martínez Esquivel, Ricardo. "Composición socio-ocupacional de los masones del siglo XIX." In *Diálogos Revista Electrónica de Historia* 8, no. 2 (August 2007-February 2008): 124-147. Available at http://revistas.ucr.ac.cr/index.php/dialogos/article/view/18344/18536

_____. "Actividades masónicas en la Ciudad de Puntarenas (1870-1876)." In *Revista Inter Sedes* VIII, no. 15 (2007): 93-108. Available at http://revistas.ucr.ac.cr/index.php/intersedes/article/view/870/931

_____. "Un estudio comparado del establecimiento de logias masónicas en Costa Rica y Guatemala (1865-1903)." In *Número especial de Diálogos 9º Congreso de Historia Centroamericano* (2008): 2357-2382.

_____. "Masones y su participación política en Costa Rica (1865-1899)." In *Número especial de Diálogos 9º Congreso de Historia Centroamericano* (2008): 1815-1848. Short version: "¿Desmasonización de la política costarricense o despolitización de las logias masónicas costarricenses (1865-1899)?" In Eduardo Rey Tristán and Patricia Calvo González eds. *200 años de Iberoamérica (1810-2010)*. Santiago de Compostela: Universidad de Santiago de Compostela, Centro Interdisciplinario de Estudios Americanistas Gumersindo Busto, Consejo Español de Estudios Iberoamericanos 2010, 248-267. Available at https://halshs.archives-ouvertes.fr/file/index/docid/529291/filename/AT4_Martinez.pdf

_____. "Masonic Societies of Ideas and their Social Representations in Costa Rica (1865-1899)." In *CRFF Working Paper Series* (University of Sheffield) 4 (2008): 1-21. Spanish version: "Documentos y discursos católicos antimasónicos en Costa Rica (1865-1899)." In *REHMLAC* 1, no. 1 (May-November 2009): 135-154. Available at https://revistas.ucr.ac.cr/index.php/rehmlac/article/view/6860/6547

_____. "Sociedades de ideas en Puerto Limón durante la década de 1890." In *Revista Intercambio. Revista sobre Centroamérica y el Caribe* 7 (2009): 157-186. Available at http://revistas.ucr.ac.cr/index.php/intercambio/article/view/3221/3127. Short version: "Sociabilidades modernas: sociedades fraternales secretas en el Caribe costarricense a finales del siglo XIX." In

Memorias. Revista Digital de Historia y Arqueología desde el Caribe 11 (2010): 128-143. Available at http://rcientificas. uninorte.edu.co/index.php/memorias/ article/view/516/277. French version: « La Franc-maçonnerie à Puerto Limon : un espace de réception privilégié du cosmopolitisme dans une ville portuaire. » In Cécile Révauger and Éric Saunier. *La Franc-Maçonnerie dans les ports.* Bordeaux : Presses Universitaires de Bordeaux, 2012, 105-122.

_____. "Conspiradores políticos y sectas misteriosas: Imaginarios sociales sobre la masonería en Costa Rica (1865-1899)." In *Revista Estudios* 22 (December 2009): 13-32. Available at http://revistas.ucr.ac.cr/index.php/ estudios/article/view/24182/24810

_____. "Sociabilidad moderna, impugnación católica y redes masónicas en la Ciudad de Puntarenas (1870-1951)." In Oriester Abarca Hernández, Jorge Bartels Villanueva and Juan José Marín Hernández eds. *De Puerto a Región: El Pacífico Central y Sur de Costa Rica 1821-2007.* San José: Editorial de la Universidad de Costa Rica, 2010, 105-142.

_____. "La masonería y el establecimiento de la Sociedad Teosófica en Costa Rica (1904-1910)." In José Antonio Ferrer Benimeli ed. *La Masonería Española: Represión y Exilios.* Zaragoza: Gobierno de Aragón, Departamento de Educación, Cultura y Deporte, Centro de Estudios Históricos de la Masonería Española, Universidad de Zaragoza, 2010, Vol. I, 369-392.

_____. *Estudios Históricos de la Masonería Latinoamericana y Caribeña.* Edited with the collaboration of Yván Pozuelo Andrés. Paris: Publibook, 2011.

_____. "*El Fantasma de Bolívar en la Masonería Venezolana* de Eloy Enrique Reverón García." In *REHMLAC* 3, no. 1 (May-November 2011): 209-218. Available at https://revistas.ucr.ac.cr/index. php/rehmlac/article/view/22483/22721

_____. "*Las logias de ultramar. En torno a los orígenes de la Francmasonería en Chile, 1850-1862* de Felipe Santiago del Solar." In *REHMLAC* 5, no. 1 (May-November 2013): 237-255. Available at https://revistas.ucr.ac.cr/index.php/ rehmlac/article/view/22498/22732

_____. "Sociability, Religiosity and New Cosmovisions in Costa Rica at the turn of the Nineteenth to Twentieth Centuries." English translation by Sylvia Hottinger Craig. In *REHMLAC. Hors série nº1. Special Issue UCLA– Grand Lodge of California*, guest editor María Eugenia Vázquez-Semadeni, (October 2013): 155-191. Available at http:// rehmlac.com/recursos/vols/numsesp /201310ucla/rehmlac.uclaspecial.rich_ eng.pdf [Spanish version: "Sociabilidad, religiosidad y nuevas cosmovisiones en la Costa Rica del cambio de siglo (XIX-XX)." Available at http://revistas.ucr.ac. cr/index.php/rehmlac/article/ view/22482/22695].

_____. "Hacia la construcción de una historia social de la masonería en Centroamérica." In *Revista Estudios* 27 (December 2013): 127-151. Available at http://revistas.ucr.ac.cr/index.php/estudios/article/view/12703/11951

_____. "Sociedad civil, esfera pública y masonería en Centroamérica (1865-1876)." In José Miguel Delgado Idarreta and Antonio Morales Benítez eds. *Gibraltar, Cádiz, América y la masonería. Constitucionalismo y libertad de prensa, 1812-2012*. Gibraltar: Gobierno de Gibraltar - Centro de Estudios Históricos de la Masonería Española, Universidad de Zaragoza, 2014, Vol. I, 541-580.

_____. "Prosopografía y redes sociales: notas metodológicas sobre el estudio de la masonería en Costa Rica." In *REHMLAC+* 7, n. 2 (December 2015-April 2016): 1-25, doi: http://dx.doi.org/10.15517/rehmlac.v7i2.22689

_____. "Entre sotanas y mandiles: el proyecto masónico centroamericano de Francisco Calvo (1865-1876)". En *300 años: masonerías y masones, 1717-2017. Tomo I: Migraciones*. Edited by Ricardo Martínez Esquivel, Yván Pozuelo Andrés and Rogelio Aragón. Ciudad de México: Palabra de Clío, 2017, 91-116.

_____. *Masones y masonería en la Costa Rica de los albores de la Modernidad (1865-1899)*. San José: Editorial de la Universidad de Costa Rica, 2017.

_____. "Inmigrantes sirio-libaneses, sus mecanismos de inserción social y la masonería en Costa Rica durante la primera mitad del siglo XX." In monographic issue on "La Masonería y Centroamérica en los proyectos republicanos: logias, redes y conflictos en un mundo en transformación (1850-1950). A 300 años de la fundación de la Masonería," guest editor Miguel Guzmán-Stein, *AFEHC Boletín* 73, forthcoming (June 2017). Preview (short) version (advanced research): "Inmigrantes libaneses en Costa Rica y sus participaciones en la masonería del país (primera mitad del siglo XX)." In Eduardo Rey Tristán and Patricia Calvo González eds. *200 años de Iberoamérica (1810-2010)*. Santiago de Compostela: Universidad de Santiago de Compostela, Centro Interdisciplinario de Estudios Americanistas Gumersindo Busto, Consejo Español de Estudios Iberoamericanos 2010, 268-280. Available at https://halshs.archives-ouvertes.fr/file/index/docid/529294/filename/AT4_MartinezEsquivel.pdf

Martínez Esquivel, Ricardo, and Yván Pozuelo Andrés, eds. *Estudios Históricos de la Masonería Latinoamericana y Caribeña*. Paris: Publibook, 2011.

Martínez Esquivel, Ricardo, Yván Pozuelo Andrés, and Rogelio Aragón, eds. *300 años: masonerías y masones, 1717-2017*. Ciudad de México: Palabra de Clío, 2017. Five Volumes [*Tomo I. Migraciones, Tomo II. Silencios, Tomo III. Artes, Tomo IV. Exclusión*, y *Tomo V. Cosmopolitismo*].

Martínez Millán, José. "Fuentes para el estudio de la masonería en la Sección de Inquisición del Archivo Histórico Nacional." In *La Masonería en la Historia de España*, 349–358. Zaragoza, Spain: Gobierno de Aragón, 1985.

_____. "Juan José Díaz de la Espada, obispo de La Habana ¿un prelado masón?" In *Masonería Española y América*, edited by José Antonio Ferrer Benimeli, 1:169–179. Zaragoza, Spain: CEHME, 1993.

Martínez Moreno, Carlos Francisco. "Benito Juárez: ¿más que un Aprendiz de Masón?" In *En-Claves del Pensamiento. Revista de Humanidades* 2, no. 3 (June 2008): 127–196.

_____. "Dos perspectivas sobre los esfuerzos de la secularización en la Masonería Simbólica en México durante los siglos XIX y XX." *Revista El poder de la razón* [Gran Logia Valle de México] (2009).

_____. "¿Es correcto hablar de sociedades patrióticas paramasónicas?" Mexico City: n.p., 2008.

_____. "El establecimiento de las masonerías en México en el siglo XIX." Master's dissertation, UNAM, Mexico City, 2011. 132.248.9.195/ptb2011/junio/0670201/Index.html

_____. "Estado Nación laico y secularización masónica en México." *REHMLAC* 3, no. 2 (December 2011–April 2012): 43–65. https://revistas.ucr.ac.cr/index.php/rehmlac/article/view/6575/6266

_____. "III Symposium internacional de historia de las masonerías y las sociedades patrióticas latinoamericanas y caribeñas: masonería, independencia, revolución y secularización."

REHMLAC 3, no. 2 (December 2011–April 2012): 330–345. https://revistas.ucr.ac.cr/index.php/rehmlac/article/view/22485/22723

_____. "Geopolíticas masónicas y paramasónicas en México, vías de secularización de la sociedad y consolidación del proyecto de Estado Nación republicano, federal, liberal y laico," Paper presented at the III Symposium de historia de las masonerías y las sociedades patrióticas latinoamericanas y caribeñas: Masonería, Independencia, Revolución y Secularización, Universidad Nacional Autónoma de México, Museo Nacional de Arte, Recinto de homenaje a don Benito Juárez del Palacio Nacional, Centro de Estudios Históricos de la Masonería Latinoamericana y Caribeña, Grupo México, Mexico City, December 2–4, 2010.

_____. "Las Logias masónicas en la Nueva España." *REHMLAC* 3, no. 2 (December 2011–April 2012): 223–297. https://revistas.ucr.ac.cr/index.php/rehmlac/article/view/6582/6273

_____. "La Masonería española en el exilio de México. Masones españoles regularizados y afiliados en logias bajo la jurisdicción de la Gran Logia Valle de México (1920–1959)." In *La Masonería Española: Represión y Exilios*, edited by José Antonio Ferrer Benimeli, 1:211–230. Zaragoza, Spain: CEHME, 2010.

_____. "Masones en defensa de la República y de la Constitución mexicana. Dos sociedades patrióticas paramasónicas en el siglo XIX." In *Secular-*

ización del Estado y la Sociedad. 150 Aniversario de las Leyes de Reforma*, edited by Patricia Galdeana, 127–140. Mexico City: Siglo XXI Ed., 2010.

_____. "La secularización de la masonería como vía para la formación de un nuevo ciudadano que coadyuvó a la construcción de un Estado Nación laico. Una revisión de la *Constitución y Estatutos Generales del Rito Masónico Nacional Mexicano* de 1868." Paper presented at the Masonería Sociedades Patrióticas panel of the X Congreso Centroamericano de Historia, Universidad Nacional Autónoma de Nicaragua, Managua, July 12–16, 2010.

_____. "La Sociedad de los Yorkinos Federalistas. 1834. Una propuesta hermenéutica de sus estatutos y reglamentos generales a la luz de la historia de la Masonería." *REHMLAC* 1, no. 1 (May–November 2009): 212–233. https://revistas.ucr.ac.cr/index.php/rehmlac/article/view/6864/6551

Martínez Zaldúa, Ramón. *Historia de la Masonería en Hispanoamérica. ¿Es o no religión la Masonería?* Mexico City: Ed. Valle de México, n.d.

_____. *Historia de la masonería en México y en el mundo*. Mexico City: n.p., 1977.

_____. *La Masonería en Hispanoamérica. Su influencia decisiva en la Revolución mexicana*. Mexico City: Ed. B. Costa-Amie, 1965.

_____. *Masonería es ...* Mexico City: Herbasa, 1999.

_____. *¿Qué es la masonería? Pasado, presente y futuro*. Mexico City: Ed. B. Costa-Amie, 1980.

Mateos, José María. *Historia de la Masonería en México desde 1806 hasta 1884, México, "La Tolerancia" periódico oficial del G.O. del Rito Nacional Mexicano*. Mexico City: n.p., 1884 / Mexico City: Ed. Herbasa, 1994.

Medal, Francisco. *La historia de la Francmasonería en Nicaragua*. Managua: Gran Logia de Nicaragua, 1927.

Medina, José Toribio. *Historia del Santo Oficio de la Inquisición en Chile*. Santiago, Chile: Medina, 1952.

_____. *Historia del Tribunal del Santo Oficio de la Inquisición de Cartagena de Indias*. Santiago, Chile: Elzeviriana, 1909.

_____. *Historia del Tribunal del Santo Oficio de la Inquisición en México*. Santiago, Chile: Elzeviriana, 1905.

_____. *El Tribunal del Santo Oficio de la Inquisición en las Provincias del Plata*. Santiago, Chile: n.p. 1899.

Mejía, Yasmina. *Historia Social de la Masonería en el Estado Lara: Respetable Logia "Estrella de Occidente n° 50 (1856–1960)*. Barquisimeto, Venezuela: Universidad Centroccidental Lisandro Alvarado, 2005.

Melo, Mário. *A maçonaria e a revolução*

republicana de 1817. Recife: n.p., 1912.

_____. *A Maçonaria no Brasil. Prioridade de Pernambuco*. Recife: n.p., 1909.

Melo, Osvaldo Ferreira de. *A Maçonaria Catarinense no Período Imperial (1822–1889)*. Florianópolis, Brazil: O prumo, 1997.

Mellado Rubio, Carmen, and Concha Ponce Aura. "La masonería valenciana ante la guerra hispano-cubana, 1895–1896." In *Masonería Española y América*, edited by José Antonio Ferrer Benimeli, 1:471–480. Zaragoza, Spain: CEHME, 1993.

Mendoza Silva, Eduardo. *La historia de la masonería en Perú*. Lima: Ed. Tipografía, 1966.

_____. *La Inquisición en Hispanoamérica*. Buenos Aires: n.p., 1967.

Menezes, Manoel Joaquim de. *Exposição Histórica de Maçonaria no Brasil*. Rio de Janeiro: O Diario, 1872.

Miranda, Francisco. *Archivo del General Miranda*. Caracas: Ed. Sur-América, 1929–1940.

Miranda y Álvarez, Aurelio. *Cien años de actividad masónica*. Havana: n.p., 1961.

_____. *Historia de la francmasonería en Cuba*. Havana: Orientación Masónica, 1944.

_____. *Historia documentada de la Masonería en Cuba (1762–1920)*. Havana: Molina, 1933.

_____. *Origen cubano de la masonería regular mexicana*. Havana: n.p., 1951.

_____. *Historia moderna de la masonería en Cuba. Su influencia en la independencia cubana*. Havana: Academia Cubana de Estudios Masónicos, 1985.

_____. *Primera manifestación pública masónica de carácter independiente*. Havana: n.p., 1951.

Mola, Aldo A. "Las logias italianas en Latinoamérica (1860–1940)." In *Masonería Española y América*, edited by José Antonio Ferrer Benimeli, 1:323–343. Zaragoza, Spain: CEHME, 1993.

Molina, Eugenia. "Las modernas prácticas asociativas como ámbitos de defensa de lazos objetivos políticos durante el proceso revolucionario (1810–1820)" In *Universum* 16, Talca-Chile: n.p., 2010.

Mollès, Dévrig. "Exiliados, emigrados y modernización: el crisol masónico euro-argentino. Europa-Río de la Plata (1840–1880)." In *La Masonería Española: Represión y Exilios*, edited by José Antonio Ferrer Benimeli, 1:47–70. Zaragoza, Spain: CEHME, 2010.

"La franc-maçonnerie espagnole en Argentine : les origines du Grand Orient Fédéral Argentin (1925–1935)." Master's dissertation, Université de Haute Bretagne, Rennes II, France, 2000.

———. "Un puente transatlántico: la Gran Logia Filial Hispano-Argentina del Grande Oriente Español en la circunstancia euro-americana de Entre-Guerras." In *La masonería española en la época de Sagasta (1825–1903)*, edited by José Antonio Ferrer Benimeli, 1:809–842. Zaragoza, Spain: CEHME and the Fundación Práxedes Mateo-Sagasta, 2006.

Monduc, Guy. *Essai sur l'origine de l'histoire de la Francmaçonnerie en Guadeloupe*. Paris : n.p., 1985.

Montes de Oca Choy, María Teresa and Yasmín Ydoy Ortiz. "Chee Kung Tong. ¿Vínculos masónicos?" *REHMLAC* 1, no. 1 (May–November 2009): 234–246. https://revistas.ucr.ac.cr/index.php/rehmlac/article/view/6865/6552

Molina Jiménez, Iván. "Ateísmo y descreimiento en la ciudad de San José (Costa Rica) a inicios del siglo XX. Una aproximación preliminar." *Estudos Ibero-Americanos* 30, no. 2 (2004).

———. *La ciencia del momento. Astrología y espiritismo en Costa Rica durante los siglos XIX y XX*. Heredia, Costa Rica: EUNA, 2011.

———. *La ciudad de los monos. Roberto Brenes Mesén, los católicos heredianos y el conflicto cultural de 1907 en Costa Rica*. Heredia, Costa Rica: EUNA and EUCR, 2001.

Montoya, Jaime. *Masonería íntima*. Bogotá, Colombia, 1988.

Mora García, José Pascual. "Los comuneros, Francisco De Miranda y la francmasonería en Venezuela (1779–1810)." *Heurística 11 (January–June 2009)*: 74–92. saber.ula.ve/bitstream/123456789/30649/1/articulo7.pdf

Mora García, José Pascual. "La Masonería. Su historia y su contribución en la construcción simbólica de la nación venezolana." In *Liberalismo, Masonería e Independencia en Hispanoamérica*, edited by Moisés Guzmán Pérez. Morelia, Mexico, in press.

Mora Mérida, José Luis. "Ideario laicista-masónico e Iglesia católica en la formación de las nacionalidades hispano-americanas." In *La Masonería Española entre Europa y América*, edited by José Antonio Ferrer Benimeli, 1:503–522. Zaragoza: CEHME, 1995.

Morales Benítez, Antonio, and Fernando Sigler Silvera. "La masonería gaditana de Obediencia cubana: la logia Tolerancia y Fraternidad." In *Masonería Española y América*, edited by José Antonio Ferrer Benimeli, 1:313–322. Zaragoza, Spain: CEHME, 1993.

Morales Ruiz, Juan José. "Masones menorquines en América latina durante el siglo XIX." In *Masonería Española y América*, edited by José Antonio Ferrer Benimeli, 1:495–512. Zaragoza, Spain: CEHME, 1993.

Morel, Mario, and Françoise Jean Oliveira Souza. *O poder da Maçonaria: a história de uma sociedade secreta no Brasil*. Rio de Janeiro: Nova Frontera, 2008.

Morel, Marco. "Sociabilidades entre Luzes e sombras: apontamentos para o estudo histórico das maçonarias da primeira metade do século XIX." *Estudos Históricos* 28 (2001).

Moreno Alonso, Manuel. "La 'Santa Trinidad' de la democracia en Lima en el I Centenario de la Revolución Francesa." In *Masonería Española y América*, edited by José Antonio Ferrer Benimeli, 2:727–736. Zaragoza, Spain: CEHME, 1993.

Moreno Egas, Jorge. "Preguntas y comentarios sobre la masonería." In *Instituto de Historia Eclesiástica Ecuatoriana* 17 (1997): 207–215.

Muñoz Echeverría, Mª Elena, and Mª Jesús Ocaña Vázquez. "Elementos indígenas y de ultramar en los sellos de las logias de Cuba y Filipinas." In *Masonería Española y América*, edited by José Antonio Ferrer Benimeli, 2:1005–1008. Zaragoza, Spain: CEHME, 1993.

Nadra, Fernando. *San Martín, hoy.* Buenos Aires: Ed. Cartago, 1974.

Navajas Zubeldua, Carlos. "Biografía masónica y militar de Julio Mangada Rosenörn." In *Masonería Española y América*, edited by José Antonio Ferrer Benimeli, 2:718–720. Zaragoza, Spain: CEHME, 1993.

Navarrete, Félix [Jesús García Gutiérrez]. *La masonería en la historia y en las leyes de México.* Mexico City: Jus, 1957.

Navarro García, Jesús Raúl. "El desprestigio masónico en Puerto Rico durante la década ominosa." In *Masonería, revolución y reacción*, edited by José Antonio Ferrer Benimeli, 2:905–1006. Alicante, Spain: Institución Cultural "Juan Gil Albert," 1990.

Navarro, Nicolás. *La Masonería y la Independencia.* Caracas: n.p., 1928.

Nascimento, Carlos Eduardo. "O Qué a Maçonaria?" *Revista História Catarina* 22 (2010): 52–56.

_____. "A Maçonaria em Santa Catarina no século XIX." *Revista História Catarina* 22 (2010): 57–61.

Novarino, Marco. "La masonería italiana y la independencia de Cuba." In *Masonería Española y América*, edited by José Antonio Ferrer Benimeli, 2:1039–1056. Zaragoza, Spain: CEHME, 1993.

Obregón Loría, Rafael. *Actividades Masónicas en Centro América antes de 1865.* San José: Gran Logia de Costa Rica, 1965.

_____. "Apuntes Acerca de la Masonería Antigua en Costa Rica (1824–1865)." *Revista de los Archivos Nacionales* 1–2 (1944): 29–48.

_____. "Apuntes Acerca de la Masonería Antigua en Costa Rica (1824–1865)." In *Rafael Obregón Loría*, edited by Rafael Ángel Méndez Alfaro and Silvia Elena Molina Vargas, 107–126. San José, Costa Rica: UNED, 2010.

_____. *Ganganelli: organizador de la Masonería en Costa Rica*. San José, Costa Rica: Trejos Hermanos, 1941.

_____. *José Quirce Filguera, fundador de la masonería en la República de Guatemala*. San José, Costa Rica: Imprenta Tormo, 1951.

_____. *Porqué se trasladó a Guatemala el Supremo Consejo Centroamericano*. San José, Costa Rica: Imprenta Tormo, 1952.

_____. *Presbítero Doctor Francisco Calvo (Ganganelli). Organizador de la Masonería en Costa Rica*. San José, Costa Rica, Imprenta Borrase, 1968.

Obregón Loría, Rafael, and George Bowden. *La Masonería en Costa Rica*. 4 vols. San José, Costa Rica: Trejos Hermanos, 1938–1940; San José, Costa Rica: Imprenta Tormo, 1950. granlogiadecostarica.org/doc/Historia_De_La_Masoneria_Costarricense-Primer_Periodo.pdf; granlogiadecostarica.org/doc/Historia_De_La_Masoneria_Costarricense-Segundo_Periodo.pdf.; granlogiadecostarica.org/doc/Historia_De_La_Masoneria_Costarricense-Tercer_Periodo.pdf

Ocampo, Emilio. *Alvear en la Guerra con el Imperio del Brasil*. Buenos Aires: Ed. Claridad, 2003.

_____. "Inglaterra, la masonería y la independencia de América." *Todo Es Historia* 463 (2006): 194–202.

Oliveira Marqués, A. H. "Las Sociedades Patrióticas." In *La Masonería Española entre Europa y América*, edited by José Antonio Ferrer Benimeli, 1:289–300. Zaragoza: CEHME, 1995.

Oliveira, Ramos de. *O conflito maçonico-religioso de 1812*. Petrópolis, Brazil: Ed. Vozes, 1952.

Oliveira Sousa, Eufran and Paulo Viana Nunes. *O Aeropago de Itambé e a revolução de 1817: Padre Miguelinho e André de Albuquerque, dois herois-mártires norte-rio-grandeses*. Natal: Delta Ed., 1997.

Oller, José. *Historia del Supremo Consejo Nacional de Panamá*. Panama City: Ediciones de la Imprenta Hernández, 1934.

Olmos Sánchez, Isabel. *La sociedad mexicana en vísperas de la independencia (1787–1821)*. Murcia, Spain: Universidad de Murcia, 1989.

Olveda Cencio, Jaime. "Las logias en los primeros años republicanos, 1822–1828." In *Liberalismo, Masonería e Independencias en Hispanoamérica*, edited by Moisés Guzmán Pérez. Morelia, Mexico, in press.

Önnefors, Andreas. "Swedish Freemasonry in the Caribbean: How St. Barthélemy turned into an Island of the IXth Province." *REHMLAC* 1, no. 1 (May–November 2009): 16–41. https://revistas.ucr.ac.cr/index.php/rehmlac/article/view/6854/6541

Onsari, Fabian. *San Martín, la logia Lautaro y la Francmasonería*. Avellaneda, Argentina: n.p., 1951.

Oropeza Alfaro, Ana. "La masonería autóctona y española ante la esclavitud." In *La Masonería Española: Represión y Exilios*, edited by José Antonio Ferrer Benimeli, 1:393–410. Zaragoza, Spain: CEHME, 2010.

_____. "El proyecto político yorkino: la política popular en la campaña presidencial de Vicente Guerrero." Undergraduate dissertation, Mexico, 2010.

Oropeza Villavicencio, Eduardo Adolfo. "Masones en la Nueva España. Libros prohibidos y liberalismo." In *Liberalismo, Masonería e Independencias en Hispanoamérica*, edited by Moisés Guzmán Pérez. Morelia, Mexico, in press.

Otero González, Luis Antonio. "La Universidad Interamericana de Puerto Rico y su relación con la Masonería." *Acacia* (October–November 2008): 2–10.

Oviedo Martínez, Benjamín. "La logia Lautarina." *Rev. Chilena de Historia y Geografía* 62 (1929): 105–126.

_____. *La masonería en Chile. Bosquejo histórico. La colonia, la independencia, la república*. Santiago, Chile: Impr. Universo. 1929.

Pace, Carlo. *Resumo Histórico da Maçonaria no Brasil*. Rio de Janeiro: n.p., 1896.

Pacheco Quintero, Jorge. *La Masonería en la emancipación de América*. Bogotá: n.p., 1943.

Padilla Bolívar, Antonio. "La lucha de José Martí." *Historia 16* 131 (March 1987): 62.

Padilla, Washington J. "La actividad de las sociedades bíblicas en Ecuador durante el primer liberalismo." In *Protestantes, liberales y francmasones. Sociedades de ideas y modernidad en América Latina, siglo XIX*, edited by Jean Pierre Bastian, 97–118. Mexico City: Fondo de Cultura Económica, 1990.

Palti, Elías J. *La invención de una legitimidad. Razón y retórica en el pensamiento mexicano del siglo XIX (un estudio sobre las formas del discurso político)*. Mexico City: Fondo Económico de Cultura, 2005.

Pascual Martínez, Pedro. "La prensa masónica de España y Cuba (1868–1898)." In *La Masonería Española y la crisis colonial del 98*, edited by José Antonio Ferrer Benimeli, 1:681–698. Zaragoza, Spain: CEHME, 1999.

Pascual, Pedro. "Ausencia de periódicos y libros masónicos en la Independencia de América." In *Actas del XII Congreso de la Asociación Internacional de Hispanistas [AIH]*, 194–202. Mexico City: n.p., 1995.

Pasquali, Bolívar. "San Martín y la masonería en la independencia americana." *Todo Es Historia* 405 (2001): 6–23.

Paz Sánchez, Manuel de. "Aspectos generales y principales características de la implantación sistemática de la francmasonería en la Gran Antilla durante el último tercio del siglo XIX." *Anuario de Estudios Americanos* 36 (1979): 531–568.

_____. "Crónica y semblanza wangüemertiana de Mercedes Pinto: una feminista canaria en Cuba (1935–36)." *Boletín Millares Carlo*, 457–473. Las Palmas, Spain: UNED, 1980. Also in: *Masones en el Atlántico*, 2:103–121. Santa Cruz de Tenerife, Spain: Idea, 2010.

_____. "El enigma Sandoval y otros "enigmas" militares españoles: Bayo, Giroud, Rodríguez Lozano ..." In *La masonería española en la época de Sagasta (1825-1903)*, edited by José Antonio Ferrer Benimeli, 1:545–570. Zaragoza, Spain: CEHME and the Fundación Práxedes Mateo-Sagasta, 2006).

_____. "España, Cuba y Marruecos. Masonería, identidades y construcción nacional." In *Anuario de Estudios Atlánticos* 55 (2009): 273–310.

_____. "Españolismo versus separatismo en la masonería puertorriqueña: la logia Borinquen nº 81 de Mayagüez (1889–1897)." *Boletín Millares Caro* 4, no. 7–8 (1985): 199–227.

_____. "Hipótesis en torno a un desarrollo paralelo de la masonería canaria y cubana durante el primer tercio del presente siglo. Acotación para un estudio." *IV Coloquio de Historia Canario-Americana*, 2:567–602. Las Palmas, Spain: Cabildo Insular de Gran Canaria, 1982.

_____. "Luis Felipe Gómez Wangüemert y la masonería palmera y cubana de la década de 1930. Notas para un estudio." In *II Jornadas de Estudios Canarias América*, 29–63. Santa Cruz de Tenerife, España, 1981.

_____. *Martí, España y la Masonería*. Santa Cruz de Tenerife, Spain: Idea, 2008.

_____. "Masonería española y emancipación colonial." In *La Masonería en España. Memoria y razón*, 59–79. Barcelona: Ed. mra, 2009. Also in: *Zeitschrift für Internationale Freimaurer-Forschung* 7, no. 13 (2005): 79–92.

_____. "La masonería y la pérdida de las colonias: impresiones sobre el caso cubano." In *Masonería Española y América*, edited by José Antonio Ferrer Benimeli, 2:1107–1126. Zaragoza, Spain: CEHME, 1993.

_____. "Masones y anticlericales en Luis F. Gómez Wangüemert." In *La Masonería Española entre Europa y América*, edited by José Antonio Ferrer Benimeli, 1:453–468. Zaragoza: CEHME, 1995. Also in: *Masones en el Atlántico*, 2:155–176. (Santa Cruz de Tenerife, Spain: Idea, 2010).

_____. "La muerte de José Martí: un debate historiográfico." *Cuadernos de Investigación. Brocar* 17 (1990): 7–21/ *El Caimán Barbudo* (Havana: n.p., 1990): 10–14.

_____. "Los residentes españoles en Cuba y la masonería después de la independencia." *Cuadernos de Investigación Histórica* 10 (1986): 41–56.

_____. *Wangüemert y Cuba*. La Laguna, Cuba: Centro de Cultura Popular Canaria, 1991.

_____. "Wangüemert y la masonería palmera y cubana 1930." In *Masones en el Atlántico*, 2:123–154. Santa Cruz de Tenerife, Spain: Idea, 2010.

Paz Sánchez, Manuel de, and José Manuel Castellano. "Martí, masón y otras crónicas wangüemertianas." In *Masonería Española y América*, edited by José Antonio Ferrer Benimeli, 2:671–688. Zaragoza, Spain: CEHME, 1993.

Paz Soldan, Mariano F. "La Logia Lautaro." In *Historia del Perú independiente*, 228–232. Lima: n.p., 1868–70.

Pelúas, Daniel. *El ojo que todo lo ve. Ritos, símbolos y lenguajes de la masonería / Para entender a las logias uruguayas*. Montevideo: Fin de Siglo, 2012.

Pérez Fontana, Daoiz. "La Masonería y los masones en la organización de la República. Apuntes para la historia." Montevideo, Uruguay, s/d, unpublished.

Pérez Vila, Manuel. *La experiencia masónica de Bolívar en París*. Caracas: Pesquiven, 1983.

Pereira, Eduardo Carlos. *A maçonaria e a igreja cristã*. Sao Paulo: Livraria Independiente, 1945.

Pereira Henriquez, Oscar, Uwe Kramp de Negri, and Jorge Carvajal Muñoz. *Universidad La República*. Santiago, Chile: Univ. La República, 1996.

Pereira, Miguel A. "La modernidad en el periodismo masónico puertorriqueño del siglo XIX." *Acacia* (January–March 2009): 4–32.

Pereira, Nilo. *Conflitos entre a Igreja e o Estado no Brasil*. Recife: Universidade Federal de Pernambuco, 1970.

_____. *Dom Vital e a questão religiosa no Brasil*. Recife: Imprensa Universitária, 1966.

Pérez Escutia, Ramón Alonso. "Los orígenes de la Masonería en Michoacán, 1821–1834." In *Liberalismo, Masonería e Independencias en Hispanoamérica*, edited by Moisés Guzmán Pérez. Morelia, Mexico, in press.

Pérez Marchand, M. L. *Dos etapas ideológicas del siglo XVIII en México a través de los papeles de la Inquisición*. Mexico City: n.p., 1945.

Pérez Vila, Manuel. "La experiencia masónica de Bolívar en París." In *Visión diversa de Bolívar (Ciclo de conferencias en homenaje al Libertador con motivo del bicentenario de su natalicio)*. Caracas: Pequiven, 1983.

Perramón, Edgar. *Breve Historia de la Masonería en Venezuela*. Caracas: Talleres Tipográficos Cultural, 1997.

Piccirelli, Ricardo. *San Martín y la política de los pueblos*. Buenos Aires: Ed. Gure, 1957.

Picón, Mariano. *Miranda*. Caracas: Monte Avila, 1997.

Piedra Solano, Arturo. "Notas sobre la relación entre liberalismo, francmasonería y penetración protestante en Centroamérica." In *Protestantes, liberales y francmasones. Sociedades de ideas y modernidad en América Latina, siglo XIX*, edited by Jean Pierre Bastian, 119–131. México: Fondo de Cultura Económica, 1990.

Pinto Lagaride, Fernando. *La masonería, su influencia en Chile*. Santiago, Chile: Orbe, 1973.

Piñeiro y Del Cueto, Carlos M. *La ideología martiana frente a la doctrina comunista*. San Juan, Puerto Rico: n.p., 1979.

_____. *Mensaje Anual (del 22 de marzo 1959)*. Havana: n.p., 1959.

Piñuela García, Dionisio, Cristina Vicente López, and Mª Natividad Ortiz Albear. "Fuentes para el estudio de la masonería antillana conservadas en el A.H.N., Sección 'Guerra Civil.'" In *La Masonería Española y la crisis colonial del 98*, edited by José Antonio Ferrer Benimeli, 2:839–848. Zaragoza, Spain: CEHME, 1999.

Pizarro Llorente, Henar. "La represión de la masonería en el Tribunal del Santo Oficio de Cartagena de Indias a prin-cipios del siglo XIX." In *La Masonería Española entre Europa y América*, edited by José Antonio Ferrer Benimeli, 1:53–72. Zaragoza: CEHME, 1995.

Polanco, Hugo. *La Masonería en la República Dominicana*. Santo Domingo, Dominican Republic: Universidad Católica Madre y Maestra, 1985.

Polanco Alcántara, Tomás. *Miranda, el Precursor. Bello el maestro de primer orden*. Madrid: Embajada de Venezuela, 1973.

Polo Friz, Luigi. "Albert A. Goodall, un enviado especial del Supremo Consejo de Boston al mundo masónico sudamericano y europeo en la segunda mitad del siglo XIX." In *Masonería Española y América*, edited by José Antonio Ferrer Benimeli, 2:763–774. Zaragoza, Spain: CEHME, 1993.

Ponte Domínguez, Francisco J. *El delito de francmasonería en Cuba: estudio histórico acerca de la alianza del altar y el trono, su persecución de la francmasonería en Cuba*. Mexico City: n.p., 1951.

_____. *Historia de la Masonería del Rito Escocés en Cuba*. Havana: Impr. Institución M. Inclan, 1961.

_____. *Historia de la Masonería Salvadoreña*. Sonsonate, El Salvador: Imprenta Excélsior, 1962.

Porset, Charles. "La Francmasonería en Santo Domingo (siglos XVIII–XIX)." In *Masonería Española y América*, edited by José Antonio Ferrer Benimeli, 1:191–204. Zaragoza, Spain: CEHME, 1993.

Pozuelo Andrés, Yván. "La historiografía masónica latinoamericanista actual. Presente y futuro." *200 años de Iberoamérica (1810–2010). Congreso Internacional. Actas del XIV Encuentro de Latinoamericanistas Españoles*, edited by Eduardo Rey Tristán and Patricia Calvo González, 281–288. Santiago de Compostela: Universidad de Santiago de Compostela, 2010. halshs. archives-ouvertes.fr/docs/00/52/92/98/ PDF/AT4_Pozuelo.pdf

_____. "Masonería en los periódicos digitales hispanoamericanos (2006–2007)." *REHMLAC* 1, no. 1 (May–No-vember 2009): 247–260. https:// revistas.ucr.ac.cr/index.php/rehmlac/ article/view/6866/6553

_____. "La masonería: ¿una organización discreta?" *Taller de Ediciones. La historia sin "buenos" y "malos,"* April 20, 2008. talleredeciones. com/cuza/modules.php?name =News&file=article&sid=309

_____. "La masonería: ¿una organización discreta? Cuestión de definición." *REHMLAC* 1, no. 2 (December 2009–April 2010): 62–87. https://revistas.ucr.ac.cr/index.php/rehmlac/article/view/6618/6307

_____. "Una muestra de famosos escritores liberales antimasones." *Revista de Arte, Historia y Literatura* 35 (2009). actuallynotes.com/Una-muestra -de-famosos-escritores-liberales-antimasones.html

_____. "Los nombres simbólicos hispanoamericanos como fuente de información de la identidad proyectada de los masones transatlánticos sobre sí mismos: el caso de los asturianos (siglos XIX–XX)." Paper presented at the III Symposium de historia las masonerías y las sociedades patrióticas latinoamericanas y caribeñas: Masonería, Independencia, Revolución y Secularización, Universidad Nacional Autónoma de México, Museo Nacional de Arte, Recinto de homenaje a don Benito Juárez del Palacio Nacional, Centro de Estudios Históricos de la Masonería Latinoamericana y Caribeña, Grupo México, Mexico City, December 2–4, 2010.

_____. "Notas sobre el "nombre simbólico" en Hispanoamérica." *REHMLAC* 3, no. 2 (December 2011–April 2012): 206–242. https://revistas.ucr.ac.cr/index.php/rehmlac/article/view/6581/6272

_____. "Presentación del debate "Masonería y Política" de Managua 2010." *REHMLAC* 4, no. 1 (May–November 2012): 158–188. https://revistas.ucr.ac.cr/index.php/rehmlac/article/view/12147/11422

_____. "Las relaciones masónicas entre Asturias e Hispanoamérica en los siglos XIX y XX. Estado de la cuestión." *REHMLAC* 1, no. 1 (May–November 2009): 261–281. https://revistas.ucr.ac.cr/index.php/rehmlac/article/view/6867/6554

_____. "Relaciones y opiniones oficiales de las masonerías españolas sobre Iberoamérica durante la II República (1931–1935)." *REHMLAC* 2, no. 2 (December 2010–April 2011): 123–150. https://revistas.ucr.ac.cr/index.php/rehmlac/article/view/6600/6291

Prien, Hans-Jürgen. "Protestantismo, Liberalismo y Francmasonería en América Latina durante el siglo XIX: Problemas de investigación." In *Protestantes, liberales y francmasones. Sociedades de ideas y modernidad en América Latina, siglo XIX*, edited by Jean Pierre Bastian, 15–23. Mexico City: Fondo de Cultura Económica, 1990.

Prober, Kurt. *Cadastro geral das Lojas Maçônicas do Brasil*. Paquetá, Brazil: n.p., 1975.

_____. *Catalogo das Duas Maiores Coleçoes de Medalhas Maçônicas Brasileiras. Coleção Eureka e Coleção Gonçalves Ledo*. Rio de Janeiro: n.p., 1988.

_____. *Catalogo das Medalhas Maçônico-Brasileiras*. Rio de Janeiro: n.p., 1989.

_____. "História do Supremo Conselho do Rito Escocés Antigo e Aceito no Brasil." *O Aprendiz: Boletim Informativo da Loja Duque de Caxias* (1979).

Ramírez Benito, Penélope. "El exilio republicano en Chile. Antonio de Lezama, escritor, periodista y masón." In *La Masonería Española: Represión y Exilios*, edited by José Antonio Ferrer Benimeli, 1:767–776. Zaragoza, Spain:

CEHME, 2010.

_____. "La masonería postsagastina: el caso de Antonio de Lezama (1882–1971)." In *La masonería española en la época de Sagasta*, 1:637–650. Zaragoza, Spain: Gobierno de Aragón, 2007.

Ramos Gómez Pérez, Luis. *Bibliografía masónica en bibliotecas de la ciudad de México*. Mexico City: UNAM, 1990.

Ramsay, Allison Olivia. "The Roots/Routes of the Ancient Order of Foresters in the Anglophone Caribbean with Special Emphasis on Barbados." *History in Action* 2, no. 1 (2011): 1–13.

Randouyer, Françoise. "Fondos documentales de la masonería española en la Biblioteca Nacional de París." In *La Masonería en la Historia de España*, edited by José Antonio Ferrer Benimeli, 359–364. Zaragoza, Spain: Gobierno de Aragón, 1985.

_____. "Ideología masónica a través de los nombres simbólicos." In *La masonería en la España del siglo XIX*, edited by José Antonio Ferrer Benimeli, 1:425–439. Salamanca, Spain: Junta de Castilla y León, 1987.

_____. "Les noms symboliques des Maçons espagnols." In *Chroniques d'histoire maçonnique* 29–30 (1982) : 56–61.

Rangel, Nicolás. *Los precursores ideológicos de la guerra de Independencia: la masonería en México, siglo XVIII*. Mexico City: Publicaciones del Archivo General de la Nación, 1932.

Raynaud De La Ferrerie, Serge. *El libro negro de la Francmasonería*. Lima: Ed. Nueva Era, 1981.

Redondo Díaz, Fernando. "La prensa militar y el papel de la masonería en ultramar." In *La Masonería Española y la crisis colonial del 98*, edited by José Antonio Ferrer Benimeli, 2:711–716. Zaragoza, Spain: CEHME, 1999.

Rego Mello, Mario C. de. "A Maçoneria no Brasil." In *Livro maçônico do centenario*. Rio de Janeiro: Ed. Octaviano Bastos, 1922.

Renault, Agnès. Los francmasones franceses de la jurisdicción de Cuba a principios del siglo XIX." *REHMLAC* 1, no. 1 (May–November 2009): 59–72. https://revistas.ucr.ac.cr/index.php/rehmlac/article/view/6857/6544

———. "La influencia de la masonería francesa en el Departamento Oriental de Cuba en los años veinte del siglo XIX. Los aportes de la prosopografía." *REHMLAC* 1, no. 1 (May–November 2009): 74–89. https://revistas.ucr.ac.cr/index.php/rehmlac/article/view/6856/6543

———. "L'influence de la franc-maçonnerie française dans le Département Oriental de Cuba dans les années 1820—Les apports de la prosopographie." *REHMLAC* 1, no. 1 (May–November 2009): 74–89. https://revistas.ucr.ac.cr/index.php/rehmlac/article/view/6856/26721

Restrepo Canal, Carlos. *Informe sobre la Masonería y la Independencia*. Bogotá: n.p., 1959.

Revauger, Cécile. "Freemasonry in Barbados, Trinidad and Grenada: British or Homemade?" *Journal for Research into Freemasonry and Fraternalism* 1, no. 1 (March 2010): 79–93.

Reverón García, Eloy Enrique. *Crisis de la masonería venezolana (siglo XX)*. Caracas: Instituto de Altos Estudios Diplomáticos "Pedro Gual," 1995.

———. "El fantasma de Bolívar en la masonería venezolana" en *Bolivarium*, N VI, Sartenejas, U.S.B., 1997.

———. *El fantasma de Bolívar en la masonería venezolana*. Caracas: Publicaciones Monfort S.A., 2001.

———. *Influjos masónicos en la instauración del matrimonio civil en Venezuela (1867–1877)*. Caracas: Ed. Masones Unidos, 1990.

———. *Influjos masónicos en la instauración del matrimonio civil, y registros civiles para macimientos, matrimonios y defunciones*. Caracas: Academia Nacional de la Historia, 1988.

———. *Masonería desnuda*. Caracas: Ed. IVEM, 1994.

———. "Masonería en Venezuela, 1850–1867." Undergraduate dissertation, Universidad Central de Venezuela, Caracas, Venezuela, 1992.

———. "Memoria masónica de Venezuela." In *Historia para todos* 17 (1996).

_____. "Mito y realidad en la historiografía masónica (1808–1830)." *Anuario de Estudios Bolivarianos* 4 (1995).

Rich, Paul John. "Civil Society and Freemasonry: The Cardenista Rite and Mexico" (2002).

_____. "Kim and the Magic House: Freemasonry and Kipling." In *Secret Texts: The Literature of Secret Societies Marie M. Roberts y Hugh Ormsby-Lennon.* New York: AMS Press, 1995.

_____. "Mexican Freemasonry and Porfirism." *The Philalethes* 48, no. 1 (1995).

_____. "Mexican Grand Masters and Presidents." *The Philalethes* 48, no. 1 (1995).

_____. "The Mexican Viceroy's French Cooks: Masonic Mysteries in the Palace Kitchens." *The Scottish Rite Research Society* 16, no. 1 (2009).

_____. "Reapraising Scottist Rite Freemasonry in Latin America." *Heredom* 4 (1995): 241–268.

Rich, Paul John, and Antonio Lara. "The Mystery of Matthew Carrey: Continuing Adventures in Masonic Bibliography." *Heredom: The Transactions of the Scottish Rite Research Society* 8 (1999–2000): 219–223.

Rich, Paul John, and Guillermo de los Reyes Heredia. "Mexican Freemasonry. The Devil's Government." *The Philalethes* 47, no. 6 (1994).

_____. "Towards a Revisionist view of Poinsett: Problems in the Historiography of Mexican Freemasonry, Part II." *The Philalethes: Journal of the Philethes Society* (1995): 1–5.

_____, and Guillermo De los Reyes Heredia. "Freemasonry's Educational Role." *American Behavioral Scientist* 40 (1997): 957–967.

Rich, Paul John, Guillermo De los Reyes Heredia, and Antonio Lara. "Smuggling Masonic Books to Mexico." In *Freemasonry in Context: History, Ritual and Controversy.* New York: Lexigton Books, 2003.

_____. "Smuggling Masonic Books to Mexico." In *Freemasonry in Context: History, Ritual and Controversy,* edited by Arturo de Hoyos and S. Brent Morris. New York: Lexington Books, 2003.

Rodríguez Carrasco, Pedro. "El problema de las sectas: criterios para una aproximación analítica." *Ciencias Religiosas* 14 (2005): 43–62.

Rodríguez Dobles, Esteban. "Conflictos en torno a las representaciones sociales del alma y los milagros. La confrontación entre la Iglesia Católica y la Sociedad Teosófica en Costa Rica (1904–1917)." *REHMLAC* 2, no. 2 (December 2010–April 2011): 85–110. https://revistas.ucr.ac.cr/index.php/rehmlac/article/view/6598/6289

Rodríguez Jiménez, Carlos. "La Francmasonería en Venezuela." In *Vida y acción en varios mundos*, 63–85. Caracas: Gráficas Acea, 1990.

Rodríguez Lettieri, Mª Elena. "El exilio español en la Primera República y la masonería argentina." In en *La Masonería Española: Represión y Exilios*, edited by José Antonio Ferrer Benimeli, 1:117–136. Zaragoza, Spain: CEHME, 2010.

"La masonería española en la República argentina (1890–1931)." In *La masonería española en la época de Sagasta (1825–1903)*, edited by José Antonio Ferrer Benimeli, 1:747–774. Zaragoza, Spain: CEHME and the Fundación Práxedes Mateo-Sagasta, 2006.

Rojas, Rafael. *La escritura de la independencia. El surgimiento de la oposición pública en México*. Mexico City: Taurus, 2003.

_____. "Una maldición silenciada. El panfleto político en el México independiente." *Historia Mexicana* 47, no. 1 (July–September 1997): 35–67.

_____. *La nueva sociabilidad: facciones parlamentarias, grupos de opinión y logias masónicas en los orígenes de México*. Mexico City: n.p., 1998.

Romero, Celestino. *Raíz histórica de la masonería en Venezuela*. Caracas: Empresa El Cojo, 1957.

Romeu Beltrán, Jorge Luis. "Challenges and Characteristics of Cuban Freema- sons in the 20th Century: A Demographic Approach." Paper presented at the International Conference on American and Latin American Freemasonry: A New Past and a New Future— Freemasonry and Civil Society Program of the History Department of the University of California at Los Angeles (UCLA), The Grand Lodge of California, California's Institute for Masonic Studies, Los Angeles, December 3, 2011.

_____. "Estudios estadísticos del auge y declive de la Gran Logia de Cuba (1945–1980)." *REHMLAC* 3, no. 2 (December 2011–April 2012): 157–184. https://revistas.ucr.ac.cr/index.php/rehmlac/article/view/6579/6270

Romo, Manuel. "Concepción y sus primeras logias, 1856–1810." Unpublished.

_____. *¿Fue masón el Papa Pío IX?* Santiago, Chile: Aposthropes, 2011.

_____. "El masón Ventura Blanco Encalada (1782–1856)." *Archivo Masónico* 23 (2011).

Rotjer, Aníbal A. *La Masonería en la Argentina y en el mundo*. Buenos Aires: n.p., 1973.

Rubio Sánchez, Manuel. "La influencia de la masonería en la vida política del reino de Guatemala. Primera parte (1717–1821)." *Anales de la Academia de Geografía e Historia de Guatemala* 68 (1994): 71–98.

Ruiz y Ruiz, Raúl A. "La logia Lautaro

y la Independencia de América." *Revista de la Junta Provincial de Estudios Históricos* 15 (1946): 73–82.

Ruiz Sánchez, José Leonardo. "Independentismo y sociedades secretas en Cuba bajo el reinado de Fernando VII." In *Masonería Española y América*, edited by José Antonio Ferrer Benimeli, 1:147–159. Zaragoza, Spain: CEHME, 1993.

Sabater i Pie, Joan. "La crisis del 98 en la filatelia masónica." In *La Masonería Española y la crisis colonial del 98*, edited by José Antonio Ferrer Benimeli, 1:159–175. Zaragoza, Spain: CEHME, 1999.

_____. "Sociedad, Masonería y Filatelia. Historia de la filatelia masónica mundial." In *La Masonería española en el 2000. Una revisión histórica*, edited by José Antonio Ferrer Benimeli, 2:1001–1026. Zaragoza, Spain: Gobierno de Aragón, Departamento de Educación, Cultura y Deporte, 2001.

Sala, Céline. "Los archivos del desengaño: Las luces y el mundo de las fuentes "ultra marinas." *REHMLAC* 2, no. 2 (December 2010–April 2011): 111–122. https://revistas.ucr.ac.cr/index.php/rehmlac/article/view/6599/6290

Salazar Páez, Antonio. "Historia de la Gran Logia Unida Mexicana." In *Logia de Estudios e Investigaciones Duque de Wharton nº 18. G.L.E.* (1996–1997): 289–296.

Salcedo, José. *Miranda (1781–1981).* Caracas: Italgráfica, 1981.

Salcedo Bastardo, Luis. *Simón Bolívar. La vita e il pensiero político.* Rome: Enciclopedia Italiana, 1983.

Salsamendi, Miguel. *Crónicas del levantamiento de Columnas de las logias nacidas bajo la jurisdicción masónica uruguaya y datos biográficos de sus fundadores, desde el 21 de enero de 1830 al 30 de junio de 2000.* Montevideo: n.p., 2001.

Sanabria Martínez, Víctor Manuel. *Los orígenes de la Masonería en Costa Rica. Documentos Históricos de la Masonería Centroamericana.* San José, Costa Rica: n.p., 1928.

Sánchez Ferré, Pere. "Del exilio a la resistencia. Las logias Luis Companys." In en *La Masonería Española: Represión y Exilios*, edited by José Antonio Ferrer Benimeli, 2:1131–1149. Zaragoza, Spain: CEHME, 2010.

_____. "La maçonerie catalana i el conflicte colonial a Cuba al darrer del segle XIX." *Primeres Jornades d'Estudis Catalano-Americans* (1985): 241–255. Also in: *L'Avenç* 76 (1984): 62–69.

_____. "Masonería y colonialismo español." In *La masonería y su impacto internacional*, 11–26. Madrid: Universidad Complutense de Madrid, 1989.

Sánchez Gálvez, Samuel. "Ciencia y cultura en Fernandina de Jagua." *REHMLAC, Revista de Estudios Históricos de la Masonería Latinoamericana y Caribeña*

1, no. 1 (May–November 2009): 172–190. https://revistas.ucr.ac.cr/index.php/rehmlac/article/view/6862/6549

_____. "Institucionalización de la masonería en Cienfuegos." *REHMLAC, Revista de Estudios Históricos de la Masonería Latinoamericana y Caribeña* 1, no. 1 (May–November 2009): 191–211. https://revistas.ucr.ac.cr/index.php/rehmlac/article/view/6863/6550

_____. *Legados perdurables: masonería en Cienfuegos (1878–1902)*. Cienfuegos, Cuba: Ed. Mercurio, 2010.

_____. "La logia masónica cienfueguera Fernandina de Jagua (1878–1902). Un estudio de caso." Doctoral dissertation, Universidad Carlos Rafael Rodríguez de Cienfuegos, Cuba, 2010.

_____. "La logia masónica cienfueguera Fernandina de Jagua (1878–1902). Un estudio de caso." *REHMLAC, Revista de Estudios Históricos de la Masonería Latinoamericana y Caribeña* 2, no. 1 (May–November 2010): 85–92. rehmlac.com/recursos/vols/v2/n1/rehmlac.vol2.n1-ssanchez.pdf

_____. *Martí ciñó el mandil. Prueba documental de su filiación masónica*. Havana: Ediciones Bachiller, 2007.

_____. "Los nombres simbólicos en la logia masónica cienfueguera Fernandina de Jagua: expresiones de pensamiento." *Anuario 2007* (Cienfuegos, Cuba, 2007).

_____. "Los nombres simbólicos en la logia masónica cienfueguera Fernandina de Jagua. 1878–1902." *Universidad y Sociedad* 2, no. 2 (2007): 45–47.

Sánchez Hita, Beatriz. *Los periódicos del Cádiz de la Guerra de la Independencia (1808–1814). Catálogo comentado*. Cádiz: Diputación de Cádiz, 2008.

Sánchez, Juan Francisco. *Historia sintética de la Masonería Dominicana*. Ciudad Trujillo, Dominican Republic: Ed. Montalvo, 1998.

Sánchez Montoya, Francisco. "La represión al catedrático Manuel Martínez Pedroso, masón, diputado por Ceuta y miembro de las Cortes en el exilio mexicano." In *La Masonería Española: Represión y Exilios*, edited by José Antonio Ferrer Benimeli, 1:777–784. Zaragoza, Spain: CEHME, 2010.

Sánchez Solano, Esteban. "La identificación del desarticulador del mundo católico: el liberalismo, la masonería y el protestantismo en la prensa católica en Costa Rica (1880–1900)." *REHMLAC* 2, no. 2 (December 2010–April 2011): 34–52. https://revistas.ucr.ac.cr/index.php/rehmlac/article/view/6595/6286

Santos, Fernanda, and José Eduardo Franco. "A insustentável leveza das fronteiras: Clero Católico na Maçonaria e a questão do Anticlericalismo e do Antimaçonismo em Portugal." *REHMLAC* 2, no. 2 (December 2010–April 2011): 53–65. https://revistas.ucr.ac.cr/index.php/rehmlac/article/view/6596/6287

Santos Molano, Enrique. *Antonio Na-*

riño, *filósofo revolucionario*. Bogotá: n.p., 1999.

Sappez, Delphine. "Antonio Govin y Torres: nexo entre masonería y autonomismo en Cuba." In *La Masonería Española: Represión y Exilios*, edited by José Antonio Ferrer Benimeli, 1:559–572. Zaragoza, Spain: CEHME, 2010.

Saunier, Eric. *Encyclopédie de la Franc-maçonnerie*. Rome : La Tipografica Varese S.p.A., 2000.

_____. "L'espace caribéen : un enjeu de pouvoir pour la francmaçonnerie française." *REHMLAC* 1, no. 1 (May–November 2009) : 41–56. https://revistas.ucr.ac.cr/index.php/rehmlac/article/view/6855/6542

_____. "El espacio caribeño: un reto de poder para la francmasonería francesa." *REHMLAC* 1, no. 1 (May–November 2009): 42–58. https://revistas.ucr.ac.cr/index.php/rehmlac/article/view/6855/26720

_____. "La prosopografia, una vía para la historia de la masonería." *REHMLAC* 1, no. 2 (December 2009–April 2010): 37–43. https://revistas.ucr.ac.cr/index.php/rehmlac/article/view/6616/6305

_____. "La prosopographie : une nouvelle voie pour l'histoire de la Franc-maçonnerie." *REHMLAC* 1, no. 2 (December 2009–April 2010) : 37–43. https://revistas.ucr.ac.cr/index.php/rehmlac/article/view/6616/26723

Scardino, Humberto, and Luis Pérez

Martela. *Biografías Masónicas*. Montevideo: n.p., 1991.

Seal-Coon, Frederic W. *An Historical Account of Jamaican Freemasonry*. Kingston: n.p., 1976.

_____. "La isla de Jamaica y su influencia masónica en la región." In *Masonería Española y América*, edited by José Antonio Ferrer Benimeli, 1:205–226. Zaragoza, Spain: CEHME, 1993.

_____. "The Island of Jamaica and Its Regional Masonic Influence." *Ars Quatuor Coronatorum* 104 (1991): 165–178.

_____. "La Mítica masonería de Francisco de Miranda." In *La masonería española entre Europa y América*, edited by José Antonio Ferrer Benimeli, 1:107–126. *Zaragoza, Spain: CEHME*, 1995. Also in: *Logia de Estudios e Investigación Duque de Wharton* 18 (1996–1997): 245–268.

_____. "Simon Bolívar, Freemason." *Ars Quatuor Coronatorum* 90 (1978): 231–248; 92 (1979): 202–215.

_____. *Spanish-American Revolutionary Masonry. The Mythical Masonry of Francisco de Miranda*. London: n.p., 1981.

_____. "Wellwood Hyslop-Jamaican Freemason." *Ars Quatuor Coronatorum* 89 (1976): 92–112.

Sepúlveda Chavarría, Manuel. *Crónicas de la Masonería Chilena (1750–1944)*. Santiago, Chile: Ed. de la G.L. de Chile, 1994.

Sepúlveda Muñoz, Isidro. "Hostos y Martí: Análisis comparado de los nacionalismos antillanos finiseculares." In *La Masonería Española y la crisis colonial del 98*, edited by José Antonio Ferrer Benimeli, 1:303–324. Zaragoza, Spain: CEHME, 1999.

Sievens Irizarry, Otto. "La masonería vista por autores puertorriqueños." *Acacia* (July–September 2010): 8–25.

Silva, Eduardo. *Historia de la masonería en el Perú*. Lima: n.p., 1966.

Silva, Joao Nepomuceno. "En torno da abolição." *A Trolha* 18, no. 35 (May–June 1988): 63 et seq.

Silva Mendes, Asdrúbal. "A Abolição." *A Trolha* 18, no. 35 (May–June 1988): 45 et seq.

Silveira, José Luiz. *Revelações Históricas da Maçonaria*. Santa María, Brazil: n.p., 1985.

Soler, Mariano. *La Masonería y el catolicismo*. Montevideo: Ed. Andrés Rius, 1884.

Soucy, Dominique. "La diffusion des concepts maçonniques dans la société cubaine du XIXe siècle." (Etudes Hispaniques et Latinoaméricaines, Université Paris VII, France, 1999).

_____. "Hacia una mediología de la masonería cubana." In en *La Masonería española en el 2000. Una revisión histórica*, edited by José Antonio Ferrer Benimeli, 2:993–1000. Zaragoza, Spain: Gobierno de Aragón, Departamento de Educación, Cultura y Deporte, 2001.

_____. "Intervención del Gran Oriente de Francia en la historia de la masonería cubana." In *La masonería española en la época de Sagasta (1825–1903)*, edited by José Antonio Ferrer Benimeli, 1:693–700. Zaragoza, Spain: CEHME and the Fundación Práxedes Mateo-Sagasta, 2006.

_____. *Masonería y nación (1811–1902). Redes masónicas y políticas en la construcción identitaria cubana*. Santa Cruz de Tenerife, Spain: Ediciones Idea, 2006.

_____. "El Palenque Literario": Un testimonio de la realidad masónica de Cuba (1876–1883)." In *La Masonería en Madrid y en España del siglo XVIII al XXI*, edited by José Antonio Ferrer Benimeli, 1:535–550. Zaragoza, Spain: CEHME, 2004.

_____. "Vicente Antonio de Castro y la opción reformista: desde 'La Cartera Cubana' hasta Yara." In *La Masonería española. Represión y exilios*, edited by José Antonio Ferrer Benimeli, 1:411–422. Zaragoza, Spain: CEHME, Gobierno de Aragón, Departamento de Educación, Cultura y Deporte, 2011.

Soucy, Dominique, and Delphine Sappez. "Autonomismo y masonería en Cuba." *REHMLAC* 1, no. 1 (May–November 2009): 90–99. https://revistas.ucr.ac.cr/index.php/rehmlac/article/view/6858/6545

Spencer Robertson, William. "Francisco de Miranda and the Revolutionizing of Spanish America." *American Historical Association Report* (1907): 189–540.

_____. *La vida de Miranda.* Caracas: Academia Nacional de la Historia, 2006.

Stolper, Edward. "More ligth on Simon Bolívar, Freemason." *Ars Quatuor Coronatorum* 92 (1979): 202–205.

Subero, Efrain. "Bibliografía masónica de Venezuela." In *La masonería en Venezuela*, 1:41–88. Caracas: Gran Logia República Venezuela, n.d.

_____. "La Masonería como origen de la Independencia de Venezuela." In *La masonería en Venezuela*, 1:17–38. Caracas: Gran Logia República Venezuela, n.d.

_____. *La masonería en Venezuela.* Caracas: Gran Logia República Venezuela, 2000.

Supremo Consejo Centroamericano. *Constitución del Gran Oriente y Supremo Consejo Centro Americano.* San José, Costa Rica: Imprenta de la Paz, 1871.

Tacón, Laurence. *Simon Bolívar.* Paris : L'Herne, 1986.

Tavares Barbosa, Antonio Carlos. "Os primordios da Maçonaria Brasileira [Crítica al trabajo del mismo título de Rizzardo da Camino]." In *Formação Histórica da Maçonaria*, 87–101. Rio de Janeiro: Ed. Esperanto, 1983.

Tellez-Cuevas, Rodolfo. "La masonería en el proceso de formación del estado laico mexicano." Paper presented at the III Symposium de historia las masonerías y las sociedades patrióticas latinoamericanas y caribeñas: Masonería, Independencia, Revolución y Secularización, Universidad Nacional Autónoma de México, Museo Nacional de Arte, Recinto de homenaje a don Benito Juárez del Palacio Nacional, Centro de Estudios Históricos de la Masonería Latinoamericana y Caribeña, Grupo México, Mexico City, December 2–4, 2010.

_____. *El papel de la masonería en la política y la administración mexicana.* Toluca, Mexico: Instituto de Administración Pública del Estado de México, 2009.

Thornton, Sister Mary Crescentia. *The Church and Freemasonry in Brazil, 1872–1875: A Study in Regalism.* Washington, DC: The Catholic University of America Press, 1948.

Timmons, Wilbert H. "Los Guadalupes. A Secret Society in the Mexican Revolution for Independence." *Hispanic American Historical Review* 30, no. 4 (1950): 453–479.

Tonelli, Armando. *El general San Martín y la masonería.* Buenos Aires: Talleres Gráficos A Arcelta, 1943.

Torre Villar, Ernesto de la, ed. *Los Guadalupes y la independencia, con una selección de documentos inéditos.* Mexico City: Jus, 1985.

Torres Cuevas, Eduardo. "El 98, Cuba y la masonería cubana." In *La masonería española y la crisis colonial del 98*, edited by José Antonio Ferrer Benimeli, 2:1089–1114. Zaragoza, Spain: CEHME, 1999.

_____. *El alma visible de Cuba: José Martí y el partido revolucionario cubano*. Havana: Ed. Ciencias Sociales, 1984.

_____. "Los cuerpos masónicos cubanos durante el siglo XIX." In *Masonería española y América*, edited by José Antonio Ferrer Benimeli, 1:229–256. Zaragoza, Spain: CEHME, 1993.

_____. "El Gran Oriente de Cuba y las Antillas y la ruptura del 68." In *Historia de la masonería cubana. Seis ensayos*, 84–101. Havana: Imagen Contemporánea, 2005.

_____. *Historia de Cuba 1868–1898*. Havana: Editorial Política, 1994–1996.

_____. *Historia de la masonería cubana. Seis ensayos*. Havana: Imagen Contemporánea, 2005.

_____. "José Martí y la masonería española." In *Historia de la masonería cubana. Seis ensayos*, 247–283. Havana: Imagen Contemporánea, 2005.

_____. "La masonería cubana en las décadas finales del siglo XIX: escenario y alternativas ante el nuevo milenio." In *La masonería española en el 2000. Una revisión histórica*, edited by José Antonio Ferrer Benimeli, 1:185–206. Zaragoza, Spain: Gobierno de Aragón, Departamento de Educación, Cultura y Deporte, 2001.

_____. *La masonería en Cuba durante la Primera República (1902–1933)*. Havana: n.p., 1991.

_____. "Masonerías en Cuba durante el siglo XIX." *REHMLAC* 3, no. 2 (December 2011–April 2012): 65–104. https://revistas.ucr.ac.cr/index.php/rehmlac/article/view/6576/6267

_____. "Origins and Development of Freemasonry in Cuba." Paper presented at the International Conference on American and Latin American Freemasonry: A New Past and a New Future, Freemasonry and Civil Society Program of the History Department of the University of California at Los Angeles (UCLA), The Grand Lodge of California, California's Institute for Masonic Studies, Los Angeles, December 3, 2011.

_____. "Presencia republicana española en Cuba." In *La Masonería Española: Represión y Exilios*, edited by José Antonio Ferrer Benimeli, 1:327–335. Zaragoza, Spain: CEHME, 2010.

_____. "Sagasta, Cuba y las masonerías cubana y española." In *La masonería española en la época de Sagasta (1825–1903)*, edited by José Antonio Ferrer Benimeli, 1:681–692. Zaragoza, Spain: CEHME and the Fundación Práxedes Mateo-Sagasta, 2006.

Torres Puga, Gabriel. "Centinela mexicano contra Francmasones. Un enredo detectivesco del licenciado Borunda en las causas judiciales contra franceses de 1794." *Estudios de Historia Novohispana* 33 (July–December 2005): 57–94.

Treviño Montemayor, Rebeca. "Historiografía de la masonería en México." *Ciencia y Arte* 7 (1991): 153–169.

Trueba Lara, José Luis. *Masones en México. Historia del poder oculto.* Mexico City: n.p., 2007.

Urbina Gaitán, Chester. "Teosofía, intelectuales y sociedad en Costa Rica (1908–1929)." *Revista de Ciencias Sociales* 88 (2000): 139–144.

Urias Horcasitas, Beatriz. *De moral y regeneración: el programa de "ingeniería social" postrevolucionario visto a través de las revistas masónicas mexicanas, 1930–1945.* Mexico City: n.p., 2004.

Valdés Valle, Roberto Armando. "Anti-masonismo en las páginas del periódico salvadoreño *El Católico* durante el año 1885." In *La masonería española: represión y exilios*, edited by José Antonio Ferrer Benimeli, 2:1187–1204. Zaragoza, Spain: CEHME, 2010.

_____. "*El Católico y El Porvenir*: controversia periodística y judicial, 1892." Paper presented at the Masonería y Sociedades Patrióticas panel at the X Congreso Centroamericano de Historia, Universidad Nacional Autónoma de Nicaragua, Managua, July 12–16, 2010.

_____. "Elementos para la discusión sobre masonería, política y secular-

ización en la Centroamérica del siglo XIX." *REHMLAC* 2, no. 2 (December 2010–April 2011): 66–84. https://revistas.ucr.ac.cr/index.php/rehmlac/article/view/6597/6288

_____. "La masonería y el Gobierno de Rafael Zaldívar (1876–1885)." *Boletín AFEHC* 37 (2008). afehc-historia-centroamericana.org/index.php?action=fi_aff&id=1976

_____. "Masones, Liberales y Ultramontanos salvadoreños: Debate político y constitucional en algunas publicaciones impresas, durante la etapa final del proceso de secularización del Estado salvadoreño (1885–1886)." Doctoral dissertation, Universidad Centroamericana "José Simeón Cañas," El Salvador, 2010. uca.edu.sv/deptos/filosofia/web/admin/files/1260825405.pdf

_____. "Masones, Liberales y Ultramontanos salvadoreños: Debate político y constitucional en algunas publicaciones impresas, durante la etapa final del proceso de secularización del Estado salvadoreño (1885–1886)." *REHMLAC* 2, no. 1 (May–November 2010): 79–84. https://revistas.ucr.ac.cr/index.php/rehmlac/article/view/6612/6301

_____. "Origen, miembros y primeras acciones de la masonería en El Salvador (1871–1872)." *REHMLAC* 1, no. 1 (May–November 2009): 155–171. https://revistas.ucr.ac.cr/index.php/rehmlac/article/view/6861/6548

_____. "Origen, miembros y primeras acciones de la masonería en El Salvador (1871–1872)." *Cultura. Revista de la Secretaría de Cultura de la Presidencia. Edición dedicada a Monseñor Romero* 102 (January–July 2010): 107–126.

_____. "Relevancia política de los masones salvadoreños durante el año 1885." II Simposio Internacional de Historia de la Masonería y Sociedades Patrióticas Latinoamericanas y Caribeñas, Cátedra Transdisciplinaria de Estudios Históricos de la Masonería Cubana Vicente Antonio de Castro (CTEHMAC), Casa de Altos Estudios Don Fernando Ortiz, Universidad de La Habana, Oficina del Historiador de la Ciudad de La Habana, Gran Logia de Cuba de A.L y A.M, and Centro de Estudios Históricos de la Masonería Española (CEHME) of the Universidad de Zaragoza, Havana, Cuba, December 2–6, 2008.

Valdivieso Montano, Acislio. *Un capítulo de historia masónica venezolana.* Caracas: Ed. Patria, 1930.

_____. *Introducción a la masonería venezolana.* Caracas: Trip. Americana, 1928.

Valín Fernández, Alberto. "L'emigració gallega i asturiana en la maçoneria cubana del segle XIX." *L'Avenç* 218 (1997): 60–63.

_____. "A emigración galega e a masoneria en Cuba no derradeiro tercio do século XIX." In *Entre nos. Estudios de Arte, Xeografía e Historia en homenaje o profesor Xosé Manuel Pose Antelo,* 749–756. Santiago de Composte-la, Spain: Universidade de Santiago de Compostela, 2001.

_____. "Galicia y su emigración en la masonería cubana." In *Masonería Española y América,* edited by José Antonio Ferrer Benimeli, 1:513–520. Zaragoza, Spain: CEHME, 1993.

Valverde, Jaime. *Las sectas en Costa Rica. Pentecostalismo y conflicto social.* San José, Costa Rica: Ed. DEI, 1990.

Vaquero Iglesias, Julio Antonio. "Masonería e independencia americana según la historiografía decimonónica española." In *Masonería Española y América,* edited by José Antonio Ferrer Benimeli, 1:1083–1096. Zaragoza, Spain: CEHME, 1993.

Vargas Márquez, Wenceslao. *La Masonería en la Presidencia de México.* Mexico City: Ed. Surco de Letras, 2010.

Vásquez, José V. *Semblanza del Presbítero Doctor Francisco Calvo, grado 33, fundador de la Masonería en Centroamérica.* Tegucigalpa: n.p., 1966.

Vázquez Ibáñez, Paloma. "La masonería y su influencia política en el Puerto Rico del siglo XIX y principios del XX." Master's dissertation, Pontificia Universidad Católica de Puerto Rico, 2004.

_____. "Política sagastina en las colonias de ultramar a finales del siglo XIX: Puerto Rico, la carta autonómica de 1897 y su breve instauración." In *La masonería española en la época de Sagasta (1825–1903),* edited by José Antonio

Ferrer Benimeli, 1:701–711. Zaragoza, Spain: CEHME and the Fundación Práxedes Mateo-Sagasta, 2006.

Vázquez Mantecón, Carmen. *Muerte y vida eterna de Benito Juárez*. Mexico City: n.p., 2006.

Vázquez Semadeni, María Eugenia. "American Origins of Mexican Freemasonry." Paper presented at the International Conference on American and Latin American Freemasonry: A New Past and a New Future, Freemasonry and Civil Society Program of the History Department of the University of California at Los Angeles (UCLA), The Grand Lodge of California, California's Institute for Masonic Studies, Los Angeles, December 3, 2011.

_____. "Criminal seguida a Luis Zuloaga por infiel al Rito de York." In *La Masonería española. Represión y exilios*, edited by José Antonio Ferrer Benimeli, 1:497–508. Zaragoza, Spain: CEHME, Gobierno de Aragón, Departamento de Educación, Cultura y Deporte, 2011.

_____. "Del mar a la política. Masonería en Nueva España. México, 1816–1823." In *Liberalismo, Masonería e Independencias en Hispanoamérica*, edited by Moisés Guzmán Pérez. Morelia, Mexico, in press.

_____. *La formación de una cultura política republicana. El debate público sobre la masonería en México, 1821–1830*. Mexico City: Universidad Nacional Autónoma de México y Colegio de Michoacán, 2010.

_____. "La Gran Legión del Águila Negra. Documentos sobre su fundación, estatutos y objetivos." *Relaciones* 28, no. 111 (2007): 143–166.

_____. "Historiografía sobre la masonería en México. Breve revisión." *REHMLAC* 2, no. 1 (May–November 2010): 16–29. https://revistas.ucr.ac.cr/index.php/rehmlac/article/view/6608/6297

_____. "La interacción entre el debate público sobre la masonería y la cultura política, 1761–1830." Doctoral dissertation, Colegio de Michoacán, Mexico, 2008

_____. "La interacción entre el debate público sobre la masonería y la cultura política, 1761–1830." *REHMLAC* 2, no. 1 (May–November 2010): 74–78. https://revistas.ucr.ac.cr/index.php/rehmlac/article/view/6611/6300

_____. "Juárez y la masonería." *Metapolítica* 10, no. 46 (March–April 2006).

_____. "La masonería durante el período juarista." In *Las rupturas de Juárez*, edited by Conrado Hernández López and Israel Arroyo, 287–312. Oaxaca, Mexico: Universidad Autónoma "Benito Juárez," 2007.

_____. "La masonería en México, entre las sociedades secretas y patrióticas, 1813–1830." *REHMLAC* 2, no. 2 (December 2010–April 2011): 18–33. https://revistas.ucr.ac.cr/index.php/rehmlac/article/view/6594/6285

_____. "La masonería mexicana en el debate público 1808–1830." In *La masonería española en la época de Sagasta (1825–1903)*, edited by José Antonio Ferrer Benimeli, 2:861–882. Zaragoza, Spain: CEHME and the Fundación Práxedes Mateo-Sagasta, 2006.

_____. "Masonería, Papeles públicos y cultura política." *Estudios de Historia Moderna y Contemporánea de México* 38 (July–December 2009): 35–83.

_____. "Las Obediencias masónicas del rito de York como centro de acción política, México 1825–1830" (Chiapas, México, 2009).

_____. "The Public Debate about Freemasonry, United States/Mexico, 1730–1840." Paper presented at the International Conference of the History of Freemasonry, Centre interdisciplinaire bordelais d'étude des lumières-Lumières Nature Société, Université de Bordeaux III Centre d'étude de la Littérature Françaises des XVIIe et XVIIIe Siècles (CELLF), Sorbonne IV. Paris Chair of Freemassonary, Faculty of Religious Studies, University of Leiden, Centre de la Méditerrannée Moderne et Contemporaine, Université de Nice Sophia-Antipolis, The Interdisciplinary Research Group Freemasonry, Free University of Brussels, The George Washington Masonic Memorial, Alexandria, VA, May 26–30, 2011.

Verges, J.M. Miguel. *La independencia mexicana y la prensa insurgente*. Mexico City: Instituto Nacional de Estudios Históricos de las Revoluciones de México, 1985.

Vescio, Luiz Eugênio. *O Crime do Padre Sorio: Maçonaria e Igreja Católica no Rio Grande do Sul (1893–1928)*. Santa María-Porto Alegre, Brazil: n.p., 2001.

Villa, Gustavo E. *Artigas, las instrucciones del año XIII y la masonería*. Montevideo: Arca, 2010.

Villasana, Angel Raúl. "Repertorio Bibliográfico de Venezuela [Entradas masónicas]." In *Efrain Subero, La Masonería en Venezuela*, 1:89–102. Caracas: Gran Logia de la República de Venezuela, 2000.

Weisberger, R. William, Wallace McLeod, and S. Brent Morris, eds. *Freemasonry on Both Sides of the Atlantic: Essays Concerning the Craft in the British Isles, Europe, the United States, and Mexico*. Boulder, CO: East European Monographs, 2002.

Werneck Gonçalves, Thiago. "O hábito e o avental: a Igreja católica e a maçonaria na Questão Religiosa (1872–1875)." In *Anais da V Semana de História Política. II Semana Nacional de Historia: Política e Cultura. Política e Sociedades*. Rio de Janeiro: Universidade Estatal de Rio de Janeiro, 2010.

_____. "O periodismo maçônico oitocentista da Corte imperial brasileira: notas de pesquisa." *REHMLAC* 3. no. 1 (May–November 2011): 142–156. https://revistas.ucr.ac.cr/index.php/rehmlac/article/view/6590/6281

_____. *Periodismo maçônico. Política e opinião pública na Corte imperial brasileira (1870–1875)*. Rio de Janeiro: Universidade Federal Fluminense, 2011.

Wünderich, Volker. "Digresión: la dimensión espiritual del nacionalismo." In *Sandino. Una biografía política*, 150–180. Managua: IHNCA-UCA, 2009.

Young, F.E. "Mexican Masonry in 1909." *Ars Quatuor Coronatorum* 22 (1909): 214–217.

Zalce y Rodríguez, Luis. *Apuntes para la historia de la masonería en México. De mis lecturas y recuerdos*. Mexico City: n.p., 1950.

Zabala, Iris. *Masones, comuneros y carbonarios*. Madrid: Siglo XXI Editores, 1971.

Zavala, Lorenzo de. *Ensayo histórico de las revoluciones de México desde 1808 hasta 1830*. Paris: F. Dupont et G. Laguionis, 1831–1832.

Zeldis, León. *La Francmasonería en la independencia de Chile y América*. Madrid: n.p., 1997.

_____. *Freemasonry's contribution of South American Independence. A factual Approach*. London: n.p., 1998.

_____. "Joel Poinsett. Masón, diplomático y revolucionario." In *La Masonería en Madrid y en España del siglo XVIII al XXI*, edited by José Antonio Ferrer Benimeli, 1:479–488. Zaragoza, Spain: CEHME, 2004.

Zubizarreta, Ignacio. "Una sociedad secreta en el exilio: los unitarios y la articulación de políticas conspirativas antirrosistas en el Uruguay, 1835–1836." *Boletín del Instituto de Historia Argentina y Americana Dr. Emilio Ravignani* 31 (2009).

Zuñiga, Antonio R. *La logia Lautaro y la independencia de América*. Buenos Aires: n.p., 1922.

Freemasonry in Cuba in the Nineteenth Century[1]

Eduardo Torres Cuevas[2]

Abstract

This article analyzes the development of Cuban Freemasonry during the 19th century and its relations with the principal political, economic and cultural processes of the Island, in particular with those of emancipation and of the arrival of liberal, civic, lay and secular ideas. This paper also serves as literature review about what it has been written on this specific topic.

Keywords: Cubans Freemasonry, 19ᵗʰ century, liberalism, secularism, emancipation

Resumen

Esta investigación analiza el desarrollo de las masonerías cubanas durante el siglo XIX y sus relaciones con los principales procesos políticos, económicos y sociales de la Isla, en especial con los de emancipación y de llegada de ideas liberales, civilistas, laicas y seculares. Asimismo, este trabajo funciona como un estado de cuestión sobre lo escrito con respecto al específico objeto de estudio.

Palabras clave: Masonerías cubanas, siglo XIX, liberalismo, secularismo, emancipación

1 This article was previously published in *REHMLAC*, Vol. 3, No. 2, December 2011-April 2012. I would like to thank the *REHMLAC* editorial committee for authorizing the publication of this article in English. A first version was presented at the *V Symposium Internacional de la Masonería Española*, Cáceres, España, held from 16-20 June 1990, and published in José Antonio Ferrer Benimeli (collator), *Masonería Española y América* (Zaragoza: CEHME, 1993), Vol 1, 229-256.

2 Eduardo Torres Cuevas. Cuban. Doctor of History from Havana University, Cuba. Professor of History, Havana University, Cuba. Director of the José Martí National Library in Havana, Cuba. Director of the Casa de Altos Estudios Don Fernando Ortíz and the Transdisciplinary Professor of Historical Studies of the Vicente Antonio de Castro Cuban Masonry, Havana University, Cuba. Email: torres-cuevas@cubarte.cult.cu.

19世纪的古巴共济会

摘要

本研究分析了19世纪期间古巴共济会的发展及其与古巴岛主要政治、经济和文化进程的关系，特别是和解放进程以及新观念（包括自由观念、公民观念、外行观念以及世俗观念）到来之间的关系。本文同时对有关该研究的文字记录提出了疑问。

关键词：古巴共济会，19世纪，自由主义，世俗主义，解放

Introduction

Cuba is not exactly lacking in systematic works on the history of Freemasonry and its influence on processes of national construction. Since the middle of the nineteenth century, both the extensive and persistent efforts to recruit new members and to disseminate Freemasonry, and the criticisms and attacks on the institution gave rise to an extensive bibliography of books and pamphlets, augmented by numerous journal and newspaper articles. The quality, however, is highly uneven and the trustworthiness of the information with regard to historic facts even appears to be intentionally distorted for sectarian reasons, both in favor of and against the institution. Nevertheless, Cuban Masons made a concerted effort to produce works that were rigorous in content, information, and interpretation, and allowed them to support the institution's role in society, culture, and the national political arena. Thus, if one discounts low-quality propaganda, the student of Cuban Freemasonry can find a collection of works which amount to an intellectual tradition on the subject. This was partly due to the fact that during the twentieth century the institution enjoyed prestige for its involvement in the wars of independence and its fraternal, philanthropic and ethical principles, as well as being associated with republican, democratic, secular and anti-racist ideals. To this, one has to add that Freemasonry has functioned normally in Cuba without being persecuted or prohibited and, in certain periods of history, its social tenets became predominant, as was the case between 1902 and 1933.

To give an idea of the extensive Cuban Masonic bibliography, it suffices to cite here some of its most important works: the *Manual de la Masonería, o sea el Tejedor de los Ritos Antiguos Escocés, Francés y de Adopción* by Andrés Cassard,[3] whose first edition, published by the New York publisher George R. Lock-

---

3   Andrés Cassard: Founder of the upper bodies of the Scottish Rite of Regular Cuban Freemasonry. He was born in Santiago de Cuba in 1823. At 22 years of age he moved to Havana. In 1852 he fled

wood, dates from the end of the 1850s. It was written for Columbus Freemasonry, the original name of the regular Cuban Freemasonry, whose high degrees were founded by Cassard in Cuba in the same year. No less important are the following three works: the compilation of *Liturgias y rituales* by Vicente Antonio de Castro y Bermúdez for the Grand Orient of Cuba and the Antilles, issued in 1862,[4] *El consultor del masón,* written by Aurelio Almeida González in 1883,[5] and the *Diccionario enciclopédico de la Masonería* by Lorenzo Frau Abrines and Rosendo Arús Arderiú, which was first published in Havana in 1883 and later published in Spain in 1891, Mexico in 1955 and Argentina in 1956. Important twentieth century works include the *Manual masónico,* written and published by Francisco de Paula Rodríguez and Gerardo L. Betancourt in 1919, *La historia documentada de la Masonería en Cuba* by Aurelio Miranda y Álvarez,[6] published in 1933,

to the United States of America. According to the Masonic historian Aurelio Miranda, his flight was precipitated by his involvement, together with Eduardo Facciolo, in editing the clandestine publication *La Voz del Pueblo.* The North American Charles Brockway asserts that he wasn't involved in any political event and that he was sentenced to death "merely for his Masonic activities." This seems unlikely as this wasn't a period particularly noted for excesses against Masons. The year following his arrival in North America, he received the 33rd degree of Scottish Freemasonry. In 1855, he founded the first lodge in New York working in Spanish, La Fraternidad No. 387, and he is also attributed with having founded the Amor Fraternal Lodge No. 4 in New Orleans. The book referred to in the text, disseminated widely in Latin America and Spain, has been found to have many important Masonic errors. In addition, the work has been edited a number of times in various countries. Cassard died on February 3, 1894 at the age of 70 in New York City. Important figures in the Cuban independence movement and the Cuban Revolutionary Party were active in or participated in the meetings of La Fraternidad Lodge. An analysis of this unique individual can be found in Lorenzo Frau Abrines & Rosendo Arús Arderiú, *Diccionario Enciclopédico de la Masonería* (La Habana: Propaganda Literaria, 1883), Volume I, 274-278; and in Miguel Guzmán Stein, "Andrés Cassard y su vida en Nueva York. Tres nuevas facetas de un masón polifacético," in *La Masonería española. Represión y exilios,* collated by Ferrer Benimeli (Zaragoza: Gobierno de Aragón, 2010), Volume I, 509-544.

4   Vicente Antonio de Castro y Bermúdez: Founded the Grand Orient of Cuba and the Antilles. He is the highest-ranking Masonic leader in the history of Cuba of all the various Masonic bodies established on the island. For more on this figure, see: Eduardo Torres Cuevas, *Historia de la Masonería cubana. Seis ensayos* (La Habana: Imagen Contemporánea, 2005), 68-160; and Dominique Soucy, "Vicente Antonio de Castro y la opción reformista: desde *La Cartera Cubana* hasta *Yara,*" in *La Masonería española. Represión y exilios,* Vol I, 411-423.

5   Aurelio Almeida González: The most important figure in the regulation of Cuban Masonry and in its unification during the Ten Years' War and the post-war period. Author of the works noted in the text, in which he argues in favor of Masonic use of the revolutionary liturgies of Vicente Antonio de Castro. His work endowed Cuban Masonry with legal, philosophical, and organizational foundations, which were respected by all subsequent Masonic bodies who continued his work. He was born in the province of Matanzas on October 10, 1843 and died in Havana on June 25, 1885 at the young age of 42.

6   Aurelio Miranda y Álvarez: One of the most notable figures in the history of Cuban Masonry and one of the founders of the magazine *La Gran Logia,* which may be considered the oldest Cuban periodical. He took part in a number of important events in the reorganization of the Cuban nation. Endowed with pro-independence ideology and intellectual rigor, the book quoted is without doubt

Historia de la Masonería en Cuba by Roger Fernández Callejas, and, lastly, *La Masonería en la independencia de Cuba* (1954) and *Historia de la Masonería del Rito Escocés en Cuba* by Francisco J. Ponte Domínguez, (1961).

All the books referred to above, and others excluded for reasons of space, were written by Masons at different times in history and they all speak highly of Freemasonry. As a result, the information is selective and the interpretation is colored by the prism through which the authors view their object of study, the times they wrote in, and the philosophical, political and social ideas they shared. Their motivation was not only that of the historian whose objective was to study the impact of Freemasonry on the history of Cuban

society but that of the Mason who, from within the institution, observes only that which reflects well upon it. For this reason, what is missing from Cuban historiography is a tradition of academic study and a search for documentation which makes it possible to reconstruct the true role of the organization in the history of Cuba objectively, from more than a purely institutional perspective. Part of the reason for this is that, for various reasons, Cuban non-Masonic historians have not selected Freemasonry as a subject of study. Now, however, first steps in this type of social and historical work are being made and the work of the following researchers should be highlighted: Manuel de Paz Sánchez,[7] Dominique Soucy,[8] Delphine Sappez,[9] Agnès Renault,[10] Samuel Sánchez

---

one of the most rigorous books on Cuban Masonic history and also the outcome of a life dedicated to research and the search for documents.

7   "L. F. Gómez Wangüemert y la Masonería palmera y cubana de la década de 1930," *Jornadas de estudios Canarias-América* (1981): 31-67; "Los residentes españoles en Cuba y la Masonería después de la independencia," *Cuadernos de investigación histórica* 10 (1986): 41-56; *Ibid.* & José Manuel Castellano Gil, "Martí, masón y otras crónicas wangüemeretianas," collated by Ferrer Benimeli, *Masonería española y americana* (Zaragoza: CEHME, 1993), Vol II, 671-687; "La Masonería y la pérdida de las colonias: impresiones sobre el caso cubano," *Masonería española y americana*, Vol II, 1107-1125; "La gran decepción de José Martí. Sobre su vinculación a la Masonería en España, 1871-1874," *Nuevo Mundo Mundos Nuevos, Debates* (2008): 1-38. nuevomundo.revues.org/index30883. html. (Revised September 15, 2011); *Martí, España y la Masonería* (Canarias: Ediciones Idea, 2008); "España, Cuba y Marruecos: Masonería, identidades y construcción nacional," *Anuario de estudios atlánticos* 55 (2009): 273-310.

8   *La Gran Legión del Águila Negra: Un Águila de dos cabezas (México-Cuba, 1823-1830)* (Francia: Universidad de París VIII), *Ibid., Masonería y nación. Redes masónicas y políticas en la construcción identitaria cubana (1811-1902)* (España: Ediciones Idea, 2006); *Ibid.*, "Vicente Antonio de Castro y la opción reformista: desde *La Cartera Cubana* hasta *Yara*"; *Ibid.* & Delphine Sappez, "Autonomismo y Masonería en Cuba," *REHMLAC, Revista de Estudios Históricos de la Masonería Latinoamericana y Caribeña* (San José, Costa Rica) 1, n. 1 (mayo-noviembre 2009): 90-99. https://revistas.ucr. ac.cr/index.php/rehmlac/article/view/6858/6545. (Revised September 15, 2011).

9   "Antonio Govín y Torres, nexo entre Masonería y autonomismo en Cuba," en *La Masonería española. Represión y exilios*, Vol I, 559-572.

10   "Los francmasones franceses de la jurisdicción de Cuba al principio del siglo XIX," *REHMLAC, Revista de Estudios Históricos de la Masonería Latinoamericana y Caribeña* (San José, Costa Rica) 1, n. 1 (mayo-noviembre 2009): 59-72. https://revistas.ucr.ac.cr/index.php/rehmlac/arti-

Gálvez,[11] Janet Iglesias Cruz y Javiher Gutiérrez Forte,[12] Paul Estrade,[13] María Dolores Domingo Acebrón,[14] María Teresa Montes de Oca Choy, Yasmín Ydoy Ortiz,[15] Haens Beltrán,[16] my own,[17] and other unpublished works presented within the context of the international symposia on historical studies of Latin American and Caribbean Freemasonry held at Havana University in 2007 and 2008.[18]

The role of Masonic institutions

cle/view/6857/6544; y "La influencia de la Masonería francesa en el Departamento de Cuba en los años veinte del siglo XIX. Los aportes de la prosopografía," *REHMLAC, Revista de Estudios Históricos de la Masonería Latinoamericana y Caribeña* (San José, Costa Rica) 1, n. 1 (mayo-noviembre 2009): 74-89. https://revistas.ucr.ac.cr/index.php/rehmlac/article/view/6856/6543. (Revised September 15, 2011).

11 *Martí ciñó el mandil. Prueba documental de su filiación masónica* (La Habana: Ediciones Bachiller, 2007); "Ciencia y cultura en Fernandina de Jagua," *REHMLAC, Revista de Estudios Históricos de la Masonería Latinoamericana y Caribeña* (San José, Costa Rica) 1, n. 1 (mayo-noviembre 2009): 172-190. : https://revistas.ucr.ac.cr/index.php/rehmlac/article/view/6862/6549; "Institucionalización de la Masonería en Cienfuegos," *REHMLAC, Revista de Estudios Históricos de la Masonería Latinoamericana y Caribeña* (San José, Costa Rica) 1, n. 1 (mayo-noviembre 2009): 191-211. https://revistas.ucr.ac.cr/index.php/rehmlac/article/view/6863/6550; y "La logia masónica cienfueguera Fernandina de Jagua (1878-1902). Un estudio de caso" (Tesis doctoral en Historia, Universidad Carlos Rafael Rodríguez de Cienfuegos, 2010), Una entrevista a Sánchez Gálvez sobre su experiencia doctoral en *REHMLAC, Revista de Estudios Históricos de la Masonería Latinoamericana y Caribeña* (San José, Costa Rica) 2, n. 1 (mayo-noviembre 2010): 85-92. https://revistas.ucr.ac.cr/index.php/rehmlac/article/view/6613/6302; (Revised September 15, 2011).

12 "Españoles y Cubanos en la Masonería. Manuel Curros Enríquez," *REHMLAC, Revista de Estudios Históricos de la Masonería Latinoamericana y Caribeña* (San José, Costa Rica) 1, n. 2 (diciembre 2009-abril 2010): 121-129. https://revistas.ucr.ac.cr/index.php/rehmlac/article/view/6620/6309; "La simbología masónica en el Cementerio de Colón," *REHMLAC, Revista de Estudios Históricos de la Masonería Latinoamericana y Caribeña* (San José, Costa Rica) 2, n. 1 (mayo-noviembre 2010): 59-73. https://revistas.ucr.ac.cr/index.php/rehmlac/article/view/6610/6299; y "La Masonería en los albores de la República. Las elecciones de 1908: Los Masones y sus logias en la política de los primeros años de la República cubana," *Congreso Internacional. Actas del XIV Encuentro de Latinoamericanistas Españoles*, eds. Eduardo Rey Tristán & Patricia Calvo González (Santiago de Compostela: Universidad de Santiago de Compostela, 2010), 225-235. hal.archives-ouvertes.fr/docs/00/52/92/78/PDF/AT4_Gutierrez-Iglesias.pdf; (Revised September 15, 2011).

13 "Un masón audaz y conformista, paradigmático del Gran Oriente de Francia: el franco-cubano Severiano de Heredia (1836-1901)," en *La Masonería española. Represión y exilios*, Tomo I, 545-558.

14 "Independencia en el Caribe, Cuba: José de Armas y Céspedes: masón," en *La Masonería española. Represión y exilios*, Tomo I, 573-580.

15 "Chee Kung Tong ¿Vínculos masónicos?" *REHMLAC, Revista de Estudios Históricos de la Masonería Latinoamericana y Caribeña* (San José, Costa Rica) 1, n. 1 (mayo-noviembre 2009): 234-246. https://revistas.ucr.ac.cr/index.php/rehmlac/article/view/6865/6552. (Revised September 15, 2011).

16 "" (Tesis de Maestría en Historia, Universidad Carlos Rafael Rodríguez de Cienfuegos, 2011).

17 *Historia de la Masonería cubana. Seis ensayos*; y "Presencia republicana española en Cuba," en *La Masonería española. Represión y exilios*, Tomo I, 327-336.

18 See Ricardo Martínez Esquivel, "Simposios Internacionales de Historia de la Masonería Latinoamericana y Caribeña (La Habana, Cuba, 2007 y 2008)," *REHMLAC, Revista de Estudios*

in Cuba cannot be denied nor underestimated. In the nineteenth and twentieth centuries, Freemasonry played an important role in Cuban political, social, religious, and cultural history. The aim of this paper is to present a brief outline of the significance of Masonic institutions in the formation and development of Cuba. It will not be possible to include very specific aspects which cannot be dealt with here for lack of space and to avoid the risk of making serious omissions.

The Origins of Freemasonry in Cuba

I have to confess that, despite my interest in discovering evidence of possible operative, labor-craft Freemasonry in the sixteenth and seventeenth centuries in Cuba, no documentary or archeological evidence has yet come to light which would allow me to confirm its presence at that time. But it is a search which must be continued, so we will continue to carry out research into brotherhoods established in Cuba at that time. The truth is that the control the Church had over the brotherhoods was extremely tight. One also has to add that there were few monuments and religious buildings at that time. I wrote

the above in 1975, but, in revising the text, I am obliged to add that Eusebio Leal Spengler, a historian based in Havana, recently showed me evidence of operative Freemasonry in the stones of the Monastery of San Francisco in Havana, which can be dated from the first half of the eighteenth century. These discoveries raise questions never before broached. At least two things can be asserted: Firstly, as far as I can establish by comparing these marks with those appearing in the work of Jean Louis Van Bell,[19] the signs are similar to those of stoneworkers (operative Masons) in Europe. These marks were occasionally made in the stones in order for builders to know where and how the stones should be placed, and others were the mark of the builder, a kind of signature, which made it possible to recognize the work he had done so he could be paid for it. Secondly, we have the proof of the presence of this type of Freemasonry in the first works on Cuban monuments from the beginning of the eighteenth century. Further studies will doubtless throw light on their origins and meaning.

Much more unsettling, but at the same time appealing, is the situation in the eighteenth century with regard to speculative Freemasonry. It is known

Históricos de la Masonería Latinoamericana y Caribeña (San José, Costa Rica) 1, n. 2 (diciembre 2009-abril 2010): 159-167. https://revistas.ucr.ac.cr/index.php/rehmlac/article/view/22250/22417). In relation to this historiographical renewal in Latin America, see also: Yván Pozuelo Andrés, "La historiografía masónica latinoamericanista actual. Presente y futuro," *Congreso Internacional. Actas del XIV Encuentro de Latinoamericanistas Españoles*, eds. Eduardo Rey Tristán & Patricia Calvo González (Santiago de Compostela: Universidad de Santiago de Compostela, 2010), 281-288. halshs.archives-ouvertes.fr/docs/00/52/92/98/PDF/AT4_Pozuelo.pdf; (Revised September 15, 2011).

19 *Dictionnaire des signes lapidaires Belgique et nord de la France* (Éditions Braine le Chateau, 1984-1994).

that, following the foundation of the Grand Lodge of England in 1717, traders, sailors and English agents disseminated Freemasonry throughout the world. French Freemasonry was spread in the same way. Cuba was at the heart of both legal and illegal imperial and commercial struggles between these powers in America, and in particular in the turbulent Caribbean. There was close contact with people of both nationalities, but there is no documentary proof that there were modern Masons in Cuba before 1750.[20]

The first reference to Freemasonry in Cuba I have found comes from the historian Joseph Gabriel Findel's *Historia de la Francmasonería* and relates to the period between 1751 and 1754. According to Findel, between those dates, the Grand Lodge of England appointed eight provincial Grand Masters, including one for Cuba.[21] If one looks at the dates and places selected, one can see that they were key points in the expansion of the British Empire or places where it had important economic or political interests. What cannot be overlooked is that, in the case of Cuba, this ran parallel to the English preparations for the capture of Havana. The invasion and occupation of Havana in 1762 confirms the relationship between the ambitions of the Grand Lodge of England and those of the British Empire, the more so if one takes into account that the post of Grand Master was occupied by Lord Carnarvon, who had close links to the English government. There is sufficient evidence to show that this Freemasonry never managed to found lodges in Cuba, but, at the same time, it is possible to say that Cuba was one of the first places in Latin America where English Freemasonry considered creating a grand lodge.

What has been called the first "Cuban" Masonic document dates from the British occupation of Havana. It was published by the English Masonic review *Ars Quatuor Coronatorun* and is a parchment manuscript 8 ¾ inches long and 8 ½ wide, with a red lacre seal featuring an arm with a trowel in the hand in relief. The text, written in English, is the initiation certificate of a member of the occupying British troops named Alexander Cockburn. He was initiated into the Irish Register No. 218 Lodge.[22] The lodge belonged to the Infantry Reg-

---

20 Eric Saunier, "L'espace caribéen: un enjeu de pouvoir pour la franc-maçonnerie française," *REHMLAC, Revista de Estudios Históricos de la Masonería Latinoamericana y Caribeña* (San José, Costa Rica) 1, n. 1 (mayo-noviembre 2009): 41-56. https://revistas.ucr.ac.cr/index.php/rehmlac/article/view/6855/6542; José Antonio Ferrer Benimeli, "Vías de penetración de la Masonería en el Caribe," *REHMLAC, Revista de Estudios Históricos de la Masonería Latinoamericana y Caribeña* (San José, Costa Rica) 1, n. 1 (mayo-noviembre 2009): 2-19. https://revistas.ucr.ac.cr/index.php/rehmlac/article/view/6853/6540. (Revised November 11, 2009).

21 Joseph Gabriel Findel, *Historia de la Francmasonería* (La Habana: Editorial Acacia, 1946), Tomo I, 160. The places which, according to this author, were selected for the eight planned provincial Grand Masters were South Carolina, South Wales, Barbados, North America, Antigua, Sicily, Germany, Chester and Cuba.

22 Francisco de Paula Rodríguez & Gerardo L. Betancourt, *Manual masónico* (La Habana: Imprenta El Siglo XX, 1919); Aurelio Miranda y Álvarez, *Historia documentada de la Masonería en Cuba* (La

iment No. 48, known as the De Webb Regiment, commanded by Lieutenant Colonel Teesdale.[23]

Following the withdrawal of English troops from Havana on July 8, 1763, there is no evidence of any functioning Masonic lodge remaining. This confirms the thesis that the Masons active during this period belonged to the occupying British troops and they did not—or were not able to—recruit anyone from the Havana cultural elite. At any rate, relationships were personal, rare, and generally circumstantial.

We have only found one document referring to Freemasonry from the period between 1763 and 1790. This is dated December 7, 1769 and refers to the release from prison of the Englishman John FitzGerald, who had been sent by the Governor of Cuba to prison in Cadiz for having "held a degree as Freemason."[24] As can be seen in this case, there is no relationship here between Freemasonry and the activities of the Creoles in Cuba either.

One question should be raised about this period of history: Might there have been people linked to Freemasonry within the group in power on the island? There is much work still to be done on this question. Those in the political governance of Cuba at this time, as well as many of the future Havana oligarchy, were closely linked to the group of the Count of Aranda in Spain. This gives rise to the hypothesis that some of them

may have been Masons and that, hence, they may have had meetings in Cuba. This is based on the fact that Aranda was one of the founders and promoters of Freemasonry in Spain and the fact that many of the people in power on the island were followers of Enlightenment ideas. This idea appears to be supported particularly by the fact that the Governor Ambrosio de Funes y Villalpando, Count of Ricla, was a first cousin of Aranda, and General Alejandro O'Reilly, who led the military reorganization of the island, was the great-uncle of Pedro Pablo O'Reilly, one of the most powerful Cuban landowners and, in the 1820s, the Grand Master of the Spanish American Territorial Grand Orient of the Scottish Rite. This hypothesis, however, seems to break down, if one consults the work of José Antonio Ferrer Benimeli, who raises doubts about whether the Conde de Aranda was even a Mason. If the famous Count did not promote Freemasonry in Spain, there is no reason to suppose that his close collaborators did so in Cuba. Furthermore, the much-discussed link between Enlightenment thinkers and Masons seems increasingly unsustainable. Not all Masons were Enlightenment thinkers and not all Enlightenment thinkers were Masons. This would explain the lack of documentary evidence of Masonic activity from this period. It was not until 1792 that the conditions were right for the foundation of the first lodges on the island.

Habana: Molina, 1933), 13.

23 *Documentos, inéditos sobre la toma de La Habana por los ingleses en 1762* (Biblioteca Nacional José Martí, Departamento Colección Cubana, s.a.), 104.

24 Ponte Domínguez, *La Masonería en la independencia de Cuba*, 11.

First Period of Freemasonry in Cuba (1798-1830)

In the last decade of the eighteenth century there was a profound change in the structure of the Cuban economy, with the spread of a plantation system based on slave labor. Cuba became a slave-owning society, but at the same time there was an increase in the peasant population and in the middle classes. The Cuban oligarchy marked out its structures and its ideas for the future. The Creole tradition and the Enlightenment, in its Spanish incarnation, formed the basis of the thinking and the plans of this hegemonic group. This context was strongly influenced by three revolutionary processes: the North American, the French, and—the one which made the most impact—the Haitian.

As a consequence of the slave uprising on what was then Saint Domingue, numerous French residents moved to Cuba. With them arrived the first Masonic lodges active in the Caribbean. These were *La Persévérance, La Concorde, L'Amitié* and *La Bénéfique Concorde.* The creation of these lodges can be accurately dated to 1798. The two first lodges were established in Santiago de Cuba and the two last in Havana. Their founding charters, issued by the Grand Orient of France, were not addressed to Cuba but to Saint Domingue and the lodges kept their names and continued to hold meet-ings in French. Some Creoles and Spaniards joined them, and the effect of the lodges' presence in Cuba was profound and lasting. With these lodges also arrived the Scottish Rite, which was the rite followed by the French lodges. This rite would be adhered to by the majority of subsequent Cuban Masonic lodges. The other aspect to highlight is that this Freemasonry was within the sphere of influence of the Grand Orient of France and not the Grand Lodge of England, and would therefore be strongly influenced by the social and philosophical thinking of the French Orient.[25]

On December 17, 1804, a founding charter was granted to the first Masonic lodge created in Cuba. The lodge was called Le Temple des Vertus Théologales and had been operative since 1802 of the "vulgar era." Significantly, its charter, numbered 103, was not issued by the Grand Orient of France but came from the Grand Lodge of Pennsylvania, at that time the most important political center of the recently created United States of America.[26] This lodge, rarely referred to in Cuban history books, nevertheless played an important role in Cuban national processes. The members of the group that constituted it were all French and its Worshipful Master, Joseph Cerneau, was particularly interesting and has been described by some historians of North American Freemasonry as "the Mason who did most harm to United States Freemasonry."[27] Other Masonic

---

25 Renault, "Los francmasones franceses de la jurisdicción de Cuba al principio del siglo XIX"; *Ibid.*, "La influencia de la Masonería francesa en el Departamento de Cuba en los años veinte del siglo XIX. Los aportes de la prosopografía."

26 Archivo Nacional de Cuba: *Fondo Capitanes Generales,* leg. 32.

27 Aurelio Miranda y Álvarez, *La historia documentada de la Masonería en Cuba,* 30.

authors, however, called him an "enthusiastic and disputatious brother,"[28] while the governor of the island, Salvador del Muro y Salazar, Marquess of Someruelos, said that he had a "revolutionary character."[29] Cerneau was expelled from North American Freemasonry in 1813 by the Charleston Supreme Council in South Carolina, but the lodge he created in Cuba remained active and some of its members were linked to the first separatist plots, such as the plot headed by Román de la Luz. It is worth pointing out that another member of the lodge, Joaquín de Infante, wrote the first constitution for a republic in an independent Cuba in the year that the Cádiz constitution was approved in Spain (1812).

In addition to those already mentioned, another lodge from Haiti, called the *Réunion de Coeurs,* was established on November 18, 1805 in Santiago de Cuba.

As proof of the importance of these lodges within Cuban society, it is worth mentioning that the *Amistad, Concordia* and *Virtud* streets in the center of Havana are named after the three lodges active in the city during this period.

The political conflict in Spain, sparked by the French occupation in 1808, the outbreak of the Spanish War of Independence, the Junta movements, the Constitutional process of 1812, and the political unrest of the period were mirrored in Cuba. The socio-political world in Cuba played a particularly important role in the beginnings of the Latin American independence process.

The lodges I have referred to as being active in Cuba at that time were not under the jurisdiction of any Spanish Masonic body. The French invasion of Spain provoked a strong anti-French movement which forced many of the French who had even become citizens in Cuba to flee to Louisiana. They took with them the lodges which had been active until 1808. The only lodge to remain active was El Templo de las Virtudes Teologales, which now bore a Spanish name and included a majority of Creoles amongst its initiates. This lodge managed to survive beyond 1814, when, as a result of the restoration of the Ancien Régime in the person of Ferdinand VII, all lodges were prohibited within the Spanish empire. It resurfaced in 1820, after many years of secret activity, as we shall see below.

Despite the royal decree issued on January 19, 1814 by the Regency Council making Freemasonry an offence in all Spanish dominions, it is true that between 1814 and 1820 the number of Masonic institutions and lodges grew, albeit in secret. It must also be noted that in terms of content, and regardless of the Masonic bodies which created them, the new lodges served to affiliate members of different sectors of creole society, with clearly defined political profiles. Two schools of thinking can be detected within the new lodges: one is pro-independence and creole and the other liberal and constitution-

---

28 Ponte Domínguez, 14.

29 Miranda y Álvarez, 30.

alist. These currents can be observed in numerous documents. The mere fact of running afoul of the official prohibition by joining a lodge was, in itself, a political act. For example, a famous critical mural painted on the external and internal walls of a house in Havana, described in the *Diario cicla Habana* on March 24, 1812, not only provides an insight into the presence of Masonic symbolism but also anti-slavery and American patriotic feeling in what must have been an active lodge. These words describe a part of the mural:

> At the corner, there is a black man wearing a torn shirt and long pants prostrated at a white man's feet, hugging his knees. He has a book in his hand which reads: True patriotism is a profound hatred of injustice, and all kinds of unfairness or tyranny. Underneath: The American patriot who loves man, his homeland, and truth. There is another figure pointing at a book which reads: The holy freedom of press authorizes us to speak and write in favor of our just cause.[30]

On Saturday April 15, 1820, the news of the victory in Spain of the liberal constitutionalist Rafael del Riego reached Cuba. The Captain General of the island, Don Juan Manuel Cajigal was immediately obliged to swear loyalty to the 1812 constitution by the regiments from Málaga and Catalonia who were passing through Havana on their way to fight against independence forces in Latin America. Within days, a number of Masonic lodges came to light as well as a number of other secret societies which were not Masonic, but which imitated their structures and organizational practices. The number of lodges and societies, and the large number of members, lead one to believe that many of them had been active in the preceding years. Taking advantage of the freedoms decreed, two new Masonic bodies were established. They were the Spanish Grand Lodge of Ancient and Accepted Masons of York, whose members came to be known as Yorkinos, and the Spanish American Territorial Grand Orient of the Scottish Rite, known as Escocistas. Amongst the non-Masonic societies which were organized along Masonic lines and were therefore often confused with them were the following: Comuneros, Carbonarios, Anilleros, Cadena Triangular, Soles, and Caballeros Racionales. Each one of these institutions and organizations, Masonic or not, had different political ideas.

The Grand Spanish Lodge of Ancient and Accepted Masons of York was officially constituted on November 30, 1820. This branch of Freemasonry had certain characteristics on the American continent during that period, which I will describe in brief. Its principal breeding ground was the United States of America and, in particular, Pennsylvania. The content of its liturgies and the ideas of its main figures had clear liberal connotations. In the North American, not Spanish ver-

---

30 *Diario de La Habana* 594 (March 24, 1812): 1.

sion, it was Protestant, and therefore profoundly critical of Catholicism and its social and ethical content, and it was strongly American, more North American than Latin American. Under the guise of extending the "area of liberty," North American Yorkinos attempted to influence the development of the Latin American independence movement, in particular in Mexico and Cuba, regions which were in the sights of North American territorial expansion.[31]

The creation of Yorkino lodges in Latin America was linked to the US Government secret agent, Joel Robert Poinsett, amongst others. He was crucial in the creation of Yorkino Freemasonry and was in Cuba in the years in which it appeared on the island. Among Poinsett's papers there is a letter dated October 14, 1825, which confirms the political character of the York Rite Freemasonry, spurred on by the North Americans and his own personal role in the creation of this type of Freemasonry in Mexico:

> With the purpose of counteracting the action of the fanatic party in Mexico City, and if not possible, to spread the liberal principles more widely amongst those who have to govern this country, I incited and helped a certain number of respectable people to form a Grand Lodge of Yorkino Masons.[32]

While the Poinsett papers don't contain direct references to Yorkino Freemasonry in Cuba as they do for Freemasonry in Mexico, there is doubtless much in common between the two institutions and it is true the North American agent was highly active in attempting to annex Cuba to the United States.[33] The Cuban Grand Yorkino Lodge was constituted with a group of lodges that had been active prior to its creation. Importantly, all of them had been founded by North American grand lodges: two by the Pennsylvania Grand Lodge—Poinsett's home lodge— and one by the South Carolina Grand Lodge. It was Pennsylvania that authorized the creation of the Yorkino Grand Lodge.

It can be deduced from the list of people who took part in the constitution of the Yorkino Grand Lodge that the lodges they represented had been active for many years, albeit secret-

---

31 Soucy, *La Gran Legión del Águila Negra: Un Águila de dos cabezas (México-Cuba, 1823-1830)*; Carlos Francisco Martínez Moreno, "La Sociedad de los Yorkinos Federalistas, 1834. Un acercamiento hermenéutico a sus estatutos y reglamentos generales a la luz de la historia de la Masonería," *REHMLAC, Revista de Estudios Históricos de la Masonería Latinoamericana y Caribeña* (San José, Costa Rica) 1, n. 1 (mayo-noviembre 2009): 212-233. https://revistas.ucr.ac.cr/index.php/rehmlac/article/view/6864/6551. (Revised May 17, 2011).

32 José Fuentes Mares, *Poinsett, Historia de una gran intriga* (México: Editorial Jus, 1951), 103. For greater clarity on Poinsett's actions, see Joel Robert Poinsett, *Notas sobre México* (México: Editorial Jus, 1950), prologue and notes by Eduardo Enrique Ríos, translation by Pablo Martínez.

33 There are other papers in the Library of Congress of the United States where the Poinsett papers are located, which include the letters sent to Félix Varela in which Poinsett attempted to incite the annexation of Cuba.

ly. This is confirmed by the number of former worshipful masters that appear in the list. Despite the fact that the first chapter, first article of its *General Regulations* stipulates that "The good Mason must not become involved in plots against the state: he must be faithful and obedient to the authorities of the country he resides in: he must be a peaceful and cool-headed citizen," the same chapter and article also point out: "Love of the homeland must be the first object to occupy his heart. All sacrifice is as nothing compared to the worth and merits of the homeland."[34]

Despite the above statements, the Yorkinos did play an active role in politics and at that time they were commonly known as the "Creole party."[35] The Yorkinos demanded a set of requirements for membership which are summarized in article 75 of the regulations.

To be accepted as a Mason not only must the aspirant comply with the requirements expressed in the first article (they must believe in the Great Architect of the Universe and must never have committed a crime) but they must not be "officially" poor, must have a good reputation, must be at least 21 years old, must be freeborn, must possess all four limbs, must not be disfigured in any way, must have all their sentient faculties in perfect working order, and must not be eunuchs. Women are not admitted.[36]

According to a document dated March 5, 1822, the Yorkino Grand Lodge already had 30 associated lodges: seven under Pennsylvania, two under South Carolina, and three under Louisiana. It is not known how nor when the remaining eighteen were established, but it is reasonable to suppose they were created or regularized by the Grand Lodge established in Cuba.[37]

The other Masonic body active at this time, the Grand Spanish American Territorial Orient of the Scottish Rite, had started to constitute itself prior to the Yorkino Grand Lodge. It was based around the Grand Consistory of the 32nd degree created in Havana on April 2, 1818 by Luis Juan Lorenzo D'Clouet, a colonel of French origin.[38] Its authorization came from the Grand Orient of France. Its constituent lodges were related to the French Grand Orient and were the Unión Fraternal and Rectitud in Havana and Divina Pastora in Matanzas. The Constante Sophie Lodge was founded shortly afterward. Officially, the Territorial Grand Orient started its work on May 14, 1821. Its initial leadership was composed of a group of Spanish officers and merchants in Havana. Unlike the Yorkinos, the members of this body were initially mainly

34 A reproduction of the document cited can be found in Miranda y **Álvarez**, 43-44.

35 Félix Varela, *Escritos Políticos* (La Habana: Editorial de Ciencias Sociales, 1977), 122.

36 Miranda y Álvarez, 30.

37 *Ibid.*

38 Biblioteca Nacional José Martí, Sala Cubana, *Colección Manuscritos Vidal Morales*, Tomo V, n. 43.

Spanish, and so it was dubbed the "Peninsular party." Although they shared the same liberal principles as the Yorkinos, there was French influence in their liturgies. What was conspicuous at this time were the debates between the two Masonic bodies, many of which were public. Perhaps the most significant aspect of the development of the Territorial Grand Orient was that during 1822 its membership began to change and by the middle of the year it was made up mainly of Creoles. These belonged to some of the most eminent families in the country. The Grand Mastership fell to the powerful Conde de O'Reilly, and one of the most important figures, Nicolás de Escovedo, was a follower and close collaborator of Félix Vareal and Bishop Espada.

The initial differences between the two Masonic bodies led to mutual accusations, but the increasing dominance of the Creoles led to both bodies being accused of seeking the independence of the country. The following paragraph can be found in one of the Escocista documents of the time.

> The Chamber also considered that, at this time, we should not encourage malice, resentment, and vengeance to accompany the plan which has been launched so openly, that is to say, ideas and plans of political independence, when Freemasonry is the only thing that has been and could have been discussed, because this is what respect, the good

of the island, and true knowledge of Freemasonry in Spain demands.[39]

Whilst there was no independence plot within Escocista Freemasonry, it is true that it did refuse to affiliate Cuban Freemasonry to the bodies existing in Spain. What could explain these differences—above all if one takes into account the personalities leading Escocista symbolic Freemasonry—seems to be the chaos in which Spanish Freemasonry was immersed at the time and the struggle of the Havana oligarchy against Spanish liberals, and, in particular, the Cadiz merchants. This can be confirmed if one studies the non-Masonic documents of the Conde de O'Reilly, a resolute subject of Ferdinand VII. The Escocistas aspired to the sovereignty of their Grand Orient, according to the strict formulations of Masonic constitutions. In 1823, Yorkinos and Escocistas attempted a union which never became effective, owing to the fall of the constitutional regime and the reinstatement of absolutism.

Special reference must be made to the non-Masonic secret societies which had clearly political profiles and were often referred to as Masonic organizations. They can be grouped in the following way: The Comuneros, Carbonarios and Anilleros. Despite their differences in Spain, they were fairly united in Cuba and even worked together, since they were constituted by army officers or Spanish merchants who found themselves opposing the Creoles.

---

39 Paula Rodríguez & Betancourt, D. 22.

On the other hand, the Cadena Triangular, active in Camagüey, Caballeros Racionales,[40] active in Matanzas, and Los Soles, based in Havana, had clear independence sympathies. There is plenty of evidence that these latter three organizations acted in a coordinated manner, and were also linked to the Bolivarian independence movement in Latin America. Suffice it to say that the Soles—also known as the Soles y Rayos de Bolívar—was founded by Latin American residents in Cuba, all distinguished leaders in Latin American independence movements. They included the Argentine José Antonio Miralla, who would die later while attempting to carry out an invasion to achieve the independence of Cuba, Vicente Rocafuerte, subsequently president of independent Ecuador, and the Columbian José Fernández Madrid, who had been president of the first republic of Colombia.[41] The Peruvian Manel Lorenzo Vidaurre was also linked to the Cadena Triangular in Camagüey.

Rocafuerte wrote the following about the Soles:

> In Havana, there is a very secret society which is in frequent contact with another in Caracas. It is headed by Dr. J. Fernández Madrid, who is well-known amongst us for his virtues, his outstanding talents, and his sincere patriotism. He did me the honor of initiating me into the mysteries of this patriotic association.[42]

Another factor links these secret societies to the Lautaro lodges in the South American cone. The full name of the lodges was Logia de Lautaro o de los Caballeros Racionales. Can it have been pure chance that the lodge in Matanzas was also called the Caballeros Racionales? Furthermore, the first letters of the mystic legend of the Lautaro lodges was U.F.V (*Unión, Fe, Victoria*) and those of the Soles was also U.F.V (*Unión, Firmeza, Valor*). The Venezuelan general José Antonio Páez wrote in his *Memoria*: "In 1823, the Minister of War, Señor Pedraza, authorized Don Pedro Hojas to carry out anti-piracy operations and to establish relations with the inhabitants of Cuba, in order to foment the revolution which on that island goes by the name of 'Soles de Bolivar.'"[43]

As can be seen, neither the Carbonarios, Comuneros and Anilleros, nor the Caballeros Racionales, Cadena Triangular and Soles were Masonic institutions, but organizations with specific political aims, even if they modeled their initiation ceremonies,

---

40 Ferrer Benimeli, « Les Caballeros Racionales, les loges lautariennes et les formes déviées de la Franc-maçonnerie dans le monde hispanique », dans *Les révolutions ibériques et Ibéro-Américaines à l'aube du XIXe siècle, Actes du colloque de Bordeaux 2-4 juillet 1989* (Paris, Editions CNRS, 1991).

41 Torres Cuevas, *Historia de la Masonería cubana. Seis ensayos*, 163.

42 José Antonio Fernández de Castro, *José Fernández Madrid, prócer colombiano de la independencia de Cuba* (La Habana: Colección Órbita, UNEAC, 1966), 213-214.

43 Julián Vivanco, *José Antonio Miralla. Precursor de la independencia de Cuba* (La Habana: Editorial El Sol, 1958), Tomo I, 38.

organization and structures on those of the Masons.

The fall of the constitutional regime in 1823 was accompanied by the prohibition of Freemasonry and of the other organizations referred to in the Royal Decree of August 1, 1824. However, the Captain General of the island, Francisco Dionisio Vives, had to act with great care and no small measure of energy to quell the insubordination of the lodges in Cuba. The Yorkino Grand Lodge sent out a circular to all its affiliates to find out if they were ready to "declare their allegiance to the constitution on this island in the likelihood of Spain falling to the despotic system protected by the French government."[44]

Similarly, there were lodges in Havana which flaunted their disobedience. But, in some cases using persuasion, and in other cases wielding a machete (as was the case of a lodge in the Havana town of Vereda Nueva), Vives managed to achieve the dissolution, or at least the inactivity, of the Masonic groups and some of the secret societies, most of which his secret agents had infiltrated.[45] Shortly afterwards he uncovered the Soles conspiracy (which he put down), and later, in 1829, the plot of the Gran Legión del Águila Negra, which by then had almost collapsed before it was able to take action.[46] There are ample documents to prove that the Águila Negra conspiracy was related to members of the Yorkino Rite, albeit not directly with the lodge. It was based in Mexico, and its chief instigator, whose alias was Varón Fuerte o Protomédico de Londres, was the Mexican president, Guadalupe Victoria.[47] The Gran Legión was active during the armed conflict between Mexico and Spain, but when this came to an end, support received by its members started to diminish, until, by 1826, it only existed in name. The inefficiency of both the Soles and Águila Negra conspiracies was due to the fact that their plans to separate Cuba politically from Spain were based on intervention by independence armies from the American continent, either Venezuela or Mexico, and never on the island's own capacity to achieve and maintain independence.

Perhaps the most debated period of the history of Cuban Freemasonry is that which we have just referred to, though it should be said it did not leave a very deep imprint on the history of the institution in Cuba. The period is important as it raises questions about the social action of Freemasonry, its foundations, and its historical role. Some authors, such as Paula Rodríguez y Betancourt, assert that the "accusation of being conspiratorial, with which Cuban Freemasonry is often branded" is unjust,[48] whilst others, such

---

44 Ponte Domínguez, 25.

45 *Ibid.*, 32.

46 Roque Garrigó, *Historia documentada de la Conspiración de los Soles y Rayos de Bolívar* (La Habana, Editorial El Siglo XX, 1929), 260.

47 Adrián del Valle, *Historia documentada de la Conspiración de La Gran Legión del Águila Negra* (La Habana, Editorial El Siglo XX, 1930), 100-120.

48 Paula Rodríguez & Betancourt, XVIII.

as Ponte Domínguez, maintain that "It can be seen that, throughout the nineteenth century, the Creole Masons in Cuba were, at all times, either within the heart of the brotherly lodges or outside the main independence conspirators on the island."[49] Both authors were Masons, although a generation divides the two writers. I believe that, in the history of Cuban Freemasonry, there are stages and periods which run parallel to those in the history of Universal Freemasonry. They are not only determined by historic times, but also in the way Masonic ideas and practices developed. Whilst the general principles of the Freemasonry were formulated in the early years of the eighteenth century, during the creation of the Grand Lodge of England, it was during the rest of the eighteenth and the beginning of the nineteenth century that the system of degrees and the rites themselves were developed, and this created a tension between Masonic ethics and their practical implementation. For this reason, it was not always possible to set clear boundaries between the sphere of Masonic action and political practice. The identification of Freemasonry with the Enlightenment—from which Freemasonry clearly sprang—and, in some cases, with liberalism, explains why many, both inside and outside the institution, saw no sense in sharing the same basic ideas but behaving differently when putting the ideas into practice. One should add, however, that the specific circumstances of countries and epochs were not defined by general trends, but rather by specific trends belonging to different geographical areas and social milieus. This is particularly clear if one compares Latin American and North American, or English and French, Masonic traditions.

Although this is not the place—nor the objective of this paper—to analyze the relationship of Freemasonry with certain groups in power, it must, nevertheless, be pointed out that Freemasonry's presence and influence on politics declined systematically during the nineteenth and twentieth centuries. The period we are dealing with here was, in fact, one of the periods in which Freemasonry exerted most political pressure. Neither is this the place to speak of the role of Masonic institutions during this period in disseminating liberal-republican ideas, and with them the development of ideas of a secular democratic society, although this is in fact one of the most important aspects in the study of this period of Cuban Freemasonry. What is necessary is to establish the existence of two different currents within Freemasonry, which were manifested as two different rites. Yorkino Freemasonry had clear Protestant, secular, North American and biblical features, while Escocista Freemasonry, though also secular, was more Latin, and was free of anti-Catholic sentiment. Both were guided by universal Masonic principles, but demonstrated clear political—liberal—leanings, not so much in their regulations as in the documentation which accompanied their activities. Furthermore, it is necessary to distinguish from Freemasonry

---

49 Ponte Domínguez, 10.

the secret societies of a political nature which at that time took on Masonic elements or imitated features of Freemasonry. This type of association would disappear subsequently, giving way to the new modern political parties. The mistake has been in confusing Freemasonry with the politically-motivated secret societies. What divided Masons from each other and Masons from the secret societies was the defense of the interests, perspectives and projects of new societies opposed to the Ancien Régime, which underlay but were also above the truisms of the constitutionalist movement. Masonic lodges were not free of political concerns during this period, and this would not be the only period in Cuba's history that this was so.

Second Period of Freemasonry in Cuba (1830-1868)

There were no regular or irregular Masonic bodies established in Cuba between 1830 and 1857. Despite the rise of the liberal movement in Spain, Masonic activity continued to be prohibited. Ferdinand VII had created the crime of Freemasonry, so it was persecuted in Spain and in its colonies. Tensions decreased gradually, and the moderate liberal government of Francisco Martínez de la Rosa reduced sanctions for the crime of Freemasonry in the Royal Decree of April 23, 1834. While the crime continued to exist in the penal code, it did not put an end to the active and ongoing presence of Masons in Cuba.

Another feature of this period was the membership of Cubans in foreign Masonic institutions, above all, in the United States, Mexico, and France. Also active were a number of secret societies, whose aim was the independence of Cuba from Spain. As in the previous period, these political organizations adopted Masonic initiation rites and structures, so they were often identified incorrectly as Masonic. While some of them sought independence, others sought annexation to the United States of America. Amongst these organizations, one can cite the Sociedad Libertadora de Puerto Príncipe, la Orden Estrella Solitaria, La Unión (whose name reflects the desire of its members to see the annexation of Cuba to the United States). Some of these organizations called themselves "lodges" owing to the way they were organized and the need for an initiation rite. Their clear political nature can be seen in their activities, and even in some cases they both call themselves "Masons" and declare themselves in favor of independence. Nevertheless, they were not constituted according to "regular" Freemasonry precepts, nor did they respect the formulations of the established constitutions. During the rise of the annexationist movement between 1848 and 1855, there was an increase in conspiratorial groups, which almost always imitated the organization of Freemasonry. During this period, which sprang from a crisis in the development of Cuban national consciousness, one can note clear North American influence and this is also reflected in some members of Masonic institutions.[50]

The victory of Unión Liberal in Spain in 1855 and the links of its leading figures with the Cuban oligarchy, mainly generals Leopoldo O' Donnell y Jorris, José Gutiérrez de la Concha e Irigoyen, Domingo Dulce y Garay and Francisco Serrano y Cuenca Guevara Domínguez—all in the Cuban governing body—opened the door to reform in Cuba and the opening of society to certain social, political and press freedoms. Thanks to the new conditions, the first two lodges, *Fraternidad* No. 1 and *Prudencia* No. 2, were established in Santiago de Cuba. These would give new life to Masonic institutions in Cuba.

While Freemasonry prior to 1855 had been subject to considerable North American influence, these new lodges leant more towards Spain, and, for this reason, attempted to join the Gran Oriente Hispérico Reformado de España. They were not able to establish this relationship, as by that time the Gran Oriente no longer existed.[51] The truth was that there were no longer any Masonic bodies in Spain. In fact, the Gran Oriente Nacional de España did not come into existence until six years after the establishment of the Columbus Freemasonry. Since the aim of these first lodges was to constitute a Grand Lodge for the island of Cuba, they resorted to one of the most exciting and controversial figures in the history of North American Freemasonry, Albert Pike, then Grand Commander of the Supreme Council of the South of the United States for the Ancient and Accepted Scottish Rite. At least three Masonic lodges were needed for the creation of a grand lodge, so the *San Andrés* No. 3 lodge was created on November 18, 1859, also in Santiago de Cuba. On December 5, the three lodges met to constitute their governing body, which they named the Columbus Grand Lodge.[52]

Prior to this, on March 26, 1859, the French-born Andrés Cassard, now living in the United States, had been authorized to create the upper positions, degrees and bodies of Scottish Rite Freemasonry in Cuba. Curiously, and independently of the powers given to the Santiago lodges to create the Grand Lodge, it was Albert Pike and Albert G. Mackey—the latter being the author of one of the most important works on Masonic jurisprudence in Cuba—who granted these powers. In December 1859, Cassard arrived in Santiago de Cuba from New York. He decided not to disembark, being under threat of the death sentence from the Spanish authorities. And on December 27, in his cabin, he founded the Supreme Council of the 33rd Degree for the island of Cuba and the rest of the Spanish Antilles.[53] This fact is momentous, as Columbus Freemasonry, which takes its name

50 An explanation of this process can be found in Torres Cuevas, *De la Ilustración reformista al Reformismo liberal* (La Habana: Instituto de Historia de Cuba. La Colonia, Editora Política, 1994), 314-394.

51 Miranda y Álvarez, 202.

52 *Ibid.*, 206.

53 Julio César Llopiz, "Columna Fraternales," *Excelsior* (October 21, 1950).

from the document, would have jurisdiction not only over Cuba, but also over Puerto Rico and, potentially, over Santo Domingo, which is to say, over all the Spanish Antilles.

Although the Supreme Council and the Grand Lodge had been constituted to govern different degrees of Columbus Freemasonry, the irregularity with which the Supreme Council had been founded caused intense rivalry in terms of jurisdiction and authority between the two bodies.

The most important feature of Columbus Freemasonry was that, despite having obtained their letters of patent from North American Masonic bodies, its members and their ideas were linked to what came to be known as "Latin" Freemasonry, which was characterized by a desire to distance itself from Protestant, mystic and elitist ideas of Anglo-Saxon Freemasonry. In the case of Columbus Freemasonry, however, there was also a strong Spanish element, so one cannot ascribe to the institution any political action against the existing regime on the island. This is particularly clear when one considers the first Masonic leaders. The first Grand Commander of the Supreme Council was the Spanish merchant and one of the richest landowners in the east of the island, Antonio Vinent y Gola, Marquess of Palomares del Duero, a title he was granted for his services against the Cuban independence movement. And the first Grand Master of the Columbus Grand Lodge was Francisco de Griñan, another important landown-

er in the eastern region and also active against the independence movement.

Perhaps as a result of the North American influence, and despite its clear Latin vision, Columbus Freemasonry bore a feature which was absent from future Cuban Masonic bodies. It was distinctly racist. One of its documents runs as follows:

> Finding ourselves in a country where it is not possible for people of color to mix with whites, as the line which divides society is very clear, and people of color are not admitted freely, let the Master of the Regular Grand Lodge be informed that it is not possible to receive anyone not considered to be white, though he may be free, to avoid the upset it could provoke, and the conflict in which all would be involved by admitting a host of brown and dark people who we know to be in possession of the best qualities. Let it be told to the Regular Grand Lodges so that it can be communicated to the other symbolic lodges in their jurisdiction; and article 115 is understood to be revised in this respect.[54]

In 1862, Cuban Freemasonry was divided when a new institution, the Grand Orient of Cuba and the Antilles, was created. It was, in essence, patriotic, ethical and reformist, and the Cuban Revolution of 1868 was hatched within it. Its creator was the doctor, scientist

54 Miranda y Álvarez, 206.

and distinguished intellectual Vicente Antonio de Castro y Bermúdez.[55]

Authorized by Albert Pike,[56] in whose North American Masonic body he had regularized his degrees, de Castro returned to Cuba to review and regularize Cuban Freemasonry. There is no doubt that those involved in these events were motivated by intentions which have yet to be fully cleared up. Albert Pike, in particular, was responsible for having created a totally irregular situation. First, he had authorized the Santiago lodges to found a grand lodge, but independently, he authorized André Cassard to create the upper degrees, which provoked rivalry between the grand lodge and the Supreme Council. Now, he was granting Vicente Antonio de Castro full powers to reorganize Cuban Freemasonry. Pike wanted to convert the Supreme Council of the South of the United States into the center of Freemasonry. Even at that time, it called itself the "First Masonic power in the world." The leanings of the Cuban institution, however, were towards the creation of fraternal links and not dependency.

Vicente Antonio de Castro returned to the island in 1861, taking advantage of the political amnesty decreed by the colonial government. He went immediately to Santiago de Cuba, where the governing Masonic bodies of Columbus Freemasonry were based. His objective became clear when he decided to return to Havana and to break with the established Masonic organization by creating a new body. The historian Roger Fernández Callejas maintains that he did so, as the Columbus Masonic leadership, both in the grand lodge and the Supreme Council, was dominated by supporters of the colonial authorities. On March 28, 1862, de Castro founded the Grand Orient of Cuba and the Antilles. From then until 1868, there was conflict between the two Masonic bodies in Cuba, caused by their differing political convictions.[57]

Between 1862 and 1868, the

---

55 Torres Cuevas, *Historia de la Masonería cubana. Seis ensayos*, 130-160.

56 Albert Pike: One of the most important figures in the history of North American Freemasonry was involved in the beginnings of all the initial bodies in Cuban Freemasonry. His influence and contentious interventions in Cuban Freemasonry still need to be studied. He was initiated as a Mason in 1850, after having played an important role in North American territorial expansion. As a leader of a cavalry detachment, he played an active part in Mexico's loss of its North American territories. He was one of the first to propose the construction of a railway from coast to coast to ensure expansion to the west. During the Civil War he fought for the South, and reached the rank of Brigadier General, responsible for the Indian territory situated to the west of Arkansas. Later he took refuge in Canada, as he feared being arrested. On August 30, 1865, the president of the United States permitted him to return to his country on condition of swearing loyalty to the nation. He was 56 years old. From then on, he devoted himself to his profession as a lawyer, the administration of his property, and to Freemasonry. He died on April 2, 1891 at the Holy House of the Temple of the Scottish Rite in Washington. The Supreme Council erected a statue in his name in Washington. From 1859, he was the Grand Perpetual Commander of the Supreme Council of the 33rd Degree for the South Jurisdiction of the United States and lived at the Holy House of the Temple (3rd and East; N.W., Washington, D.C.).

57 Torres Cuevas, *Historia de la Masonería cubana. Seis ensayos*, 68-139.

Grand Orient continued to create lodges in the main towns and settlements of the island until there were about twenty, some of which had shifted obedience from Columbus to the Grand Orient. The two figures who attacked Vicente Antonio de Castro's insubordination most vociferously were Andrés Cassard and Albert Pike. Pike, unhappy with the character the Grand Orient was adopting and spurred on by Columbus Freemasonry, demonstrated his disapproval of all of de Castro's acts in a letter dated November 17, 1865. In the letter, he accused the Grand Orient of being none other than a political, non-Masonic, "Jacobin club headquarters." But the problem was even more complex. The Grand Orient liturgies were essentially Masonic, but they included numerous definitions and analyses of a political nature. One comes to the inevitable conclusion that they represented a markedly ethical project to transform society. Another prominent nineteenth century Cuban Mason, Aurelio Almeida, wrote:

> Its system, surpassing the strict biblical-moral sphere which the English and American rituals revolve around, especially in the symbolic degrees, took in the vast field of social and political sciences (...). Castro's Scottish system (...) introduced into the work of the brotherhood an element which all its modern and ancient laws shunned completely: the political element.[58]

Another aspect which particularly irritated Pike was the criticism of the elitism of North American Freemasonry and the enthusiasm for Latin American Masonic traditions. The Grand Orient liturgies were rationalist, enlightened, liberal, democratic, anticlerical, internationalist, secular, in favor of secular education, deist, and, above all, patriotic. Moreover, their motto was the same one adopted by the Grand Orient of France in 1848: Liberty, Equality, Fraternity.

The most important characteristic of the Grand Orient lay in the fact that it was responsible for generating a patriotic vision based on democratic republicanism, which could only be achieved through the creation of an independent state. Many of those who participated in the revolutionary independence movement of 1868 sprang from this Masonic body. The patriotic leaders who launched the War of Independence were members of the Grand Orient. However, the famous assertion—widespread in Spanish historiography—that "if Spain loses the Spanish Antilles, it will be the September revolution and Freemasonry which are to blame,"[59] is false, as the leaders of the regularly constituted Masonic body —Columbus Freemasonry—not only kept well out of any plots, but also open-

---

58 Aurelio Almeida, *El consultor del masón. Colección de tratados sobre todas las materias de la Francmasonería* (Madrid: Puente, Godoy y Loureiro Editores, 1883), Vol. I, 75.

59 Vicente de la Fuente, *Historia de las sociedades secretas antiguas y modernas, especialmente de la francmasonería* (Lugo: Soto Freire, 1870-1871), (Apéndice de 1881), 275.

ly demonstrated their opposition to the independence movement. The members of the Grand Orient, on the other hand, dedicated their lives to the independence of Cuba.

The Grand Orient of Cuba and the Antilles was dissolved on October 10, 1868, the day the revolution, known as the Grito de Demajagua or Grito de Yara, broke out. Shortly afterwards, on May 12, 1869, the founder of the Grand Orient, Vicente Antonio de Castro, died. As we have indicated, the independence movement immediately joined ranks with Freemasonry. The revolution, linked to the internal problems of Columbus Freemasonry, opened a period of important readjustments and redefinitions in Cuban Freemasonry. In both Spain and Cuba, Freemasonry was acquiring a much wider social and political dimension than in previous periods. But it was characterized by its splintering into tendencies and groups, and internationally there were conflicts between the Grand Lodge of England and the Grand Orient of France. In Cuba, the Masons who supported independence, those who continued the work of the Grand Orient, created itinerant lodges in the "manigua," such as the Tínima and Camagüey lodges, and the Independencia Lodge—created by the worshipful president of the Republic of Cuba in Arms, don Carlos Manuel de Céspedes.[60] Many of their passwords were versions of text from the liturgies of the Grand Orient. When the first

Cuban constitution, the Guáimaro, was drawn up in 1869, many of the secular, social, and political ideas proclaimed by the Grand Orient were written into law and would leave an enduring mark on the history of Cuba.

Third Period of Freemasonry in Cuba (1868-1898)

The dissolution of the Grand Orient was not enough to stop the repression against Freemasonry, as Masons were associated with the independence movement. Considering all Masons to be conspirators, the Body of Volunteers—a Spanish paramilitary force on the island—drew up a list of leading figures, not only from the irregular Grand Orient, but also from Columbus Freemasonry. The most wantonly violent acts were committed in Santiago de Cuba. On the Spanish volunteers' list in the town were José Andrés Puente Badell, then Grand Master of the Grand Lodge of Columbus, Esteban Miniet, Grand Treasurer, and other prominent personalities belonging to both groups, along with many who were not Masons. With no trial or legal process of any kind, they were taken to the camp at the San Juan de Wilson factory, seven leagues from Santiago de Cuba, and murdered on February 13, 14, and 15, 1870. The order was given by Carlos González Boet, who, paradoxically, was also a Mason.[61] Numerous Masons were also arrested in Havana, the event most

---

60   Fernando Figueredo Socarrás, "Logia militante Independencia," in *La Gran Logia* (La Habana) 3 (1901): 23-25.

61   Buenaventura Cruz, *Cómo murió nuestro Gran Maestro Andrés Puente. Relato del único superviviente*; Paula Rodríguez & Betancourt, Apéndice XV, LXXVI1-LXXXI.

worthy of note being the attack on the San Andrés Lodge— whose members included Martí's teacher, Rafael María Mendive—and the imprisonment of 52 Cuban, Spanish and foreign Masons who were found there.[62]

Freemasonry underwent trying circumstances during the First Cuban War of Independence (1868-1878), but it was also a time of restructuring. This process involved much more than simple reorganization. It implied a profound redefinition of the identity of the institution. On May 26, 1870, the lodges in the capital, who wished to be independent of the Supreme Council and the Grand Columbus Lodge, both based in Santiago de Cuba, created the First Provincial Mother Lodge of Havana.[63] Its Grand Master was the Spaniard Severino Fernández Mora, a doctor of military health in the Spanish army, who, for his activities and ideas, was forced by the colonial authorities to abandon the island "within 24 hours."[64] On May 23, 1875, the Second Provincial Mother Lodge was constituted, with a wider base than the previous one. There is no doubt that both attempts were motivated by those formerly active in the Grand Orient and certain sectors within the Columbus Freemasonry who had different ideas from those leading the Grand Lodge based in Santiago. Other reasons included the impracticality of the center of Freemasonry being so far from the political and economic center

of the country.

In 1875, the Columbus Supreme Council took a step which had special connotations for the future of Cuban Freemasonry. It sent two delegates, David Elías Pierre and Benjamín Odio, to the Convention of the Supreme Councils of the Scottish Rite in Lausanne in Switzerland. At the convention, the men signed the Confederation Agreement of the World Regular Supreme Councils. At the time, this event made an impact in Cuba, firstly because the Cuban delegation had been accepted, whilst the Spanish delegation had been refused, the reason being that the Spanish delegation was so disorganized that accepting one delegation would have meant the exclusion of others, and secondly because the Masonic rules established at the Convention were adopted and accepted. This was particularly important with regard to politics. Although Freemasonry had always defined itself as being detached from political practice, it could not avoid being caught up in the maelstrom of political events.[65] The Lausanne definitions reinforced its philanthropic-fraternal character, defining its basic tenets and providing it with a framework for social action. This was seen clearly in the replacement of its openly political mottos, such as the French revolutionary *Liberty, Equality, Fraternity*, with the new mottos of *Brotherly Love, Relief and Truth*. The guidelines which underlay the change

---

62   Vicente Rumbaut y Yáñez, *La Masonería, y el odfelismo en Cienfuegos* (Cienfuegos: Taller Tipográfico de Rafael Caro, 1938), 104.

63   Torres Cuevas, *Historia de la Masonería cubana. Seis ensayos*, 237.

64   *Ibid.*

65   Frau Abrines & Arús Arderiú, Vol I, 134.

in Cuban Freemasonry's positions were expressed in 1875 by Francisco de Paula Rodríguez, one of the most important figures in the institution at the end of the nineteenth and the beginning of the twentieth century:

> Because of this presumptuous error, we were believed to be playing a political role (...) which led to continued harassment and persecution of the institution. In this respect, we have learnt a lot. The motto *Liberty, Equality and Fraternity,* which is a clearly political motto, has been replaced with the one used in England and in the United States, *Brotherly Love, Relief and Truth.*[66]

This meant that Freemasonry gained a more significant social presence, leading to the joining of new members who didn't wish to be linked to political action but who did share Freemasonry's social ideas and wished to play a part in its cultural or ethical-philanthropic-fraternal work. In addition, North American influence within the institution diminished and was replaced by the presence of a strong core of members with a strong Hispanic cultural background, and, above all, an increasing expression of Cuban intellectual ideas.

In 1876, one of Vicente Antonio de Castro's followers and the person who doubtless was responsible for the creation of the definitive organization and objectives of Cuban Freemasonry, Aurelio Almeida y González, then one of the main figures of the Second Provincial Mother Lodge of Havana, prepared what some Mason historians have come to consider a veritable "coup d'état" against Columbus Freemasonry.[67] First, he went on a lengthy journey around the United States of America to gain the support of the main North American Masonic bodies. Then, on July 28, 1876, several days after his return to Havana, he dissolved the Provincial Mother Lodge and, on August 1, to great jubilation, announced the creation of a new independent Masonic body, the Grand Lodge of the Island of Cuba. Thus, once again, there were two separate Masonic bodies. The situation became even more complex when further lodges linked to different Spanish Masonic bodies began to function.

The Masonic body created by Almeida dedicated itself immediately to reorganizing the lodges and establishing relationships with Freemasonry in other countries. Not only did it obtain the recognition of the North American Grand Lodges, but also that of the Spanish Masonic body of Práxedes Mateo Sagasta.[68] In fact, the new Masonic institution was the reorganized Grand Orient of Cuba and the Antilles, now regularized, under a new name, and missing its direct links with political ideas and action. Under the influence of

---

66 *Revista La Gran Logia* (La Habana) 6 (1904).

67 Torres Cuevas, *Historia de la Masonería cubana. Seis ensayos,* 237-238.

68 Ferrer Benimeli (coord.), *La Masonería española en la época de Sagasta (1825-1903)* (Zaragoza: CEHME y la Fundación Práxedes Mateo-Sagasta, 2006).

the Spanish restoration and certain liberties conceded with the aim of achieving the end of the war in Cuba, both Masonries, that of Columbus and that of the Island of Cuba, were able to converge and develop a joint vision of Freemasonry that was essentially cultural and based on the developing elements of nascent Cubanness, free thought, the trend towards a secular society and a broad spectrum of liberal ideas, more ideological than political.

It is necessary to explain in more detail Almeida's aims for the organization. Freemasonry was, above all, an institution with ethical aims, dedicated to philanthropic social and cultural action, to the establishing of national roots and international fraternal links. According to this view, the institution was not permitted to become involved in politics, but it is true to say that a certain model of politics did, nevertheless, favor the social action of Freemasonry. This model was a liberal model, whose tenets were compatible with the ethics of Freemasonry. This explains why liberals and Masons were identified as being opposed to conservatism, but, at the same time, why there should be different trends within liberalism and Freemasonry. On an individual level, the ethical-philanthropic-fraternal work of the Mason complemented and was correlated with liberal political practice. Thus, Freemasonry excluded itself from politics, but in ideological terms continued to correspond to certain political ideas. In Cuba, however, this was not the most important dimension. Although the traditional rivalry between conservatism and liberalism existed, the main division was between independence and union with Spain. And, faced with this issue, although the institution aimed to be a center of unity and fraternity, the Masons were once again divided, and this division was reflected in the debate about the tenets of Freemasonry. These were the issues of the day and modern ideas of the institution must not be extrapolated to those times, because current ideas are the result of more than a century of Masonic practice and thought.

On November 24, 1876, the Grand Lodge and Supreme Council of Columbus signed what came afterwards to be known as the *Treaty of Peace and Friendship*. This has been renewed in all subsequent Cuban Masonic codes and is based on the agreements of the Lausanne Congress of Supreme Councils. This agreement eliminated the mystic, aristocratic, and authoritarian posts within the organization and the high degrees lost a large part of the importance they had enjoyed. According to the agreement, the Supreme Council recognized the Grand Lodge as the "regular, competent, and sovereign" authority over all the first three degrees or symbolic degrees, and, at the same time, the Grand Lodge recognized the Supreme Council as being the only body authorized to govern degrees 4 to 33. The leadership of both organizations would have their own laws and regulations and would not fall within the jurisdiction of the other.[69] This

---

69 This document is reproduced in *Código masónico de la Isla de Cuba* (La Habana: Edición F. Verdugo, 1931).

agreement can be considered to be a model for overcoming internal conflicts and one of the most valuable instruments for achieving Masonic unity and brotherhood.

The internal contradictions within the Grand Lodge of Columbus continued to cause clashes between the leadership of the Grand Lodge based in Santiago de Cuba and the lodges in the west of the island, led by José Fernández Pellón y Castellanos. Fernández Pellón, the representative of the 27 western lodges, managed to gain acceptance for the move of the Grand Lodge to Havana, whilst the Supreme Council remained in Santiago de Cuba. If one takes into account that the Grand Lodge governed the symbolic lodges—the majority—it made sense to move to the capital. But some of the eastern lodges were resisting the move, preferring the Grand Lodge of Columbus to stay in Santiago de Cuba.

On July 20, 1877, the Columbus Grand Lodge was proclaimed in the capital.[70] The majority of the leadership was in the hands of a strong group linked to Cuban liberalism. The group had clear reforming aims and a year later it would give rise to the Liberal Party, later, the Autonomist Liberal Party. Moreover, the character of the Masonic lodges made it possible for both reformists and secessionists to work together for the cultural and social development and transformation of the country. The Grand Master was

Antonio Govín y Torres,[71] who was also the secretary and one of the administrators of the Autonomist Liberal Party.[72] Alongside the conflicts within Columbus Freemasonry, the Grand Lodge of the Island of Cuba had achieved a depth and a strength which transcended the regionalist limitations of its rival. Almeida created and proclaimed a Masonic code, until then unfamiliar to Cuban lodges, which has been recognized by other Spanish-speaking countries. Moreover, Alameida authorized the creation of lodges in Spain under the jurisdiction of the Grand Lodge of the Island of Cuba. Amongst Almeida's most significant works are *El Consultor del Masón* and *Jurisprudencia masónica,* which were widely disseminated amongst Latin American Masons. The first of the works includes the liturgies of the Grand Orient of Cuba and the Antilles written by Vicente Antonio de Castro.

The First Cuban War of Independence, also known as the Ten Years' War, was concluded in 1878, and in the same year the first political parties in the history of the country were founded. The most important of these was the Liberal Party, but as we have already said, shortly afterwards it started to call itself the Autonomist Party. Its leaders included key figures from the two Masonic bodies. Amongst these were Antonio Govín y Torres, party secretary and Grand Master of the Columbus Grand Lodge, José Fernández

---

70   Torres Cuevas, *Historia de la Masonería cubana. Seis ensayos*, 120.

71   Sappez, "Antonio Govín y Torres, nexo entre Masonería y autonomismo en Cuba," 559-572.

72   Soucy & Sappez, "Autonomismo y Masonería en Cuba," 90-99.

Pellón, José María Gálvez, president of the party, and Rafael Montoro, the most renowned intellectual of the liberal-autonomist movement and worshipful master of the Plus Ultra lodge.

The autonomist program contained important aspects which were promoted by Cuban lodges. Their political beliefs were expressed as follows:

> *The necessary freedoms:* Extension of individual rights guaranteed in Clause 1 of the Constitution: Freedom of press, of assembly and association, Inviolability of dwelling, person, correspondence and property. Right of petition. Also, freedom of religion and science in education.[73]

All the aspects contained within the autonomist program were the result of forceful Masonic propaganda. The most illuminating of these refers to the different manifestations of freedom of conscience, which Masons and liberals boldly included under religious freedom and scientific education, that is to say, secular education. This exacerbated the conflicts and debates between Catholics and Masons, and between liberals and conservatives. It is important to highlight the fact that, although Masons were often identified with liberals, not all the members of the institution were liberals nor all liberals, Masons. Nor were all the autonomists Masons, nor all Masons autonomists. And the Masons were particularly careful to open their ranks to Spanish residents in Cuba.

Under these conditions, it now no longer made sense to maintain two Masonic organizations. This, however, did not put an end to the presence of internal tendencies and the still unsettled problems of regionalist tendencies, differing political views, and different ideas about the limits of Freemasonry in its social involvement, issues of nationality and other important questions. On October 8, 1878, little more than two months after the creation of the Autonomist party, work was started on the unification of the two Masonic institutions. This was concluded on January 25, 1880 with the unification of the two Masonic bodies under the name Grand United Lodge of Columbus and the Island of Cuba. As a consequence, 46 lodges were merged and the new Cuban Masonic organization obtained the recognition of 34 foreign Masonic bodies. On September 4, 1881, the new institution was joined by the lodges of Camagüey and Oriente, which had separated when the Columbus Grand Lodge moved to Havana. 25 more lodges joined the Grand Lodge, although there were still some lodges in these regions that held out. In 1881, there were 71 lodges active in Cuba under the jurisdiction of the Grand Lodge.

This was a period of strong Masonic influence in Cuban thinking. Many of the most distinguished intellectuals of the time, both autonomist

---

73   Luis Estévez Romero, *Desde el Zanjón hasta Baire* (La Habana: Editorial de Ciencias Sociales, 1974), 56.

and pro-independence, were Masons. The lodge membership lists reveal that many of them were professionals or highly qualified workers. And many of these were also figures from Cuban public life, such as journalists, doctors, engineers, pharmacists, teachers and lawyers. The ideas held by the institution—freedom of conscience, of press, of association, separation of Church and state, secular education and secular civil life, civil marriage, burial, and other social acts—created a common background for the social consciousness of the country and the people's aspirations to overcome the traditional colonial system. This was expressed in the new conflict between Masons and Catholics, although many Masons were also true to the tenets of the Church. The Church had lost social presence and power. It is worth transcribing the opinion that a bishop of Havana, monsignor Ramón Fernández Piérola y López de Luzuriaga, expressed in a letter on August 4, 1880 about the state of religion on the island.

> The state of indifference, if it can be expressed thus, is such that since everyone is so involved in the soul of business that no one thinks of the business of the soul. Of the 200,000 souls in Havana, not more than 3,000 attend mass. If you add to this that there are more than fifty Masonic lodges you will have an exact idea of the state of the country from a moral and religious point of view.[74]

It is an over-simplification to say that Masonic tradition was at the origin of the Cuban independence movement. Whilst it is true that the 1868 conspiracy was bred within the lodges of the Grand Orient of Cuba and the Antilles, this was an irregular Masonic body and disowned as a "Jacobin club headquarters" both by regular Cuban Freemasonry, as well as by the most important North American Masonic figures. The dissolution of the Grand Orient and the absorption of the remaining lodges into the Grand Lodge of the Island of Cuba fed into a complex process. Many of the original members of the Grand Orient were involved in the wars of independence and either died during the conflict or subsequently fled into exile. A Masonic diaspora thus emerged which was also involved in the independence activities of the 1880s and 1890s. These Masons were not members of any one particular conspiratorial body which might be described as Masonic; rather, they participated in lodges in the countries they lived in, and, as patriots, they joined other non-Masons in creating and maintaining an independence movement which would culminate in the creation of the Cuban Revolutionary Party.

Those who remained in Cuba joined the lodges, where they found many members who were in favor of independence. The lodges were essentially given over to cultural and social work, which was a way of demonstrating patriotism under the prevailing circumstances. By regularizing their con-

---

74 Manuel S. J. Maza Miquel, *El alma del negocio y el negocio del alma* (República Dominicana: PUCMN, 1990), 12.

dition as Masons and creating a new grand lodge, the conditions were now right for the unification of Freemasonry in a new, unified direction. Within this Cuban world view were subsumed the disagreements between reformist-autonomists and pro-independence advocates. Despite the existence of different tendencies within Cuban Freemasonry, it is true that a certain skepticism over the chance of achieving independence and the rise of certain political ideas emerging from the social tendencies of the time led to a general preference for more autonomist views at the beginning of the 1880s. Politically, the idea emerged that it was preferable to achieve by *"evolution* what had not been possible to achieve by *revolution."*

The evolutionary approach was the main weapon the autonomists used against those in favor of independence, but the autonomists were also part of the Cuban intellectual movement in their criticism of the colonial system's structural lack of freedoms and modernity. Cuban Freemasonry was strongly influenced by the scientific and liberal thinking displayed in the final decades of the nineteenth century. Whilst in some Masonic lodges there were some groups in favor of national liberation, most of them were primarily dedicated to philanthropic, fraternal, scientific and cultural activities.

The Masonic lodges in this period were particularly active in the main cities on the island. Amongst other activities, they focused on creating and maintaining libraries, schools, lecture halls, and scientific and literary journals. Many members of the Cuban intellectual élite were Masons. Three lodges in Havana—Amor Fraternal, San Andrés, and Plus Ultra—were notable for their cultural activities and for their role in modernizing education, science and culture. Their most prominent intellectual figures included Antonio Govín, Grand Master of the Grand Lodge; Rafael Montoro, Worshipful Master of Plus Ultra; Aurelio Almeida; José Antonio Cortina; José Fernández Pellón; José María Gálvez; the son of the famous French painter Juan Bautista Vermay, Claudio; Rafael Fernández de Castro; Aurelio Miranda; Enrique José Varona and the person who, for many reasons, would be linked to the best of Cuban pro-independence youth, Rafael María Mendive, Martí's teacher.

Compared to Spanish-influenced Catholic schools, the best schools in Havana inherited the best of the Cuban historical tradition and were strongly influenced by active Mason intellectuals. It is important to point out that the school of Rafael María Mendive, where José Martí was educated, had one of the most illustrious teaching bodies, and was a worthy successor to the "El Salvador" school created by José de la Luz y Caballero. These teachers included the distinguished Masons Claudio J. Vermay and Joaquín Fabián Aenlle y Monjiotti—assistant to Vicente Antonio de Castro in the Grand Orient of Cuba and the Antilles—a renowned chemist who became Dean of the Faculty of Pharmacy in the University of Havana, and whose image is on one of the seven medallions in the Aula Magna of the University of Havana. The best of the generation of José Martí owe their vision of society to these teachers. They imparted a vision of a secular society which was anti-colonial, scientifically inquisitive, free-thinking, and favored freedom of conscience against religious absolutism. Moreover, they had their own view of God, free of the traditional pieties, the creator of a universe in which only virtue, truth, and good could generate advanced societies.

The two most renowned journals of the second half of the nineteenth century, the *Revista Cubana* and the *Revista de Cuba,* were run by leading Masons José Antonio Cortina and Enrique José Varona. Both publications covered a wide range of issues. Legal, philosophical, and scientific studies, as well as literary pieces lent depth, topicality and open-mindedness to the thought and tastes of the new Cuban society. More than one essay was written by outstanding Mason intellectuals. Darwin's theories, Hegelian aesthetics, Cuban and world history were all submitted to the rigorous and informed analysis of the most lucid and cultured minds in the country. Faced with old and conservative ideas—colonialism was largely based on conservative ideas, which the editors viewed as the strange behavior of a country which had nothing to con-

serve and much to redeem and reanalyze—the publications, together with lodges, lyceums and other associations, opened up new spaces in which a new type of mentality and knowledge could be mapped out. They were attempting to create the basis for a new, secular, free-thinking, democratic, Cuban society, and were deeply convinced that society must be founded on science. They also proposed a new secular morality. The lodges served as an environment for the new concerns of those who thought, lived, and participated in Cuban society. Alone, however, they were not sufficient to break with the Cuban class system.

Furthermore, exiled pro-independence Masons were active in a wide number of different ways. Some regularized their degrees in foreign Masonic bodies, above all in Mexico, Central America (Honduras, Costa Rica[75]), around the Caribbean (the Dominican Republic, Colombia, Jamaica and Haiti), and in the United States. In many cases, they founded lodges within the jurisdiction of the Masonic bodies of those countries. These include those named after important figures in the earlier war of independence, such as the Francisco Vicente Aguilera Lodge and the Ignacio Agramonte Lodge in Florida. Nevertheless, the focus and prin-

---

75 Guzmán-Stein, "Masones y liberales, españoles y cubanos: Intervención y aporte al desarrollo social, político y cultural de Costa Rica en el siglo XIX," *La Masonería Española entre Europa y América*, collated by Ferrer Benimeli (Zaragoza: CEHME, 1995), Vol I, 41-50; *Ibid.*, "Costa Rica, España y Cuba: Antecedentes, desarrollo e impacto del movimiento de independencia en la sociedad costarricense finisecular y la Masonería," *La Masonería Española entre Europa y América*, Vol II, 1041-1087; y Martínez Esquivel, "Composición socio-ocupacional de los Masones del siglo XIX," *Diálogos Revista Electrónica de Historia* (San José, Costa Rica) 8, n. 2 (agosto 2007-febrero 2008): 137-141. historia.fcs.ucr.ac.cr/articulos/2007/vol2/6vol8n2martinez.pdf. (Revised March 16, 2010).

ciple activities of these Masonic lodges did not involve conspiracy, attempts to recommence the armed struggle and the reorganization of the pro-independence movement. These were separate activities. While the conspiracies dealt with a specific political objective, the independence of Cuba, Freemasonry and fraternal activities confined themselves to the human solidarity necessary amongst men united in a common destiny.

One of the most notable Masons connected to the independence movement was the Cuban National Hero José Martí y Pérez. He was not active in the regular bodies of Cuban Freemasonry, but rather started his Masonic career in the Madrid Lodge Armonía during his first stay in Spain between 1871and 1874.[76] Martí's connection with Freemasonry requires a study all of its own, but what must be mentioned here is his definition of the institution: "Freemasonry is no more than the active form of liberal thought."[77] As is evident, he too connects Freemasonry with liberalism, as might be expected from his relationship with Spain, the period in which he lived, and the lodge in which he started his Masonic career. What is also indisputable is the influence of the Mason José María Mendive and the social thinking of the latter decades of

the nineteenth century. Another influence which may have been decisive is his clear link with Mexican Freemasonry during his stay in Mexico. Many of his speeches were made in the Masonic Temple in New York and there is evidence of his visits to lodges in Florida.

José Martí was one of the most perceptive analysts of the Cuban reality of his time and the person who carried out the most profound analysis of North American pretensions with regard to Cuba and Latin America. His vision, imbued with love for Spain, his parents' home country, led him to see the independence of Cuba as a way of guaranteeing the independence of all of what he called Our America, to differentiate it from "that which is not ours." In 1895, a day before he fell in battle, he wrote what can be considered his political last will and testament, his legacy to us as Cubans.

> Every day I am in danger of giving my life for my country, as is my duty. I am ready and willing to do so, so that with the timely independence of Cuba, the hold of the United States may be prevented from spreading over the Antilles and falling upon our lands in America. All I have done up to this day and what I will do

---

76　This assertion was made for the first time by Martí's close friend, Fermín Valdés Domínguez, in his work *Ofrenda de Hermano* (La Habana: Ediciones Quesada y Aróstegui, s.a.), 24. For more information about Martí, the Mason, see the following: Torres Cuevas, *Historia de la Masonería cubana. Seis ensayos*, 279-316; De Paz Sánchez & Castellano Gil, "Martí, masón y otras crónicas wangüemeretianas," 671-687; De Paz Sánchez, "La gran decepción de José Martí. Sobre su vinculación a la Masonería en España, 1871-1874," 1-38; *Ibid.*, *Martí, España y la Masonería*; Sánchez Gálvez, *Martí ciñó el mandil. Prueba documental de su filiación masónica.*

77　Emilio Roig de Leuchsenring, *Martí y las Religiones* (La Habana: Sección de Impresión Capitolio Nacional, s.a.), 59.

in the future is for this (...) to prevent the actions of the North American imperialists and the Spanish in Cuba leading down a path which must be barred, and which, with our blood, is being barred, a path which leads to the annexation of the peoples of our America to the turbulent and brutal North which so despises us (...). I have lived within the heart of the monster (United States) and I know what is within its belly: my slingshot is the slingshot of David against Goliath.[78]

Unlike the revolutionary movement of 1868, the revolution of 1895 was not associated with an irregular Masonic body. Although its main figures, José Martí, Máximo Gómez and Antonio Maceo, were Masons, the movement originated in a new type of organization, the political party. This was no longer merely "a gathering of those in favor of an idea," but was now endowed with the structures capable of aspiring to and holding on to power. This was a sign of the times. Political parties had now developed the practical experience, the thinking, and the political propaganda which, up to now, had been exercised by secret organizations or elite groups. The presence of popular masses in the destiny of the country made it impossible to operate within small, closed, clandestine groups. It was time to use the force of argument to win and, at the same time, to win in order to use the force of argument.

Furthermore, Freemasonry took on a more specific role, which had been in its tenets since its beginnings. It was dedicated to fraternal and philanthropic action and the ethical and moral education of citizens, but it also encouraged theoretical, cultural and intellectual debate. This mix provided a basis for the development of political ideas whilst remaining outside politics. The Plus Ultra Lodge, for example, was a veritable seedbed for new ideas, and figures such as Rafael Montoro and José Fernández Pellón took part in the wide-ranging debate about Cuban society, the times, and universal thought.

If, on a conceptual and human level, José Martí's plans for revolution in Cuba had much in common with the Grand United Lodge of Columbus and the Island of Cuba, it was because they shared the same ethical, secular, fraternal and philanthropic ideas which underlay Masonic social action and the education of the citizen for a secular democratic republic. As with any abstract truth, however, many of the tenets could be interpreted in a wide range of different ways. For Martí, equality occupied the same space as freedom; a society of free equals, the political aim, was not infrequently both a central declaration of methods and their results. And, grounded in the purest Cuban traditions, Martí paved the way for this thinking to reach its logical conclusions, moving from a state of oppression, whether it affected particular

---

78 José Martí, "Carta inconclusa a Manuel Mercado, 18 de mayo de 1895," in *Obras Completas* (La Habana: Editorial Nacional de Cuba, 1963-1965), Vol IV, 167.

groups of people or whole nations, to the birth of the ideas of Cuban, Latin American, and Third World emancipation. The Cuban Revolutionary Party, created by the Cuban National Hero in 1892, with a social base much wider than that provided by Freemasonry and with its own ideas for society, bred the revolution of 1895.

Epilogue

Freemasonry was prohibited on the island during the War of Independence (1895-1898) by order of the Captain General Emilio Callejas on April 4, 1895. When, on January 1, 1899, Spanish sovereignty in Cuba ended and North American power began, Freemasonry underwent a rigorous overhaul, both in its leadership and in its plans. Prestigious figures in the independence movement and in Cuban Freemasonry, such as Aurelio Miranda y Álvarez and Fernando Figueredo Socarrás, returned to Cuba, and, together with other longstanding Masons in the Masonic bodies on the island such as José Fernández Pellón, Francisco de Paula Rodríguez, Gerardo L Betancourt, Juan Bautista Hernández Barreiro and Miguel Gener, gave a clear patriotic, civic direction to Cuban Freemasonry, in favor of republican principles and secular social life and thinking. Theirs, in particular, was the liberal, republican model of politics which was being drawn up with the new constitution.

Aside from any assessments, judgements and criticisms of Cuban Freemasonry, one of its most beautiful traditions was that it created and maintained links of brotherhood and solidarity with the Latin American peoples during their early years and provided them with unity in their cultural, social, and political journeys. Masonic brotherhood was directed at all the people of the world, but, in particular, North Americans, Spaniards and Latin Americans. By setting the objectives of Freemasonry at the forefront of its mission, the Cuban institution was able to maintain its continued search for unity, a feature which marked it out from the Spanish version, characterized by fragmentation, infighting, and the personalization of its many Masonic bodies. Cuban Freemasonry's ethical work, its civic education, and its secular ideas made it the institution which contributed most to democratic republicanism and the development of civil secular society in the nineteenth century, a foundation which led on to the aspirations of the twentieth century. While Masonic ideology is neither unique to nor a prerequisite for national processes, it did give certain characteristics to its social and cultural results. I believe that one of the core features underlying the plurality of the Latin American world is the contribution of Masons and Masonic institutions to the development of patriotic national consciousness and the individual civic consciousness which led many nineteenth century Masons to advocate a unique identity for Latin American peoples within a universal, humanist world view.

Bibliography

Almeida, Aurelio, *El consultor del masón. Colección de tratados sobre todas las materias de la Francmasonería* (Madrid: Puente, Godoy y Loureiro Editores, 1883).

Cassard, Andrés, *Manual de Masonería. El Tejedor de los Ritos Antiguo, Escocés, Francés y de Adopción* (New York, 1871).

De Paula Rodríguez, Francisco & Betancourt, Gerardo L., *Manual masónico* (La Habana: Imprenta El Siglo XX, 1919).

De Paz Sánchez, Manuel, "L. F. Gómez Wangüemert y la Masonería palmera y cubana de la década de 1930," *Jornadas de estudios Canarias-América* (1981): 31-67.

_____, "Los residentes españoles en Cuba y la Masonería después de la independencia," *Cuadernos de investigación histórica* 10 (1986): 41-56.

_____ & Castellano Gil, José Manuel, "Martí, masón y otras crónicas wangüemeretianas," collated by Ferrer Benimeli, José Antonio, *Masonería española y americana* (Zaragoza: CEHME, 1993), Tomo II, 671-687.

_____, "La Masonería y la pérdida de las colonias: impresiones sobre el caso cubano," collated by Ferrer Benimeli, José Antonio, *Masonería española y americana* (Zaragoza: CEHME, 1993), Tomo II, 1107-1125.

_____, "La gran decepción de José Martí. Sobre su vinculación a la Masonería en España, 1871-1874," *Nuevo Mundo Mundos Nuevos, Debates* (2008): 1-38. nuevomundo.revues.org/index30883.html.

_____, *Martí, España y la Masonería* (Canarias: Ediciones Idea, 2008).

_____, "España, Cuba y Marruecos: Masonería, identidades y construcción nacional," *Anuario de estudios atlánticos* 55 (2009): 273-310.

De la Fuente, Vicente, *Historia de las sociedades secretas antiguas y modernas, especialmente de la francmasonería* (Lugo: Soto Freire, 1870-1871).

Del Valle, Adrián, *Historia documentada de la Conspiración de La Gran Legión del Águila Negra* (La Habana, Editorial El Siglo XX, 1930).

Documentos, inéditos sobre la toma de La Habana por los ingleses en 1762 (Biblioteca Nacional José Martí, Departamento Colección Cubana, s.a.).

Domingo Acebrón, María Dolores, "Independencia en el Caribe, Cuba: José de Armas y Céspedes: masón," en *La Masonería española. Represión y exilios*, collated by Ferrer Benimeli, José Antonio (Zaragoza: Gobierno de Aragón, 2010), Tomo I, 573-580.

Estévez Romero, Luis, *Desde el Zanjón hasta Baire* (La Habana: Editorial de Ciencias Sociales, 1974).

Estrade, Paul, "Un masón audaz y conformista, paradigmático del Gran Oriente de Francia: el franco-cubano Severiano de Heredia (1836-1901)," en *La Masonería española. Represión y exilios*, collated by Ferrer Benimeli, José Antonio (Zaragoza: Gobierno de Aragón, 2010), Tomo I, 545-558.

Fernández de Castro, José Antonio, *José Fernández Madrid, prócer colombiano de la independencia de Cuba* (La Habana: Colección Órbita, UNEAC, 1966).

Ferrer Benimeli, José Antonio, Ferrer Benimeli, « Les Caballeros Racionales, les loges lautariennes et les formes déviées de la Franc-maçonnerie dans le monde hispanique », dans *Les révolutions ibériques et Ibéro-Américaines à l'aube du XIXe siècle, Actes du colloque de Bordeaux 2-4 juillet 1989* (Paris, Editions CNRS, 1991).

_____, *Masonería Española y América* (Zaragoza: CEHME, 1993).

_____, *La Masonería española en la época de Sagasta (1825-1903)* (Zaragoza: CEHME y la Fundación Práxedes Mateo-Sagasta, 2006).

_____, "Vías de penetración de la Masonería en el Caribe," *REHMLAC, Revista de Estudios Históricos de la Masonería Latinoamericana y Caribeña* (San José, Costa Rica) 1, n. 1 (mayo-noviembre 2009): 2-19. https://revistas. ucr.ac.cr/index.php/rehmlac/article/ view/6853/6540

Figueredo Socarrás, Fernando, "Logia militante Independencia," en *La Gran Logia* (La Habana) 3 (1901): 23-25.

Findel, Joseph Gabriel, *Historia de la Francmasonería* (La Habana: Editorial Acacia, 1946).

Frau Abrines, Lorenzo & Arús Arderiú, Rosendo, *Diccionario Enciclopédico de la Masonería* (La Habana: Propaganda Literaria, 1883).

Fuentes Mares, José, *Poinsett, Historia de una gran intriga* (México: Editorial Jus, 1951).

Garrigó, Roque, *Historia documentada de la Conspiración de los Soles y Rayos de Bolívar* (La Habana, Editorial El Siglo XX, 1929).

Guzmán Stein, Miguel, "Masones y liberales, españoles y cubanos: Intervención y aporte al desarrollo social, político y cultural de Costa Rica en el siglo XIX," *La Masonería Española entre Europa y América*, collated by Ferrer Benimeli (Zaragoza: CEHME, 1995), Tomo I, 41-50.

_____, "Costa Rica, España y Cuba: Antecedentes, desarrollo e impacto del movimiento de independencia en la sociedad costarricense finisecular y la Masonería," *La Masonería Española entre Europa y América*, collated by Ferrer Benimeli (Zaragoza: CEHME, 1995), Tomo II, 1041-1087.

_____, "Andrés Cassard y su vida en Nueva York. Tres nuevas facetas de un masón polifacético," en *La*

Masonería española. Represión y exilios, collated by Ferrer Benimeli, José Antonio (Zaragoza: Gobierno de Aragón, 2010), Tomo I, 509-544.

Iglesias Cruz, Janet & Gutiérrez Forte, Javiher, "Españoles y Cubanos en la Masonería. Manuel Curros Enríquez," *REHMLAC, Revista de Estudios Históricos de la Masonería Latinoamericana y Caribeña* (San José, Costa Rica) 1, n. 2 (diciembre 2009-abril 2010): 121-129. https://revistas.ucr.ac.cr/index.php/rehmlac/article/view/6620/6309

_____, "La simbología masónica en el Cementerio de Colón," *REHMLAC, Revista de Estudios Históricos de la Masonería Latinoamericana y Caribeña* (San José, Costa Rica) 2, n. 1 (mayo-noviembre 2010): 59-73. https://revistas.ucr.ac.cr/index.php/rehmlac/article/view/6610/6299

_____, "La Masonería en los albores de la República. Las elecciones de 1908: Los Masones y sus logias en la política de los primeros años de la República cubana," *Congreso Internacional. Actas del XIV Encuentro de Latinoamericanistas Españoles,* eds. Eduardo Rey Tristán & Patricia Calvo González (Santiago de Compostela: Universidad de Santiago de Compostela, 2010), 225-235. hal.archives-ouvertes.fr/docs/00/52/92/78/PDF/AT4_Gutierrez-Iglesias.pdf.

Martí, José, "Carta inconclusa a Manuel Mercado, 18 de mayo de 1895," en *Obras Completas* (La Habana: Editorial Nacional de Cuba, 1963-1965).

Martínez Esquivel, Ricardo, "Composición socio-ocupacional de los Masones del siglo XIX," *Diálogos Revista Electrónica de Historia* (San José, Costa Rica) 8, n. 2 (agosto 2007-febrero 2008): 137-141. historia.fcs.ucr.ac.cr/articulos/2007/vol2/6vol8n2martinez.pdf

_____, "Simposios Internacionales de Historia de la Masonería Latinoamericana y Caribeña (La Habana, Cuba, 2007 y 2008)," *REHMLAC, Revista de Estudios Históricos de la Masonería Latinoamericana y Caribeña* (San José, Costa Rica) 1, n. 2 (diciembre 2009-abril 2010): 159-167. https://revistas.ucr.ac.cr/index.php/rehmlac/article/view/22250/22417

Martínez Moreno, Carlos Francisco, "La Sociedad de los Yorkinos Federalistas, 1834. Un acercamiento hermenéutico a sus estatutos y reglamentos generales a la luz de la historia de la Masonería," *REHMLAC, Revista de Estudios Históricos de la Masonería Latinoamericana y Caribeña* (San José, Costa Rica) 1, n. 1 (mayo-noviembre 2009): 212-233. https://revistas.ucr.ac.cr/index.php/rehmlac/article/view/6864/6551

Maza Miquel, Manuel S. J., *El alma del negocio y el negocio del alma* (República Dominicana: PUCMN, 1990).

Miranda y Álvarez, Aurelio, *Historia documentada de la Masonería en Cuba* (La Habana: Molina, 1933).

Montes de Oca Choy, María Teresa &

Ydoy Ortiz, Yasmín, "Chee Kung Tong ¿Vínculos masónicos?" *REHMLAC, Revista de Estudios Históricos de la Masonería Latinoamericana y Caribeña* (San José, Costa Rica) 1, n. 1 (mayo-noviembre 2009): 234-246. https://revistas.ucr.ac.cr/index.php/rehmlac/article/view/6865/6552

Ponte Domínguez, Francisco J., *La Masonería en la independencia de Cuba* (La Habana: Editorial Modas Magazines, 1954).

Poinsett, Joel Robert, *Notas sobre México* (México: Editorial Jus, 1950).

Pozuelo Andrés, Yván, "La historiografía masónica latinoamericanista actual. Presente y futuro," *Congreso Internacional. Actas del XIV Encuentro de Latinoamericanistas Españoles*, eds. Eduardo Rey Tristán & Patricia Calvo González (Santiago de Compostela: Universidad de Santiago de Compostela, 2010), 281-288. halshs.archives-ouvertes.fr/docs/00/52/92/98/PDF/AT4_Pozuelo.pdf

Renault, Agnès, "Los francmasones franceses de la jurisdicción de Cuba al principio del siglo XIX," *REHMLAC, Revista de Estudios Históricos de la Masonería Latinoamericana y Caribeña* (San José, Costa Rica) 1, n. 1 (mayo-noviembre 2009): 59-72. https://revistas.ucr.ac.cr/index.php/rehmlac/article/view/6857/6544

_____, "La influencia de la Masonería francesa en el Departamento de Cuba en los años veinte del siglo XIX. Los aportes de la prosopografía," *REHMLAC, Revista de Estudios Históricos de la Masonería Latinoamericana y Caribeña* (San José, Costa Rica) 1, n. 1 (mayo-noviembre 2009): 74-89. https://revistas.ucr.ac.cr/index.php/rehmlac/article/view/6856/6543

Roig de Leuchsenring, Emilio, *Martí y las Religiones* (La Habana: Sección de Impresión Capitolio Nacional, s.a.).

Rumbaut y Yáñez, Vicente, *La Masonería, y el odfelismo en Cienfuegos* (Cienfuegos: Taller Tipográfico de Rafael Caro, 1938).

Sánchez Gálvez, Samuel, *Martí ciñó el mandil. Prueba documental de su filiación masónica* (La Habana: Ediciones Bachiller, 2007).

_____, "Ciencia y cultura en Fernandina de Jagua," *REHMLAC, Revista de Estudios Históricos de la Masonería Latinoamericana y Caribeña* (San José, Costa Rica) 1, n. 1 (mayo-noviembre 2009): 172-190. https://revistas.ucr.ac.cr/index.php/rehmlac/article/view/6862/6549

_____, "Institucionalización de la Masonería en Cienfuegos," *REHMLAC, Revista de Estudios Históricos de la Masonería Latinoamericana y Caribeña* (San José, Costa Rica) 1, n. 1 (mayo-noviembre 2009): 191-211. https://revistas.ucr.ac.cr/index.php/rehmlac/article/view/6863/6550

_____, "La logia masónica cienfueguera Fernandina de Jagua (1878-

1902). Un estudio de caso" (Tesis doctoral en Historia, Universidad Carlos Rafael Rodríguez de Cienfuegos, 2010).

_____, "La logia masónica cienfueguera Fernandina de Jagua (1878-1902). Un estudio de caso," *REHMLAC, Revista de Estudios Históricos de la Masonería Latinoamericana y Caribeña* (San José, Costa Rica) 2, n. 1 (mayo-noviembre 2010): 85-92. https://revistas.ucr.ac.cr/index.php/rehmlac/article/view/6613

Sappez, Delphine, "Antonio Govín y Torres, nexo entre Masonería y autonomismo en Cuba," en *La Masonería española. Represión y exilios*, collated by Ferrer Benimeli, José Antonio (Zaragoza: Gobierno de Aragón, 2010), Tomo I, 559-572.

Saunier, Eric, "L'espace caribéen: un enjeu de pouvoir pour la franc-maçonnerie française," *REHMLAC, Revista de Estudios Históricos de la Masonería Latinoamericana y Caribeña* (San José, Costa Rica) 1, n. 1 (mayo-noviembre 2009): 41-56. https://revistas.ucr.ac.cr/index.php/rehmlac/article/view/6855/6542

Soucy, Dominique, *La Gran Legión del Águila Negra: Un Águila de dos cabezas (México-Cuba, 1823-1830)* (Francia: Universidad de París VIII).

_____, *Masonería y nación. Redes masónicas y políticas en la construcción identitaria cubana (1811-1902)* (España: Ediciones Idea, 2006).

_____ & Sappez, Delphine,

"Autonomismo y Masonería en Cuba," *REHMLAC, Revista de Estudios Históricos de la Masonería Latinoamericana y Caribeña* (San José, Costa Rica) 1, n. 1 (mayo-noviembre 2009): 90-99. rehmlac.com/recursos/vols/v1/n1/rehmlac.vol1.n1-dsoucyydsappez.pdf (Revised September 15, 2011).

_____, "Vicente Antonio de Castro y la opción reformista: desde *La Cartera Cubana* hasta *Yara*," en *La Masonería española. Represión y exilios*, collated by Ferrer Benimeli, José Antonio (Zaragoza: Gobierno de Aragón, 2010), Tomo I, 411-423.

Torres Cuevas, Eduardo, "Los cuerpos masónicos cubanos durante el siglo XIX," *Masonería Española y América*, collated by Ferrer Benimeli, José Antonio (Zaragoza: CEHME, 1993), Tomo I, 229-256.

_____, *De la Ilustración reformista al Reformismo liberal* (La Habana: Instituto de Historia de Cuba. La Colonia, Editora Política, 1994).

_____, *Historia de la Masonería cubana. Seis ensayos* (La Habana: Imagen Contemporánea, 2005).

Valdés Domínguez, Fermín, *Ofrenda de Hermano* (La Habana: Ediciones Quesada y Aróstegui, s.a.).

Van Bell, Jean Louis, *Dictionnaire des signes lapidaires Belgique et nord de la France* (Éditions Braine le Chanteau, 1984-1994).

Varela, Félix, *Escritos Políticos* (La Habana: Editorial de Ciencias Sociales, 1977).

Vivanco, Julián, *José Antonio Miralla. Precursor de la independencia de Cuba* (La Habana: Editorial El Sol, 1958).

Notes on the "Symbolic Name" in Latin America[1]

Yván Pozuelo Andrés[2]

ABSTRACT

At the time of initiation, Masons choose a symbolic name that will identify them in their actions within the Order. In the initiation process, Masons have the opportunity to choose a symbolic name different from their birth name. These symbolic names reveal their perception of the world and transmit a vital aspect of something they wanted to inform other members of. Why was the use of symbolic names exclusive of Spanish-American Freemasonry? When and why did this custom spread? The case study analyzed was the Asturian community, since it was one of the most important groups of Spanish immigrants in America. With these notes and regional study we seek to answer these questions: Was the symbolic name a use originated by the Masons? Was it exclusive of Freemasonry? What information distinguishes the symbolic Hispanic American names from the Masons of Asturias? What data reveals the Hispanic American symbolic names of Asturian Mason residents in Hispanic America?

Keywords: Freemasonry, Symbolic name, methodology, repression, Asturias

RESUMEN

En el momento de la iniciación, los masones eligen un nombre simbólico que les identificará en sus acciones dentro de la Orden. En el proceso de iniciación, los masones poseen la oportunidad de escoger un nombre simbólico diferente a su nombre de pila. Estos nombres simbólicos revelan sus percepciones del mundo y transmiten un aspecto vital del que quisieron informar a los demás miembros. ¿Por qué este uso fue exclusivo de las masonerías hispanoamericanas? ¿Cuándo y por

---

1   This article was originally published in the journal *REHMLAC*, Vol. 3, No. 2, December 2011–April 2012. We would like to thank the editorial board for permission to reprint this article in English.

2   Yván Pozuelo Andrés. Spanish. Doctor of History. Instructor at the IES Universidad Laboral in Gijón, Spain. Editor at *REHMLAC*. Member of the Spanish Masonry Historic Studies Center (Centro de Estudios Históricos de la Masonería Española, CEHME) at the University of Zaragoza, Spain. Email: yvan@telecable.es.

qué se extendió la costumbre? El estudio de caso analizado fue la comunidad asturiana, ya que fue una de los más importantes grupos de inmigrantes españoles en América. Con estas notas y el estudio regional se pretende contestar a estos interrogantes: ¿Fue el nombre simbólico un uso originad o por los masones? ¿Fue exclusivo de la masonería? ¿Qué informaciones destacan de los nombres simbólicos hispanoamericanos de los masones de Asturias? ¿Qué datos revelan los nombres simbólicos Hispanoamérica nos de los masones asturianos residentes en Hispanoamérica?

Palabras clave: *Masonería, nombre simbólico, metodología, represión, Asturias*

拉美 "象征名字" 的注释

摘要

在入会之时，共济会成员会选择一个象征名（symbolic name）帮助其在共济会规则内实施不同行为时识别彼此。成员有机会选择一个不同于出生名的象征名。这些象征名揭示了他们对世界的感知，同时向其他会员传播某个重要信息。然而，为何象征名的使用曾经并未出现在拉美共济会呢？这一习俗是在何时，出于何种原因得以传播呢？本文对阿斯图里亚社区（Asturian community）进行案例研究分析，因为其是美国最重要的西班牙移民团体之一。本文试图通过这些注释和区域研究来回答下列问题：象征名的使用是共济会成员发起的吗？共济会曾经没有使用过象征名吗？区别拉美象征名和阿斯图利亚斯共济会成员的信息是什么？什么信息会揭示拉美地区阿斯图利亚共济会居民的象征名？

关键词：共济会，象征名字，方法论，抑制，Asturias

Introduction

Against all odds, in a field with so rich a bibliography as the history of Freemasonry, there are no papers on the use of the symbolic name for identification purposes by members. This is unusual, in light of the fact that, in theory, placing an aspect of this history under the researcher's magnifying glass typically entails consulting a large number of works from the lodges themselves, from its staunchest detractors and from academia, which began studying the phenomenon in the last quarter of the twentieth century.

Its origin has not concerned historians, nor Freemasons themselves.[3] It is well known that for religious Anti-Masons, the symbolic name represented further proof that the secret society was conspiring against the Church and the Crown. A later section will offer a few examples of this.

Thus, very few methodological articles have been written on this subject from a Spanish historiographical perspective. Brief conceptual descriptions can also be found in the various regional studies that have been done on the Spanish Masonic panorama. In these, a few lines can be found on the historic periods to which the symbolic names chosen by Masonic neophytes belong and the frequency and categorization of certain symbols. I will cite examples from these sources throughout this article.

Thus, this study remains an approximation, which hopes to play its part in broadening the spectrum of research on this question. Consequently, the first part of this paper approaches the question by attempting to clear up the origins of, and reasoning behind, the use of the symbolic name in Latin American Freemasonry, which was absent in the rest of the world. After I present theory in the first section, I will use the second and final sections to lay out the practice of symbolic naming among Masonic initiates and members in As-

turias (Spain) and in Latin America in the nineteenth and twentieth centuries as a source of information on the identity that these Masons projected upon themselves. The sample I will use to carry out this study is drawn from the five hundred Asturian Masons in the nineteenth century and the five hundred in the twentieth century (1911-1939) that appear on the tracing boards held by the Historic Memory Archives in Salamanca (Spain) and from the list of nineteenth-century Asturian Masons in Cuba recorded by Professor Ferrer Benimeli.[4]

I hope to answer several theoretical questions: What is a symbolic name? What is it for? When and how did they start being used within Freemasonry? Were the Masons the first to use the symbolic name? What sort of information does study of symbolic names yield? Was the symbolic name exclusive to Freemasonry? Why was it practiced only in Latin American Freemasonry? How is a neophyte's chosen symbolic name to be interpreted in relation to his personality? Where practice is concerned, I will address other questions: What information stands out when we examine Asturian Masons' Latin American symbolic names? What can we draw from the Latin American and Asturian symbolic names of Asturian Masons living in Latin America? What do they mean?

---

3   The symbolic name is absent even from most lodges' web pages with a separate section on "Masonic terms." On the few pages on which it is described, "pseudonym" is also used in its place. In these cases, they simply state that the symbolic name is used in Iberian Freemasonry, without specifying its origin.

4   For this last group, José Antonio Ferrer Benimeli's study "Masones asturianos en la Cuba y Puerto Rico del siglo XIX," *Ástura* (Oviedo, Spain) 9 (1993): 61-69, was used for reference.

The Symbolic Name

For Historiography

Several historians have discussed the importance of the symbolic name as a means of investigating the personality of Masons and, more specifically, their ideological ascription, at the symposia held by the CEHME.[5] The Masonic candidate adopts this new identity at the moment of his initiation, a custom of which Spanish historiography is aware thanks to the Masonic documents preserved in Spain, which have been used in numerous regional studies on the history of Freemasonry. Nevertheless, historians have failed to find any description of the symbolic name in the diverse Masonic manuals that describe the initiation mechanism.

In strictly academic terms, the first pioneering works were published by Professors Randouyer and Roldán. In her study on symbolic names given at the 1985 symposium on nineteenth-century Spanish Freemasonry, French historian Françoise Randouyer noted that on a fundamental level, in Spanish Freemasonry, symbolic names spoke to the will to hide from anti-Masonic power, suggesting that such names were not, in fact, chosen in advance as a principled mark of identity. We could say, then, that it was the profane world that imposed this practice upon the Masons. What's more, nineteenth- and twentieth-century Freemasons did not know why symbolic names were used. Randouyer specified that despite attempts to do away with symbolic names in tolerant eras, the practice was kept, given the two-way relationship with former Spanish holdings and colonies overseas, territories in which symbolic names were supposedly necessary as a safeguard against the oppression of those territories' respective executives.[6] In that and several later explanations, the symbolic name was considered to reflect only the initiate's ideological, political and mental dimensions, failing to acknowledge that they may have also reflected toponymical dimensions, national, regional or local cultural dimensions, or family or professional dimensions.

The symbolic name's importance depends upon being chosen by an in-

5   Françoise Randouyer, "Ideología masónica a través de los nombres simbólicos," *La masonería en la España del siglo XIX*, coord. Ferrer Benimeli, José Antonio (Salamanca: Junta of Castile and León, 1987), Vol. I, 425-439. First published in France, « Les noms symboliques des Maçons espagnols ," in *Chroniques d'histoire maçonnique* (Paris, France) 29-30 (1982). Daniel Ligou uses the same explanation in the wording of the note dedicated to "Spain" in the Dictionary of Freemasonry: *Dictionnaire de la Franc-maçonnerie* (Paris: PUF, 2006), 414. In this dictionary, the symbolic name is associated exclusively with "Spain" and "repression," 855. María Teresa Roldán Rabadán, "Análisis y estudio de los 'nombres simbólicos' utilizados por los miembros de cuatro logias madrileñas," in *La masonería en la España del siglo XIX*, Vol. II, 529-539; Pilar Amador, "Mensajes de mentalidad expresados a través de los nombres simbólicos de los masones de América: Cuba," *La Masonería española y América*, in Ferrer Benimeli (Zaragoza: CEHME, 1992), Vol. II, 967-981; Joâo José Alves Dias, "La presencia de España en la Masonería portuguesa: los nombres simbólicos (1892)," in *La Masonería española entre Europa y América*, Vol. I, 319-322.

6   Randouyer, 426.

dividual who has reached sufficient maturity to decide to become a Masonic candidate. This entailed a series of personal reflections on what the future Freemason would like to be called in this Hiramist circle that, at least from the outside, certainly attracted men who wished to satisfy and share their broad intellectual doubts in relation to the organization of the society in their neighborhood, locality, region, country and even continent. Professor Roldán Rabadán fine-tuned our understanding of how the symbolic name was used in Spain by linking it to the context of illegality, which plagued Freemasonry until the transition to democracy in the last quarter of the twentieth century.

Around the same time as Randouyer and Roldán were writing, historian Eduardo Enríquez del Árbol published his best attempt at a studied approximation of what the symbolic name's place in the association might be.[7] He grouped members into economic sectors (primary, secondary and tertiary), classified them based on their time period (Antiquity and the Middle, Modern and Contemporary Ages), placed them into six provisional conceptual groups (spiritual-religious, intellectual-philosophical, power-government, hero-rebel, Republicanism and inventor-artist), joined these categories in the chronological section, created several charts on which he intersected the categories with the chronology and

added the time period and country of origin. As Enríquez del Árbol pointed out, the categorization varied, based on the context of each lodge, and his methodological proposal was one of the best starting points for this sort of research.

Some symbolic names are harder to catalog into different categories. For example, the *Sagastas* and *Thiers* could be situated in Power-Government and Republicanism. *Lima* could refer to the capital of Peru or to an individual who grows limes. One of the greatest challenges is, after duly cataloging the names, explaining the meaning of these schematizations, which in most academic studies are limited to speculation. How can we move from speculation to certainty?

Later, historian Pilar Amador analyzed the symbolic names of 6,000 Freemasons in Madrid, and concluded that the symbolic name is "a means of expressing and symbolizing concepts" and differed from Randouyer in suggesting that name choice "belonged more to the field of mentality than to the field of ideology." Amador argued that mentality preceded ideology. She highlighted three categories in which the symbolic name revealed information of some sort, to wit, the individual, the socio-historic context and Freemasons as a group.[8] It was probably Amador who attempted to follow up on Enríquez del Árbol's steps by organizing a specific methodology that made use of

---

7   Eduardo Enríquez del Árbol, "Aproximación metodológica a los nombres simbólicos masónicos en un caso particular: la logia 'Moralidad n°160' de Huelva," in *Del Antiguo al Nuevo Régimen: estudios en homenaje al profesor Cepeda Adán* (Granada: Universidad de Granada, 1986), 213-242. Thanks to Professor Ferrer Benimeli for consulting this study.

8   Pilar Amador, 968.

a digital tool to cover all possible meanings behind why a Freemason would choose a symbolic name, crossing between such diverse fields as art, politics, religion and professions.

Another theoretical nuance was uncovered by the historian Pedro Álvarez Lázaro, for whom the symbolic name holds special meaning because "it cradled the bearer's code of values and beliefs," [9] a conclusion that he reached when studying Freemasons who were influenced by, or sympathetic with, Krausoinstitutionism. Nevertheless, not everything depends on ideologies, values and beliefs. What code of values and beliefs would incorporate a symbolic name that refers to a place or to a Freemason's vital toponymical performance setting, apart from a code of patrio-regionalism (patrio-localism) or of simple nostalgia?

There are also cases in which Masons ask to change their symbolic names. The case of Diego Martínez Barrio, an important Republican figure in the Second Spanish Republic (1931-39) and the Spanish Civil War (1936-39), is among the most illustrative, due to the transcendent mark it left on Spain's historic path: his symbolic name was changed from *Justicia* to *Vergniaud*, an event that needs no explanation. [10]

Among the notes on this issue, the version put forth by Professor Jean-Pierre Bastian argues that the study of symbolic names ought not limit itself to the names that were chosen, but also to those that were *not* chosen—that is, attention should be paid to the absence of names with roots in Catholic culture and the Catholic Church. [11] When we extend this sort of reflection to the task of this paper, we must ask ourselves: Why did some Freemasons decide not to carry on with this widespread practice—that is, the symbolic name—by identifying themselves by only their given first name? One such case was that of the First Venerable Master of the lodge Aurora No. 82, in San Pedro de Macorís (Dominican Republic), whose last name and symbolic name was Bobea.

Explanations of this Iberian custom can also be found in the "Lexicons of Freemasonry" published by Spanish historians in their respective regional and local studies, although more than a few fail to mention the "symbolic name" or any of its possible synonyms. After consulting those lexicons that do

---

9   Pedro Álvarez Lázaro, "Krausistas, institucionistas y masones en la España del siglo XIX," *Krause, Giner y la Institución Libre de Enseñanza. Nuevos estudios*, in Vázquez Romero & Álvarez Lázaro (Madrid: Colección del Instituto de Investigación sobre Liberalismo, Krausismo y Masonería, Universidad Pontificia Comillas, 2005), 154.

10   Leandro Álvarez Rey, "Diego Martínez Barrios y la masonería andaluza y española del siglo XX," *REHMLAC, Revista de Estudios Históricos de la Masonería Latinoamericana y Caribeña* (San José, Costa Rica) 1, No. 2 (December 2009-April 2010): 138-139. https://revistas.ucr.ac.cr/index.php/rehmlac/article/view/6621/6310. (Accessed August 15, 2011).

11   Jean-Pierre Bastian, "Las logias francmasonas españolas del siglo XX, ¿Qué tipo de sociabilidad?" *La Masonería en la España del siglo XX*, coord. Ferrer Benimeli (Toledo: Cortes de Castilla-La Mancha, 1996), Vol. I, 24.

include the symbolic name, no further explanations were found, beyond those mentioned here.

Consequently, historiography's most oft-repeated reasoning is that there is a preference for protection in the face of repression. Nevertheless, this speculation-based explanation presents a number of origin-related questions. If, for example, as the historian Roldán asserted, the symbolic name was a response to repression, it would not be a symbolic name at all, but a pseudonym that turned symbolic whenever the institution did not fear prohibition. As with many questions in the history of Freemasonry, we must research its characteristics while paying attention to the framework of sociability as a whole. Then we can ask (in the hope of shedding light on the usual explanation) whether secret societies—such as those with an anarchist or communist bent, for example—that have typically been forbidden and persecuted by governments, used symbolic names rather than pseudonyms. By way of example, we could compare the emblems of certain nineteenth-century anarchists who signed their names as *a friend of Robespierre, a supporter of dynamite, a head chopper, an arsonist*, and so on.[12] Does this mean that historians ought to reject the term "symbolic" when describing the history of Freemasonry in a repressive context?

Defining Freemasonry and its traits requires definition of other associations, and vice-versa. Its uniqueness and its mimesis are framed by the sociability of every era. As I understand it, this framing is essential to defining Freemasonry. The repressive explanation was not correct, given that Freemasons were arrested when they gathered, uncovering, then, the given first name and the symbolic name, cases that Spanish historiography describes in diverse works applied to the history of Spanish regional Freemasonry in the nineteenth century and the first half of the twentieth century. Government forces were not desperate to discover who hid behind the symbolic name, as would have been the case with clandestine organizations. Hispanic Freemasons did not learn of this circumstance and continued to use symbolic names in every time period. Let us now examine these theories on the origin of the symbolic name in the context of Spanish Masonic history.

According to the historian Alberto Valín Fernández, the use of the symbolic name as a "security measure" began with the first Galician lodge, The Constitutional Lodge of the Spanish Meeting, which operated from 1814 to 1816. He attributes this first adoption of the name to the influence of Philadelphian secret societies. He even sees this pioneer practice as the starting point for the use of pseudonyms not just by Freemasons, but also for the later European revolutionary networks.[13] On several occasions, Freemasons and Masonic organizations used more attractive phras-

---

12 Jean Maitron, *Le mouvement anarchiste en France. Des origines à 1914* (Paris: Gallimard, 2007), Vol. I, 123.

13 Alberto Valín Fernández, *Masonería y revolución. Del mito literario a la realidad histórica* (Las Pal-

ing than other entities and individuals. Their balusters, letters sent to Masonic or civil authorities, their official bulletins where the Masonic writing style—we could call it "rococo"—can be seen in all its glory. Still, the concept of the symbolic name remains a pseudonym, a *nom de guerre*, even though, in this specific case, the selection by members of the Galician lodge selected names such as *Aristóteles, Rómulo, Diocles, Scipion, Phyladelpho* and *Aquiles*, suggesting that they were more than a mere pseudonym to safeguard against government persecution. These are not anagrams, toponymical names or meaningless, made-up words. There was a clear desire for each member to choose a name that captured their intellectual, ideological or mental feeling, with a predilection for Greco-Roman Antiquity. A predilection which, as Spanish historiography would show— consistently present in the majority of lodges, especially in the nineteenth century, but also in the first half of the twentieth. However, this practice did not begin with speculative Iberian Freemasonry.

The Symbolic Name Outside of Freemasonry

It suffices to remember the Christian tradition, beginning with Peter, whose name was given to Simon, and Boanerges ("sons of thunder"), the name given to the brothers James and John. In these examples, the fundamental difference lies in the fact that, in the Christian tradition, these names were given by Christ, not chosen by the interested party. We could also mention the names taken by popes. The first to change his name when elected to head the Church was John II (533-35). His true name, Mercurius, was too pagan. But this formula was later abandoned, with the exception of John III (561-74), until the tenth century, when the heirs to the Throne of Saint Peter adopted the custom of taking a new name, which has continued until the present day. This custom has also been used by women when they take their vows to become nuns—Mother Teresa of Calcutta, for example, was born Agnes Gonxha. The practice has also been used, and still is used, by religious converts. Moving away from the Biblical and religious sphere, at other latitudes and in other cultures, actors use pseudonyms, the best-known case being Molière (seventeenth century). Writers, such as Voltaire (eighteenth century), too, have taken false names. The term has also evolved, and today, in the realm of culture, we refer to this practice as taking a pen name, stage name, artistic name, etc. Even during the Enlightenment, there were cases of nicknames that had toponymical connotations, such as Condorcet. Examining semantics and etymology, we see that the word

mas de Gran Canaria: IDEA, 2008), 24 and 98. Shifting the supposition to the distinctive names of anarchist lodges, for example, the ideological and social differences of both organizations can be seen. By way of example, in 184, the groups of "collectivists" (the name used at the time by anarchists in France) identified themselves as *The Rebels, The Indignant Ones, The Panther, The Wretched, The Revolver-in-hand, The Hatred*, and so forth, clearly without sharing signs with the lodges. See Maitron.

pseudonym existed long before speculative Spanish Freemasonry. It comes from Greek; the Latin term is a*lias*.[14] Thus, we know that the practice of using false names goes back centuries. It is a practice that is rooted in most civilizations and their societies, given that every civilization has had an individual or a group of individuals that wished to hide their identity at some moment, for one reason or another—not always out of fear of repression. Indigenous people of the Americas, Africa and Asia had double identities, with a proper name, given by the community, and another based on the dominant religion of the colonizers: two worlds, two names. Today, new technology has brought with it the extensive use of pseudonyms on the Internet and social networks, in which the user can even create several names of varying falsity and symbolism, based on how much or how little information, and how much or how little anonymity, he or she wishes to communicate. Even the expression "symbolic name" was commonly used on numerous occasions entirely outside of Masonic influence, as we can see in Spanish press and literature of the nineteenth and twentieth centuries.

For example, the Madrid-based publication *La Ilustración* from October 2, 1852 writes: "... there are various evocations to Our Lady of the Abandoned, a symbolic name that is so often heard with such sweetness on the lips of the Andalusians." In the Palma de Mallorca-based newspaper *El Genio de la Libertad*, the first line of the front page on May 21, 1854 reads "El Heraldo, our colleague El Heraldo, whose symbolic name harkens back to the middle ages ..." In the Madrid-based liberal newspaper *La Iberia* on November 1, 1857: "Under the symbolic name Dalila, the author has suggested testing the Satanic influence that this sort of corrupt woman exercises on the souls of artists ..." In the Madrid-based cultural magazine *El Museo Universal* on February 15, 1858: "His success, in Milan's Te-

---

14 *(Translator's note: this footnote has been adapted to reflect Spanish terms and definitions in the Spanish Royal Academy's* Dictionary of the Spanish Language *accurately in English, though such an adaptation is naturally limited; consult the dictionary for precise definitions.)*

According to the Dictionary of the Spanish Language of the Spanish Royal Academy (2001 edition), *pseudo-* means false. "Symbolic name" is understood to sound more virtuous than "false name," "nickname" and "alias." Pseudonym: "said of an author who hides his true name behind a false one. // 2. Said of a work by such an author. // 3. Name used by an artist when carrying out his artistry, instead of his true name." The connotations are more generic for *nom de guerre*: "a nickname adopted by someone in order to carry out an activity." In this sense, the second definition of "nickname" should be considered: "name sometimes added to the surname to distinguish between two individuals with the same first name. // 2. Descriptive name with which one person is especially distinguished." Finally, there is the frequently used *alias*: "By another name. // 2. In another fashion. 3. Nickname." *Nickname* is also listed as a synonym of *pseudonym*, a fact that is less relevant to the case of the Freemasons, as it is chosen by others and not by the person who will bear the name himself: "name that is typically given to a person, based on his physical defects or some other circumstance. // 2. Joke or humorous expression by which someone or something is described, normally serving as a sort of ingenious comparison." This last case also includes the subdefinition "term given to a person for a quality or condition he or she possesses."

atro alla Scala, was noisier than that of Adelson e Salvina, leaving established, in that temple of European art, the symbolic name of delicacy and passion." In the Madrid-based monarchic newspaper *La Esperanza* on April 11, 1859: "... the symbolic name that the Dutch have given to this region is Spitzberg (pointy mountains)." In the Havana-based satirical publication *El Moro Muza* on September 23, 1860: "I have called you Xitragupten, when your symbolic name is Délio; but I have believed that I could take such a liberty, because, if, as a poet, you are Délio, as a journalist you are better suited to the name Xitragupten." In the Madrid-based *La Voz* on June 30, 1920: "Right here, we read, yesterday, the statements of the Italian beauty in the recent American competition, where she represented her classic land, under the symbolic name Miss Italy."

These quotes confirm that the expression was used in various ideologically distinct media before the golden age of Spanish Freemasonry, which blossomed after the 1868 revolution. Before that point, with very few exceptions, there were no Masonic lodges in Spain. Of those few exceptions, such as the lodge in Gijón, *Los Amigos de la Naturaleza y Humanidad*, which operated from 1850-54, not all used the Masonic term.[15]

To wrap up this brief survey of profane *noms de guerre*, it is worth mentioning that such names have been found among individuals who led two lives or work in two fields, who take those names to hide that duality: spies, individuals who do nocturnal work that is publicly and commonly taken for reprehensible, and even people who wish to outwit an exclusivity agreement with a certain media outlet and earn money under a different identity, as Guy de Maupassant and many others have done. This reality, which makes Freemasonry and Freemasons a society that examines, selects and defends ideas that originated in society at large through a ritual structure based on ancestral practices, fits with what I have confirmed about Freemasons on several occasions: they did not invent or discover anything, but they have nevertheless obsessively defended the ideas— always created in the profane world— that they deem just. Thus, Freemasonry acted as a filter for ideas, knowledge and practices that originated in the profane world—and not in the contrary sophist sense—ultimately advocating in favor of, or against, aspects of society, joining other associations with these struggles.

Ultimately, all names with a subjective or historic meaning are symbolic names. Even newborns' given names are symbolic, though they are chosen by a third party. All have a meaning that implies ascription to a past or present cultural context, depending on the individual. "Why did you pick that name?" is a common question posed by family and friends of the parents. They ask because there are always numerous explanations, that span from the familiar (homage to earlier generations) to the historic, passing through

---

15 Victoria Hidalgo Nieto, *La masonería en Asturias en el siglo XIX* (Oviedo: Ministry of Education, Culture and Sport of the Principality of Asturias, 1985), 72-74.

various sensibilities.

Returning to the history of Spanish Freemasonry, the symbolic name was not used in the heart of the lodges in their earliest days. For example, in the same period as the Galician lodge already mentioned was operating, a Bonapartist lodge called *Beneficencia de Josefina* was opened in Madrid, and its members were persecuted by Ferdinand VII's Inquisition. No reference to symbolic names was preserved from that lodge or from any other Bonapartist lodge from that era.[16] The initiative launched in Galicia was apparently not continued. Nor was it used in other parts of the world, such as the Canary Islands or the first Scottish lodge of *San Juan y Soberano Capítulo Metropolitano de Comendadores del Teide* (1817-1820).[17] This may be due to the fact that this lodge was within the Grand Orient of France, a grand lodge that never used this means of identification. Did the Inquisition's power stay clear of the French lodge's affiliates? It certainly did not, leading one to question why it did not opt for that supposedly defensive strategy. Between 1850 and 1854, approximately, Gijón, Asturias, housed the lodge *Los Amigos de la Naturaleza y Humanidad* (already mentioned), where

symbolic names were never used, and which was forced to close due to government persecution. In that same city, many years later, at in the first stage of the golden age of Spanish Freemasonry, Freemasons from the first Asturian lodge founded the lodge *Los Amigos de la Humanidad* (1871-75), which once again belonged to the Grand Orient of France, without using any aliases.[18] It was when it joined other, later lodges within Spanish grand lodges that these Freemasons began using the symbolic name. In Murcia, Freemasonry was established in the port city of Cartagena with the founding of the lodge *Hijos de Hiram*, which operated from 1869 or 1870 until 1873. Its members did not use symbolic names; they practiced the French rite under the Grand Orient of France. As in Asturias, they began using symbolic names when they began to join Spanish grand lodges.[19] In the 1870s, in Madrid, a lodge known as *L'Hospitalière* was founded within the Grand Orient of Spain; its members—Frenchmen—apparently did not use symbolic names.[20]

One of the more recent revelations of Spanish historiography is that lodges in Andalucía began by "studying the life, work, and personality of the

---

16 Manuel M. Júlbez Campos & Henar Pizarro Llorente, "Masonería bonapartista en Madrid (1812-1820) a través de los papeles inquisitoriales," in *Masonería, Revolución y Reacción*, coord. Ferrer Benimeli (Alicante: Instituto Alicantino Juan Gil-Albert, 1991), Vol. I, 71-78.

17 Manuel de Paz Sánchez, *Historia de la francmasonería en Canarias* (Las Palmas: IDEA, 2008), Vol. I, 135-136.

18 Hidalgo Nieto.

19 José Antonio Ayala, *La Masonería en la región de Murcia* (Murcia: Ediciones Mediterráneo, 1986), 58-75.

20 Francisco Sanllorente Barragán, "Dos logias francesas fundadas en Madrid durante la I República y la Restauración canovista: Logia Osiris y L'Hospitalière (1870-1880)," in *La Masonería en Ma-*

individual to whom a symbolic name was bestowed by the Venerable Master on the day of his initiation."[21] The value of the symbolic name was reaffirmed once again as the first explanatory statement made by the apprentice in that new world. The most important detail of this quote is the fact that the Venerable Master *bestows* the symbolic name; he does not merely endorse it. We cannot generalize this fact to other Spanish regions, but we must ask, why did this custom emerge in Spain, and not in other countries where Freemasons were persecuted? Why, when it was used in this early stage, was its function and use never mentioned in the official documents of the grand lodges at any point in the nineteenth century?

From the Freemasons

*E*l Espejo Masónico, a nineteenth-century Latin American Masonic journal that enjoyed some prestige in its day, which was led by the controversial Andrés Cassard,[22] can be used to determine where the symbolic name was and was not used in Latin America and the Caribbean, even though the "symbolic name" was not the exclusive subject of a single article

or review in a journal that discussed and offered commentary on a wide variety of Masonic and Masonic-historical topics. Nevertheless, the journal's publication of balusters and letters by Freemasons, lodges and grand lodges gives the reader insight into their signatories. We do possess letters to the director of the journal sent by Masonic entities to civil authorities with the signature of Masonic authors. The overwhelming majority of Latin American Freemasons cited in this *El Espejo Masónico* were called by their given names. For example, when the Grand National Orient of Venezuela wrote to the entire Masonic world, its authorities signed with their given names. Every member of the Venezuelan *Toleranica* and *Armonía* lodges do the same in their letter to the president of the State of Yaracuy.[23]

Generally speaking, wherever Masonic authors are concerned, researchers find themselves dealing with myths, legends and fantasy. In 1890, one such author, the Spaniard Nicolás Díaz y Pérez, penned a history of Freemasonry,[24] in which he says that Pablo Antonio Olavide—an individual for whom there is no evidence that he was a Freemason[25]—used the symbolic name *Colón* (Columbus ... in 1771. He pushed

drid y en España del siglo XVIII al XXI, coord. Ferrer Benimeli (Zaragoza: Government of Aragon, 2004), Vol. I, 48-49.

21 Fernando Martínez López, *Masones, republicanos y librepensadores en la Almería contemporánea (1868-1945)* (Seville: Editorial Corduba, 2009), 261.

22 See the last paper by the same in Miguel Guzmán Stein, "Andrés Cassard y su vida en Nueva York. Tres nuevas facetas de un masón polifacético," in *La Masonería española. Represión y exilios*, coord. Ferrer Benimeli (Zaragoza: Government of Aragon, 2010), Vol. I, 509-544.

23 Cassard, Andrés, *El Espejo Masónico* (España: Extramuros, 2007), Vol. I, 179-183.

24 Published in *La Revista de España* (January-February 1891), 290.

25 Ferrer Benimeli, *La Masonería española en el siglo XVIII* (Madrid: Siglo XXI, 1986), 278.

use of the symbolic name back by over 40 years, undermining the notion that the practice began in Galicia in 1814. It is well known that Freemasonry had not yet begun in Spain in the eighteenth century, and that the grand lodges that operated in Europe did not use aliases.[26]

No official or unofficial Masonic body ever explained the importance of the symbolic name for Freemasons. It is an issue that was overlooked by official Masonic documents and by the association's official leaders during its first few centuries of existence and particularly in the Spanish context, where the symbolic name was more broadly used. Or at least, that is, no trace of such documentation has been found to date, despite the tremendous number of Masonic documents that have been distributed across the globe. The symbol is absent from the various grand lodges' manuals describing rites and rituals, and from their constitutions.[27] Despite being a custom practiced on the day of the initiation, it was not reflected in the numerous versions of the initiation

ritual that were created. It is surprising, on the one hand, to see its importance, given that it was always used in Latin American Freemasonry regardless of the era, degree of persecution or legitimacy conceded to it, and it is more surprising still to see that importance not being reflected in writing, given the obsession that the adherents of the Order of the Great Architect of the Universe had with writing, describing, rewriting and redescribing. For example, the term "symbolic name" cannot be found in the "Masonic vocabulary" that was published by *Latomia*, the most serious Spanish Masonic journal, until the first half of the twentieth century.[28]

At face value, it would seem that the symbolic name was not taken entirely seriously, even by Freemasons themselves, where researching its nature and origin were concerned. Ultimately, more than a few internal discourses that were published in the bulletins of Spanish grand lodges identify members by their given names and make no mention of symbolic names.[29]

---

26   *Ibid.*

27   This can be confirmed in the texts compiled by historian Pere Sánchez Ferré, *La Constitución de 1723. Compilación de las marcas (Landmarks) de la masonería* (Barcelona: Alta Fulla, 1998). Furthermore, the texts referred to in the title include Anglo-Saxon references that obviously were not going to be concerned about an issue that was unknown in their own way of practicing their rites and rituals, such as Mackey's *Traditional Law*, and the accounts of the landmarks by Roscoe Pound, J.W. Simons, H.B. Grant, A.S. McBride, G.F. Moore, J.A. Poignaut, W.B. Hextall and A.S. Bacon, and Albert Pike's opinion of Mackey's account. Román Goicoerrotea was also consulted, as he wrote one of the earliest articles on the subject in Spain, "Los masones," *Revista de España* (Madrid, 1870), Vol. XIII, 481-503.

28   *Latomia* (Madrid, 1932), Vol. I, 166-169. No shred of an explanation can be found in any of the "Miscellaneous notes," "Brief notes" or "Masonic consultations" (in the journal's different volumes), or in the "Succinct History of Spanish Freemasonry" (Vol. III, 1933). The intention of the authors of the journal was to break with the sophist tradition of Masons such as Díaz Pérez and Morayta (Vol. II, 1932, 44 and 114). Nevertheless, rather than use the Masonic sources that Díaz Pérez and Morayta had turned to, they used sources exclusively from Latin American and Anglo-Saxon grand lodges.

29   One example is the speech given by the Grand Master of the Regional Grand Lodge of Northeastern

For the Anti-Masons

On November 21, 1908, in its "Anti-Masonic Section," the Spanish Catholic newspaper *La Lectura Dominical* presented the correlation between the symbolic name and the supposedly secret goings-on at meetings: "Masonic meetings must be kept secret, and in meetings, members must use only their symbolic names, and not their profane name in any way."

Religious anti-Freemasons linked the symbolic name with secrecy as yet another proof of the "perversion" of the society, particularly in relation to Latin American Freemasonry. This accusation has been repeated with varying degrees of emphasis whenever Anti-Masons have sought to libel Masons.

But it was in another sort of Anti-Masonry, the liberal court, where this usage was dug up. One of the greatest Spanish literary historians of the nineteenth century, Benito Pérez Galdós, a liberal Anti-Mason who nevertheless tolerated the society,[30] expressed a quite subjective opinion on this custom. In particular, he used the term "symbolic name" in his work entitled *Amadeo I* when describing the burial of General Prim. That said, he confused it with the 18th Masonic degree "Knight of the Rose Croix." Still, in his work on *The First Republic*, he correctly noted that

some Masons identified themselves with the "symbolic names" of *Licurgo* and *Epaminondas*.

Still, in his work that deals most directly with Freemasonry, *The Grand Orient*, published before those mentioned above, Galdós used only the generic distinctive "name," never "symbolic name." But it is here that he expresses his critical opinion on the matter, subtly condemning the Freemasons as pretentious: "This individual chose to no longer be known as Juan or Pedro, and chose, with singular modesty, the name of Cato, Horatius Cocles, Leibniz or some other celebrated figure." In another passage, he writes "'Brother Aristides, or, better put, Pipaón, since I cannot get used to dispensing with real names,' said Salvador, without losing his sincerity for a moment." He continued in this vein later in the book, writing "While various brothers were filing in—brothers who, in the profane world, went by Quintana, Argüelles, Valdés, San Miguel and so on, different men left, among whom you could also find names that later were quite distinguished, but which we keep quiet about for various reasons." On later pages, he delves deeper still into the subject, writing:

To add insult to injury, those of the Arte-Real viewed the naming of an Infant in the lodges, who received the name of Draco, as such a ludicrous act

Spain (Asturias, Galicia, León and Santander) at one of the regional assemblies, which was published in the *Bulletin of the Grand Orient of Spain* in March, 1930, on the title page.

30 I have published a study on liberal Anti-Masonry, or Anti-Masonic Liberalism, which came on the scene to complete the Anti-Masonic spectrum, which already featured religious Anti-Masonry and labor Anti-Masonry. Yván Pozuelo Andrés, "Una muestra de famosos escritores liberales antimasones," *Revista de Arte, Historia y Literatura* 35 (2009). actuallynotes.com/Una-muestra-de-famosos-escritores-liberales-antimasones.html. (Accessed May 13, 2010).

that they called him "Braco." A quite celebrated General was designated Brutus II. There may be doubts that Ferdinand VII received a Masonic salary, but there is no doubt that the most distinguished and respectable names of this century, the names of Argüelles, Calatrava, Quintana, San Miguel, Flores Estrada, Galiano and others are listed among the Masters—and it is quite likely that they were all perfect Sublimes.

The symbolic name of Freemasons was the subject of Galdós' ridicule—he saw it as immodest, a ridiculous custom practiced by blowhards.

In these few lines, we can appreciate that the "symbolic name" is much more closely linked to an expression that summarizes different characteristics of the individual Freemason's identity than it is to repression. Furthermore, its use was not exclusive to Freemasonry; all the Freemasons did in Latin America was to integrate it and make it fundamental to understanding their brand of Freemasonry, an element that distinguished them from other Freemasons in the United Kingdom, France, Germany and elsewhere.

SYMBOLIC NAMES: ASTURIAS AND LATIN AMERICA

Masons in Asturias and Symbolic Names in Latin America (Nineteenth–Twentieth Centuries)

Trying to establish a relationship, or find some indication of a relationship, between Freemasons in Asturias (Northeastern Spain) and in Latin America is somewhat difficult. It is not a matter of choosing from among all the symbolic names whose meanings would lead us to historic figures who, at some point, had some connection with Latin America, but rather of selecting those figures whose lives or work left a notable impact in relation to both territories—thus, this category would include any liberal Spaniard who had governed any colonial or independent territory overseas. There were Spanish soldiers whose lives and works were notable in the Spanish War for Independence but who failed to distinguish themselves in the wars for independence in Spanish-controlled Latin America.

We have come across this issue in relation to several lodges, though always with the same Freemasons, who kept their symbolic names as they moved from lodge to lodge. Thus, there were three *Colón*s, but they were, in fact, the same individual who had passed through three lodges. And that "one," along with the rest of the "Latin America" category, represents a greater or lesser percentage, depending on the total number of Freemasons there, making statistics something that we must use cautiously.

The Nineteenth Century

Few symbolic names refer to an individual, historic or toponymical element (Annex 1). This confirms that Freemasons in Asturias had other identity priorities that they wished to highlight. The lodge *Nueva Luz* in Oviedo had the greatest number of Latin American symbolic names—eight, out of a total of nearly one hundred members. Of the seventeen lodges that kept information on their members, five had no Latin American references in their *noms de guerre* (Annex 1).[31] Of all the locations in Asturias where Freemasons operated, the capital of the principality, Oviedo, had the largest number, with twelve having Latin American references—that is to say, half of the group of these Freemasons, with the rest distributed among five other locations (Annex 2).

The number of symbolic names is not cumulative, as there were several cases of the same Freemasons who were involved in various lodges. Thus, there were only twenty-four Freemasons in Asturias, out of a total of over five hundred, who used a pseudonym with a Latin American connection (Annex 3).[32] The overwhelming majority preferred to identify themselves with figures from Greco-Roman Antiquity and mythology, past and present liberals or individuals who were notable in the profession in which they worked for the Masons. For our purposes, we will prioritize qualitative factors over quantitative factors. Figures who were important in the history of the Spanish colonization of the Americas and, conversely, in the resistance to that colonization, and figures who favored the

independence process in the nineteenth century make up the majority of the Latin American symbolic names used (Annex 3), distributed equally between the modern era of the conquest and the contemporary era of independence (Annex 4). The symbolic name that figures most prominently is *Colón* (Columbus), with seven uses. It is followed by *Cortés*, *Méndez Núñez* and *Mina*, with three uses each, and *Pizarro*, with two (Annex 5). *Mitre, Bolívar, Céspedes, Nataniel, Moctezuma* and *Hatuey* were each used once. Thus, half of the twenty-four names taken were the names of conquistadors. What are we to make of this? Colonialist Freemasons? This is a weak interpretation, as would be an interpretation that the Freemasons who chose to call themselves Hatuey, Bolívar and Moctezuma were, without a doubt, taking a pro-Latin American independence position, without considering the nuances that global independence provoked for all of the individuals situated in the broad and diverse sphere of liberalism. One could be in favor of the independence of countries that had already gained independence and opposed to that of those that had not, thus using the symbolic name to represent the past, but not the present or future. How can we settle these doubts? By consulting the baluster in which the initiate explained the reasoning behind his choice. In this specific case, such balusters were not kept. The two examples that are included in Annex 16 correspond to a socialist Argentine

---

31 This paper examines only lodges and triangles.

32 There are doubts about a few that were not considered without altering their general or specific historical description.

leader, *Juan B. Justo*, and to a celebrated author, *Cervantes*. They are from other eras, and they are included here to illustrate the difficulty of ascribing meaning to the choice of such names, and to provide a sample of the sort of information that can be drawn from such balusters. In the first example, the certainty of finding yourself face-to-face with a socialist, not immune from ideological nonsense, and in the second, despite all of the possible speculation over the possible meaning of the choice of name, it can be simply explained as homage to the father of the individual in question, who had also been a Freemason with that name. Reading these balusters does not enable us to untangle the reasons behind the adoption of the adopted name, as the lodge's documentation confines itself to praising and discussing the name selected. Some Freemasons even signed their given names to their explanations of the symbolic name chosen.[33] Nevertheless, the shortage of documentation on this question, as in the Asturian case, does not prevent us from discerning certain characteristics.

The vast majority of references to Latin America from Asturian Freemasons focus, through historical figures, on colonialism and decolonization. Only the symbolic name *Nataniel* departs from the political sphere of empire and fallen empire to offer a cultural connotation, although even here he does so by referring to the Bolivian writer Nataniel Aguirre, who discussed independence and gained fame in his work *Juan de la Rosa*. This last case, too, places us in the field of speculation whenever our guesswork is not corroborated by the explanatory baluster of the Freemason himself, or by other sorts of information that give us sufficient indication or confirmation—such sources might include the personal library of the member, an essay or articles, etc. In the case of *Nataniel*, the originality of the name—which was not at all common in Asturias—supports our hypothesis.

The Twentieth Century

At least seventeen Freemasons referred to Latin America in their symbolic name. Based on the particulars of the symbolic name or the information that we are trying to draw from them, we can remove or add new parameters to our search. For example, unlike in the nineteenth century, only two Freemasons in the twentieth used the same symbolic name with Latin American connotations: Martí. The rest made use of symbolic names without reusing them among themselves. Thus, the chart included for the nineteenth century on the use of a single symbolic name by more than one Freemason (Annex 5) has no equivalent for the twentieth. It has been replaced by another, to adjust for a phenomenon that had not taken place in the previous century: the selection of toponymical names such as *Cienfuegos, Bejucal, Caibarién* and *Argentina* (Annex 10).

---

33   For example, the work read in a lodge by U. Álvarez Portal, whose symbolic name was *Dostoiewski*, published in the *Bulletin of the Grand Orient of Spain* (Madrid, Spain) VI, No. 67 (December 10, 1932): 3-7.

Annex 11 has been added to relate the symbolic name, regardless of type, with the Latin American territory to which it refers. The few Asturian Freemasons who chose a pseudonym that referred to Latin America tended to relate that name more to a territory than to an idea or event, unlike their counterparts in the previous century. In the twentieth century, only four Freemasons mentioned political leaders who were committed, in one way or another, to the independence of people in Spanish colonies (*Bolívar, Rubén Darío, Martí* and *Juárez*), and *Lempira* is the only symbolic name that refers to resistance against the fifteenth-century invader.[34] Thus, we can conclude that the Asturian Freemasons of the nineteenth century were more influenced by politics and history, and less concerned with toponymical concerns, a trend that would be inverted in the twentieth century.

In Gijón, at *Jovellanos*, the Asturian mother lodge of the twentieth century, fourteen Freemasons with symbolic names related to Latin America (out of a total of seventeen)[35] adding to all of the Asturian lodges, with six out of eleven lodges lacking this sort of name (Annex 6). The other three Masons with symbolic names referencing Latin America joined the ranks of the Riego Lodge, also located in Gijón (Annex 7). In the end, Gijón had seventeen

references, nearly all of the Latin American symbolic names, while Oviedo had one (Annex 8). Most of those symbolic names referred to the Contemporary Age (Annex 9). In the twentieth century, the Asturian migratory movement was stable, consolidated and permanent. It was a movement that began in the second half of the nineteenth century, with one in five Asturians emigrating, resulting in the geographical references that began appearing in the symbolic names of Freemasons in the twentieth century, as family and sentimental relationships had begun forming on both sides of the Atlantic, with the nostalgia inherent to immigration and emigration. Cuba was the most referred-to territory, ahead of Mexico (Annex 11).

Asturian Freemasons in Cuba in the Nineteenth Century and their Asturian Symbolic Names

Asturian Freemasons joined at least twenty-six Cuban lodges in the nineteenth century (Annex 12). One in every five Spanish Freemasons was Asturian, with regional Spanish ascription becoming more frequent.[36] Except for the lodges *Los Girondinos 16* and *Los Templarios 26*, every lodge welcomed at least one Asturian Freemason who mentioned his region of origin in his symbolic name.

---

34 This name could have referred to the name of the currency in Honduras, except the Freemason was initiated five years before this was made the official name of that currency.

35 The Freemason who used the symbolic name *Argentina* in the *Amese* Triangle was the same individual who used it at *Jovellanos*. Thus, I have listed seventeen Freemasons, although there are eighteen references.

36 José Manuel Castellano Gil, *La masonería española en Cuba* (Santa Cruz de Tenerife: Taller de Historia, 1996), 342.

The lodges in which the most Asturian Freemasons chose region-based symbolic names were *Obreros del Progreso 174* in Cienfuegos, with twenty-seven, *La Unión Universal 266* in Cárdenas, with fifteen, and *La Unión Hispano Americana 132* in Havana, with thirteen (Annex 12).[37]

The nature and number of symbolic names point the researcher toward the important information that they reflect. For example, in this specific case, it is notable that 80% of symbolic names chosen by Asturian Freemasons in Cuba reflect their region of origin. Out of a total of 222 Asturian Freemasons accounted for by Professor Ferrer Benimeli, 59% (130) took a name with an Asturian connotation. Eighty-eight of these opted for the name of their place of birth, and thirty-two chose names pertaining to historical figures who are very well known among Asturians, such as *Pelayo* (16), *Jovellanos* (7), *Riego* (5), *Favila* (2) and *Covadonga* (2). There was a preference for names from the Middle Ages (Annex 13). These names in and of themselves are not a surefire guarantee of Asturian origin, as these individuals also left a fairly major mark on the history of Spain as a whole, and here we must reinforce this information with other pieces of prosopographic information such as their place of birth. The geographical data enables us to know the general dynamic of this group's migratory movement. In most cases, their places of birth do not coincide with places in Asturias where there were Masonic lodges, so we may conclude that it was in Cuba that they first came across this network. As for the geographical symbolic names, sixty-four came from the central region, fourteen from the east and ten from the west (annex 14). Although the three largest cities, Gijón, Oviedo and Avilés, are grouped in the center, the Freemasons, like those from the other two regions, came not just from towns, but from little villages. This fact (Annex 15) is one of the main characteristics to emerge from the study of these pseudonyms.[38] In total, they had roots in sixty-three locations. Considering the fact that Asturias had 600,000 residents at that time, making it one of the least populated parts of Spain, this amounted to a mass exodus, a profoundly rural movement of people. Once they arrived in Cuba, they moved into another economic sector as they became involved in different branches of commerce.

Conclusion

All symbolic names are pseudonyms, but not all pseudonyms are symbolic names.

37 For more on symbolic names in Cienfuegos, see: Samuel Sánchez Gálvez, "Los nombres simbólicos en la logia masónica cienfueguera Fernandina de Jagua. 1878-1902," *Universidad y Sociedad* (Cienfuegos, Cuba) II, No. 2 (2007): 45-47; *Ibid.*, "Los nombres simbólicos en la logia masónica cienfueguera Fernandina de Jagua: expresiones de pensamiento," *Anuario 2007* (Cienfuegos, Cuba, 2007).

38 In his paper, Professor Ferrer Benimeli describes the distribution of Asturian Freemasons in Cuba: "We find 98 in Havana, 77 in Las Villas, 26 in Oriente, 18 in Matanzas and three in Camagüey." Ferrer Benimeli, "Masones asturianos en la Cuba y Puerto Rico del siglo XIX," 61.

In the lodges, you could find *Victor Hugo, Bakunin, Goethe, Marx, Lavoisier, Cervantes, Marat, Danton* and even *Christ*, all gathered in one spot. Asturians regularly added *Jovellanos, Pelayo* and *Covadonga* to this illustrious list. Freemasons have taken everything short of *Great Architect of the Universe* as a symbolic name. All the rest, even *Hiram*, have been chosen a few, if not many times. This Latin American Masonic custom was not practiced in other organizations whose members also used aliases: anarchist, socialist and communist societies which, with the usual exceptions that prove the rule, used the names of their historic leaders and celebrated figures.

In her first study on the adoption of the symbolic name, Professor Randouyer wrote that "Freemasonry, as an institution, has no defined policy line and it embraces all trends."[39] This is true in part; it largely depends on the policy that we are looking at. For example, *La Plaine* of the French Revolution did not have a "defined policy line" in terms of Montagnards and Girondists, and they embraced "all trends," certainly, in the revolutionary sense, but not in the absolute sense, as *La Plaine* rejected the model of the *Ancien* Régime. We need not take the "policy line" to mean the political partisanship that characterizes political parties in the present day, but as another sort of *Plaine* that could form a broad "policy line" with increasingly clear boundaries, thanks to the work of university research.

The lodges that chose to publicize their positions acted in the same way. They framed themselves in a broad political context within "Liberalism," something acknowledged by all current historiography, thus rejecting other ideological ways of organizing society. On the Iberian Peninsula and, later, in Latin America, the symbolic name acted as a gauge that enabled researchers to detect certain details about the individual who took it. These individual details lead to other sorts of generalizations, beyond the recurring question of politics, identifying Freemasons' collective attitudes based on the historical context being studied, as has been profiled in the case of Asturian Freemasons.

We can say that the symbolic name was a "Latin American hallmark without a hallmark," in the Masonic sense, given that that custom is now nearly two hundred years old, but was never examined in Masonic manuals.[40]

The importance of the origin, history and study of the symbolic name was not beyond the scope of historiographic scrutiny. Still, for Freemasons initiated into Hispanic Freemasonry, it was their first decision, and was how they presented themselves to the new world they had just joined.

It is also worth noting that other countries' lodges did not allow this attitude to influence them, a sort of impermeability that also means that in all centuries, those lodges did not value this custom as proper or tolerable in their territories/homeland or as

---

39   Randouyer, 439.

40   "Marca" for "Landmarks," old unwritten core laws of Freemasonry.

being pertinent to the internal history of Freemasonry. At best, these lodges sometimes tolerated the practice in Spanish-controlled and formerly Spanish-controlled territories.

The peculiarities of symbolic names open the door to transversal research, as the novice hopes to identify himself with historical figures, through which ideological or mental hints can be gleaned, or, alternatively, through which he draws attention to the territory of his birth, his profession, etc., all of which influence the researcher when the time comes to catalog, schematize and describe.

The fact that a single symbolic name was chosen by several Freemasons does not imply that a particularly strong bond was formed between those Freemasons. A single symbolic name can have various meanings or shades of meaning, depending on the initiate. For example, Covadonga could refer to toponomy, to the Virgin Mary, to the Battle of Covadonga, to the Reconquista or to Spanish nationalist stances. In a nineteenth-century context, any or all of these might apply to an Asturian in Cuba. It is the initiate who reveals the meaning, generally during his first involvement with the lodge. It would be quite daring for a historian without documentation of this interaction to propose an ideological interpretation of the name chosen with any sort of rigidity.

The annexes included in this paper give an idea of the breadth of cataloging that symbolic names individually and collectively offer the researcher:

by lodge, by symbolic name, by era, by location, they can be expanded by ages, by responsibilities at lodges, and so on.

In Asturias, Latin American references in symbolic names were few and far between in both the nineteenth and the twentieth centuries. Still, study of these symbolic names offers insight into the fact that in the nineteenth century, Freemasons who wanted to convey a certain Latin American connotation through their identity chose symbolic names inspired by historic figures involved in the Conquest of the Americas, involved in the indigenous resistance, or in the independence process. In the twentieth century, references to the conquistadors disappeared entirely, though names of independence leaders remained, while toponymical names skyrocketed as a result of Asturian migration. In both centuries, Oviedo and Gijón, respectively, were hotbeds of this sort of Freemason, corroborating the position that each of these cities held in the history of Freemasonry in the Principality of Asturias.

It is clear that Asturian Freemasons who were involved in this network in nineteenth-century Cuba placed a premium on being recognized and identified as Asturians, as witnessed by the overwhelming number of symbolic names that pay homage to the places of their birth—largely in villages or in the center of the principality. The name *Pelayo*, after the king, predominated among historical figures chosen for symbolic names.

To conclude, in response to the questions that I posed at the outset of this study (What is a symbolic name? What is it for? Was it particular to Latin American Freemasons?), I can offer these provisional answers: the symbolic name is the name by which Freemasons wanted to be identified by the rest of their coreligionists, a name, accepted by prior consultation with the lodge, with the care that is offered by the power to consciously decide the information that one wishes to convey through a single word. While the symbolic name did not begin with the Freemasons—the practice was widespread among various sorts of groups—it was at the beginning in the nineteenth century, with or without government oppression, that it became a hallmark of Latin American Freemasonry that continues to this day.

When and how did symbolic names start being used within Freemasonry? Was it a response to oppression or, as Galdós posited, an exercise in vanity?

Its use was adopted on the Iberian Peninsula, in 1814, in Galicia. This was not the only region in Spain in which Freemasonry was repressed. Nevertheless, it was the only region, at that time, where the practice of symbolic names was adopted. Repression of Freemasons in Galicia was, until now, only speculation offered by historiography as a means of explaining the symbolic name's use, despite the fact that several lodges—largely those belonging to French grand lodges—did not engage in the practice during periods of particularly harsh repression. Nor is there evidence that this practice offered Freemasons any sort of defense against

persecution. Furthermore, repression does not justify the integration of this practice into the ritualistic customs of Latin American versions of Freemasonry, as it was not a mere pseudonym—it also implied political, ideological, mental, philosophical or toponymical information that went well beyond its use as mere protection from repression. Thus, repression was not the primordial element of this widespread custom in Latin American Freemasonry. Vanity may have been real in some extreme cases, though this is difficult to evaluate, as it is such a subjective matter, and millions of individuals became Freemasons.

Why only in Latin American Freemasonry? This is the thorniest question of all, as, obviously, some Latin American cultural characteristic must have influenced this practice, just as the cultural characteristics of other human groups influence their non-use of pseudonyms. This makes this a difficult matter to work through without falling into the trap of stereotyping. Neither would a taste for the clandestine, nor for the occult or "occultism," nor Faith or romance, nor literature nor thoughts of chivalry be considered academic answers. Thus far, no documents have been found that offer any sort of explanation, leaving this question open to speculation. Still, the symbolic weight, which is so pronounced at the time of initiation (after the novice has stepped through the chamber of reflection in which he decides whether he is willing to leave one world in order to be reborn in another) seems to suggest that this practice fits organically within its context, in the image and likeness of what is done in other sorts of initiation (as in religious initiations, for example).

What source enables us to know the motivations behind a novice's selection? How is a neophyte's chosen symbolic name to be interpreted in relation to his personality?

The baluster, which in Masonic terminology means "written work read in a lodge," is the document on which the initiate explains the reasoning behind his choice. Therefore, the baluster is the fundamental source that enables us to know the novice's motivations (Annex 16), even though such documents do not always contain clear explanations, as the apprentice sometimes chooses to wax poetic over the individual or idea chosen, rather than offer reasons. Still, without the baluster we would be in the realm of mere speculation, which, places us in an honorable starting point.

How can we begin to know the meaning of symbolic names with certainty, and leave off with mere speculation?

Prosopographic study[41] and knowledge of historical contexts, along with the writings of the Freemasons in question, offer us, in this sense, the critical tools necessary to minimize possible interpretations.

Bibliography

Álvarez Lázaro, Pedro, "Krausistas, institucionistas y masones en la España del siglo XIX," in *Krause, Giner y la Institución Libre de Enseñanza. Nuevos estudios*, eds. Vázquez Romero & Álvarez Lázaro (Madrid: Colección del Instituto de Investigación sobre Liberalismo, Krausismo y Masonería, Universidad Pontificia Comillas, 2005).

Álvarez Rey, Leandro, "Diego Martínez Barrios y la masonería andaluza y española del siglo XX," *REHMLAC, Revista de Estudios Históricos de la Masonería Latinoamericana y Caribeña* (San Jose, Costa Rica) 1, no. 2 (December 2009-April 2010): 138-139. https://revistas.ucr.ac.cr/index.php/rehmlac/article/view/6621/6310

Alves Dias, Joâo José, "La presencia de España en la Masonería portuguesa: los nombres simbólicos (1892)," *La Masonería Española entre Europa y América*, coord. Ferrer Benimeli, José Antonio (Zaragoza: CEHME, 1995), Vol. I, 319-322.

Amador, Pilar, "Mensajes de mentalidad expresados a través de los nombres simbólicos de los masones de América: Cuba," in *La Masonería española y América*, coord. Ferrer Benimeli, José Antonio (Zaragoza: CEHME, 1992), Vol. II, 967-981.

---

41 Éric Saunier, « La prosopographie: une nouvelle voie pour l'Histoire de la Franc-maçonnerie », *REHMLAC, Revista de Estudios Históricos de la Masonería Latinoamericana y Caribeña* (San Jose, Costa Rica) 1, No. 2 (December 2009-April 2010): 37-43. https://revistas.ucr.ac.cr/index.php/rehmlac/article/view/6616/26723. (Accessed April 11, 2011).

Ayala, José Antonio, *La Masonería en la región de Murcia* (Murcia: Ediciones Mediterráneo, 1986).

Bastian, Jean-Pierre, "Las logias francmasonas españolas del siglo XX, ¿Qué tipo de sociabilidad?" in *La Masonería en la España del siglo XX*, coord. Ferrer Benimeli, José Antonio (Toledo: Cortes de Castilla-La Mancha, 1996).

Boletín Oficial del Grande Oriente Español (Madrid, España) VI, No. 67 (December 10, 1932).

Cassard, Andrés, *El Espejo Masónico* (España: Extramuros, 2007), Vol. I.

Castellano Gil, José Manuel, *La masonería española en Cuba* (Santa Cruz de Tenerife: Taller de Historia, 1996).

De Paz Sánchez, Manuel, *Historia de la francmasonería en Canarias* (Las Palmas de Gran Canaria: IDEA, 2008).

Enríquez del Árbol, Eduardo, "Aproximación metodológica a los nombres simbólicos masónicos en un caso particular: la logia "Moralidad n°160" de Huelva," in *Del Antiguo al Nuevo Régimen: estudios en homenaje al profesor Cepeda Adán* (Granada: Universidad de Granada, 1986), 213-242.

Ferrer Benimeli, José Antonio, *La Masonería española en el siglo XVIII* (Madrid: Siglo XXI, 1986).

_____, "Masones asturianos en la Cuba y Puerto Rico del siglo XIX," in *Ástura* (Oviedo, España) 9 (1993): 61-69.

Goicoerrotea, Román, "Los masones," *Revista de España* (Madrid, 1870), Vol. XIII, 481-503.

Guzmán Stein, Miguel, "Andrés Cassard y su vida en Nueva York. Tres nuevas facetas de un masón polifacético," in *La Masonería española. Represión y exilios*, coord. Ferrer Benimeli, José Antonio (Zaragoza: Government of Aragon, 2010), Vol. I, 509-544.

Hidalgo Nieto, Victoria, *La masonería en Asturias en el siglo XIX* (Oviedo: Ministry of Education, Culture and Sport of the Principality of Asturias, 1985).

Júlbez Campos, Manuel M. & Pizarro Llorente, Henar, "Masonería bonapartista en Madrid (1812-1820) a través de los papeles inquisitoriales," in *Masonería, Revolución y Reacción*, coord. Ferrer Benimeli, José Antonio (Alicante: Instituto Alicantino Juan Gil-Albert, 1991), Vol. I, 71-78.

Latomia (Madrid, 1932-1934), Vol. I-IV.

Ligou, Daniel, *Dictionnaire de la Franc-maçonnerie* (Paris: PUF, 2006).

Maitron, Jean, *Le mouvement anarchiste en France. Des origines à 1914* (Paris : Gallimard, 2007).

Martínez López, Fernando, *Masones, republicanos y librepensadores en la Almería contemporánea (1868-1945)* (Seville: Editorial Corduba, 2009).

Pozuelo Andrés, Yván, "Una muestra

de famosos escritores liberales antimasones," *Revista de Arte, Historia y Literatura* 35 (2009). actuallynotes.com/Una-muestra-de-famosos-escritores-liberales-antimasones.html

Randouyer, Françoise, « Les noms symboliques des Maçons espagnols," in *Chroniques d'histoire maçonnique* (Paris, France) 29-30 (1982).

_____, "Ideología masónica a través de los nombres simbólicos," in *La masonería en la España del siglo XIX*, coord. Ferrer Benimeli, José Antonio (Salamanca: Junta of Castile and León, 1987), Vol. I, 425-439.

Roldán Rabadán, María Teresa, "Análisis y estudio de los "nombres simbólicos utilizados por los miembros de cuatro logias madrileñas," in *La masonería en la España del siglo XIX*, coord. Ferrer Benimeli, José Antonio (Salamanca: Junta of Castile and León, 1987), Vol. II, 529-539.

Sánchez Ferré, Pere, *La Constitución de 1723. Compilación de las marcas (Landmarks) de la masonería* (Barcelona: Alta Fulla, 1998).

Sánchez Gálvez, Samuel "Los nombres simbólicos en la logia masónica cienfueguera Fernandina de Jagua. 1878-1902," *Universidad y Sociedad* (Cienfuegos, Cuba) II, No. 2 (2007): 45-47.

_____, "Los nombres simbólicos en la logia masónica cienfueguera Fernandina de Jagua: expresiones de pensamiento," *Anuario 2007* (Cienfuegos, Cuba, 2007).

Sanllorente Barragán, Francisco, Francisco "Dos logias francesas fundadas en Madrid durante la I República y la Restauración canovista: Logia Osiris y L'Hospitalière (1870-1880)," in *La Masonería en Madrid y en España del siglo XVIII al XXI*, coord. Ferrer Benimeli, José Antonio (Zaragoza: Government of Aragon, 2004), Vol. I, 48-49.

Saunier, Éric, « La prosopographie: une nouvelle voie pour l'Histoire de la Franc-maçonnerie », *REHMLAC, Revista de Estudios Históricos de la Masonería Latinoamericana y Caribeña* (San Jose, Costa Rica) 1, No. 2 (December 2009-April 2010): 37-43. https://revistas.ucr.ac.cr/index.php/rehmlac/article/view/6616/26723

Valín Fernández, Alberto, *Masonería y revolución. Del mito literario a la realidad histórica* (Las Palmas de Gran Canaria: IDEA, 2008).

ANNEXES

Annex 1

Number of Symbolic Names making reference to Latin America in Asturian Lodges
(Nineteenth Century)

Number of Lodges	Number of Symbolic Names
5	0
2	1
6	2
2	3
1	6
1	8

Source: Hidalgo Nieto, 196-236.

Annex 2

Number of Freemasons in Asturias with Symbolic Names by Location
(Nineteenth Century)

City	Number
Oviedo	12
Gijón	3
Avilés	3
Trubia	3
Navia	2
Luarca	1

Source: Hidalgo Nieto, 196-236.

Annex 3

Latin American Symbolic Names in Asturias (Nineteenth Century) by Era

Modern (Fifteenth–Sixteenth Centuries)	Number	Contemporary (Nineteenth Century)	Number
Colón, Cortés, Pizarro, Moctezuma, Haute	5	Méndez Núñez, Bolivar, Mina, Mitre, Céspedes, Nataniel	6

Source: Hidalgo Nieto, 196-236.

Annex 4

Frequency of Latin American Symbolic Names in Asturias
(Nineteenth Century)

Symbolic Name	Number of Freemasons
Colón	7
Cortés	3
Méndez Núñez	3
Mina	3
Pizarro	2
Moctezuma	1
Bolivar	1
Mitre	1
Céspedes	1
Nataniel	1
Hatuey	1
Total	24

Source: Hidalgo Nieto, 196-236.

Annex 5

Name of Asturian Lodges and Symbolic Names Used
(Nineteenth Century)

Name of Lodge	City	Total Freemasons	Symbolic Names	Number
Nueva Luz (1878-1888)	Oviedo	98	Colón, Mina, Céspedes, Méndez Núñez, Hatuey, Bolivar, Mina, Nataniel	8
Juan González Río (1888-1893)	Oviedo	130	Mina, Nataniel, Céspedes, Moctezuma, Colón, Méndez Núñez	6
Vigilante de Asturias (1889-1892)	Oviedo	29	Mina, Céspedes, Méndez Núñez	3
El Trabajo (1876-1890)	Trubia	54	Cortés, Méndez Núñez, Colón	3
Los Caballeros de la Luz (1886)	Oviedo	11	Mina, Nataniel	2
La Justicia (1879-1880)	Avilés	40	Colón, Cortés	2

Concordia (1887-1888)	Avilés	24	Pizarro, Cortés	2
Antorcha Civiliza-dora (1879-1888)	Navia	20	Colón, Pizarro	2
Amigos de la Naturaleza y de la Humanidad (1879-1886)	Gijón	76	Colón, Mina	2
Amigos de la Humanidad (1889-1894)	Gijón	48	Cristóbal Colón, Mina	2
Luz Ovetense (1874-1877)	Oviedo	53	Colón	1
Jovellanos (1891-1892)	Luarca	18	Mitre	1

Source: Hidalgo Nieto, 196-236.

Annex 6

Number of Freemasons with Latin American Symbolic Names by Location
(Twentieth Century)

City	Number
Oviedo	1
Gijón	17

Sources: Historical Memory Archives in Salamanca (Spain). *Amese* Triangle, SE-MASONERIA_A,C.737,EXP.2; Jovellanos Lodge, SE-MASONERIA_A,C.737,EXP.4; Riego Lodge, SE-MASONERIA_A,C.737,EXP.8; López del Villar Lodge, SE-MASONERIA_A,C.737,EXP.5; Argüelles Lodge, SE-MASONERIA_A,C.739,EXP.1.

Annex 7

Number of Latin American Symbolic Names by Lodge (Twentieth Century)

Number of Lodges	Number of Symbolic Names
6	0
1	14
1	3
3	1

* The Jovellanos Lodge No. 37, which later changed its number to one with the reorganization of the Grand Orient of Spain in 1923, is counted as a single lodge. The Astúrica Lodge of the Grand Spanish Lodge is not included for lack of a reliable list.

Sources: Historical Memory Archives in Salamanca (Spain). *Amese* Triangle, SE-MASONERIA_A,C.737,EXP.2; Jovellanos Lodge, SE-MASONERIA_A,C.737,EXP.4; Riego Lodge, SE-MASONERIA_A,C.737,EXP.8; López del Villar Lodge, SE-MASONERIA_A,C.737,EXP.5; Argüelles Lodge, SE-MASONERIA_A,C.739,EXP.1; *Costa* Triangle, SE-MASONERIA_A,C.739,EXP.19; *Amor y Trabajo* Triangle, SE-MASONERIA_A,C.739,EXP.11; *José Rizal* Triangle, SE-MASONERIA_A,C.739,EXP.8; *Ferrer* Triangle, SE-MASONERIA_A,C.739,EXP.14; *Evaristo San Miguel* Triangle, SE-MASONERIA_A,C.739,EXP.12; *Alberto de Lera* Rose-Croix Chapter, SE-MASONERIA_A,C.737,EXP.1.

Annex 8

Name of Asturian Lodges and Symbolic Names Used (Twentieth Century)

Name of Lodges	City	Total Freemasons	Symbolic Names	Number
Jovellanos	Gijón	321	Argentina, Americano, Bolivar, Rubén Darío, Buenos Aires, Martí (2), Cienfuegos, Caibarién, América, Lempira, Méjico, Monterrey, Juárez	13
Riego	Gijón	74	Siboney, Cárdenas, Bejucal	3
Amese	Gijón	18	Argentina	1
Argüelles	Oviedo	40	Méjico	1
López del Villar	Gijón	15	Méjico	1

Sources: Historical Memory Archives in Salamanca (Spain). *Amese* Triangle, SE-MASONERIA_A,C.737,EXP.2; Jovellanos Lodge, SE-MASONERIA_A,C.737,EXP.4; Riego Lodge, SE-MASONERIA_A,C.737,EXP.8; López del Villar Lodge, SE-MASONERIA_A,C.737,EXP.5; Argüelles Lodge, SE-MASONERIA_A,C.739,EXP.1.

Annex 9

Latin American Symbolic Names in Asturias (Twentieth Century) by Corresponding Era

Modern (Fifteenth–Sixteenth Centuries)	Number	Contemporary (Nineteenth-Twentieth centuries)	Number
Siboney, Lempira	2	Americano, Bolivar, Rubén Darío, Martí (2), Méjico, Juárez	7

Sources: Historic Memory Archives in Salamanca (Spain). *Amese* Triangle, SE-MASONERIA_A,C.737,EXP.2; Jovellanos Lodge, SE-MASONERIA_A,C.737,EXP.4; Riego Lodge, SE-MASONERIA_A,C.737,EXP.8; López del Villar Lodge, SE-MASONERIA_A,C.737,EXP.5; Argüelles Lodge, SE-MASONERIA_A,C.739,EXP.1.

Annex 10

Nature of Latin American Symbolic Names Chosen by Freemasons in Asturias (Twentieth Century)

Five Historical Figures	Ten Toponymical Names	Two Villages
Bolivar, Rubén Darío, Juárez, Martí y Lempira	Argentina, Cárdenas, Bejucal, Buenos Aires, Cienfuegos, Caibarién, América, Méjico y Monterrey	Siboney y Americano

Sources: Historic Memory Archives in Salamanca (Spain). *Amese* Triangle, SE-MASONERIA_A,C.737,EXP.2; Jovellanos Lodge, SE-MASONERIA_A,C.737,EXP.4; Riego Lodge, SE-MASONERIA_A,C.737,EXP.8; López del Villar Lodge, SE-MASONERIA_A,C.737,EXP.5; Argüelles Lodge, SE-MASONERIA_A,C.739,EXP.1.

Annex 11

Latin American Symbolic Names of Freemasons in Asturias (Twentieth Century) and their Latin American Territorial Reference

Symbolic Name	Territory	Total Symbolic Names
Siboney, Cárdenas,* Bejucal, Martí, Cienfuegos, Caibarién	Cuba	6
Americano, Lempira, América	America	3
Méjico, Monterrey y Juárez	Mexico	3
Bolivar	Venezuela	1
Rubén Darío	Nicaragua	1

| Argentina | Argentina | 1 |

* This name could refer to several municipalities in Central American countries. Sources: Historical Memory Archives in Salamanca (Spain). *Amese* Triangle, SE-MASONERIA_A,C.737,EXP.2; *Jovellanos* Lodge, SE-MASONERIA_A,C.737,EXP.4; *Riego* Lodge, SE-MASONERIA_A,C.737,EXP.8; *López del Villar* Lodge, SE-MASONERIA_A,C.737,EXP.5; *Argüelles* Lodge, SE-MASONERIA_A,C.739,EXP.1.

Annex 12

Asturian Freemasons in Cuba with Asturian Symbolic Names (Nineteenth Century)

Name of Lodge	City	Symbolic Names	Number
Obreros del Progreso 174	Cienfuegos	Ribadesella, Oviedo, Carbayón, Granja, Navas, Avilés, Riego (2), Nalón, Pravia, Rebollada, Mallecina, Peñaflor (2), Ceres, Infiesto (2), Valdemora, San Miguel, Lay, Luarca, Villalegre, Villanueva, Amandi, San Martín, Gijón, Laviana	27
Unión Universal 266	Cárdenas	Pino, Belmonte, Jovellanos (2), Infiesto, Villahormes, Aller, Nalón, Navia (2), Soto, Santianes, Trelles, Pelayo, Trubia	15
Unión Hispano Americana 132	Havana	Jovellanos (2), Riego, Villazón, Villaviciosa, Navia, Contranquil, San Román, Pelayo, Favila, Granda, Nalón, Bances	13
Comuneros de Castilla 15	Havana	Carrea, Teverga, Covadonga, Camas,* Purón, Oviedo (2), Peñaflor, Quirós	9
Reforma 112	Havana	Cangas, Santianes, Piñera, Castro, Labarrera, Villamayor, Pelayo	7
España 40	San Juan de los Remedios	Mieres, Avilés (2), Alea, Sella, Pelayo	6
Hijos de Hiram 50	Bejucal	Muros, Colunga, Nalón, Jovellanos, Caldueño, Sella	6
Hijos de la Luz 123	Santiago	Llanes, Oviedo, Pelayo (2), Villanueva	5
Iberia 2	Caibarién	Sella, Somado, Navia, Pelayo, Viavelez	5
Hijos de Cosmopolita 161	Sagua La Grande	Balmes, Jovellanos, Pelayo, Siero, Gijón	5
Asilo de la Virtud 140	Cienfuegos	Ribadesella, Villanueva, Arlós, Colunga	4
Constancia 121	Havana	Reconco, Pelayo, Granda, Riego	4
Unión y Concordia 121	Matanzas	Pelayo (3), Cartabio	4
Esther 239	Havana	Gijón, Carangas, Asturias	3

Unión Latina 148	Guantánamo	Tarín, Serín, Mieres	3
Padilla 38	Havana	Pravia, Covadonga, Jovellanos	3
Porvenir 94	Gíbara	Pelayo, Noreña	2
Alianza 211	Santo Domingo	Pelayo, Gijón	2
Lazo de Unión 126	Regla	Favila, Nalón	2
Rosacruz Morayta 8	Espejo	Muros	1
Hijos Unión Universal 182	Benaguises	Pelayo	1
Minerva 278	Sagua de Tánamo	Pelayo	1
Fe Masónica 153	Havana	Trubia	1
El mundo Marcha	Havana	Riego	1
Los Templarios 26	Santiago de las Vegas		0
Los Girondinos 16	Victoria de las Tunas		0
		Total	130

* Written in the text "Camar."
Source: Ferrer Benimeli, "Masones asturianos en la Cuba y Puerto Rico del siglo XIX,"
61-69.

Annex 13

Asturian Symbolic Names in Cuba (Nineteenth Century) by Era

Medieval (Eighth Century)	Number	Contemporary (Nineteenth Century)	Number	Total
Pelayo (16), Favila (2), Covadonga (2)	20	Jovellanos (7), Riego (5)	12	32

Source: Ferrer Benimeli, "Masones asturianos en la Cuba y Puerto Rico del siglo XIX,"
61-69.

Annex 14

Place of Birth of the Eighty-Eight Asturian Freemasons of Cuba (Nineteenth Century) through their Toponymical Symbolic Names

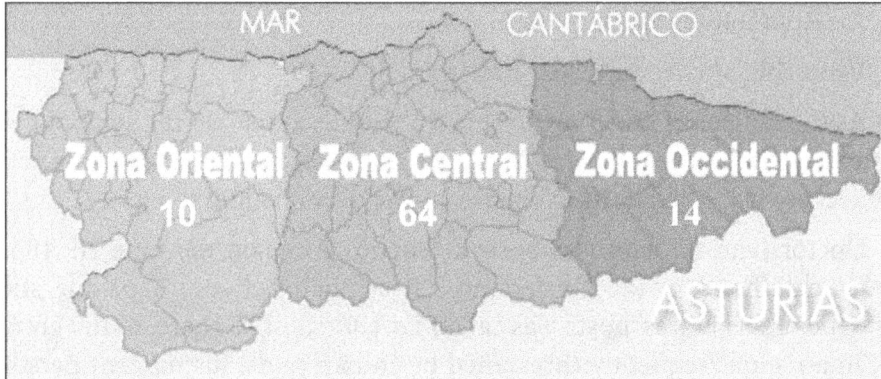

* One additional Freemason took the symbolic name "Asturias."
Source: Ferrer Benimeli, "Masones asturianos en la Cuba y Puerto Rico del siglo XIX," 61-69.

Annex 15

Frequency of Symbolic Names with Asturian Connotations by Asturian Freemasons in Cuba

Symbolic Names	Frequency of Use
Pelayo	16
Jovellanos	7
Riego, Nalón	5
Gijón, Oviedo, Navia	4
Avilés, Peñaflor, Infiesto, Villanueva	3
Favila, Covadonga, Ribadesella, Trubia, Sella, Santianes, Pravia, Colunga, Muros, Granda, Mieres	2
Granja, Carbayón, Navas, Rebollada, Mallecina, Ceres, Valdemora, San Miguel, Lay, Luarca, Villalegre, Noreña, Amandi, San Martín, Laviana, Pino, Belmonte, Villahormes, Aller, Soto, Trelles, Mieres, Alea, Camas, Purón, Quirós, Carangas, Asturias, Carrea, Teverga, Reconco, Llanes, Somado, Viavelez, Cartabio, Caldueño, Tarín, Serín, Cangas, Piñera, Castro, Labarrera, Villamayor, Balmes, Siero, Arlós, Villazón, Villaviciosa, Contranquil, San Román, Bances	1

Source: Ferrer Benimeli, "Masones asturianos en la Cuba y Puerto Rico del siglo XIX," 61-69.

Annex 16

Sample of a Baluster Explaining the Symbolic Name Juan B. Justo

An Apprentice's Work

Venerable Master and Dear Brothers:

As the lodge has asked me to present this discourse on my symbolic name, I am pleased to read the following lines, asking for forgiveness if my comments on the subject are not sufficiently extensive, as they justly ought to be.

Doctor Juan B. Justo was born in Buenos Aires on the June 28, 1865. He spent his childhood in the borderlands, at a ranch between Tapalqué and Las Flores. One of Las Flores' posts was called *La Vanguardia*. There, in the great out-doors, in a region frequently threatened by Indian raids, his nascent personality must have absorbed something of the crude environment where his parents dedicated themselves to rural chores. It may have been there that he learned to be alert, to fight, to face danger head-on and to live with sobriety and firm faith in his own strength.

As Argentina develops as a nation, there are citizens who count a series of struggles and efforts in their favor. They mark the ever-ascending line of progress, which could be synthesized in the eminent figures of Moreno, Rivadavia, Eche-varría, Alberdi and Sarmiento, Juan B. Busto [sic], organizing and directing the popular masses, awakening in them the hope for a better life, urging them into a fecund, constantly renewing struggle for their liberation. This is the worthy con-tinuation of the Argentine tradition in its libertarian and progressive aspects, and it launched a new historic cycle for our country: the cycle of dynamic and con-structive proletarian agitation.

He had the social masses in mind, a concept that until that point was un-known, and he raised concerns. Claiming rights and spreading the notion of histor-ic justice, he launched a formidable movement to emancipate the working masses, who had formerly been unacknowledged and disrupted by the political barbarism prevalent at that time, a movement today consecrated as the work that leads us to the highest of destinies. This movement responded to the relatively progressive state of our economic development. The foundation was in its development stage, but Doctor Justo, with a precise vision of the future, in a magnificent constructive, organizational effort, gave it shape, guided it and encouraged it. It was he who translated *Das Kapital*, which, together with his study and criticism, enabled him to penetrate to its roots and to share its historical meaning. Another product of his profound, constant studies, of his objective observation of the national and international reality, and of the experience he acquired over years of heroic, fero-cious struggle, was his book, *The Theory and Practice of History*, in which, clearly, methodically, and with unmatched erudition—characteristic of all his work—he studies the development of historical forces to instruct the people in his command, to whom he dedicates the book, which is fundamental to the culture of Argentina as a sort of continuation of Karl Marx's *Das Kapital*.

He hoped that the people would consciously make history, that they would work with their own strength, their own destiny. In this sense, Justo is the summary and symbol of a broad period in Argentine life that continues to this day, like the route to the future, demanding endeavor from its pioneers and from new generations. It would be futile, in this discussion, even to attempt to describe his projects, his questions, his discourses, his contributions to parliamentary debates during his sixteen-year struggle. His works would provide enough focus for study for an entire lifetime. Thanks to his presence, Congress underwent a marked transformation, with the immediate result that the nature of ordinary matters that were routinely at the center of parliamentary discussion changed substantively. From conventional issues of policies and oligarchical finances, they moved onto social questions, to the political class war, to the conflict between pure and sincere universal suffrage and fraudulent, corrupt elections. He organized and launched the renewing force of international socialism in this Republic, meaning that he gave part of the working class of his country the consciousness of its historic mission, along with teaching them to take the lead and become a living factor in the social and political history of human solidarity. In these regions, he began building a workers' organization to struggle for socialism. When I say that Doctor Justo is the father of the Argentine socialist movement, I do not mean that with him socialism emerged fully developed, as Minerva emerged from the head of Jupiter. I do not deny, and am not ignorant of the fact that without him the movement would still have been created, though later and undoubtedly with less force for expansion, and with a shallower sense of reality. Let us remember, meanwhile, that there was a seed in that workers' group—mostly or entirely foreigners—that Juan B. Justo brought together and nurtured into the first shoots of the Socialist Party. Thus, the embryo of the movement had already been fathered in the country, before Doctor Justo threw himself into the struggle for socialism. The ideological seed had come from Europe in the form of books and in the spirit of the German and Italian workers who integrated into that workers' group, but that seed was able to develop, because this was where all of the elements and social conditions that gave a *raison d'être* to its materialization in acts existed, and where these elements could be proclaimed as a factor necessary to the destiny of working people and of the nation. Justo brought the political organization of workers into being so that they would bring into the struggle for Argentine democracy a breath of idealism, a burst of ideas and ideals and an aspiration to improve the material, moral and intellectual status of the masses; a sense of civic rectitude and of public morality—in a word, a spirit of civilization and political culture. This organization came into being by its own initiative, by its counsel and by its own personal activity, a great school by the people and for the people. He achieved this by means of libraries, cultural institutions and cooperatives, all of them workshops where the spirit of the masses was forged in order to create a collective soul and the spirit of a nationality. Dealing with a nation that grew in cosmopolitanism, his spirit had to be universalist, and the national feeling for excellence therein had to be internationalist. The destiny of the Americas is to open itself up to the currents of the world and to hold in its heart, and in its territory, all of the races and all of the people of the earth. Internationalist ideas, then, must form in this region more than elsewhere—it must be a healthy nationalism. To this nationalism, he dedicated his life as a thinker and a fighter for this vast region. In his own words, a good part of the future is going to come about, by virtue of manual labor and the star of good will in the soul. He served an ideal with self-sacrifice, and—the part that remains most important to this day— he did so with efficacy and an evidently practical and positive spirit. He aimed to get as close as possible to the fertile state of realization, which is, ultimately, the best way of holding ideas and being an idealist.

His life and work were inextricably linked. In his writings, and when he taught the intellectuals and the masses, whom he uplifted with his tireless work as an organizer, he was a living example of pure and austere existence, which is no more than an uninterrupted succession of courageous truths, affirmations of character and expressions of virile conscience. Every word was an act of integrity, of honor and of sincerity, in the journalistic arena, on the street or in Congress; at all times, he preached his teachings. A master of rectitude and honesty, what he was, and what he did, the example he offered to generations and the popular power of renovation and moral restructuring that he created, all amounted to an outburst of national purification.

Someone once said that all Spaniards carry a dead man within them, a man that could have been born but was not, and who would emerge one day when all dead men decide it is time to rise. There is no doubt that this happens not just to Spaniards, but to men all across the globe. Justo's mission in Argentina and on the Río de la Plata was precisely that of a great awakener of dead men; even more than that, he breathed life into the man who remains unborn in so many men. Thanks to his influence, thousands of citizens have felt that other man arise within them, awakening in their consciousness in order to be one of the new men, called to bury forever the corpse of tradition and to banish the individual or collective spirit, that other man who, like cattle in the herd, does not lift his head so he does not lose sight of his food.

He loved the nation without proclaiming it but guided all of his work toward the nation. "We are continuing the independence movement," he said truly and justly in a party manifesto, launched during a difficult period of social conflict. He wanted the nation to be a strong, industrious, instructed and conscious race. He wanted our language to be the language of works worthy of being read and admired, and wanted the Argentine flag to represent peace and, where work was concerned, high ideals of national and international solidarity. He relentlessly battled human exploitation and privilege in order to liberate the nation's mass producers. He wanted to use intelligently all of the nation's resources to eradicate illiteracy; he decried falsehood; he highlighted and combated all mistakes and aspired to, and planned, great essential reforms for the material and intellectual betterment of the people. Such was the far-reaching and comprehensive work he wished for the nation. He worked like a laborer who does his task without complaint, because his conscience drove him to build for his fellow man and for humanity.

I have attempted—perhaps with overly vague strokes—to outline the most general trends of thought concerning this man, whose work is a faithful expression of his ideals. Others will have the last word, the final judgment on his work and on the breeding ground where his ideas and social doctrines evolved. These pages are left as a stumbling essay, albeit one which will stimulate the work that my dear brothers will resume with enthusiasm.

Buenos Aires, March 1931

Juan B. Justo

First Degree

*It is worth mentioning that Juan Bautista Justo was not a Mason.

Source: *Boletín del Grande Oriente Español* (Seville) V, No. 55 (June 10, 1931): 18-20.

Annex 17

Sample of a Baluster Explaining the Symbolic Name Cervantes

Lodge Papers

The Masonic Spirit of Cervantes

Work of an Apprentice Freemason read on February 3, 1933, by H. "Cervantes" of the "Patria Nueva" Lodge in Valencia

TO THE DGDU,

YOUR MAJESTY AND DEAR BROTHERS,

It is with joy that today I carry out the task of reading my Apprentice Freemason paper on the symbolic name "Cervantes."

Speaking to you of Cervantes and his literary output would be too much for me, and inadequate for such a tremendously enlightened man.

Furthermore, I would consider it an insult to your patriotic sentiments to now attempt to unveil, for you, the glorious personage who penned *Don Quixote de la Mancha*. NO. I will not make such a blunder. I shall simply express to you all something that I believe to be a new nuance, a suggestion that is unknown or not very well known within the formidable body of Cervantes' work. With the title of this modest paper of mine, which I submit for your benevolent attention, I indicate the subject which I hope to discuss and which is entirely unpublished.

"The Masonic Spirit of Cervantes." Yes, I must tell you that as I gained deep satisfaction—nurtured for many years—from receiving enlightenment from your tutelage and being honored as your beloved brother, I opted for a purely spiritual sentimentalism with the symbolic name of Cervantes, which was used by my father, and I hope you will permit me to dedicate this moment of respectful homage to my first moment of being touched by Masonic thought, when I immediately felt that I had made an unsuspected discovery that filled me with joyous astonishment.

I was familiar, through my literary interests, with the whole of Cervantes' work and a good proportion of the opinions put forth by those who commented on it. I believed, honestly, that I knew about Cervantes and everything about his work. That, at a minimum, there was nothing left to say. Yes here, Your Highness and my dear brothers, I find that there is still much more, that the sentimental thinking had to be considered, as well as the psychological thought, the moral foundation and the philosophical origin, the creative essence of the portentous creations. And what I had yet to appreciate and consider was simply the Masonic spirit that I didn't know, and which lives and will go on living forever, as a perennial lesson of great humanity in the magnificent work of the Prince of Wits.

Cervantes was a Freemason. Oh, of course, you could argue that not a single lodge existed in Spain in his time, that Cervantes was never initiated as a Freemason. But I insist that he was a Freemason. All I need to substantiate my assertion is a single one of his works, the best-known, the one that earned him a place in history: *Don Quixote*.

Men are judged by their works, as trees are judged by their fruit. Let us remember the Masonic Code, the Rule of our Order, and compare the precepts that sustain our legal texts with the immortal, humorous novel, *Don Quixote de la Mancha*.

Even someone with the slightest experience of literary disquisition immediately understands that he is face-to-face with a manual of good customs, like our own Masonic manual. It attempts to perfect Humankind through instruction. To educate by providing pleasure. To come to the aid of Humankind and establish, in brief, basic principles for a perfect future society based on liberty, brotherhood and the rule of law.

Miguel de Cervantes chose the only road that befits the light, exceedingly difficult and superficial character of Spaniards. To ridicule. To make people see the grotesque consequences of bad deeds. And thus, he presents us with the figure of a madman. And in the mouth of a madman, facing apparently trivial but profoundly incomprehensible situations, he puts forward concepts disguised as wise pronouncements that constitute a crude, heroic, deeply dangerous attack, for those times, on all of the hypocrisy and vice of a society that, unfortunately, have yet to be corrected, because Freemasonry still has not triumphed.

The day that the duly propagated Masonic Spirit enlightens the entire universe shall be the day that the work of the clairvoyant one-armed man's work will have triumphed, and these things shall be his well-deserved homage.

Let's take a look at a few randomly selected paragraphs from *Don Quixote*. Certainly, all are maxims of an irrefutable truth. Here are a few:

In the dedication to the Duke of Béjar, he presents his book with fear, he says, of those who, "not restraining themselves within the limits of their own ignorance, are accustomed to condemn with more severity and less justice the labors of others." In these first lines, he hits a virtuously Masonic value on the head: the tolerance and respect that we must have toward the works of others. How true it is that the most scathing criticism is typically no more than a mask for ignorance!

And now let us delve into the prodigious work.

The protagonist (as I've already mentioned, and you all already know) is a madman, and his madness is motivated by intellectual hyperesthesia, mental fatigue, since he reads without understanding; he embraces a pathological culture, acquired by chance, as he chose to read harmful, damaging, ridiculous books. Thus, Cervantes places Humankind on guard, at the dawn of the age of print, against the noxious effects of ill-chosen reading. Today, we continue to struggle desperately against the selfishness of unfortunate Spaniards who, guided by cowardly commercial zeal, gratify the passions and the lowest, instincts of the public, publishing books, pamphlets and pornographic periodicals, or low politics, which vilify society and diminish its morality, with no greater positive results than enrichment or advancement of a handful of wicked ghouls.

In Valencia, there is such a man, who exclusively publishes pornographic pamphlets and periodicals on a large scale, earning between 30,000 and 40,000 *duros* a year. I, incidentally, have been able to verify the horrendous effects of his terrible literature.

Opposite the home of this lecherous publisher, whose name I prefer to keep to myself, lives a barber with whom I have been acquainted for many years. His son, a boy of fourteen years, began reading these publications which, as a neighbor, he had been given. Having surrendered to the solitary vice, he has contracted the terrible disease known as tuberculosis, and he is now at death's door.

How many lives have been ruined by reading these fatal publications!

Cervantes identified an evil that required strict legislation—and he did this centuries ago! Today, things have scarcely changed, despite the good intentions of our new governors. Freemasonry has a clear road to follow here; and, likewise, if we continue examining all of the splendid literary output of Cervantes, we will be guided by an unmistakable Masonic spirit.

For example: Don Quixote's first adventure, after becoming a knight-errant, consists of freeing a young lad from a master who has tied him to a tree and is whipping him for the crime of demanding a just salary.

The symbolism is surprising.

Thanks to him, in a dangerous era, Cervantes was able to say that it was cowardly to hurt those who cannot defend themselves, and with heroic words wrote emphatically against those who cannot be self-made men, because they deny their servants' pay, and do not acknowledge their sweat and work.

Neither sociology nor Freemasonry has anything further to add.

Helping the weak and bringing justice are sacred principles to all good Freemasons.

Thus, all of *Don Quixote* is a program of Masonic works that, unfortunately, have yet to be carried out.

I firmly believe that one can be a Freemason by one's works. Thus, Cervantes, whose entire work is imbued with underlying Masonic values, was a Freemason. A Freemason as I have dreamed him. Tolerant, discrete, understanding, generous, reaching a state of madness in order to defend, if necessary, the needy and the afflicted.

Sublime madness! Always striving to perfect the coarse stone in order to make it a pyramid.

His *Exemplary Novels* are so human, so utterly perfect, that, in embracing them, it is as if one were abiding by the very Code of our Masonic Ritual. All of society's scourges are wisely revealed.

There, in "La Tía Fingida" a hapless woman is exploited, and in these beautiful paragraphs one can see the first ideas that later were used to write the liberal legislation concerning so-called "white slavery."

And there, when the jealous Extremaduran tortures his wife, turning marital happiness into an unfeeling abyss of slavery and misery, Cervantes ingeniously deduces the first foundations of modern laws on divorce.

And in theater, Cervantes' comedy *La elección de los alcaldes*, assumes the role of sociologist. The author points the finger at the eternal ulcer of rural despotism, with which he reached absolute and definitive success.

I do not want to tire your fraternal and benevolent attention with the type of vainly erudite quotes which Cervantes himself criticizes in his inimitable *Don Quixote de la Mancha*; inimitable, yes, with his forgiveness of the impudent Rodríguez de Avellaneda.

I would like to fit my entire profane life within the admirable Masonic teachings of Cervantes. And, as Cervantes' protagonist, even when it is the true work of madmen by the immeasurable obstacles and uncommon difficulties that we must encounter on our journey, let us take up the lance of our illusion, and—shielded by the fervent enthusiasm of unwavering fraternal affection—let us go out to the profane field and undo the wrongs and offenses of the world, to attain, inspired by the Masonic spirit of Cervantes, the full triumph of Liberty, Equality and Fraternity.

Your brother,

CERVANTES

Valles de Valencia, February 3, 1933

Source: *Boletín Oficial del Grande Oriente Español* (Madrid) VII, No. 69
(February 10, 1933): 4-7.

On the Origins of Freemasonry in Chile[1]

Felipe Santiago del Solar[2]

Abstract

This article analyzes the process of implantation of Freemasonry in Chile with an emphasis on the ways in which this kind of sociability became part of the social contexts that eventually enhanced its institutionalization. To accomplish this goal, we have focused on two periods: independence, where the Military Freemasonry had some presence but did not achieve its establishment, and the period of liberal revolts in the middle of 19th century where it produces its final institutionalization. Two important questions are addressed in this article: Why didn't Masonry succeed in establishing itself at the beginning of the nineteenth century? And Which factors made its institutionalization possible in 1862? In order to answer these queries, we need to examine the political culture of the era, analyze its movements, and expand the scope of observation in such a way that marries the local Chilean experience to the processes of international circulation, which put it into perspective.

Keywords: Grand Lodge of Chile, l'etoile du pacifique, Lodge Lautaro, Lodge Filantropía, Grand Orient of France, Manuel Blanco Encalada

Resumen

El presente artículo analiza el proceso de implantación de la masonería en Chile poniendo énfasis en las vías de ingreso de este tipo de sociabilidad y en los contextos sociales que permitieron su institucionalización. Para ello, nos hemos centrado en dos periodos: el de la independencia, donde la masonería militar tuvo cierta presencia pero no logró su establecimiento; y el periodo de las revueltas liberales a mediados del siglo XIX, donde se produce su institucionalización definitiva. Dos cuestiones importantes se abordan en este artículo: ¿Por qué la Masonería no

---

1 Some of the ideas developed in this article were previously published in the journal REHM-LAC, Vol. 1, No. 1, May-November 2009. I am grateful for the generosity of its director, historian Ricardo Martínez Esquivel, for authorizing my use of this material.

2 Political Scientist, Master in History, and PHD student in history, of the University of Paris Diderot—Paris 7, and the Pontificia Universidad Católica de Chile. Member of the Centro de Estudios de la Masonería Española (CEHME) [Spanish Centre of Masonic Studies].

logró establecerse a principios del siglo XIX? Y ¿Qué factores hicieron posible su institucionalización en 1862? Para responder a estas preguntas, necesitamos examinar la cultura política de la época, analizar los movimientos y ampliar el alcance de la observación de tal manera que se pueda entender la experiencia chilena local a los procesos de circulación internacional que la ponen en perspectiva.

Palabras clave: Gran Logia de Chile, l'etoile du pacifique, logia Lautaro, logia Filantropía, Gran Oriente de Francia, Manue Blanco Encalada

论智利共济会的起源

摘要

本文分析了共济会在智利的成立过程，重点强调了共济会社交性（sociability）在智利的进入途径，同时分析了多个社会情境下成立的共济会，这些社会情境都促进了共济会的制度化。因此，本文聚焦于两个阶段，第一阶段描述军事共济会（Military Freemasonry）的独立，虽然其已经出现但并未正式成立。第二阶段描述19世纪中期的自由反抗（liberal revolts），在此期间共济会建立了最终的制度。

关键词：智利共济会总会所，l'etoile du pacifique，劳塔罗会所，Lodge Filantropía，法兰西大东方社，曼努埃尔·布兰科·恩卡拉达

Introduction

There is a certain consensus among the classic historians of Chilean Freemasonry,[3] for the most part members of the Order themselves, that its origins date back to the wars of independence, later becoming institutionalized with the creation of the *Gran Logia de Chile* in the mid-nineteenth century.

Although this affirmation is not

---

3   There are four classic works of the history of Freemasonry in Chile: Benjamín Oviedo, *La Masonería en Chile. Bosquejo histórico, la colonia, la independencia, la República*, Soc. Imp. y Lit. Universo, Santiago, 1929; René García Valenzuela, *El origen aparente de la Francmasonería en Chile y la respetable Logia Simbólica "Filantropía chilena." Contribución al estudio de la Francmasonería en Chile y sus precursores*, Ed. Imprenta Universitaria, Santiago, 1949; Fernando Pinto Lagarrigue, *La Masonería y su influencia en Chile (ensayo histórico, político y social)*, Ed. Orbe, Santiago, 1966; Manuel Sepúlveda Chavarría, *Crónicas de la Masonería Chilena (1750- 1944)* 5 Vols., Ed. Gran Logia de Chile, Santiago, 1994- 1995.

totally erroneous, it is necessary to put the connection between both processes into context (which otherwise are absolutely unconnected), and to reflect, at least, on two problems: 'Why didn't Masonry succeed in establishing itself at the beginning of the nineteenth century?' and 'Which factors made its institutionalization possible in 1862?'

To answer these questions, it is essential to examine them within the political culture of the era, analyze its movements, and expand the scope of observation in such a way that marries the local Chilean experience to the processes of international circulation, which put it into perspective.

To do this, we will use as a temporal reference the two founding moments of Masonry's history in Chile. The first, benefiting from the wars of independence, was possible because of the opening up of the country and the military mobility that transferred this type of sociability from Europe to America, connecting different processes of masonic implementation in the continental sphere. However, in the case of Chile, the Masonry's presence was weak due to factors such as the strong presence of a traditional Catholic culture, usually excluding of these types of sociability, and because of the exogenous character of the phenomenon, which did not allow for its reproduction on a local level.

In the second phase, conversely, and thanks to the incorporation of Chile into the global economy, the migratory processes increased. With this came the importation of associative practices that not only allowed the rise of Masonry, but also the existence of Chileans inclined to join it.

The process of modernization, which began with Hispanic reformism and intensified with the wars of independence, nurtured the creation of a modern political culture whose fruits were perceivable as early as the mid-nineteenth century. Moreover, the overt nature of French Masonry allowed the local recruitment of liberal youths who, taken under the wing of the *Grand Orient de France*, underwent an associative pedagogical process, subsequently becoming independent and nationalizing this kind of sociability among Chilean elites.

In summary, the Spanish Enlightenment was not in itself enough to create a generation which was inclined to be part of Masonry, among other reasons, because of the anti-Masonic discourse firmly rooted in imperial political culture. In spite of this, it paved the way into the territory and initiated a process of modernization that influenced the aforementioned situation to the extent that the model of Hispanic modernity was replaced by another model, this one of French origin.

Chilean Enlightenment in Hispanic Modernity

Despite the rulings that were put in place to prevent it, especially after the French Revolution, the Age of Enlightenment succeeded in spreading through Spain in a limited and controlled manner.

Without calling the political or religious order into question, the Enlightenment sought, in science, a tool for development (principally of the economy) and was reduced to a group of politicians and intellectuals who used their talents—during the governments of Carlos III and Carlos IV—to bring Spain to an equal standing with the rest of Europe.[4] To do this, they imposed a series of economic, political and cultural reforms aimed at strengthening the economy and the authority of the monarchy.

In social terms, the Spanish Crown encouraged the creation of economic societies composed of friends of the country, which constituted an important innovation in associative matters. Adhering to the utilitarian nature of the Spanish Enlightenment, the main purpose of these organizations was to seek improvements in the local economy through science. Despite this, they also served as spaces to share ideas,[5] where the debate about the economy soon shifted to political matters.

The second half of the eighteenth century was characterized by a significant process of transformation in the Hispanic world. Despite its eminently utilitarian nature, and the strict rule of the monarchy, science, education, culture, and the arts flourished in Spain. This was reflected also, to varying degrees, in its overseas territories.

The form that the Enlightenment took in overseas territories, for its own part, though similar to that of the motherland, focused principally on strengthening and centralizing the Crown's power in its overseas domains through military reforms, the administrative reconfiguration of the country, and tax increases, among other initiatives. Despite the fact that the Hispanic Enlightenment, in all its manifestations, spread across the whole continent, the extent to which it was adopted varied. Its greatest concentration was in the viceroyal capitals, and it extended from there to the rest of the region.

This Enlightenment was also influenced by other models of modernity, thanks to the circulation of books—a result of an active contraband trade with England, the United States, and France—as well as to the journeys that Creoles took through Europe.[6] Due to its geographical isolation, its indirect and informal relations with Atlantic commerce and its modest cultural exchange with Europe, Chile remained a closed-off and traditional enclave of colonial Spanish culture. The Catholic corporate headquarters ruled over society, defining the class bonds to which the king's subjects belonged. As a result of this, the already restricted Spanish Enlightenment had an even more tenuous connection with the far corners of the Empire.

---

4   Gérard Dufour, *Lumières et Ilustración en Espagne. Sous les règnes de Charles III et de Charles IV* (1759- 1808), Ed. Elipses, Paris, 2006, p. 11.

5   Jean Sarrailh, *La España ilustrada. De la segunda mitad del siglo XVIII, Fondo de Cultura económica*, Madrid, 1957.

6   For more on this topic, see this interesting piece: Jaime Rodríguez, *La independencia de la América española*, Fondo de Cultura Económica, México, 1996, pp. 81-102.

Nevertheless, this situation of isolation was alleviated by the Bourbon Reforms, which, despite aiming to centralize power and increase control over the colonies, by promoting openness to foreign trade with other maritime powers, eventually opened up the first cracks in the nation's insular walls. At the same time, thanks to the Royal Decree of 1778 which allowed free trade between various cities of the Southern Cone and many Spanish ports, movement increased across the Atlantic and the connection to the heart of the continent improved. This allowed Chile, a marginal part of the Empire, to improve its relations with the two neighboring viceroyal capitals, Buenos Aires and Lima, and to become a belated member of the Spanish Enlightenment.

Another important channel of communication between Chile and Europe was formed by the journeys abroad that Creoles took, where, for academic, commercial, or military reasons, they came into direct contact with European ideas and forms of sociability. As well as pursuing their own personal processes of acculturation, upon returning from their journeys, these cultural intermediaries brought with them prohibited literature, as in the case of José Antonio de Rojas, who introduced an important shipment of French books containing Diderot and D'Alambert's *"Encyclopedia."*[7]

In terms of sociability, traditional practices of "community, corporate solidarity, and ethnic identity"[8] were maintained. The only testimony that we have of any kind of intellectual social gathering dates back to the start of the nineteenth century in the city of Concepción in southern Chile. This group was made up of a limited number of members of the provincial elite, notably Bernardo O'Higgins and Luis de la Cruz, who would later become members of the Lautaro Lodge.[9]

The Chilean Enlightenment, despite acting as a vehicle of modernization for the elites, did not in itself manage to transform traditional culture, due to its small-scale and limited nature. It would not be until the start of the Revolution and particularly the government of José Miguel Carrera, that Chile would fully enter the age of Enlightenment and see the first signs of modernity flourish, such as the press in 1811 and the Sociedad Económica de Amigos del País (Economic Society of Friends of the Country) in 1812. However, this first taste of the Enlightenment ended abruptly with the violent Spanish Reconquest of 1814, which revoked these changes and brought the country back to colonial subjugation.

In spite of the evident transformations that the Enlightenment produced throughout the Hispanic world, Freemasonry was one of the things that

7   Alfredo Jocelyn-Holt, *La independencia de Chile, tradición, modernización y mito*, Ed. Planeta/Ariel, Santiago, 2001, p. 111.

8   Pilar González Bernaldo, *Civilidad y Política en los orígenes de la nación argentina*, Ed. Fondo de Cultura Económica, Buenos Aires, 2008, p. 22.

9   Benjamín Vicuña Mackenna, *Obras completas*, Vol. V, *"Vida de O'Higgins, La corona del Héroe,"* Editorial Universidad de Chile, Santiago, 1936, p. 105.

Spanish tradition rejected, condemned, and whose dissemination across the whole territory was heavily impeded. It was not until the start of the Revolution of the Peninsula in 1808 that Masonry and secret societies succeeded in taking advantage of the cracks that the Bourbon Reforms opened up in the continent's social structures.

Masonry and Secret Societies

Paradoxically, the first indictment of Masonry in Hispanic America was in the city of Valdivia, one of the southernmost regions of Chile. The accusation before the Inquisition Tribunal of Lima was against the prison governor of Valdivia, Lieutenant Colonel Ambrosio Sáez de Bustamante,[10] who was accused of the crime of

Freemasonry.[11] The indictment was presented by Friar Joseph Villamartin of the Order of San Francisco in Chile, who received the information from a soldier named Miguel de Luca:

"He was, on one occasion, playing a game of cards with some others, and upon one of his moves, I said to him: 'Sir, that is the move of a Freemason.' And he responded: 'Yes, sir, and I am a Freemason [...] Yes sir, there's no need to be shocked, because we Freemasons do not distance ourselves from the law of Christ, and if anyone speaks to the contrary, it is because they do not know the foundations of the Freemasons. And I have been interrogated twice: I have been examined and I came off well, because they found nothing that opposed the faith and law of Christ [...] We are different because our goods are shared, that is, if one of our company is in poverty, those who are rich must help and save him."[12]

Despite the possibility that Sáez de Bustamante could have in fact been

10 Ambrosio Sáez de Bustamante (Guayaquil 1710-?) was the son of General Pablo Sáez Durón, esteemed soldier and Spanish civil servant in America, and Manuela de Bustamante Osores. Early in his life, he pursued a military career and participated in military campaigns in Naples, Sicily, Lombardy and Savoy, among others. He worked in information services and he applied to be the governor of Valdivia, which he was granted by the *Real Orden* (Royal Order) in 1747. He assumed control of the government in 1753 and counted among his work the construction of a rampart of the town square, with the intention of fortifying the city, due to its strategic importance in the Empire. His government (1753-1759) was never free from conflict, mainly with the governor of the kingdom of Chile, Manuel de Amat y Juniet, because of the disagreements between them on the future fortification of the region. During the trial of residence, which ended in 1764, he was absolved of all charges, and the following year was given the title of Colonel. He was also given the honor of the habit of the Order Santiago and governance of Merida, Spain, where he died. For more information, see: Gabriel Guarda, *La sociedad en el Chile austral. Antes de la colonización alemana*, 1645-1845, Ed. Andrés Bello, Santiago, 1979, pp. 280- 281.

11 The original trial can be found in Madrid in the National Historical Archive, Inquisition section, book 1194.

12 Case against the Governor of Valdivia by the inquisition of Lima, in: José Antonio Ferrer Benimeli, *Masonería, Iglesia e Ilustración*, Fundación Universitaria española, Madrid, 1982. Vol. III. p. 466.

initiated into a lodge during his military campaigns, which took place in Italy (in Naples, for example, the first lodge dates back to 1734),[13] it is also important to place the accusation in the context of the difficult relationship that he had with the Governor of the Kingdom, Manuel de Amat y Juniet, who, in the same era, had tried fruitlessly to discredit him before the Crown. Taking this into consideration, this case is little more than an anecdote. However, it shows the state of alert that pervaded even the most remote parts of the Spanish Empire.

The threat of Masonry arrived early in Chile. Most likely its precocious rise is the result of the communication networks of the Holy Office, which alerted the authorities of the Church to the dangers of this new heresy, and both the Pope and Royal authorities warned of the punishments that existed against it.[14] The Spanish Enlightenment could also have served as a vehicle, as the works of Jerónimo de Feijoo, which were widespread in the Hispanic world and are known to have circulated in Chile,[15] dedicate a section to Masonry.[16]

In spite of this, in the Southern Cone there were only two legal cases against Freemasons, unlike in the Viceroyalty of Mexico, where they had more of a presence, although even here they hardly dominated the headlines.[17]

The Spanish Enlightenment inadvertently served as a vehicle for the dissemination of Masonry, a process that came as an unintentional result of the condemnation that was made public throughout the Empire. However, unlike the rest of Europe, in no case did it benefit the establishment of lodges in the colonies. It isn't until the fall of Fernando VII in 1808 that Masonry establishes itself and becomes socially acceptable for the enlightened elites of the Hispanic world.

In the case of Chile, extensive speculations have been made on the early establishment of Masonry. Despite the existence of some (fairly dubious) testimonies that give accounts of its presence,[18] it seems wrong to speak of its establishment in that period. At

---

13 Pierre-Yves Beaurepaire, *L'Europe des francs-maçons XVIII-XXI siècles*, Ed. Belin, 2002, p. 15.

14 The Council of the Spanish Inquisition in 1751 had already sent a notice informing on Freemasonry to which the Tribunal of Lima gave a negative response in 1753. For more information, see: Benjamín Oviedo, *La masonería en Chile: Bosquejo histórico: La colonia, la independencia, la república*. Ed. Universo, Santiago, 1929, p. 19. The documents are reproduced in: José Antonio Ferrer Benimeli, *La Masonería española en el siglo XVIII*, Ed. Siglo XXI, Madrid, 1986., pp. 402- 403.

15 Cristian Gazmuri, *El 48 chileno. Igualitarios, reformistas, radicales, masones y bomberos*, Santiago, Ed. Universitaria, 1993, p. 191.

16 Jerónimo Feijoo, *Cartas eruditas, y curiosas: en que, por la mayor parte, se continua el designio del Theatro critico universal*, volume IV, letter XVI, Real Compañía de Impresores, Madrid, 1778. pp. 187-203.

17 Rogelio Aragón, "*La masonería en las revoluciones decimonónicas de México*," in *Hispania Nova*, contemporary history magazine, No. 8, Spain, 2008.

18 The testimony that is available to us (and which is of dubious value) was told to Diego Barros Arana by General Jerónimo Espejo. The Amunátegui brothers confirm the event after a personal

most, there are some isolated cases. In fact, the only testimony that we know to be true is that of José Miguel Carrera, who joined the St John's Lodge No. 1 in New York in 1816,[19] but after his initiation he never returned to Chile.

The appearance of lodges during this period was possible because of the dissolution of the Spanish Empire, which was part of a large-scale process which became known as "Atlantic Revolutions."[20] The war was the determining factor of their establishment. It accelerated international travel and facilitated the advancement of new forms of socia-bility as an alternative to the traditional links that were dissolved after the crisis of the monarchy.

In this context, the Lautaro Lodge, which existed in Chile approximately from 1817 to 1820, was part of an associative phenomenon that began with the Napoleonic occupation of the center of the Spanish Empire. In the Spanish Empire, between 1808 and 1814, there existed 24 simultaneous yet unconnected[21] French and Spanish lodges,[22] from which arose the Caballeros Racionales[23] Lodge (Lodge of Rational Knights).

interview with José Álvarez Condarco, secretary to José de San Martin and member of the second Lautaro Lodge. According to the latter, during a mission to Chile as a member of parliament of the United Provinces of the Río de la Plata, while they dined with other Spanish officials, Condarco, as a detainee, made "A series of Masonic hand gestures of identification" in the middle of a toast. The gestures were returned to him, identifying all the present officials as Masons. This situation allowed him to escape the execution by firing squad that the royalist governor Marcó del Pont had condemned him to. For more information, see: Miguel Luis y Gregorio Víctor Amunategui, *La reconquista española*, Imprenta Barcelona, Santiago, 1912, p. 395. See also: Enrique de Gandía, *La independencia de América y las sociedades secretas*, Ed. Sudamérica Santa Fe, Argentina, 1994. p. 80; Emilio Corbière, *La masonería: Política y sociedades secretas*, Ed. Sudamericana, Buenos Aires, 1998. p. 216. Also referenced in: Luis de Amesti, *"La supuesta camarilla de Marcó del Pont,"* in the *Boletín de la Academia Chilena de la Historia* No. 63. p. 183.

19 Felipe del Solar, José Miguel Carrera, *Redes masónicas durante las guerras de independencia en América del Sur, en La masonería española represión y exilios*. Minutes in the *XII Symposium Internacional de Historia de la Masonería Española*, Almería, October 8-10, 2009, Ed. Gobierno de Aragón, departamento de educación, cultura y deporte, 2010. Vol. I, pp. 475- 495.

20 For a study of the Atlantic revolutions that include the Hispano-American world, see: María Teresa Calderón and Clément Thibaud (coord.) *Las Revoluciones en el mundo Atlántico*, Ed. Taurus, Colombia, 2006.

21 Enrique de Gandía published an interesting document of a British agent (Mariano Castilla), originally from Buenos Aires, which recounts the supposed connection between the passengers of the ship named *George Canning y Napoleón*. For more details, see: Gandía, Op. Cit. pp, 381-383.

22 There were 14 French lodges, 13 Spanish and one Latin American lodge. For more on the first two cases, see: José Antonio Ferrer Benimeli, *Masonería española contemporánea*, Siglo XXI de España Publishers, 1980, Vol. I, 228, pp.

23 In the most important existing sources on the lodge, the intercepted letters to Carlos de Alvear and the declarations of Servando Teresa de Mier before the tribunal of the Mexican Inquisition, no reference is made to Francisco de Miranda, nor any statement that the lodge was founded in England. For more information, see: Julio Guillén, "Correo insurgente de Londres capturado por una corsario puertorriqueño, 1811," In *Boletín de la academia chilena de la historia*, Santiago, No. 63, 1960, pp. 125-155; Tomás de Iriarte, *Memorias. La independencia y la anarquía*, Buenos Aires, Ediciones

From this grouping came the Lautaro Lodge of Buenos Aires, which, in its early stages, was under the leadership of Carlos de Alvear, and subsequently passed on to Juan Martín de Pueyrredón and José de San Martín. The latter was in charge of training a branch of the lodge in Mendoza,[24] where a group of exiled Chilean patriots joined. They were mainly members of the Bernardo O'Higgins faction, and, in joining, they secured the local bases for the reconquest of Chile.

Once in power, the lodge would have pushed to promote independence and a program of reforms akin to that of Buenos Aires. However, the relationship between the different lodges was not a harmonious one, due both to political differences and to local disputes. It seems that they functioned with a certain autonomy until the breakdown of relations in around 1820, caused by the refusal of José de San Martín to return with his army to Buenos Aires.

In this way, the Lautaro Lodge that existed in Chile[25] would come to be part of a process of proliferation of civil-military lodges on a regional scale. We know with certainty that at least two more of these lodges existed: Caballeros Orientales (Eastern Knights) in Montevideo and the Logia central de la paz de América del Sur (South American Central Lodge of Peace) in Upper Peru.

In the latter's case, if we are to believe the memoirs of Tomás de Iriarte[26] and the investigation that the Inquisition made against him, it was in reality the first Masonic lodge established in the region. Like the Caballeros Racionales Lodge, it arose from Spanish associative culture and moved from the Iberian Peninsula to South America where it appears to have then dissolved.

The wars of independence encouraged intense international mobility. Among the officers of the continent's liberating armies were mercenary soldiers, including veterans of the Napoleonic *Grande Armée*, as well as North American and British officers. However, secret sociability mainly arose out of Spanish influence, and its Creole adop-

---

argentinas "S.I.A.," 1944. pp. 7-13, 173-177 et 222-225; Juan E. Hernández y Dávalos, *Colección de Documentos para la Historia de la Guerra de la Independencia de México,* Mexico, 1882, Vol. 6, pp. 617-621.

24 This remains unclear. We do not know if the lodge continued to function in Mendoza or if it moved to Santiago.

25 There are multiple lists of the members of the Chilean Lautaro Lodge. If we accept the sources, which otherwise do not give categorical indications of who the members were, we have established that the Chileans who participated in the Lodge were: Bernardo O'Higgins, Ramón Freire, Luis de la Cruz, Miguel Zañartu, José Ignacio Zenteno, Manuel Borgoño, José Irizarri, and Manuel Blanco Encalada. The latter two were from Río de la Plata and Guatemala, respectively. The other members came from the United Provinces of the Río de la Plata: José de San Martín, Tomás Guido, Hilarión de la Quintana, Matías Zapiola, Gregorio de las Heras, Rudecindo Alvarado. For more information, see: *Archivo de Don Bernardo O'Higgins,* Santiago, Nascimiento, 1946. Principally volumes VI, VII, VIII, IX, XVIII and the first appendix.

26 Tomás de Iriarte, *Memorias. La independencia y la anarquía, Buenos Aires,* Ediciones argentinas "S.I.A," 1944, pp. 7-13, 173-177 y 222-225.

tion, which would probably explain its hybrid qualities. Its epicenter in the region was the Río de la Plata, a place where it found fertile soil to develop, thanks to its proximity to the Atlantic. This benefited the circulation of traders of many nationalities and allowed for the early development of modern practices such as the press, intellectual gatherings, cafés, and patriotic societies.

In the aforementioned region, the Lautaro Lodge appeared as a combination of two associative processes: an external one from the Peninsula, which moved to Buenos Aires through the members of the Caballeros Racionales society; and an internal one which had been developing since the start of the nineteenth century.

Additionally, in Buenos Aires there was previous history of lodges, such as the one founded in 1804 by the Portuguese trader Juan Silva Cordeiro, named *Logia de San Juan de Jerusalén de esta parte de América* (Lodge of Saint John of Jerusalem of this part of America), in which traders and some members of the colonial bureaucracy participated.[27] There are also testimonies that give accounts of lodges and the initiation of Creoles during the 1806-1807 English invasions.[28]

In this way, secret sociability managed to replicate itself in Buenos Aires. It assumed its own characteristics, thanks to the existence of an enlightened political culture among a Jacobin group of the Río de la Plata elite. However, the links created between its members showed early signs of wearing away. After the fall of Carlos Alvear´s government in 1815 the first split occurred between the lodge and the formation of two opposing factions that reproduced the same type of secret organization.

The creation of factions and their organization into lodges was one of the most critical factors that explain the exhaustion of the model at the beginning of the 1820s. As testimony to this, we have the correspondence between Miguel Zañartu, representative of Chile in Buenos Aires, and member of the Lautaro Lodge, who systematically informed O'Higgins of this situation:

"Members of the brotherhood do not understand each other and they have started to mistrust one another. All of them loathe San Martín and see him as nothing more than an enemy of

---

27   We have information about this lodge because of legal proceedings initiated against it after the aprons of its members were discovered. Juan Canter, for his part, mentions in a document that he attributed to Juan Ángel Vallejos, who confirms the information given by Carlos Calvo. However, he gives no information on the location of this document. Neither could we get access to the proceedings against the lodge. See Juan Canter, Op. Cit, p. 208; Carlos Calvo, *Anales históricos de la revolución de América Latina, acompañados de los documentos en su apoyo*, Paris, 1864, Vol. III, p. 103.

28   There are various testimonies that give accounts of the contact between Creoles and Masonry, which include: Enrique Martínez, "Observaciones hechas a la obra póstuma del señor Ignacio Núñez, titulada 'Noticias Históricas de la república Argentina'" In *Biblioteca de Mayo*, Vol. I Memorias, Buenos Aires, 1960. p. 527. More details in: François-Xavier Guerra and Antonio Annino, *Inventando la Nación: Iberoamérica siglo XIX*, Fondo de Cultura Económica, México, 2003. p. 575.

society, since he opposed taking part in the civil wars and he stopped his troops from marching [...] the least angry of the brothers say that whenever he was resentful or considered it necessary to separate some, or dissolve all, of the group, he could have made advances towards it and obtained it, making use of the reputation that he enjoyed without exposing the country to so many disasters.

The humiliation of Buenos Aires is now complete and rational men will shed bitter tears over the disregard that they showed for Chile's mediation. Soler has been named exterior general [...] I suppose that this would have been initiated in the greatest shroud of mysteries, and I think that for two reasons. The first is that this person shares the opinion of those unhappy with the administration, and the second because they have to take revenge on San Martín, dressing one of his enemies in robes of authority. And, of course, Soler, as his title states, is the general of the forces that San Martín ruled over. One may ask how it can be that only my speculation is possible, being part of the brotherhood. This is also for two reasons. The first is because they don't allow me into their meetings since I opposed the war of Santa Fe (which turned out so beautifully for them) and the second because I believe that in my presence they only spoke of neutral topics or of those that they considered beneficial for me to know." [29]

Parallel to the process of dissolution of the secret societies in the Southern Cone, a second process of founding lodges began due to military movement to the heart of the continent. This enabled the diffusion of the Masonic expertise of Gran Colombia,[30] linked in turn to the region of the Caribbean, which constituted an important Masonic nucleus, thus facilitating the foundation of new lodges in South America.

After the creation of a new autonomous Masonic group in the department of Venezuela, a process of expansion began in the region,[31] thus disseminating Masonry among the military elites of Gran Colombia.

This process connected with that of South America via cultural intermediaries such as Antonio Valero de Bernabé, 32nd degree of the Ancient

29 Letter from Zañartu to O'Higgins, February 5, 1820, In: *Archivo de Don Bernardo O'Higgins*, Op. Cit, Vol. VI. pp. 193-194.

30 **Translator's Note:** Gran Colombia was the name given to large areas of the north western part of the South American continent (including modern day Colombia, Venezuela and Ecuador). It was a state that emerged in 1819 out of a struggle for independence that was waged and eventually won by Simón Bolívar, a Venezuelan born revolutionary, and his associates, for the whole of Spanish America. It existed for only eleven years (until 1830), when Ecuador and Venezuela formally seceded.

31 Américo Carnicelli, *La Masonería en la independencia de América (1810–1830)*, Ed. Secretos de la Historia, Bogotá, 1970. T.II, pp. 26-35.

and Accepted Scottish Rite (AASR) who arrived in Lima in 1825 to take charge of the second auxiliary division of Peru. As well as his military functions, he was entrusted with the mission of regulating and creating new lodges in the name of the *Gran Oriente Nacional Colombiano* (National Grand Orient of Colombia), from which one can highlight the foundation of the Rosicrucian chapter, *Regeneración* (Regeneration), in Lima.

This first internal process of expansion of Masonry in South America, which benefited from the movements of the armies of Simón Bolívar and José de San Martín, allowed Manuel Blanco Encalada, a former member of the Santiago Lautaro Lodge, to receive the 18th Degree of the AASR (Knight Rose Croix) in Lima, where he was fulfilling his military duties. Later, in 1827, he founded and lead the first Masonic lodge in Chile, known as Filantropía (Philanthropy).

However, can we really speak of Chilean Masonry? The Filantropía Lodge, according to records from its founding agreement, was composed of 15 members,[32] of whom only four were from Chile.[33] Therefore (despite the fact that Chile eventually became their homeland), the birth of this group constituted a peripheral manifestation of the cosmopolitan nature of Masonry, a form of sociability in which Europeans and Americans found a medium to meet as a brotherhood.

This lodge represents a synthesis of the wars of independence. On the one hand, it included a member of the Lautaro Lodge, Manuel Blanco Encalada and another (possibly) of the Caballeros Orientales de Montevideo Lodge, Manuel Gandarillas.[34] On the other hand, many of its members were veterans of the Napoleonic Wars.

---

32 Manuel Blanco Encalada (Argentina), Manuel José Gandarillas (Chile), Manuel Rengifo (Chile), Tomás Ovejero (Spain?), Juan Francisco Zegers (France), Ventura Blanco Encalada (Argentina), Ángel Arguelles (Chile), Vicente Tur (?), Francisco Doursther (Holland), Victorino Garrido (Spain), José Manuel Gómez de Silva (Argentina), Jorge Lyon (England), Carlos Renard (France), José Domingo Otaegui (Chile), Mariano Álvarez (?). See: René García, Op. Cit, p. 13.

33 Perhaps five, considering that Tomás Ovejero, whom García Valenzuela (probably erroneously) refers to, could be the Chilean Tomás Obejero Marmolejo, who during that era acted as secretary to Blanco Encalada.

34 Although he does not appear in the registers that Tomás de Iriarte delivered, it is very likely that he was a member of that secret society, just as José Miguel Carrera was. Both of them were of great importance in the creation of the newspaper and pamphlets that they published against the ruling party of the United Provinces of the Río de la Plata, where, among other things, there was a call on Masons to abandon the Lautaro Lodge or "*Gran Logia*" as they called it, due to the crimes that it had committed. For more information, see: Tomás de Iriarte, *Op. Cit*, pp., 7-13, 173-177 y 222-225; Guillermo Feliu Cruz, *La imprenta federal de William P. Griswold y John Sharpe del general José Miguel Carrera 1818-1820*, Santiago, Editorial Universitaria, 1965. pp. 96.

* **Translator's note:** *Afrancesado* is an adjective meaning 'adopting of French culture.' It is almost impossible to translate the heavy connotations that this word carries into English. The political climate at the time, where the Napoleonic occupation of Spain had precipitated the wars of independence that raged throughout the empire, meant that an adoption of French intellectual culture was in fact a rejection of Spanish intellectual culture. Moreover, 'no intellectual or political culture exercised

Among them the *afrancesado** brother of the venerable of the lodge, Ventura Blanco Encalada, who, according to the testimony of his son, began in a lodge in Limoges during his exile in France after the fall of Joseph Bonaparte.[35]

These precedents reinforce the hypothesis that these wars were an instance of Masonic socialization between the Hispanic American armies, a project that was cut short at the end of the 1820s due to the political factions that arose within the lodges. Thus, the appearance of secret societies in the 1810s constitutes a precursor, an experience of associative education for the first failed attempt to institutionalize Masonry in South America.

The Rise of an Alternative Modernity—Chile in the Mid-Nineteenth Century

More than twenty years had to go by for Masonry to find a new way into Chile. After the civil war of 1829, which led to the authoritarian republic, there are only a few references to Masonry, and these are of little consequence.[36]

In spite of the arrival of the conservative governments and the limitations of the Catholic Enlightenment, the wars of independence began a process of modernization that would slowly replace the Hispanic model.

During the 1820s, the number of journeys that Creoles were making to Europe increased, mainly to France, which allowed the formation of a generation that was *afrancesada*, and the socialization of knowledge due to the significant number of works that made their way into the country without the former colonial restrictions. Thus, the timidity that authors showed during the period of independence contrasted with the following decade, as quotes and extracts in the Chilean press from authors such as Montesquieu, Bentham, Constant, Rousseau, Voltaire, Paine and others, were constant.[37]

its influence more directly or contradictorily over intellectual Spain than France.' For more information, see: Courtney Blaine Johnson, *(Re)Writing the Empire: The Philippines and Filipinos in the Hispanic Cultural Field 1880-1898,* The University of Texas, Austin, 2004, pp. 13-14

https://www.lib.utexas.edu/etd/d/2004/johnsonc00699/johnsonc00699.pdf

35 Manuel Romo, *"El masón Ventura Blanco Encalada (1782-1856)"* en: *Archivo Masónico N° 23*, Santiago de Chile, 2011, p. 6.

36 There are two references to Masonry: the first one was in 1828, when the statesmen Pradel y Magallanes asked congress to pass a law against secret societies. The second reference, in 1834, appears in a letter from the minister Diego Portales to his confidant Garfias (it is the last known reference). It probably refers to some members of the Filantropía (Philanthropy) lodge who were active during his governance. He mentions: "It is a matter of meeting and reestablishing the Masonic lodges, with the aim of making them serve political affairs and elections: this move scares me, because past experience has shown us the bad consequences that those meetings have brought; when withdrawing from their institution, they applied themselves to public affairs, and poor Chile, which had been free of this plague, would come to be, despite its pacifistic character, the victim of mysterious schemes." Quoted by Pinto, Op. Cit, p. 159.

37 Gazmuri, Op.Cit, p. 27.

From the 1830s, the national culture also became enriched due to the arrival of foreign scientists and intellectuals, called in to modernize the country. More notable arrivals were Andrés Bello, Claudio Gay, Rodolfo Phillipi, Ignacio Domeyko, who brought their knowledge and understanding to the scientific world and helped in the education of the local elites.

The incorporation of Chile onto the world stage, by means of a simultaneous entry and exit of cultural representatives, had an important effect in other areas. In the 1840s, it led to the expansion of the public sphere and the diversity of sociability, which was markedly French in style. Examples of this are the creation of the *Sociedad Literaria* (Literary Society) in 1842, the foundation of the markedly liberal daily newspaper *El Progreso* (Progress), the distribution of books such as Lamartine's *"Historia de los girondinos"* (A History of the Girondists), the creation of the *Club de la reforma* (Reformation Club) in 1849, the *Sociedad de la Igualdad* (Equality Society), and the publication of its newspaper *El amigo del pueblo* (The Friend of the Village) in 1850.

Somewhat anachronistically, the French Revolution, condemned by Spanish tradition, became the ideological model for the romantic generation that was led by José Victorino Lastarria, Santiago Arcos, Francisco Bilbao, among many other youths of the Creole elite. This passion for French culture, considered the main catalyst for progress, was complemented by the rejection of Spanish tradition, which was considered responsible for Chile's cultural and economic backwardness.

The appearance of this new political culture entered into direct conflict with the conservative sectors who, despite sharing the ideal of progress, differed from the young *afrancesados* with respect to the relationship between the Church and the state.

By 1848, the Church, for its part, had already condemned all forms of political modernity,[38] despite its participation in the creation of the new public sphere. Via the press, it began a campaign of containment of secular reforms, principally those that leant towards religious tolerance, in a time when, by 1850, European and North American immigration had reached around 6000 individuals in Valparaíso alone.

Thus, as the second half of the nineteenth century began, Chilean society would begin a new process of social reform that was a product of the synthesis of two opposing models that had their own strong stance on modernity: the Hispanic model, of strong Catholic roots, and the French model, which was secularizing.

---

38   Ibid., p. 84.

The Birth of Masonry in Chile[39]

The first lodges established in Chile were, for the most part, composed of traders and artisans of European and North American origin. This factor explains their proliferation in port cities—centers of national and international commerce of the Pacific.

The French lodges arose from the union of a group of Gallic residents in the city of Valparaíso, who, in 1850, requested of the *Grand Orient de France* a constitutive letter to legitimize their work.[40] Seven masters met at the initiative of brother Jean Baptiste Dubreuil, a former member of the L'Etoile de la Gironde Lodge of the *Orient de Bordeaux*. They founded the L'Etoile du Pacifique Lodge. A little after, the English-speaking group— Pacific Lodge No. 1—came into existence, which requested a patent letter from the Grand Lodge of California. However, due to the fact that this never came to pass, they made the request to the Grand Lodge of Massachusetts and, in 1853, they were recognized under the name of Bethesda.

Finally, as these lodges carried out their work in French and English respectively, a third lodge was formed in 1853 on the initiative of Manuel de Lima, a member of the L'Etoile du Pacifique Lodge, who came from Curaçao. The lodge was named the Unión Fraternal (Fraternal Union). This group opened its doors to a significant number of Chileans as well as Argentinians, Englishmen, Frenchmen, Spaniards and Germans, which gave it a distinctive international dimension.[41]

From this group of lodges came a new lodge in the south of Chile in the city of Concepción, due to the great movements of traders between the ports of Valparaíso and Talcahuano. In 1856, Enrique Pastor, of Spanish nationality, and who had been a member of the Unión Fraternal Lodge, founded the Estrella del Sur (Star of the South) Lodge, which became affiliated with the *Gran Oriente Nacional del Perú*. This lodge, which initially was composed of mainly foreign Masons,[42] in time started to open its doors to Chileans.

---

39 For a more detailed analysis of the first decade of the formation of Masonry in Chile, see: Felipe del Solar, *Las Logias de Ultramar. En torno a los Orígenes de la Francmasonería en Chile 1850-1862*, Santiago, Ed. Occidente, 2012.

40 The documentation relating to the first stable lodges in Chile can be found in the National Library of France in the section of western manuscripts, in the *Maçonnique* department, location FM2 844 y FM2 845.

41 André Combes, "*Las logias del Gran Oriente de Francia en América Latina*," in: José Antonio Ferrer Benimeli (Coord.) *Masonería Española y América, V Symposium Internacional de Historia de la Masonería Española*, Cáceres, June 16-20, 1991, Centro de Estudios Históricos de la Masonería Española, Zaragoza, 1993, p. 188.

42 The founding members were: Pedro Cancini, Italian, member of the Bethesda Lodge; Daniel Ulriksen, Danish, also member of the Bethesda Lodge; Isaac Nathan, Briton initiated in the Jehem Lodge of Sacramento, California; Guillermo Lawrence, Briton, initiated in the L'Etoile du Pacifique Lodge; Edward William Burton, North American, initiated in the Washington Lodge; and Pablo Ferreti, initiated in the San Juan Lodge of Marseille. See: Manuel Romo, *Concepción y sus primeras logias*

The same commercial mobility that allowed this type of sociability to expand to the provinces threatened the stability of its infrastructure because many of its members, especially masters, constantly had to travel for long periods of time, change homes, or return to their own countries. In this context, they had to sustain a constant process of recruitment and a rapid scheme for internal promotion in order to ensure their continued existence.

The rise of Masonry in Chile was possible thanks to two factors: the implementation of foreign forms of sociability that arrived with their native communities, and the process of associative learning undertaken by the young Chilean *afrancesados*, who wanted to participate in them.

In the case of the English-speaking lodges, despite maintaining fraternal relationships with their local equivalents, it seems that they had a more closed nature, probably due to language barriers. They constituted a fraternal refuge for foreigners of Protestant faith who came under constant attack from the Catholic Church.[43]

In the case of the French, however, they established a space of integration with the local communities. They aided the initiation of Chileans (many of whom spoke French) and supported the creation of national lodges which ended up under the guardianship of the *Grand Orient de France*.

The establishment of Masonry in Chile constituted an important innovation in terms of sociability. It marked a decisive rupture with Hispanic culture, which had condemned Chilean society and emphatically stigmatized it since the eighteenth century. Masonry's most dedicated members were to be found among the generation of young romantics, who, in a short period of time, took ownership of it and founded a national obedience.

At the start of the 1860s, Masonry continued to grow in the territory. Firstly, the Estrella del Sur Lodge broke off its relations with the *Gran Logia Nacional del Perú* and affiliated itself with the *Grand Orient de France*, changing its name to *Aurora de Chile*.[44] In the city of Copiapó in the far north, a lodge was founded in 1862 that was named Orden y Libertad (Order and Freedom). This city, like Concepción, was an important nucleus in social mobilization and soon became the epicenter of the *Partido Radical* (Radical Party). In Valparaíso, in addition to its three existing lodges, a fourth arose under the name of *Progreso* (Progress), whose first venerable master was Blas Cuevas, member of the Unión Fraternal lodge. Thus, in 1862, six lodges existed in Chile, creating an interconnected network between the center, north and south of the country.

1856- 1860, publisher unknown, pp. 232-233.

43   Ibid., p. 171

44   Gazmuri, Op. Cit, p. 164

The Schism and the Creation of the Gran Logia de Chile

Chilean "Masonology" tends to define the act of Napoleon III intervening in the designation of Mariscal Magnan as the Great Master of the *Grand Orient de France* on January 11, 1862, as a key factor in the foundation of the Gran Logia. As Cristian Gazmuri suggests, this action, instead of triggering the rupture, served as an excuse to create a national autonomous entity.[45]

The Unión Fraternal Lodge sought to group together the existing lodges in the territory. However, the lodges of Valparaíso—L'Etoile du Pacifique and Bethesda—refused to join the *Gran Logia*. A similar thing happened with the Rosicrucian Chapter of the 18th degree and with the Consistory *Caballeros (Knight Kadosh)* of the 30th degree, who belonged to those lodges.[46]

In this way, the three "separatist" lodges, facing the impossibility of joining each other, agreed that each would present three chosen brothers in order to create the *Gran Logia de Chile*,[47] choosing as Grand Master the lawyer Juan de Dios Arlegui. The Aurora de Chile Lodge, for its part, went on to call itself Fraternidad (Brotherhood), due to its break from the *Grand Orient de France*. Similarly, with the participation of members of this lodge, a new group appeared named "Aurora."[48]

In this way, Chilean Masonry began to take the first steps toward autonomy. However, its separation from the *Grand Orient de France* was not received kindly. Antide Martin, venerable master of the Chilean mother lodge L'Etoile du Pacifique, sent a letter to the *Grand Orient de France* explaining the recent schism. His main arguments referred to the Unión Fraternal Lodge proclaiming itself the Grand Lodge in an act totally outside of Masonic law, considering that it would have had to request a letter of acknowledgement from a superior power and, on the contrary, it acted "without any authority but its own will."[49] At the same time, it legalized, of its own accord, another lodge of Valparaíso and the lodges of Copiapó and Concepción. To make matters worse, they were initiating new members independently of rites or of obedience.

On December 2, 1862, the *Grand Orient de France* wrote on the subject in a printed letter sent to the L'Etoile du Pacifique Lodge, in which it stated:

---

45   Ibid., p. 164. Of the same opinion is: Combes, Op. Cit. p. 189.

46   Romo, Op. Cit., p. 289.

47   Günter Böhm, *Manuel de Lima, fundador de la masonería chilena*, Santiago, Universidad de Chile, 1979. p. no numbers, (information that appears on the back of a letter sent by Antide Martin, venerable master of the L'Etoile du Pacifique Lodge to the *Grand Orient de France* informing on the 'irregular' creation of the *Gran Logia de Chile*).

48   García, Op. Cit, p., 152.

49   BNF, FM2 844, Letter from Antide Martin to the *Grand Orient de France*, August 18, 1862. F. 2.

We thank and congratulate you on the communications that you have sent us. For us this is further proof of the excellence of your sentiments and all of your respect for the moral doctrine of the Order.

The conduct of the former Unión Fraternal and Aurora de Chile lodges is anti-Masonic. It has no precedent in the annals of Masonry; no one can justify nor lessen its gravity. We can understand their desire to see a centralized Masonic power in the countries where they were established, thanks to the *Grand Orient de France*; but we cannot understand why, to found this power, they forget their faith and their oaths, that they turn to perjury and revolt as the first foundations of the monument that they wish to erect ... sad footings for an institution of love and peace that has the principal mission of preaching to men respect of the law, sanctity of promises and universal brotherhood![50]

Having examined the aforementioned letter, the *Grand Orient de France* decided:

• "The Council declared the lodges of the Unión Fraternal del Orden de Valparaíso, and Aurora de Chile del Orden de Concepción to be abolished.

• They will be stripped of their titles, their names erased from the golden book of the *Grand Orient de France*.

• The groups that pertain to them are consequently instructed to cease all contact with the aforementioned lodges.

• This notice will be inserted into the official bulletin so that it may come to the attention of all groups and all Masons."[51]

The letters of Antide Martin, as well as the response of the *Grand Orient de France*, were spread around the globe with the aim of discrediting the new Masonic power. However, that same year the *Gran Logia de Chile* awarded itself a constitution that consolidated its operation. In this way, new lodges started to appear all over the territory from the four existing groups. In 1864, the first lodge in Santiago, Chile's capital, was founded under the name *Orden y Justicia* (Order and Justice), beginning a constant process of founding lodges from the second half of the nineteenth century, which grew at varying speeds depending on the political contexts that applied to them.

Conclusion

The two defining moments of the establishment of Masonry in Chile have a characteristic in common, in that they were both part of a process of increasing internation-

---

50   BNF, FM2 844, Letter from the *Grand Orient de France* to the L'Etoile du Pacifique Lodge, December 2, 1862, F.1.

51   Ibid. F. 2.

al travel.[52] However, they differ both in their contexts and in the way that they were received locally.

During the wars of independence, the events that took place generated a change that abruptly broke off the colonial monotony and allowed the integration of new practices into society. However, the limited process of modernization initiated by the Catholic Enlightenment did not generate the local base needed to maintain its presence in the long term. The Spanish anti-Masonic discourse in that era was yet another element that induced fear of Masonry, despite the participation of priests in secret societies and Masonic lodges.

In the mid-nineteenth century, however, the transformations initiated during the wars of independence allowed for the development of a young generation of liberal admirers of French culture who were quick to notice that Masonry was a type of organization that was in accordance with their own political projects.

In this case, Catholic discourse did not produce the same effects as during the wars of independence. One would have to measure to what extent the propaganda against Masonry let its existence become known, made it attractive to young liberals and afforded it an occasionally anticlerical appearance—something which ensured its place in public debate.

In geographical terms, there were at least three phases which helped to embed Masonry in Chile: the first, of Hispanic origin, was characterized by the liberal economic measures that improved internal connections within the continent. They promoted the movement of people, goods, and ideas. In this same vein, the journeys that Creoles took to foreign countries, acting as cultural intermediaries, increased the admission of prohibited books.

A second defining moment of Masonry was the wars of independence, which encouraged military mobility to central Latin America, connecting the Masonic Caribbean domain with South America via the mediation of the Masonry of Gran Colombia. Finally, in the mid-nineteenth century, the previous phases and the desire to leave behind colonial tradition came to fruition. This process allowed the opening of new types of modern society that were linked to intense international trade, encouraging the presence of significant foreign communities who brought in their customs and modes of sociability.

The religious tolerance practiced by the lodges corresponded perfectly to the secular reforms that the liberal sectors tried stubbornly to carry out throughout the second half of the nineteenth century. The trade routes that interconnected the country, from Valparaíso to the north and the south, allowed Masonry to spread across the land, expanding and multiplying, and above all generating a network that benefited the organization on a national level.

---

52 Pierre-Yves Beaurepaire, "La République Universelle des Francs-maçons entre « culture de la mobilité » et basculement national (XVIII-XIX siècle)," In: *Revue de Synthèse*, Vol. 123, No. 1, 2002, pp. 37-64.

Freemasonry as a Center of Political Action in Independent Mexico, 1821-1830

María Eugenia Vázquez Semadeni[*]

ABSTRACT

The main objective of this paper is to show how some of the internal practices of Freemasonry, the masonic bodies, their channels of communication and the loyalties they generated were taken advantage of by the *Yorkino*s to establish a center of political action, that is to say, a space where agreements were reached and which enabled them to undertake initiatives to achieve, preserve, and exercise political power. I will show that this was in part possible due to the institutional structure arising from the establishment of the republican, representative and federal system, but also due to the fact that the *Yorkinos* created a discourse about the political system, themselves, and their opponents which for a time endowed their political actions with considerable legitimacy.

Keywords: Mexico, public sphere, politics, York Rite, Freemasonry, Mexican Independence

RESUMEN

El objetivo principal de este trabajo es mostrar cómo algunas prácticas internas de la masonería, los cuerpos masónicos, sus canales de comunicación y las lealtades que generaron fueron aprovechadas por los Yorkinos para establecer un centro de acción política. Es decir, un espacio donde se lograron acuerdos y que les permitió emprender iniciativas para lograr, preservar y ejercer el poder político. Demostraré que esto fue en parte posible debido a la estructura institucional que surgió del establecimiento del sistema republicano, representativo y federal, pero también debido al hecho de que los Yorkinos crearon un discurso sobre el sistema político, ellos mismos y sus oponentes que por un tiempo le otorgó a sus acciones políticas de una legitimidad considerable.

* Assistant Adjunct Professor, Department of History, University of California, Los Angeles. This paper is a reworking of two previous papers published in Spanish in *LiminaR. Estudios Sociales y Humanísticos*, 7, VII, 2, Dic., pp. 41-55 and in *REHMLAC. Revista de Estudios Históricos de la Masonería Latinoamericana y Caribeña*, Numero Especial UCLA-Gran Logia de California, 2013, pp. 116-138.

Palabras clave: *México, esfera pública, política, Rito de York, Francmasonería, Independencia de México*

1821-1830年间共济会作为墨西哥独立之后的政治行动中心

摘要

本文主要目的是展示约克礼仪派（Yorkinos）如何利用共济会内部实践、共济会机构、机构间传播渠道和忠诚来建立政治行动中心。此中心用于达成协议，并能使协议主动实现、保存和行使政治权力。本文将展示上述观点成立的两点原因。首先有可能的是，制度结构从共和党、代表和联邦系统的成立中兴起。其次，事实证明，约克礼仪派创造了有关政治系统、自身和对手的话语，这在短时间内为其政治行动赋予了相当的合法性。

关键词：墨西哥，公共领域，政治，约克礼，共济会，墨西哥独立

Introduction

Mexican Freemasonry in the first decades of the nineteenth century was closely linked to political activity in the nascent country. On the one hand, the principal or most prominent masons in those years were also some of the most important political actors and on the other hand, the public images of the groups struggling for political power were constructed in part around the masonic affiliations of their members. In addition, the masons, especially those who established and promoted lodges following the York rite in Mexico, used the organizational structure of Freemasonry to obtain political support, to influence electoral results, and to legitimize their accession to power.

The main objective of this paper is to show how some of the internal practices of Freemasonry, the masonic bodies, their channels of communication and the loyalties they generated were taken advantage of by the Yorkinos to establish a center of political action, that is to say, a space where agreements were reached and which enabled them to undertake initiatives to achieve, preserve, and exercise political power.[1] I will show that this was in part possible due to the institutional structure arising from the establishment of the republican, representative and federal

---

1   Marco Antonio Flores Zavala, "La masonería en la República Federal. Apuntes sobre las logias mexicanas (1821-1840)", in Manuel Miño Grijalva, Mariana Terán Fuentes, Edgar Hurtado Hernández and Víctor Manuel González Esparza (coords.), *Raíces del federalismo mexicano*, Zacatecas, Universidad Autónoma de Zacatecas/Secretaría de Educación y Cultura del Gobierno del Estado de Zacatecas, 2005, pp. 125-136.

system, but also due to the fact that the Yorkinos created a discourse about the political system, themselves, and their opponents which for a time endowed their political actions with considerable legitimacy.

I also aim to resolve some issues concerning the origins and development of Freemasonry in New Spain/ Mexico in the 1810s and 1820s and to confirm or refute some of the stories on the subject which have been repeated in masonic and academic historiography to this day, frequently without any documentary proof. Carrying out a study of this kind is a major challenge, as masonic sources in Mexico from the first half of the nineteenth century are rare. In recent years, however, I have been able to locate a number of documents, which, together with the bibliographic and press sources, provide sufficient information to support the research. These are records from some the first lodges founded in what is now Mexico, as well as a series of letters, balusters,[2] circulars, certificates, appointments, and decrees produced by masons, mostly Yorkinos, as well as records of two trials: the masonic trial of a member of the York rite in the city of Chihuahua in 1827 and the ecclesiastical trial of the priest Antonio Arroyo in 1830 for belonging to a Yorkino lodge. Some of these documents were scattered in private collections and auctioned in recent

years by Louis C. Morton auctioneers; others are located in a number of Mexican archives, such as the Archivo General de la Nación, the Lafragua collection in the National Library of Mexico, the Archivo Histórico del Arzobispado de México and the Manuel Orozco y Berra Library. Further documents are located in US archives, in particular the collections of the Grand Lodges of Louisiana and New York.

It should be mentioned that the study of press and bibliographic sources required a deep critical analysis of sources, as frequently the newspapers or works of nineteenth century were written by authors who were involved in one way or another in the events they relate either magnify or minimize the public role of Masonry, described people as masons who were not so, imputed actions to people who did not commit them, and even published fake information. Having said this, if one compares the information contained in the above-mentioned documents with the information in the press and that written by the main writers of the period— such as Lucas Alamán, José María Luis Mora, Lorenzo de Zavala, Carlos María de Bustamante, José María Tornel, Juan Suárez y Navarro, José María Bocanegra and Francisco Ibar—it is possible to deduce with a considerable degree of certainty which information can be trusted and which cannot.[3]

---

2   Circular or other document issued by a Supreme Council.

3   The documents discovered for this research have made it possible to confirm the masonic affiliations of some of the personalities mentioned in the work; Michael Costeloe, in his work *La primera república federal de México (1824-1835). Un estudio de los partidos políticos en el México independiente*, México, FCE, 1996 was able to corroborate the membership of other followers of the York rite; for those remaining, information contained in public papers have been evaluated and have

The Origins

The first lodges for which we have trustworthy records in what is now Mexico but was then New Spain were established on the Gulf of Mexico coast in the second half of the 1810s. The oldest record refers to a lodge established in the port of Veracruz, with a letter of patent granted by the Grand Lodge of Louisiana dated 30 April 1816. The lodge was named "Los amigos reunidos" (The gathered friends) No. 8 and the Master was Miguel José Monzón, a Spaniard and a surgeon in the Royal Navy. The First Warden was Antonio Valera, also Spanish, an officer in the Royal Navy and involved in the liberal network set up to reestablish the constitution of 1812 (Cádiz) during the reign of Ferdinand VII between 1814 and 1820. The Second Warden was Felix Galán, a Veracruz trader and merchant of the frigate "El Águila".[4]

The information on this lodge coincides with the information found in the archives of the Spanish Inquisition. In 1816 there were two Inquisition trials for Freemasonry. In the first, Don Francisco Vicente Pérez Durán indicated that he met and dealt with Don Gonzalo de Ulloa—lieutenant of a frigate and commander of the body of patriots in Veracruz—who confessed to being a Freemason and referred to the existence of a lodge in that city. In the second trial, in Zacatecas, Don Juan Antonio Zarandona stated that Don Juan José Martinez—a travelling merchant originally from Vigo—affirmed that there were many masons in Veracruz, and several in Zacatecas, including José de Gayangos, the mayor, who had attended the lodge in Veracruz.[5] Unfortunately, records of these trials don't provide us with sufficient information to be certain that the Veracruz lodge was the same as the one mentioned above, but they do confirm the existence of significant, early masonic activity in Veracruz.

On 12 April 1817, again with a letter of patent from the Grand Lodge of Louisiana, the "Reunión de la Virtud" (Gathering of virtue) number 9 lodge was founded in Campeche. The Master was Juan Miguel López Duque de Estrada, the First Warden José María Machín, and the Second Warden Car-

---

been considered valid when cross-referencing seem to justify it.

4   Grand Lodge of Louisiana. Book of Grand Secretary 1812-1840, pp. 33-34. For more information on these lodges, their members and the origins of masonry in Mexico, see María Eugenia Vázquez Semadeni, "Del mar a la política. Masonería en Nueva España/México, 1816-1823" in *REHMLAC. Revista de Estudios Históricos de la Masonería Latinoamericana y Caribeña*, Numero Especial UCLA-Gran Logia de California, 2013, pp. 116-138. It should be mentioned that the existence of this lodge and the two mentioned in the following paragraphs had been noted in the nineteenth century by various masonic authors who, unfortunately, did not record their sources. Historians such as Melchor Campos García also mentioned some of them, but did not have access to the original records. In 2010, I managed to locate the records in the archive of the Grand Lodge of Louisiana, thanks to the extraordinary assistance of the librarian Sally Sinor, and I presented them in a talk to the Instituto de Investigaciones Históricas at the UNAM.

5   Archivo General de la Nación, hereafter AGN, *Inquisición*, vol. 1.461, expediente 4, fs. 129-131 and vol. 1.463, expediente 9, fs. 97-99.

los Francisco Escoffie.[6] The three were all seamen, the latter two mainly active in the merchant navy.

This information concurs with the date found by Melchor Campos García for the founding of Freemasonry in Campeche. Following Eligio Ancona's account, Campos García believes that Freemasonry started in the region around 1817, with the arrival of military personnel emigrating from Spain and the shipwreck of the frigate *Ifigenia,* amongst whose passengers there were several masons. This information does not necessarily conflict with the information from the Grand Lodge of Louisiana as it is possible that the masons who arrived in Campeche on board the *Ifigenia* may have decided to organize a lodge and requested authorization from Louisiana. It should be said, however, that none of the three first officers of the "Reunión de la Virtud" lodge arrived on the *Ifigenia* nor was a soldier coming from Spain.[7]

Finally, in March 1820, the Grand Lodge of Louisiana granted a letter of patent to the "Aurora de Yucatán" (Dawn of Yucatán) lodge No. 18, established in Mérida. The three officers in the lodge were the Worshipful Master, Luis Cañas, John Quevedo, First Warden; and Pedro Tarrazo, Second Warden.[8] Cañas was also a merchant sailor and a pioneer of maritime education in Mexico. I have not been able to locate information about the professions of Pedro Tarrazo and John Quevedo.

The "Los Amigos Reunidos", "Reunión de la Virtud" and "Aurora de Yucatán" lodges must have followed the York rite as between 1813 and 1814 a committee at the Grand Lodge of Louisiana drew up a uniform system of work following this rite for the three symbolic degrees, which had to be implemented by all the lodges within its jurisdiction.[9]

The sources indicate that, more or less at the same time and in the same area, bodies following the Scottish rite were also being formed. An authorization dated 17 Feb 1822 demonstrates that there was already a Grand Consistory of the Scottish rite in the Arcadia of Veracruz at that time (the Grand Consistory of the Scottish Rite of Ancient and Accepted Freemasons, 32nd degree).[10] The document does not mention when the Grand Consistory

6   Grand Lodge of Louisiana, Book of the Grand Secretary 1812-1840, pp. 39-40, Archive of Grand Lodge of Louisiana.

7   Melchor Campos García, *Sociabilidades políticas en Yucatán. Un estudio sobre los espacios públicos, 1780-1834*, Mérida, Universidad Autónoma de Yucatán/Conacyt, 2003. Eligio Ancona, *Historia de Yucatán desde la época más remota hasta nuestros días, parte tercera, época moderna*, Barcelona, Imprenta de Jaime J. Roviralta, 1889 t. III, p. 117.

8   Grand Lodge of Louisiana, Book of the Grand Secretary 1812-1840, p. 67, Archive of the Grand Lodge of Louisiana.

9   James B. Scot, *Outline of the Rise and Progress of Freemasonry in Louisiana. From its introduction to the reorganization of the Grand Lodge in 1850*, New Orleans, Clarck & Hofeline Book Printers, 1873, p. 20.

10 Grand Consistory of Veracruz, [Authorization granted to Melchor Álvarez], 17 Feb 1822, Biblioteca Manuel Orozco y Berra.

was established but it does affirm that it was done so with the authorization of the Supreme Council of the Inspectors General of the 33rd degree in Paris.

The authorization was granted to Melchor Álvarez, a prominent Spanish military officer who had served in the Royalist army in the struggle against the insurgents, but who in 1821 joined the Army of the Three Guarantees and supported Iturbide in achieving independence. From 1819 the Inquisition had received reports stating that Álvarez was a Freemason[11] and in 1822 he held the 32nd degree of the Scottish rite, the Sublime Prince of the Royal Secret. In the same year he was named Commander General of the Province of Yucatán and he was on his way to his new appointment when he was granted the authorization. With this authorization he was empowered to visit the lodges within the Grand Consistory's jurisdiction which were on his way to Merida. Thanks to this document we know that in 1822 there were lodges of the Scottish rite active between Veracruz and Mérida, although unfortunately we don't know how many, which ones they were, and for how long they had been in existence.

The authorization also states:

In the capital of the peninsula [of Yucatán] and in the city of Campeche, there are two [lodges] following the York rite depending on the G∴ [Lodge] M ∴ of Louisiana for which you have the particular mission to request that they join this S∴ G∴ Consistory and recognize it as the only supreme authority constituted on this Continent of the ancient and accepted Scottish rite of masonry.[12]

This paragraph indicates that by 1822 only two of the three lodges to receive a letter of patent from Louisiana in the region were still active. This is consistent with the Historical Table of Lodges of the Grand Lodge of Louisiana, according to which the "Los Amigos Reunidos" lodge in Veracruz ceased to exist in 1818.[13] This would then mean that the two lodges still active were the "Reunión de la Virtud" lodge in Campeche and the "Aurora de Yucatán" lodge in Merida. However, the Historical Table records that the Grand Lodge of Louisiana withdrew the letter of patent for the "Reunión de la Virtud" on 11 August 1821.[14] So which was the lodge in Campeche referred to in the document? If it was a new lodge authorized by Louisiana in 1817, it should have been recorded in the catalogue of the Grand Lodge, but there is no reference to it.[15] One hypothesis is that an error may have been made when compiling the Catalogue of Lodges and the

---

11 AGN, Instituciones Coloniales, *Inquisición* 61, Vol. 1416, exp. 14, fs. 193-211.

12 Grand Consistory ... [Authorization ...]

13 Grand Lodge of Louisiana, "Historical Table of Lodges". Reproduced every year in the records of the Grand Lodge.

14 Grand Lodge of Louisiana, "Historical ..."

15 The constitution of the Grand Lodge of Louisiana, formulated in 1819, prohibited masons from

patent was withdrawn in 1822 after the "Reunion de la Virtud" had agreed to join the Great Consistory of Veracruz. Such a hypothesis may be backed up by the information provided by Aznar y Carbó, according to whom there was a lodge in Campeche in 1822 called "Unión de la Virtud", which could be "Reunión de la Virtud" after it had changed its name on changing rites.[16]

This possibility seems even greater when one notes what happened with the "Aurora de Yucatán". A letter written in 1823 refers to a Scottish rite lodge active in Merida called "Aurora Yucateca" No. 5, constituted under the auspices of the Grand Consistory of Veracruz.[17] Melchor Campos García has pointed out, and I agree, that it is highly likely it was the former York rite lodge, which accepted Melchor Álvarez's invitation to join the Grand Consistory of Veracruz and adopted the Scottish rite.[18] The small change of name from Aurora de Yucatán to Aurora Yucateca is similar to the change from Reunión de la Virtud to Unión de la Virtud.

Whatever the reason, the first York rite lodges in the Gulf of Mexico did not last very long and soon declined or became absorbed into the Scottish rite Masonry in the region. Whilst there is no direct relationship between these first lodges and York rite organization established in 1825, it does seem possible that some of its founders may have "seen the masonic light" in the lodges under the authority of Louisiana, then joined the Scottish rite, and later decided to reestablish the York rite in Mexico, for reasons more political than Masonic, as we shall discover below. One of the founders may have been Lorenzo de Zavala, who has been shown to be a member of these early coastal lodges by almost all historiographical sources.

Furthermore, the lodges under the authority of Louisiana were not the only lodges to join the Veracruz Scottish rite. There was another 32nd degree Grand Consistory in Yucatán under the authority of the Grand Consistory of Havana.[19] It is not known when it was founded, but given its allegiance to Ha-

---

setting up new lodges without obtaining prior authorization from the Grand Lodge. Nevertheless, it is possible that some new lodges may have been founded in Campeche before this prohibition and that they never received their authorization from the Grand Lodge of Louisiana. This information may concur with Aznar and Carbó's assertion that around 1822 there were three lodges in Campeche, although it is also possible that two of these lodges may have been formed under the auspices of the Scottish rite Grand Consistory, or even under some other authority, and only one was under the Louisiana jurisdiction, as the authorization indicates. Tomás Aznar Barbachano and Juan Carbó, *Memoria sobre la conveniencia, utilidad y necesidad de erigir constitucionalmente en estado de la Confederación Mexicana el antiguo distrito de Campeche, constituido de hecho en estado libre y soberano desde mayo de 1848, por virtud de los convenios de división territorial que celebró con el estado de Yucatán, de que era parte*, México, Imprenta de Ignacio Cumplido, 1861, pp. 24-25.

16   Aznar, *Memoria* ... , 24-25.

17   Aurora Yucateca Lodge, [Letter to Melchor Álvarez], 1st day of 1st month m∴ a∴ d∴ l∴ v∴ l∴ 5823 (1 March 1823). Biblioteca Manuel Orozco y Berra.

18   Campos García, *Sociabilidades* ... p. 90.

19   "Discurso masónico pronunciado al abatimiento de columnas del gran consistorio de Yucatán al separarse del de la Havana [sic] y reunirse al gran consejo [sic] de Veracruz", in: *La inquisición*

vana, it cannot have been before 1818, the year in which the Havana Consistory was founded.[20] In 1822, the Grand Consistory of Yucatán decided to separate from Havana in order to join the Grand Consistory of Veracruz. In this way the two most important Scottish rite bodies active in the Gulf of Mexico in 1822 became one, and moreover absorbed the incipient York rite masonry. Thus the efforts of the Grand Consistory of Veracruz to become the supreme Masonic authority in the region, and perhaps the country, were greeted with success. In doing so, an important Scottish rite masonic force was created and, as will be seen, began to involve itself in political issues.[21]

It is important to point out that another organized Scottish rite group appears to have been active in Central Mexico between 1817 and 1818. An Inquisition record includes claims that members of the Dragoons regiment in Querétaro and Mexico City may have been masons. And this may well have given rise to Alamán's assertion that the arrival of expeditionary troops in New

Spain boosted masonry. Both Alamán and José María Chavero state that the first lodge to be established in Mexico City before independence was at the chaplaincy of the former Teresian convent in number 2 of Santa Teresa la Antigua Street. Both note that the lodge was called "Arquitectura Moral" (Moral Architecture), headed by the Judge of the Audiencia de Mexico, Felipe Martínez de Aragón and was composed mainly of Spaniards. They also state that the lodge moved later to the Coliseo Viejo street. Chavero specified that it was a Scottish rite lodge.[22]

First Steps in Politics

One traditional narrative in Mexican historiography is that, once independence was achieved, organized Masonry in Mexico was opposed to Iturbide being crowned emperor, as they would have preferred a constitutional monarchy with a Bourbon on the throne. According to this story, Scottish rite Masonry—which as I have just indicated was the dominant

se pone o la religión se acaba, no. 2, México, Oficina de Don José María Ramos Palomera, 1822. This document was published by Ruth Solis Vicarte in her work *Las sociedades secretas en el primer gobierno republicano (1824-1828)*, México, ASBE, 1997, pp. 206-208.

20   On the Grand Consistory of Havana see José Manuel Castellano Gil, *La masonería española en Cuba*, La Laguna, Ayuntamiento de La Laguna/Cabildo de Tenerife/CEHME/Centro de la Cultura Popular Canaria, 1996, p. 49.

21   From 1826, the Yorkino commentators stated that Veracruz was the bastion of Scottish masonry, and according to what has been shown here, it appears that they were not wrong.

22   AGN, Instituciones Coloniales, *Inquisición* 61, Vol. 1416, exp. 14, fs. 193-211. Lucas Alamán, *Historia de Méjico, desde los primeros movimientos que prepararon su independencia en el año de 1808 hasta la época presente*, México, Imprenta de J. L. Lara, 1852, tomo V, p. 58. José María Chavero, "Comunicado", in *Correo de la Federación Mexicana*, 26 August 1829, vol VIII, num. 449. It is imperative to mention that the Arquitectura Moral lodge is not the one which José María Mateos refers to as the first lodge in Mexico, supposedly founded in 1806 and located in Ratas street. I make this clarification as both masonic and academic historiographers have made the mistake of confusing them. For an explanation of this confusion, see Vázquez Semadeni, "Del mar ...", pp. 121-122.

form in the country—supported or even formulated the Plan de Casa Mata to overthrow Iturbide, with the intention of reviving the Treaty of Cordoba. Things got out of hand, however, and, as a result of the movement launched by Antonio López de Santa Anna and the provinces' desire for autonomy, a federal republic was established instead of a Bourbon monarchy.[23]

Sufficient proof has not yet been found to assert that this plan was formulated by masons,[24] although there is evidence that some masonic groups played a role in politics during this period, one of them being the former York rite lodge, subsequently the Scottish lodge called "Aurora Yucateca".

When Melchor Álvarez was appointed Commander General of Yucatán by the imperial government, his arrival caused concern and aroused suspicion amongst the local politicians who saw him as a civil servant imposed by central power who was not familiar with the region's problems and who was charged with submitting the regional interests to Iturbide's designs.

The distrust of Álvarez by some sectors of the political class in Campeche and Yucatán increased when Iturbide dissolved congress. The emperor began to be seen as a dictator and it seemed that Álvarez would support his

decisions and oblige those in the peninsula to respect them. The members of the "Aurora Yucateca" expressed these suspicions clearly.

When you arrived in this capital, you raised well-founded and distressing doubts, and each and every one of the inhabitants of this distinguished province feared falling victim and being sacrificed to fierce despotism and we believed you capable of sustaining the whims of the Liberator of the North, and trampling over our civil liberty, fundamental state laws and furthermore, the liberty of our corporations (illegible) and our national congress.[25]

But Álvarez did not support Iturbide's measures. On the contrary, he ordered the creation of a military junta in Becal, which lent its support to the Plan de Casa Mata.[26] The involvement of a well-known Scottish rite mason like Álvarez may have given rise to the idea that the Plan de Casa Mata was hatched by the Scottish rite masons. But, pure speculation aside, what is incontrovertible is that this is the first evidence of political activity endorsed by a masonic body in Mexico. The "Aurora Yucateca" lodge sent a letter to Álvarez assuring him that they no longer distrusted him,

23   One of the authors to maintain this version was Lucas Alamán in his *Historia de Méjico.*

24   Alfredo Ávila, *Para la libertad. Los republicanos en tiempos del imperio 1821-1823*, México, UNAM, 2004, pp. 257-258.

25   Aurora Yucateca Lodge, [Letter ...]

26   On the Becal Junta see María Cecilia Zuleta, "Raíces y razones del federalismo peninsular, 1821-1825", in Josefina Zoraida Vázquez (coord.), *El establecimiento del federalismo en México (1821-1827)*, México, El Colegio de México, pp. 155-188.

thanks to his action in the Becal junta in favour of civil calm, liberty and national independence. And they offered him the "gavel, the quill and the sword in defense of their liberties and [his] person [Melchor Álvarez] ".[27]

As I have pointed out, this is clear evidence of political action undertaken by members of the lodge. It is interesting to note that they did so, not as citizens, but as masons, from mason to mason, and they offered Álvarez the support of the lodge as a body. That is to say that they used the masonic structure to act politically, to oppose what they saw as the dictatorship of Iturbide, and to declare themselves defenders of public calm and national independence. As I have stated above, while it is not possible to assert that all Scottish rite masonry was involved in movements against the empire and in favour of the Plan de Casa Mata, it is nevertheless possible to say that at least some masons were involved in the fall of the empire in Yucatán.

The Founding of the "Yorkinos"

After the fall of Iturbide in 1823, the provincial political groupings demanded the establishment of a federal republic which would respect regional autonomy. In October of the following year, the federal constitution was declared and Guadalupe Victoria, an insurgent leader in the fight for independence, was elected president.

According to Rafael Dávila's account, Scottish rite Masonry at this time deployed all its organizational apparatus to revive the Treaty of Córdoba and to prevent the consolidation of the recently created republic. Dávila asserts that the upper bodies of the Scottish rite united into one body at the end of 1824 and organized "the repair and emancipation of Masonry in order to prevent [the] ruin [of the nation]". They called together the masonic authorities, determined the way in which the representatives were to be elected, the character they should have, the extraordinary Masonic meetings which would precede appointments, and the power which should be given to the electors. With these assertions, Dávila implies that the Scottish rite masons would be manipulating the composition and orientation of the new national congress, working in obscurity "without the authority of the people, whose fate they were determining in the depths of their caves".[28]

Dávila's account is part of the anti-Scottish rite narrative which began to appear in 1823, so one needs to treat its content with care. I have not been able to locate any other documents which might confirm the fusion of the upper bodies of the Scottish rite in 1824, but the idea is nevertheless appealing. As I mentioned above, there is evidence that at that time, in addition to the Grand Consistories of Veracruz and Yucatán, there were also lodges or other types of Scottish rite bodies in Central Mexico

---

27   Aurora Yucateca Lodge, [Letter ...]

28   Rafael Dávila, *Taller de cohetería. Diálogos crítico-alegóricos entre un cohetero y un tamborilero*, Tomo I, México, Imprenta de la ex-inquisición a cargo de Manuel Ximeno, 1827, pp. 11-12.

and in the capitol. If all those bodies decided to join forces around 1824 to form one Scottish rite organization in the country, if a large number of the Scottish rite masons were Spanish, if we believe Alamán's version claiming that many of them were in favour of a constitutional monarchy or a central republic and they had been against the election of Victoria[29], all this would help to understand why various Mexican political actors—such as José María Chavero and José María Tornel[30]—were fearful of the ascendance of Scottish rite Masonry and decided to establish new York rite lodges in the country.

The organization of what from that time onwards was known as the York rite, the Yorkinos, or the Popular Party, started in September 1825. Three lodges were created in Mexico City which sought regularization from the Grand Lodge of New York, with the mediation of the US Minister Plenipotentiary Joel R. Poinsett.

The first lodge was the "Rosa Mexicana" (Mexican Rose), which sent a request for a letter of patent on 16 September, and whose members were the famous insurgent leader and independence hero Vicente Guerrero (Worshipful Master), José Aldama, José Serrano, Manuel Jiménez, José Manuel Palomino, Pedro María Anaya, Juan Urzueta and Guillermo Gardette. The second was the "Federalista" (Federalist) lodge which sent its request on 3 October and whose members included the treasury secretary José Ignacio Esteva (Worshipful Master) Félix María Aburto, the famous journalist Antonio José Valdés, Juan Nepomuceno Pérez, José N. Téllez, the congressman José María Tornel, the military officer and later president of Mexico Anastasio Bustamante, Albino Pérez, the Greek liberal who arrived with the troops of Xavier Mina, Alexander Yhary, and the North American minister Joel R. Poinsett. The third lodge was the "Yndependencia", which sent its request on 6 October and whose members were the senator for Yucatán Lorenzo de Zavala (Worshipful Master), the Cuban émigré involved in the so-called Conspiracy of the Suns and Rays of Bolívar, José Teurbe Tolón, Vicente Filisola, W. S. Parrot, T Vidal, Antonio Campos, Ramón Rey and Fernando del Valle.[31]

According to the US periodical *The Escritoir or Masonic and Miscellaneous Album*, the Grand Lodge of New

---

29   Alamán, *Historia de Méjico ...* , pp. 89, 410, 474.

30   Both Chavero and Tornel recognize that they belonged to Scottish rite masonry and were worried by the political views it was tending towards and its possible actions to obstruct the government. Tornel asserts, however, that he did not support the idea of setting up a new York rite organization. Chavero, "Comunicado ..." José María Tornel, *Breve reseña histórica de los acontecimientos más notables de la nación mexicana, desde el año de 1821 hasta nuestros días* (México: Imprenta de Cumplido, 1852), 46.

31   "Petition for a Charter for a Lodge in Mexico, York Rite, to be called Rosa Mexicana", México, 26 September 1825, and "Petition for a Warrant for a Lodge to be known as Federalista Lodge", México, 3 October 1825, in *Collection made by committee on Antiquities of the Grand Lodge of Free and Accepted Masons, of the State of New York*, New York, Grand Lodge of Free and Accepted Masons of the State of New York, 1905, unnumbered pages. Desaguliers [Geo. Fisher], "Freemasonry

York held an extraordinary meeting on 10 February 1826 to grant the letters of patent to these lodges.[32] Meanwhile, the Mexican National Grand Lodge of Ancient, Accepted and Free Masons of the York Rite was created in Mexico City. The officers, installed by Poinsett on 25 September 1825, were José Ignacio Esteva, Grand Master; Lorenzo de Zavala, Deputy Grand Master; Vicente Guerrero, First Grand Warden; José María Alpuche, Catholic priest and senator for Tabasco, Second Grand Warden; José Teurbe Tolón, Grand secretary; Félix María Aburto, Grand treasurer; Vicente Filisola, Grand First Deacon; José Aldama, Grand Second Deacon; and Miguel Ramos Arizpe, an important and eminent Catholic priest, Grand Chaplain. The patent for the Grand Lodge was obtained from the Grand Lodge of New York thanks to the intervention of Poinsett.[33]

In addition to those mentioned above, I have been able to establish the following were also York rite masons during the period: Agustín Viesca, José Ignacio Basadre, José María Chavero, Mariano Arista, Manuel Reyes Veramendi, José María Arechaga, José Manuel Herrera and Isidro Gondra.[34]

Many of the founders of the York rite organization were distinguished Mexican politicians, including members of congress and cabinet as well as military officers and priests, all occupying public office at the time they were initiated into the rite. These men were dissatisfied with the way that independent government was developing in Mexico and wanted to consolidate the recently established republic and ensure the permanent removal of any Spaniards from public offices so their posts could be occupied by Mexicans from the middle class. In addition, they wanted to increase popular political involvement and disseminate republican principles and practices amongst the population. In other words, they were seeking a more radical transformation of the political and social order.

In order to achieve this goal, they focused on promoting the expansion of York rite masonic bodies. In 1826 there were at least 18 symbolic lodges, an itinerant lodge attached to the No. 2 regiment, the Mexican National Grand Lodge, located in Mexico City, and a Royal Arch Chapter called "La Libertad" (Liberty). For this reason, Lorenzo de Zavala was delighted with the rapid expansion that republican York

---

in Mexico. Its origin illustrated by original documents, not heretofore published", *The Masonic Review*, Cincinnati, 1859. Vease también Michael Costeloe, *La primera república federal de México (1824-1835). Un estudio de los partidos políticos en el México independiente*, México, Fondo de Cultura Económica, 1975, p. 50 and Carlos Francisco Martínez Moreno, "El establecimiento de las masonerías en México en el siglo XIX", Master's thesis, Facultad de Filosofía y Letras, UNAM, 2011, pp. 799-804.

32 *The Escritoir; or, Masonic and Miscellaneous Album*, 11 Feb 1826.

33 *Masonic Mirror: and Mechanics' Intelligencer*, 31 December 1825.

34 Mariano Arista, [Carta a Muy Excelente Capítulo de Arcos Reales La libertad], Oriente de México, a los 3 días del 6º m∴ m∴ a∴ l∴ 5826 and José Manuel Herrera, [Letter written to José Teurbe Tolón], 27 October 1826.

masonry was enjoying.[35]

During 1826 and 1827, the leaders of the Mexican National Grand Lodge dedicated their efforts to extending the rite to areas further away from the capital. To do so they took advantage of the institutional structure of the new political system and the relationships which this enabled them to enter into. For example, the fact that the system was representative and federal meant that a national congress was established in Mexico City formed with lawmakers from all the states in the federation.. The main Yorkinos who were in the capitol, many of whom also occupied important public posts, were thus able to meet the provincial political actors who came to the city and to establish links with those who had similar political ideas to theirs. Some of these state legislators became York rite masons and when they returned to their cities of origin were entrusted with establishing lodges there. This was the case with Santiago Abreu, deputy for New Mexico, to whom the Grand Master of the Mexican National Grand Lodge, Vicente Guerrero, granted the authorization to establish a symbolic lodge in Chihuahua.[36] Similarly, when the national government appointed Anastasio Busatamante Commander General of the Eastern Internal Provinces, Bustamante was entrusted with making the rite known in that part of the country.[37] In addition, itinerant lodges were established in several regiments in the army and these also contributed to the expansion of Yorkino bodies beyond the central area of the republic.

By 1828, the York rite masonic structure had grown substantially in Mexico. According to the catalogue drawn up by Agustín Viesca, then Grand Secretary of the Mexican National Grand Lodge, there were 102 symbolic lodges within its jurisdiction in that year, although some of them had "gone dark". The greatest concentrations of lodges were in the State of Mexico, Mexico City, Veracruz and Puebla. In the north and the south of the country they were less frequent, but there was at least one lodge in each state of the federation. The number of itinerant lodges in the regiments in the army had also increased significantly and there were

---

35 Lorenzo de Zavala, *Comunicado de la M∴R∴G∴L∴N∴M∴ al M∴E∴ Capítulo No 1 con el distintivo de la Libertad*, 2 April 1826. The existence of at least 18 lodges under the jurisdiction of the Mexican National Grand Lodge can be confirmed by the number given to the India Azteca lodge: José María Tornel, [Letter sent to A∴ M∴ E∴ C∴ D∴ R∴ A∴ N 1 tit. Libertad], Or∴ de Méjico a los 28 d∴del 5º m∴m∴a∴1∴5.826. For its part, it is known that there was an itinerant lodge in Regiment number 2 from Mariano Arista's letter [Letter...].

36 Vicente Guerrero, [Power granted to Santiago Abreu], 3 May 1827. The appointment of Vicente Guerrero to Grand Master of the Mexican National Grand Lodge can be confirmed in the Secretaría de la M∴ R∴ G∴ L∴ N∴ M∴, [Circular number 25 de la Mexican National Grand Lodge on the document entitled *Gracias singulares del ciudadano José María Tornel*, ruling that there was no reason to take action against Tornel], O∴ de México a los 4 días de 5∴ m∴ m∴ a∴ 1∴ 5828.

37 Anastasio Bustamante, [Letter, no recipient indicated], 3 July 1826. Letter from Servando Teresa de Mier to José Bernardino Cantú, 31 August 1826, in Adalberto Arturo Madero Quiroga (comp.), *Ensayos de David Alberto Cossío*, Monterrey, Cámara de Senadores, 2002, pp. 315-321.

now 13.[38] In the state of Puebla a Grand Lodge had been established, although it is not known how many lodges it had within its jurisdiction.[39]

The Yorkino Discourse and the Formation of Public Images

Almost since the establishment of the York rite lodges in Mexico, various writers who belonged to them, or at least shared their political ideas, dedicated themselves to constructing the public image of the Yorkino group and the image of those they considered to be their political rivals: followers of the Scottish rite. In so doing, the divisions which had been created in the Mexican political class since independence, which first were categorized in public debate as liberal or servile, and later as iturbidist-federalist and borbonist-centralist, were re-categorized in Masonic terms as Scottish and Yorkino.[40]

Debates by writers of the period around these public images revolved around the way they understood the new political system, the way in which institutions should function, the practices which underpinned them, and the need to define fundamental concepts such as sovereignty, representation, and legitimacy. The formulation of the public images took on great importance at that stage as the groups vying for power were identified with a series of principles which legitimized or discredited their political actions.

Since there were many Spaniards who followed the Scottish rite and some of them had shown themselves to be in favor of the constitutional monarchy and even of remaining united to Spain,[41] it was easy for Yorkino commentators to accuse the Scottish rite followers of being enemies of independence and the republic. In addition, many personalities, such as Nicolás Bravo,[42] who were said to be in favour of the centralized

---

38 Francisco Ibar, *Regeneración política de la República Mexicana*, vol II, number 14, Imprenta a cargo del ciudadano Tomás Uribe y Alcalde, México, 1830.

39 [Baluster circulated by Mexican National Grand Lodge], Oriente de México, a los 17 días del cuarto mes masónico año Luminar de 5.828, en Águila Mexicana, 17 de septiembre de 1828, año IV, núm. 261, México, Imprenta del Águila. This baluster was published in an antiyorkino newspaper, which casts doubt upon its authenticity; however, it may be validated by a letter sent by Juan Rodriguez to Anastasio Zerecero which refers to the baluster in question. The letter is cited in Costeloe, *La primera ...* , p. 174.

40 It is necessary to make two explanatory comments on this matter. Firstly, the divisions in the political class were not quite as unequivocal as presented in public debate at the time and later in historiography. Secondly, the public images of the political groups already existed and the yorkinos reverted to them to formulate their discourse. For a more comprehensive analysis of these subjects, see María Eugenia Vázquez Semadeni *La formación de una cultura política republicana. El debate público sobre la masonería en México, 1821-1830*, México, IIH-UNAM/Colmich, 2010.

41 Alamán, *Historia de Méjico ...* , p. 89.

42 I have not been able to located documents confirming the affiliation of Nicolás Bravo to the Scottish rite, but in the *Correo de la Federación Mexicana* he is described as Grand Master of the rite on 9 February 1828 in volume VI, number 465, Mexico, Imprenta del Correo. It should be noted that to date no response from Bravo has been found, denying his degree and affiliation, a practise that was

republic, joined the Scottish group and so the Scottish were tarred as enemies of the federation. Lastly, in the Scottish ranks there were personalities like José María Fagoaga, members of the privileged social, economic and political sectors of the capitol and so Yorkino discourse defined them as "aristocrats", who preferred a political system which would allow them to control the country in a despotic manner from the center. The Yorkinos lumped all their political opponents together under these headings, so that owing to their masonic links, the Scottish rite masons were all presumed to be "enemies of the country" and of the principles which underpinned the new political order.

At the same time, the Yorkinos constructed their own public image which identified them as the defenders of a series of principles, projects and values which were allegedly those held by the majority of the nation: independence, liberty, federalism, the republic, equality, and broad political participation. In so doing, they managed to present themselves as the spokespeople of the general will, as the protectors of national interests, and of the political system chosen by the Mexicans.[43]

This strategy was highly effective as it enabled Yorkinos to make the Scottish appear a mere faction, who in order to protect their private interests were ready to give up the achievements of the patriots, a term which the Yorkinos adopted for themselves and with which they cloaked themselves in their public roles. Their discourse was capable of thwarting their opponents politically for many years as every proposal or act coming from anyone labeled as Scottish was immediately classified as Bourbon, favouring Reconquest or, at the very least, destabilization.[44] This limited the support that the Scottish received for their projects, and even, for a time, their

common at the time when people wished to deny assertions appearing in the press.

43 As examples of this discouse see the following: *Diálogo entre un liberal moderado y un exaltado sobre los empleos* (tomado de *El Sol*, núm. 1.035), Guadalajara, Imprenta del C. Mariano Rodríguez, 1826. Simón el trompetero, *Quedaron los escoceses como el que chifló en la loma*, México, Oficina de la testamentaría de Ontiveros, 1826. *Hoy truenan los escoceses como Judas en la gloria*, México, Oficina de la testamentaría de Ontiveros, 1826. *El Patriota*, 25 April, 4 and 18 July 1827, año 1, núms. 1, 11 y 13, Puebla, Imprenta del ciudadano Pedro de la Rosa. Rafael Dávila, *Taller de cohetería. Diálogos crítico-alegóricos entre un cohetero y un tamborilero*, Tomo I, México, Imprenta de la ex-inquisición a cargo de Manuel Ximeno, 1827. L. M. Federación, *Lista de los escoceses y apunte de sus maldades*, Puebla, Reimpreso en la Liberal, 1827. *El Amigo del Pueblo*, 23 January 1828, tomo III, núm. 4, México, Imprenta del Águila. *Llegada de D. Francisco de Paula a Veracruz*, Puebla, re-impreso en la Oficina del Patriota, 1827. El costeño de Acapulco, *La ejecución de justicia contra el coronel Mangoy, la causa son los coyotes porque intentó su expulsión*, México, Imprenta del Correo, 1827. Yadspat, *Contestación a un valiente retador*, Victoria de Durango, Imprenta liberal, a cargo de Manuel González, 1827.

44 An example of this is the description made by yorkino publications of the Plan de Montaño, which was a movement led by Nicolás Bravo against secret societies and Poinsett's influence in the Mexican government. See *Correo de la Federación Mexicana*, 1 January 1828, tomo IV, núm. 426, México, Imprenta del correo. *El Amigo del Pueblo*, 2 January 1828, tomo III, núm. 1, México, Imprenta del Águila.

electoral success.

Thus it is possible to maintain that an essential aspect of the Yorkino political actions was their discourse. The public images they created of the groups vying for power, the public discussion about the characteristics of the foundations of the political system, and in general, the participation in public debate were all new ways of doing politics, as effective as direct negotiation, the formation of alliances, or influence in electoral processes. That is to say, public debate was a way of reinforcing their legitimacy which was just as important as elections or constitutional provisions.

This element of Yorkino political action, however, was not directly related to masonic structure, unlike the actions which will be analyzed in the next section.

York Rite Masonic Bodies as Centers of Political Action

Those who were initiated into the "masonic societies" who had "raised their columns under the rite of York" declared that one of the main purposes of their societies was to give their support to the new political institutions, this is, the republican, federal system.[45] This implied that the Yorkinos, not only as citizens but also as adherents of the rite, had to guard the foundations of the social edifice. This meant defending and respecting the government of Guadalupe Victoria, which had been established on these foundations. For this reason, if any member of a Yorkino lodge showed himself to be publicly against the government or attacked it in the press, he was reprimanded by the members of the Grand Lodge and ordered to desist. This happened to José María Alpuche when he criticized the measures taken by the government against the Marqués de Santángelo, an Italian who had been expelled from Mexico for his publications in favor of the Congress of Panama.[46]

Another of the main duties of the Yorkinos was to discredit the Scottish by spreading the negative public image they had created, and to try to keep them out of public office. This duty was so important that, if a Yorkino did not perform it, he was suspected of supporting the Scottish, in word or deed, and could be accused of being "unfaithful to the rite of York" and be subjected to a masonic trial. This was the case of the apprentice Luis Zuloaga in Chihuahua and José María Tornel in Mexico City.[47]

The duties of Yorkino masons also included working to enable the members of the Yorkino organization, or at least those who shared their political ideas, to be successful in the various electoral processes, which ran the gam-

---

45 Lodge number 54, "Apoteosis de Hidalgo", T∴ número 543, *Criminal seguida contra el ex- h∴ Luis Zuluaga, Aprendiz M∴, por infiel al rito de Y∴*, Chihuahua, 1827.

46 José María [Tornel], [Letter to don José D.], México, July 19 1826, in *El Sol*, 31 July 1826, año 4°, núm. 1, 143, México, Imprenta a cargo de Martín Rivera.

47 Lodge number 54, *Criminal ...* , 1827. Secretaría de la M∴ R∴ G∴ L∴ N∴ M∴, [Circular...], O∴ de México a los 4 días de 5∴ m∴ m∴ a∴ l∴ 5828.

ut from city council elections to local legislatures and the national congress. This work consisted mainly of "forming opinion" in favor of their candidates, but also involved specific activities such as drawing up and distributing printed lists with the names of those people they wished to be voted for, appropriating the lists drawn up by their opponents to prevent them reaching the electoral boards, and even committing "irregularities" in these processes, such as voting more than once.[48]

By 1828, the Yorkinos had succeeded in establishing lodges almost throughout the entire country, and had consolidated their legitimizing discourse, so now the Grand National Mexican Lodge was in a position to deploy its entire organizational apparatus with a view to winning all the elections due to take place that year, both for the legislatures and for the second presidential election.

The Yorkino leadership implemented a perfectly organized plan to this end. In June 1828, the Grand National Mexican Lodge sent a circular to all the workshops under its jurisdiction to urge them to start forming opinion in favor of the "patriots" whom they wished to be elected representatives to the legislatures. They indicated that those appointed should be enlightened individuals, men of integrity, dedicated to public service, and known adherents of independence and the federal insti-

tutions. And they imposed the prerequisite that they should be followers of the York rite both in opinions and sentiment.[49] The lodges had to reach agreement using committees to formulate their plan of action.

For its part, the Grand Lodge in the capitol created a committee of five members with whom the lodges outside the capital had to maintain contact. The lodges also had to provide information on the individuals they had agreed to name as representatives, the state of opinion about them, and of any difficulty which might occur. This committee was responsible for establishing contact with the Yorkinos living in states or territories where there was still no York rite lodge, so they could direct the elections according to the plan which had been drawn up.[50]

Despite all this organization, the plan caused problems, as numerous York rite masons wished to occupy public posts, and this made it necessary for some of the state commissioners to request the leaders of the rite to send them lists with the names of people who they believed most appropriate to run for the elections.[51]

This example alone is enough to understand the way in which the Yorkino leadership used the hierarchical and organizational structure of masonry, its loyalties and its channels of communication to carry out activities of a political nature. This was even more flagrant,

48 Lodge number 54, *Criminal ...* , 1827.

49 [Baluster circulated ...], in Águila *Mexicana*, 17 September 1828.

50 [Baluster circulated ...], in Águila *Mexicana*, 17 September 1828.

51 Costeloe, *La primera ...* p. 174.

however, in the fight for the presidency.

The election of the president was due to be held in September 1828 and would be carried out by the state legislatures. They had to name, by absolute majority, two individuals. The votes coming from all the states would be counted by the national congress and the person with the most votes would be elected president and the second placed person, vice-president of the republic.

The Yorkinos analyzed carefully which candidate they would support, as there were several members of their group who could aspire to lead the executive. These included Lorenzo de Zavala, Ignacio Esteva, José María Tornel, Anastasio Bustamante and Vicente Guerrero, then Grand Master of the Mexican National Grand Lodge. [52]

The Grand Lodge formed a committee of five individuals to examine the qualities, virtues and merits of the various candidates and decided to grant their support to the "distinguished General Vicente Guerrero".[53] From that moment on, the members of the Grand Lodge used the resources made available by the national Yorkino organization to work towards Guerrero's victory.[54]

Firstly, the Yorkino writers mounted a major campaign in the public press in which they extolled Guerrero's qualities and sought to discredit his main opponent, Manuel Gómez Pedraza, primarily by pointing out that he belonged to the Scottish group, which, as one will recall, the Yorkinos had labeled as enemies of independence, the republic and the federation. [55]

Secondly, the Grand Secretary of the Grand Lodge, José Manuel Herrera, sent messages to the symbolic lodges throughout the country, informing them that the committee had chosen Guerrero as candidate for the presidency and Anastasio Bustamante for the vice-presidency. They asked the lodges to second the plan and suggested that the members of the lodge urge the city councils—many of them composed of Yorkinos—to state that the opinion of the people was firmly in favour of Guerrero.[56] Everything seems to indicate that Herrera's request was heeded, as in several parts of the country, such as Orizaba and Veracruz, the town councils sent

---

52　Los amantes del bien público [José Manuel Herrera], *Oigan todos los congresos el voto de la República o sea, la expresión de la voluntad general, con respecto a los patriotas en quienes deben recaer los altos empleos de presidente y vicepresidente*, México, Imprenta de la testamentaría de Ontiveros, 1828. Carlos María de Bustamante claims that Herrera is the author in the entry in this Diary for 30 July 1828.

53　José Manuel Herrera, [Baluster sent to la M∴R∴L∴ núm. 54, Apoteosis de Hidalgo], México, a los 28 días del 4° mes de 5828.

54　José María Tornel, *Breve reseña histórica de los acontecimientos más notables de la nación mexicana*, México, INEHRM, México, 1985, pp. 311-312.

55　Los amantes del bien público [José Manuel Herrera], *Oigan todos los congresos ...* , 1828. El coyote manso [Andrés María Nieto], *Manuel Gómez Pedraza, segundo emperador de los mexicanos*, México, Imprenta de las escalerillas, 1828. *El Sol*, 9 de agosto de 1828, año 6, núm. 1.884, México, Imprenta a cargo de J. P. Márquez.

56　José Manuel Herrera, [Letter sent to la R∴L∴ Apoteosis de Hidalgo], Oriente de Méjico a los 13

delegations to the legislatures requesting them to vote for Guerrero.[57]

At first sight, these actions don't seem to make much sense, as it was the legislatures who would make the vote, and the city councils could not intervene in their decisions. From 1826, however, the Yorkino propagandists had disseminated an idea of the political system in which the city councils played a fundamental role, as, though they lacked political representation in the strictest sense, they were made up of people who had been elected by popular vote, they carried out important roles in the electoral processes, and they had the right to speak in the name of their people, and for this reason they had sufficient strength to consider themselves the voice of the people. Thus, the city council's demonstrations in favour of Guerrero conferred considerable legitimacy on his candidacy as well as placing significant pressure on the legislatures to vote in his favor.

Despite this, Guerrero was not elected president; the winner was Gómez Pedraza. After this failure, events moved rapidly. Antonio López de Santa Anna headed an armed movement to place Guerrero in the presidency, and shortly afterwards there was a riot in Mexico City. Gómez Pedraza fled Mexico City and gave up his claim to the presidency. In their evaluation of the elections, Congress judged that the legislatures had voted against the "will of their constituents", and thus declared the election null and void and appointed Vicente Guerrero and Anastasio Bustamante[58] president and vice-president respectively. This exceeded the powers that the constitution had given congress, but it can be understood better if one considers that in the committee set up to evaluate the elections seven out of the thirteen legislators were Yorkinos: Manuel García Tato, Vicente Güido de Güido, Ignacio Basadre, José María Bocanegra, José María Alpuche, José Sixto Berduzco and Juan Evangelista Guadalajara.[59]

Some state governors interpreted the appointment of Vicente Guerrero as president as an imposition by the center over the will of the states. When Gómez Pedraza left Mexico City he went to Jalisco, where he hoped to launch a defense of his electoral win. For their part, General Vicente Filisola—who was a Yorkino and member of the Grand Lodge, but during the fight for the presidency had decided to support Gómez Pedraza [60]—and General Melchor Múzquiz, who had been governor of the state of Mexico and was a political en-

---

días del 6º m∴m∴a∴l∴ 5.828.

57   *El Sol*, 5 October 1828, año 6, núm. 1.939, México, Imprenta a cargo de J. P. Márquez. Torcuato Di Tella, *Política nacional y popular en México, 1820-1847*, México, FCE, 1994, pp. 222.

58   José María Bocanegra, *Memorias para la historia de México Independiente*, tomo I, México, INEH-RM, 1985, pp. 505-509.

59   The names of the deputies have been taken from Costeloe and Bocanegra and were cross-checked against the lists in Ibar, Mateos, the documents in the Louis C Morton auctioneers and the circular from the office of the Mexican National Grand Lodge.

60   It is possible to corroborate the fact that Filisola belonged to the Grand Lodge in the records of

emy of Lorenzo de Zavala, had met in Puebla to march against Guerrero. But the civil militia mutinied and did not follow their orders; thus they were unable to fight Guerrero.

Something similar happened in Guanajuato. The governor Carlos Montes de Oca sought to establish an alliance with Jalisco, Michoacán, San Luis Potosí and Zacatecas, but the militiamen under the command of Luis Cortázar declared themselves in favor of the Guerrero. The documentation in the General Archive of the Nation demonstrates that Guerrero was in constant touch with medium and low-ranking officers in the militia and in the army, particularly in units with itinerant lodges.[61]

The final result shows that, although the plan implemented by the Grand Lodge may not have been sufficient to ensure Guerrero's election as president, the Yorkinos' actions were nevertheless useful, as, thanks to the city hall delegations, the Yorkino discourse in the public press and the armed and popular movements in favor of Guerrero, the Yorkinos were able to maintain – in congress and in the press – that the representatives had not respected the desires of the people they were representing, and this was sufficient motive

to discredit the election of Gómez Pedraza. With this argument they disregarded the votes of the legislatures and sought to give legitimacy to the accession of Guerrero to the presidency, even though it had not been achieved constitutionally.

Their victory did not last long, however. During the few months in 1829 when Guerrero was at the head of the executive he had to address numerous challenges, from the attempted reconquest led by Isidro Barradas to the meagerness of the public finances and the complaints about taxes which his finance minister, Lorenzo de Zavala,[62] was seeking to impose. In addition, there was a split in the Yorkino ranks. On the one hand, some of the more militant members were unhappy with the conciliatory approach of Guerrero and on the other, some Yorkinos (and many other political actors) were apprehensive about the popular mobilization which Guerrero and his supporters had resorted to.[63]

This process came to a head at the end of 1829 with the uprising to overthrow the president, headed by Anastasio Bustamente, who was acting as vice-president and who had been a well-known member of the Yorkino organization. He became head of the ex-

the office of the M∴ R∴ G∴ L∴ N∴ M∴, [Circular...], O∴ de México a los 4 días de 5∴ m∴ m∴ a∴ l∴ 5828. His motives for supporting Pedraza have been discussed by Costeloe, Di Tella, Ávila and other authors, so they will not be dealt with in this paper.

61 Alfredo Ávila, "La presidencia de Vicente Guerrero", in Will Fowler, *Presidentes mexicanos*, tomo I, México, INEHRM, 2004, pp. 70-71.

62 José Antonio Serrano Ortega, "Tensar hasta romperse, la política de Lorenzo de Zavala", en Leonor Ludlow (coord.), *Los Secretarios de Hacienda y sus proyectos (1821-1933)*, México, UNAM, 2002, pp. 87-110.

63 Vázquez Semadeni, *La formación ...* , passim.

ecutive when the government of Guerrero was brought down. The uprising, known as the Plan de Jalapa, brought to power a group who wished to close down the channels of political participation opened up in previous years and sought to apply a moderate liberalism.[64] They also needed to prevent their opponents from trying to recover control of public businesses. For this reason and others, it was necessary to break up the Yorkinos.

During 1830, the government which emerged from the Plan de Jalapa imprisoned or prosecuted renowned Yorkino writers such as Pablo de Villavicencio, Luis Espino and José Ramón García Ugarte. Lucas Alamán, who was Minister of Foreign Affairs, started to remove from office any Yorkino authorities established the previous year. As since 1828 a law had been created to prohibit secret societies, there were numerous denunciations of lodges in the states and their relationships with legislatures, city councils and the governors, such that belonging to a York rite body became a reason for losing one's office.[65] Despite this, some local lodges, such as the one in Zacatlán, remained active, but they were persecuted, both by the civil and ecclesiastical authorities.[66]

Lastly, the government initiated a clear campaign to dismantle what remained of the Yorkino leadership. Alpuche was accused of conspiracy for having invited Manuel Mier y Terán to initiate a revolt against the government and was exiled for 6 years. Anastasio Zercero, Mariano Zerecero, and Lucas Balderas were found to be involved in a conspiracy; Anastasio was exiled for five years and Mariano condemned to death, although he did receive a pardon, apparently due to the intervention of Anastasio Bustamante. Balderas was arrested, as was Manuel Reyes Veramendi. Finally, Isidro Gondra was accused of conspiracy and of contributing with Guerrero to the war being waged in the south of the country, for which he was exiled for four years.

There were also numerous cases brought against Zavala, and although they didn't prosper, he decided to leave the country for the United States. With him went two other important Yorkino writers, editors of the *Correo de la Federación*: Ramón Ceruti and the so-called Count Cornaro. Juan Nepomuceno Almonte fled into hiding when he was about to become embroiled in a case for having received secret correspondence which the government

---

64 José Antonio Serrano y Manuel Chust, "Adiós a Cádiz: el liberalismo, el doceañismo y la revolución en México, 1828-1835", in Jaime E. Rodríguez (coord.), *Las nuevas naciones. España y México 1800-1850*, Madrid, Mapfre, 2008, pp. 191-225.

65 *Representación que el ayuntamiento y vecindario de la ciudad de Toluca ha dirigido a la Cámara de Senadores, pidiendo se declare nula la legislatura actual del Estado de México*, México, Imprenta a cargo del C. Tomás Uribe y Alcalde, 1830. Andrés Videgaray, *Almoneda de las joyas, instrumentos y muebles mazónicos, que por fallecimiento del Rito Yorkino venden sus albaceas para cubrir sus infinitos acreedores*, Puebla, Imprenta del C. Pedro de la Rosa, 1830. Costeloe, *La primera ...* , p. 257.

66 *Autos formados sobre la conducta del Presbítero Antonio Arroyo, ministro de Santiago Chignahuapan, por pertenecer a la logia yorkina*, Puebla, 1830. Archivo Histórico del Arzobispado de México, Fondo *Episcopal*, Sección *Provisorato*, Serie *Autos contra eclesiásticos*, Caja 24, exp. 14, 118 f.

had found out about. Furthermore, the senator Hernández Chico, editor of *El Atleta* died on 1 April 1830.[67] Thus, the Yorkino leadership was almost destroyed.

It can therefore be maintained that, due to internal divisions, to the conflicts which the Yorkino leadership had to address when it came to power during Guerrero's presidency, and to the persecution that the Yorkinos were subjected to during the Alamán administration,[68] York rite lodges and their followers ceased to act as centers of political action from 1830 onwards. Although it is worth mentioning that this did not mean that masonry ceased to be considered an effective tool for political action, as a mere four years later the new rite of Yorkinos Federalistas was founded, with clearly political ambitions.[69]

Closing Remarks

The discursive work and the organizational apparatus implemented through the masonic and institutional structure for some years enabled the Yorkinos to grow into an important political force, which intervened on close to a national level. The Yorkino political actors in the capital were able to coordinate their actions with their supporters in the states, in large part due to the wide spread of their lodges, to their hierarchical structure and the masonic channels of communication. Membership of York rite bodies was a means which the leaders of the rite used to try to unite the wills and the efforts of its members to achieve certain political ends, such as electoral victory. In this way the Yorkinos managed to coordinate the political action of a large proportion of the political class in the country.

As Marco Flores has pointed out, the fact that a mason receives directions from his superiors doesn't necessarily mean that he complies with them, so it is important not to fall into the error of supposing that the Yorkinos always acted in a joint, coordinated manner.[70] The important thing to observe is how the masonic structure gave the recently constituted nation the spaces and the tools to link political actors in different parts of the country, to communicate plans, principles, and projects, to obtain their support and even to have some influence over local politics. The masonic structure was very useful, for a time, for numerous Mexican political actors. The

---

67   Archivo de la Suprema Corte de Justicia de la Nación, *Asuntos penales siglo XIX*, exp. 83. *Registro Oficial del Gobierno de los Estados Unidos Mexicanos*, 10 de marzo, año 1, núm. 49 y 10 September 1830, año 1, núm. 138, México, Imprenta del Águila. Ibar, Francisco, *Regeneración política ...* , 21 May 1830, tomo II, núm. 45. Bustamante, 26 March, 1 April and 17 August 1830. Costeloe, *La primera ...* , p. 265-271.

68   It was called the government of Anastasio Bustamante but many considered that it was Lucas Alamán who really directed the actions of the various authorities.

69   José María Lafragua, [Apuntes sobre su vida pública hasta 1841], s/l, s/f, Colección Lafragua, Biblioteca Nacional de México.

70   Flores Zavala, "La masonería ..." , pp. 125-136.

fact that the final result may not have been what the Yorkino leaders wished for is a secondary matter, because what did happen was that at least one sector of the politically active population of the country began to act in a joint and coordinated manner, and this contributed in some way to the formation of a national political class.

Freemasonry, Civil Society, and the Public Sphere in Central America (1865–1876)[1]

Ricardo Martínez Esquivel[2]

ABSTRACT

Due to the specific characteristics of Latin American modernity, I argue in this article that it should be regarded more as a process of socio-historical construction than as an analytical category. This will allow us to gain an understanding of the particular guise that modernity took on in Latin America, and, therefore, of the ideological construction of a Central American Freemasonry instigated and led by Catholic priest Francisco Calvo. Accordingly, this paper addresses the nature of the relationships between modernity and the establishment and evolution of Freemasonry in Central America during the initial period of its active development (1865–1876). Why did Freemasonry emerge as a space of social interaction? What contextual factors influenced the development of Masonic activity? And what social functions did it serve in the expansion of civil society and the broadening of the public sphere?

Keywords: Civil society, public sphere, Central America, Freemasonry

RESUMEN

Debido a las características específicas de la modernidad latinoamericana, en este artículo se arguye que debe considerarse más como un proceso de construcción socio-histórica que como una categoría analítica. Esto nos permitirá comprender el aspecto particular que la modernidad adquirió en América Latina y, por tanto, la construcción ideológica de una francmasonería centroamericana instigada y dirigida por el sacerdote católico Francisco Calvo. En consecuencia, este trabajo aborda la

---

1 This article was previously published in *Gibraltar, Cádiz, América y la masonería. Constitucionalismo y libertad de prensa, 1812–2012*. Coordinated by José Miguel Delgado Idarreta and Antonio Morales Benítez. Government of Gibraltar—Center for Historical Studies of Spanish Freemasonry, University of Zaragoza, 2014, Volume I, pp. 541–580. We are grateful to the coordinators for permitting us to publish this paper in English.

2 Assistant Professor of History, researcher and director of *REHMLAC, Revista de Estudios Históricos de la Masonería Latinoamericana y Caribeña* (http://rehmlac.ucr.ac.cr/), all at the University of Costa Rica. Email: ricardo.martinezesquivel@ucr.ac.cr

naturaleza de las relaciones entre la modernidad y el establecimiento y la evolución de la masonería en Centroamérica durante el período inicial de su desarrollo activo (1865-1876). ¿Por qué surgió la Francmasonería como un espacio de interacción social? ¿Qué factores contextuales influyeron en el desarrollo de la actividad masónica? ¿Y qué funciones sociales han servido en la expansión de la sociedad civil y en la ampliación de la esfera pública?

Palabras clave: Sociedad civil, esfera pública, Centroamérica, Francmasonería

1865-1876年间中美洲的共济会、公民社会和公共领域

摘要

由于拉美现代性（modernity）的具体特点，本文主张，拉美现代性应该更多地被视为一种社会历史建构，而不属于分析范畴。这将允许我们理解现代性在拉美地区呈现的伪装，进而理解中美洲共济会的意识结构。煽动并领导该共济会的是天主教牧师Francisco Calvo。相应地，本文处理了现代性和中美洲共济会初期积极成立及发展（1865-1876年）之间的关系本质。为何共济会以一种社会互动空间的方式出现？何种情境因素影响了共济会活动的发展？共济会在公民社会扩张和公共领域拓宽的进程中提供了何种社会功能？

关键词：公民社会，公共领域，中美洲，共济会

Introduction

If there is one analytical category that helps us to understand Freemasonry, it is the concept of modernity. As has been discussed in the European context by José Antonio Ferrer Benimeli, Margaret Jacob, and *Pierre-Yves Beaurepaire*, and in the context of the United States by Steven Bullock, Masonic lodges were either at the forefront of the construction of modern civil society or a consequence of the processes of modernization, as the case may be.[3]

---

3   The many works of these authors include: José Antonio Ferrer Benimeli, *La masonería como problema político religioso. Reflexiones históricas* (Mexico City: Autonomous University of Tlaxcala, 2010). Margaret Jacob, *Living the Enlightenment: Freemasonry and Politics in Eighteenth-Century Europe* (New York and Oxford: Oxford University Press, 1991). *Pierre-Yves Beaurepaire, L'espace des francs-maçons. Une sociabilité européenne au XVIIIe siècle* (Rennes: Rennes University Press, 2003).

These authors have shown that Free-masonry acted as the perfect diffusion mechanism for the ideas that would transform the various systems of social meaning in operation during the transition from the Old Regime. Freemasonry, in fact, first emerged in Britain in the eighteenth century, a time and place shaped not only by the Enlightenment but also by the early effects of the industrial revolution.[4] It is important to emphasize this point, given that Freemasonry was one of the first institutions to bring together the incipient middle classes.

In Latin America's case, François-Xavier Guerra[5] has described how the processes leading up to political independence played an important part in the transition from the Old Regime to what, following Enrique Dussel,[6] we might call the second stage of modernity.[7] These processes were pri-

---

Steven Bullock, *Revolutionary Brotherhood. Freemasonry and the Transformation of the American Social Order, 1730–1840* (Chapel Hill: University of North Carolina Press, 1996), 109–133.

4   Eric J. Hobsbawm, *La era del capitalismo*, trans. A. García Fluixá and Carlo A. Caranci (Barcelona: Guadarrama, 1981), 372–401.

5   François-Xavier Guerra, " 'De la política antigua a la política moderna': invenciones, permanencias, hibridaciones' " (paper delivered at the *19th International Congress of Historical Sciences*, Oslo, August 6–13, 2000 [accessed September 15, 2012]): available at: http://www.oslo2000.uio.no/ program/papers/s17/s17-guerra.pdf. Guerra, "De la política antigua a la política moderna: algunas proposiciones," *Anuario IEHS* 18 (2003): 208–209.

6   Dussel defines modernity as the set of new paradigms for everyday life and for understanding history, science, and religion that emerged in Europe toward the end of the fifteenth century, coinciding with European dominance over the Atlantic. This conception allows us to approach modernity as a process of socio-historical construction/reconstruction—in other words, as a process that came about through a series of historical phenomena of a "global nature," in Immanuel Wallerstein's phrase, that can be understood in terms of his "world-systems theory" or Fernand Braudel's concept of "world-economies." Such approaches allow us to locate the origins of modernity at a point in time before the eighteenth century, and to appreciate the great contrast in thinking between those who believe modernity to be a process that can be "finished" (i.e. Jürgen Habermas) and those who disagree (i.e. the postmodern school). Enrique Dussel, "Europa, modernidad y eurocentrismo" in *La Colonialidad del Poder: Eurocentrismo y Ciencias Sociales. Perspectivas latinoamericanas*, ed. Edgardo Lander (Buenos Aires: UNESCO-CLACSO, 2000 [accessed October 10, 2012]): available at: http://enriquedussel.com/txt/1993-236a.pdf. John H. Elliott, *Empires of the Atlantic World: Britain and Spain in America 1492–1830* (Connecticut: Yale University Press, 2006), 88–116. Immanuel Wallerstein, *The Modern World-System* (San Diego and New York: Academic Press, 1974). Fernand Braudel, *Civilisation matérielle, Économie et Capitalisme. XVe–XVIIIe Siècle* (Paris: Armand Colin, 1979). Jürgen Habermas, 'Modernity versus Postmodernity,' trans. Seyla Ben-Habib, *New German Critique* 22 (1981): 3–14.

7   This second stage of modernity is crucial, because it coincided with the development of modern Masonic ideology. With Great Britain established as the movement's international center, this explains its geographic reach. Paul John Rich and Jessica Harland-Jacobs have shown that, during the time when Britain was ascending and becoming established as a global hegemonic power, Freemasonry played an important role in the education of the elite, serving to disseminate the ideology of modernity as it unfolded and actively promoting empire-building and imperial control. Paul John Rich, *Elixir of Empire: The English Public Schools, Ritualism, Freemasonry, and Imperialism* (London: Regency Press Ltd., 1989). Jessica Harland-Jacobs, "Hands across the Sea: The Masonic Network,

marily driven by external factors, particularly Napoleon's invasion of Spain, the Spanish Revolution of 1808–1810, and the subsequent promulgation of the Spanish Constitution by the Cádiz Cortes (1812).[8] The heady winds of freedom blowing from the various revolutions of the late eighteenth century brought new ideas and forms of social interaction that reconfigured the ideals, mentalities, and interests of the Creole population.[9] In their discussion of the advent of modernity in Latin America in the nineteenth century, Guerra, Fernando Armas Asin, and Julio Pino Vallejos have shown that this period was characterized by the continuity and stability of structures, practices, and ideas associated with the Old Re-

gime. This meant that modernity was unable to become fully established and entrenched, resulting in a process of coexistence and hybridization between those elements that were indicative of the Old Regime and those that signified modernity. Nevertheless, by the second half of the nineteenth century, various governments were reaffirming their commitment to modernity as a project, leading them, in some cases, to work to consolidate the nation-state, enter international markets, or develop a secular culture.[10]

Due to the specific characteristics of Latin American modernity, I would argue that it should be regarded more as a process of socio-historical construction than as an analytical cat-

British Imperialism, and the North Atlantic World," *Geographical Review* 89, no. 2 (1999): 237–253. Harland-Jacobs, "All in the Family: Freemasonry and the British Empire in the Mid-Nineteenth Century," *Journal of British Studies* 42, no. 4 (2003): 448–482. See also: R. William Weisberger, Wallace McLeod, and S. Brent Morris eds., *Freemasonry on Both Sides of the Atlantic: Essays Concerning the Craft in the British Isles, Europe, the United States, and Mexico* (Boulder, CO: East European Monographs, 2002). Dévrig Mollès, *"Triangle atlantique et triangle latin: l'Amérique latine et le système-monde maçonnique (1717–1921), Éléments pour une histoire des opinions publiques internationales"* (Doctoral Dissertation in History, University of Strasbourg, France, 2012).

8   Gregorio Alonso, 'Prolegomena to Atlantic Catholic Citizenship' (paper delivered at *Liberalism and Religion: Secularisation and the Public Sphere in the Americas*, London, April 18, 2012 [accessed May 7, 2012]): available at http://sas-space.sas.ac.uk/4135/1/LIA%2C_Atlantic_Catholic_Citizenship%2C_Alonso%2C%2C_18.04.12.pdf. It is also worth noting that in New Spain (Mexico), the revolutionary press helped popularize the notion that the Cádiz Cortes were controlled by liberals and therefore Masons. María Eugenia Vázquez Semadeni, *La formación de una cultura política republicana. El debate público sobre la masonería en México, 1821–1830* (Mexico City: UNAM and El Colegio de Michoacán, 2010), 31.

9   Guerra, *Modernidad e independencias. Ensayos sobre las revoluciones hispánicas* (Madrid: Editorial MAPFRE, 1992), 227–239.

10   Guerra, 'De la política antigua a la política moderna,' 1–13. Fernando Armas Asin, 'Radicalismo liberal, modernización y tolerancia religiosa en el siglo XIX Latinoamericano' (paper delivered at the *19th International Congress of Historical Sciences*, Oslo, August 6–13, 2000 [accessed 15 September, 2012]): available at: http://oslo2000.uio.no/program/papers/s17/s17-asin.pdf. Julio Pinto Vallejos, " 'De proyectos y desarraigos': la sociedad latinoamericana frente a la experiencia de la modernidad (1780–1914)" (paper delivered at the *19th International Congress of Historical Sciences*, Oslo, August 6–13, 2000 [accessed September 15, 2012]): available at: http://oslo2000.uio.no/program/papers/s17/s17-valejos.pdf.

egory. This will allow us to gain an understanding of the particular guise that modernity took on in Latin America, and, therefore, of the ideological construction of a Central American Freemasonry instigated and led by Catholic priest Francisco Calvo.[11] Accordingly, this paper addresses the nature of the relationships between modernity and the establishment and evolution of Freemasonry in Central America[12] during the initial period of its active development (1865–1876).[13] Why did Freemasonry emerge as a space of social interaction? What contextual factors influenced the development of Masonic activity? And what social functions did it serve in the expansion of civil society and the broadening of the public sphere?

The Advent of Modernity in Central America (1821–1865)

One of the first signs of modernity to appear in Latin America during the first half of the nineteenth century was the creation of new spaces of social interaction. These included, for example, the Lodge of Rational Knights, the Lautaro Lodge, the Guadalupe Lodge, the Grand Legion of the Black Eagle, the Unitarian movement, local gatherings for patriotic discussion, utopian societies, the *comuneros*, and Freemasonry itself: groups that were persecuted and, therefore, often conducted their activities in secret. The new forms of social contact offered by modernity, whether literary, economic, political, patriotic, or, indeed, Masonic, shared certain ideological themes while retaining their own distinctive iden-

---

11 Rafael Obregón Loría, *Ganganelli: organizador de la Masonería en Costa Rica* (San José: Trejos Hermanos, 1941). Obregón Loría, *Presbítero Doctor Francisco Calvo (Ganganelli). Organizador de la Masonería en Costa Rica* (San José: Imprenta Borrase, 1968).

12 This paper understands Central America as the socio-historical construct created by the Spanish colonial project, i.e. Hispanic Central America, which, at the start of the nineteenth century, included only Guatemala, Honduras, El Salvador, Nicaragua, and Costa Rica. The analysis will therefore focus exclusively on the development of Freemasonry in Hispanic Central America, and will not address the Scottish or English forms that became established in Belize and on the Caribbean coast of Honduras and Nicaragua from the second half of the eighteenth century. Archives of the United Grand Lodge of England, "Papers Relating to Early Freemasonry in Central/South America and the Caribbean, 1773–1875" (GBR 1991 HC 22–23, 28). Carlos Granados, "Hacia una definición de Centroamérica, el peso de los factores geopolíticos," *Anuario de Estudios Centroamericanos* 11, no. 1 (1985): 59–78. Héctor Pérez-Brignoli, "Transformaciones del espacio centroamericano," in *Para una historia de América*, eds. Alicia Hernández Chávez, Ruggiero Romano and Marcello Carmagnani (Mexico City: COLMEX, 1999), Vol. 2, 55–93. Céline Sala, "Los archivos del desengaño: Las luces y el mundo de las fuentes "ultra marinas," " *REHMLAC* 2, No. 2 (December 2010–April 2011 [accessed December 15, 2010]): available at https://revistas.ucr.ac.cr/index.php/rehmlac/article/view/6599/6290.

13 On the various periods of Masonic activity in Central America during the nineteenth century, see Ricardo Martinez Esquivel, "Modernity and Freemasonry in 19th Century Central America" (paper delivered at *Liberalism and Religion: Secularisation and the Public Sphere in the Americas*, London, April 18, 2012 [accessed May 7, 2012]): available at: http://sas-space.sas.ac.uk/4146/1/LIA%2C_Modernity_and_Freemasonry%2C_Martinez%2C_18.04.12.pdf.

tities. Together, they formed a broad spectrum that offered people the opportunity to become active in several different movements at once.

Interestingly, because Masonic social activities centered around the lodge, it is there that its functions and activities became formally defined—through the construction of a normative framework accompanied by a powerful socializing effect invoking brotherhood between members, and through Freemasonry's assumption of various roles relating to education, culture, spirituality, and politics. In other words, the lodge served as a place to meet, learn, and discuss ideas, and, consequently, the main social space for its members. In order to understand the social dynamics of Freemasonry, then, it is essential to consider the lodge as a space. This is because the lodge, through a collection of symbols and rituals, expresses the ideals and discursive elements that Freemasonry has made its own.[14] That said, once we understand the significance of the lodge to its members, what is interesting is to study the social behavior of the Masonic networks to which this space gave rise, as I try to do here; in other words, to seek to understand how something created through the private social interactions between Masons helped them take a role in the development of civil society and the public sphere: the novel features of the new models of sociability that modernity brought to nineteenth-century Latin America.[15]

To take an example, Guillermo de los Reyes Heredia and María Eugenia Vázquez Semadeni describe how, in the early years of Mexican independence, Freemasonry sought to become an integral part of the new post-independence political system, serving to coordinate political support and providing a space where new ideas could circulate. Nevertheless, the Mexican Masonic movement failed in this attempt, because the political culture of the time did not look favorably on the establishment of political parties or non-state institutions that might influence public life. This was a point in the country's history where unity was equated with unanimity, and dissent with treason. Both authors remain of the opinion, however, that Freemasonry played a pivotal role in the construction and consolidation of the public sphere in Mexico.[16]

So, in contrast to what had hap-

---

14 Jacob, *Living the Enlightenment*, 96–119. Luis P. Martín, "Las logias masónicas: una sociabilidad pluriformal," *Hispania: Revista española de historia* 63, No. 214 (2003): 523–550. Martín, "La modernidad política de la masonería en la España contemporánea," *Las logias masónicas en la modernización de España, Bulletin d'Histoire Contemporaine de l'Espagne* 32– 36 (December 2000–December 2003), 19–42.

15 Guerra, *Modernidad e independencias*, 13–31. Víctor Uribe-Uran, "The Birth of a Public Sphere in Latin America During the Age of Revolution," *Comparative Studies in Society and History* 42, No. 2 (2000): 425–457. Elías José Palti, "Recent Studies on the Emergence of a Public Sphere in Latin America," *Latin American Research Review* 36, No. 2 (2001): 255–266.

16 Guillermo de los Reyes Heredia, *Masonería, política y sociedad en México* (Puebla: Meritorious Autonomous University of Puebla, 2009), 16 and 101-118. Vázquez Semadeni, *La formación de una cultura política republicana.*

pened in Europe, the establishment of Freemasonry in Latin America was a consequence of the gradual unfolding of modernity, and not the vanguard of that process. This contention is also held to apply to Central America, since, as we will see, Freemasonry did not gain a foothold here until 1865, held back by the unfavorable contextual conditions hitherto prevailing in the region.[17] This paper therefore maintains that Freemasonry began to develop as one of a number of social spaces within the broader context of the expansion of the public sphere, which occurred as part of the modernization of Central American civil society in the nineteenth century.

Central America in the nineteenth century was undergoing a unique, dynamic, and interrelational transition between the predominance of the Catholic Church and modernity, a process that was to transform the identities and cultural practices of society as a whole. This process was neither homogeneous nor linear in nature, but proceeded in fits and starts, affecting different sectors of society in different ways. Culture, ideas, and the social imagination all tended to draw on models from abroad,[18] adopting elements of liberal and Enlightenment thought associated with secular models of state and society.[19] Nonetheless, the influence of religion actually increased, and, although the Catholic Church and its institutions lost their hold over everyday behavior, Catholic morality and religious beliefs continued to guide people's social conduct at this time.[20] The

---

17 Hans-Jürgen Prien, in his discussion of nineteenth-century Latin America, in fact concluded that it was republicanism, driven by liberalism, that was at the forefront of modernity, and that liberalism in turn was given much impetus by Freemasonry. Nevertheless, Prien's hypothesis has become increasingly discredited as a result of more recent historical studies of Freemasonry in Latin America. These demonstrate that its varying forms came about as a consequence of modernity and independence, and not the reverse. Prien, "Protestantismo, Liberalismo y Francmasonería en América Latina durante el siglo XIX: Problemas de investigación," in *Protestantes, liberales y francmasones. Sociedades de ideas y modernidad en América Latina, siglo XIX*, ed. Jean Pierre Bastian (Mexico: FCE, 1990), 15–23. Yván Pozuelo Andrés, "La historiografía masónica latinoamericanista actual. Presente y future," *200 años de Iberoamérica (1810–2010). Congreso Internacional*, eds. Eduardo Rey Tristán and Patricia Calvo González (Santiago de Compostela: University of Santiago de Compostela, 2010 [accessed March 20, 2012]): available at: http://halshs.archives-ouvertes.fr/docs/00/52/92/98/PDF/AT4_Pozuelo.pdf.

18 Gerardo Morales García, *Cultura oligárquica y nueva intelectualidad en Costa Rica: 1880–1914* (Heredia: EUNA, 1995), 26–53. Patricia Fumero Vargas, "La ciudad en la aldea. Actividades y diversiones urbanas en San José a mediados del siglo XIX" and Patricia Vega Jiménez, "De la banca al sofá. La diversificación de los patrones de consumo en Costa Rica (1857–1861)," in *Héroes al gusto y libros de moda. Sociedad y cambio cultural en Costa Rica (1750–1900)*, eds. Iván Molina Jiménez and Steven Palmer (San José: Editorial Porvenir, Plumsock Mesoamerican Studies, 1992), 113–208. Molina Jiménez, *La estela de la pluma. Cultura impresa e intelectuales en Centroamérica durante los siglos XIX y XX* (Heredia: EUNA, 2004).

19 Morales García, *Cultura oligárquica y nueva intelectualidad*, 26–53. Ciro F. S. Cardoso and Pérez Brignoli, *Centro América y la Economía Occidental* (San José: EUCR, 1977), 87–111.

20 José Daniel Gil Zúñiga, *El culto a la Virgen de los Ángeles (1824–1935). Una aproximación a la mentalidad religiosa en Costa Rica* (Alajuela: MHJS, 2004), 34–42. Alfonso González Ortega, *Vida*

next part of the paper briefly explores the ways in which modernity revealed itself across different social spheres in Central America in the period between 1821 and 1865, with a view to analyzing its significance for the establishment of Freemasonry.

Following Central America's declaration of independence from Spain in 1821, the five nations developed a conception of economic "progress" that was closer to British liberalism, advancing the rise of the machine, industry, and large-scale production.[21] This was a time when Great Britain was consolidating its position as a hegemonic world power. With designs on the Atlantic, Central America was in its sights,[22] and from a very early stage the region began to build up debts with Great Britain. Indeed, in economic terms, the effects of adopting the principles of liberalism in the British tradition were clearly observable, as, in contrast to other aspects of life in Central America, all of the most powerful social groups were economic liberals.[23] Consequently, changes in agricultural legislation, land access, and crop yields throughout the nineteenth century can be understood just by looking at the impacts of the key tenets of liberal economic thought.[24]

The Central American economy, then, drew impetus from industrial Great Britain, which set up a network of mini ports in the Pacific, financed transportation and production, and provided manufacturing infrastructure for the region—all the while, of course, setting the terms on which trade took place.[25] The import trade was almost completely controlled by German

---

cotidiana en la Costa Rica del siglo XIX (San José: EUCR, 1997), 34–42. Esteban Rodríguez Dobles, "Reconsiderando el Período Liberal: Mentalidad y Sociabilidad. Propuesta teórica para un estudio de las sociedades de creencias católicas y sus conflictividades ante la modernidad en Costa Rica, 1870–1935," *Revista Estudios* 22 (2009 [accessed June 3, 2012]: available at: http://estudiosgenerales. ucr.ac.cr/estudios/no22/papers/isec2.html. Similarly, neither animism nor pantheism lost much of their cultural influence among indigenous groups. Rafael Cuevas Molina, *Identidad y Cultura en Centroamérica: Nación, Integración y Globalización a Principios Del Siglo XXI* (San José: EUCR, 2006), 1–64.

21 These achievements were won extremely slowly and gradually, in a process that continued virtually into the early years of the twentieth century. For further reading, see Mario Ramírez Boza and Manuel Solís Avendaño, "El desarrollo capitalista en la industria costarricense (1850–1930)" (Undergraduate Thesis in Sociology, University of Costa Rica, 1979).

22 Jordana Dym, "Villes et frontières: définir un territoire souverain pour la Fédération de L'Amérique centrale, 1821–1843," in *Les empires atlantiques. Des lumières au libéralisme (1763–1865)*, eds. Federica Morelli, Clément Thibaud and Geneviève Verdo (Rennes: Rennes University Press, 2009), 159–182.

23 Lowell Gudmundson Kristjanson, "Sociedad y Política (1840–1870)," in *Historia general de Centroamérica. De la Ilustración al liberalismo*, ed. Pérez Brignoli (Madrid: FLACSO-Sociedades Estatales Quinto Centenario-Ediciones Siruela, 1993), Vol. III, 212.

24 Gudmundson Kristjanson, "Sociedad y Política (1840–1870)," 212. José Antonio Salas, "La privatización de los baldíos nacionales en Costa Rica durante el siglo XIX. Legislación y procedimientos utilizados para su adjudicación," *Revista de Historia* 15 (1987): 63–118. Molina Jiménez, *La alborada del capitalismo agrario en Costa Rica* (San José: EUCR, 1988).

25 Molina Jiménez, *La alborada del capitalismo agrario*, 46–54.

merchants, very often acting as representatives for British trading houses.[26] Nonetheless, the fortunes of each of the Central American republics were very different. [27] Costa Rica managed to carve out a place in the international market solely on the basis of coffee exports. Guatemala and El Salvador enjoyed a limited resurgence from trading in crops strongly associated with the colonial period, as well as a minor boon when they too began producing coffee. Meanwhile, Honduras and Nicaragua did not become directly integrated into the global market at all, their experience being marked instead by regional isolation and the persistence of archaic structures.[28] Common to all five was the emergence of small, hegemonic groups and, consequently, the marginalization of the greater part of society. Each country sought to encourage foreign immigration, mainly from Europe and the United States, to mitigate structural deficiencies such as a lack of capital and skilled labor.[29] At this time, the region's biggest trading centers were the capital cities and major ports.[30] These were also, incidentally, the first places to acquire Masonic lodges, due to the large influx of immigrants who introduced new social practices and thus contributed to the expansion of the public sphere, as appears to have happened elsewhere in Latin America as well.[31] Among these practices were modern models of social

26   Clotilde Obregón Quesada, "Inicio del comercio británico en Costa Rica," *Revista de Ciencias Sociales* 24 (1982): 59–69. Rodrigo Quesada, "América Central y Gran Bretaña: la composición del comercio exterior (1851–1915)," *Anuario de Estudios Centroamericanos* 11, No. 2 (1985): 77–92. Robert A. Naylor, *Influencia británica en el comercio centroamericano durante las primeras décadas de la Independencia (1821–1851)* (Antigua: CIRMA, 1988).

27   Héctor Lindo Fuentes, *La Economía de El Salvador en el Siglo XIX* (San Salvador: CONCULTURA: Dirección de Publicaciones e Impresos, 2002), 213–252. Steven Topik, "Coffee anyone? Recent Research on Latin American Coffee Societies," *The Hispanic American Historical Review* 80, No. 2 (2000): 225–266. Cardoso and Pérez Brignoli, *Centroamérica y la economía occidental (1520–1930)*, 149–180. Gudmundson Kristjanson and Lindo Fuentes, *Central America, 1821–1871: Liberalism Before Liberal Reform* (Alabama: The University of Alabama Press, 1995). Robert Williams, *States and Social Evolution: Coffee and the Rise of National Governments in Central America* (Chapel Hill N.C.: The University of North Carolina Press, 1994).

28   Nicaragua saw the development of the great cattle ranches, but these barely met the needs of a dwindling domestic market, whereas mining became the main economic activity in Honduras.

29   Eugenio Herrera Balharry, *Los alemanes y el Estado cafetalero* (San José: UNED, 1988). Regina Wagner, *Los alemanes en Guatemala, 1828–1944* (Guatemala: Editorial IDEA, 1991). Anita Gregorio Murchie, *Imported Spices: A Study of Anglo-American Settlers in Costa Rica 1821–1900* (San José: Departamento de Publicaciones del Ministerio de Cultura, Juventud y Deportes, 1981). Rita Bariatti Lussetti, *Italianos en América Central. De Cristóbal Colón a la Segunda Posguerra* (San José: Editorial Alma Máter, 2011). Giselle Marín Araya, "Inmigrantes españoles en la ciudad de San José, 1850–1930" (Master's Thesis in History, University of Costa Rica, 2000).

30   It is worth noting here that port cities were also critical to the expansion of Freemasonry at a global level. For further reading, see the discussion relating to Spain, Great Britain, Costa Rica, France, the USA, Sweden, and China, among others, in the book edited by Cécile Révauger and Saunier, *La Franc-Maçonnerie dans les ports* (Bordeaux: Bordeaux University Press, 2012).

31   François-Xavier Guerra and Annick Lempériére, *Los espacio públicos en Iberoamérica. Ambigüe-*

interaction, including Freemasonry.

The economic context of this period is important for understanding the establishment and development of Central American Freemasonry for a number of reasons. First, many of the Order's leaders were drawn from the ranks of the coffee barons, who also dominated the political landscape in Central America. Although they represented only a small proportion of Freemasons region-wide, their actions both within and beyond the lodge made them key figures in this process. Second, most Masons at the time belonged to the urban middle classes that had grown up on the back of the expansion of the coffee trade. Foreign nationals, in particular, played a crucial role in bolstering Freemasonry in the region.

Finally, the process of nation-state building that continued throughout the nineteenth century was marked by the introduction of European-style institutions, the adoption of ideals associated with liberalism and the Enlightenment after the French model,[32] and, in Costa Rica's case, the promotion of new electoral practices.[33] In this process, the various elites that held civil power in Central American society were ever conscious of the need for the state to maintain its ties to the Catholic Church.[34] As a result, from a very early stage, the Central American states took on a denominational character,[35] often aligning themselves with the policies and interests of the Vatican.[36] During this period, as was the case in the rest of Latin America,[37] the Central American nations were on their way to becoming exclusionary and unequal, with the in-

---

dades y problemas. Siglos XVIII–XIX (Mexico City: FCE and CEMCA, 1998), 27–53.

32 Gudmundson Kristjanson, "Sociedad y Política (1840–1870)," 203–256. Obregón Quesada, *El proceso electoral y el Poder Ejecutivo en Costa Rica* (San José: EUCR, 2000). María de los Ángeles Palacios Robles, "La formación del ciudadano costarricense de 1821–1886," *Cuadernos para la Ciudadanía* 3 (San José: EUCR, 2005), 27–32.

33 Hugo Vargas González, "Procesos electorales y luchas de poder en Costa Rica. Estudio sobre el origen del sistema de partidos (1821–1902)" (Undergraduate Thesis in History, University of Costa Rica, 1996).

34 Dagoberto Campos Salas, *Relaciones Iglesia-Estado en Costa Rica. Estudio Histórico-Jurídico* (San José: Editorial Guayacán, 2000), 42–88.

35 One might add that Costa Rica remains a Catholic state to this day (2013).

36 Anthony Gill, *Rendering unto Caesar: The Catholic Church and the State in Latin America* (Chicago: The University of Chicago Press, 1998), 17–46. Miguel Picado Gatgens, "Los concordatos celebrados entre los países de Centro América y la Santa Sede durante el siglo XIX," *Revista de Historia* 28 (1993): 207–232. *Ricardo Bendaña Perdomo, La Iglesia en Guatemala. Síntesis histórica del catolicismo* (Guatemala: Artemis Edinter, 1996). Luis Ernesto Ayala Benítez, *La Iglesia y la independencia política de Centro América: "El caso de El Estado de El Salvador" (1808–1833)* (Rome: Gregorian & Biblical Bookshop, 2007). Campos Salas: *Relaciones Iglesia-Estado*, 42–88. José Aurelio Sandí Morales, "La Relación Estado e Iglesia católica en Costa Rica 1850–1920; en los procesos de Control del Espacio Geográfico y la Creación de un Modelo de costarricense" (Master's Thesis in History, National University of Costa Rica, 2009).

37 E. Bradford Burns, *La Miseria Del Progreso: América Latina en El Siglo XIX*, trans. Carlos L. Castro Dixon (Panama: EUPAN, 1986).

terests of the elite being pursued to the detriment of the majority of society. At the same time, they were studiously fabricating myths and idealizations intended to conceal the wretched realities of life that, in many cases, have persisted to the present day.

The first attempt at building a modern political system was the Federal Republic of Central America (1824–1839), which took "republic," "democracy," "homeland," and "citizens" as its watchwords. However, due to the region's cultural diversity and the imposition of various parochial interests, modern innovations were overpowered by the vestiges of the colonial era. As a result, there was a drive to expand sovereignty at the expense of the construction of a Central American nation-state.[38] Following the dissolution of the union, the five states gradually transformed into republics,[39] although this by no means signified that modern political projects were being consolidated. In the years between 1840 and 1865, there was in Central America an idealization of the nation-state and a will to impose it, as well as efforts to centralize power and resources, obstructing the right to development at local and regional levels. The result was a series of centralizing dictatorships imposed by *caudillos* who were the chief beneficiaries of the new agro-export economies. Traditional forms of organization, such as the municipalities,[40] survived, and "equal citizenship" did not apply to everyone, and especially not to indigenous groups. An unrelenting stream of coups d'état, peasant uprisings, and ethnic conflicts would follow in the years to come.[41]

By the middle of the 1860s, then, the Central American states had begun to modernize, under the very strong influence of the Church. This had an effect on the formation and development of Freemasonry in the region. Generally speaking, the main effects of modernity were felt in the cities, which tended towards Europeanization, acquiring a more cosmopolitan and progressive outlook that created a supportive environment for the first Masonic lodges in Central America.

---

38 Yolanda Dachner T., "Centroamerica: una nación antigua en la modernidad republican," *Anuario de Estudios Centroamericanos* 24, no. 1–2 (1998): 7–20.

39 Guatemala in 1847, Costa Rica in 1848, Nicaragua in 1854, El Salvador in 1859, and Honduras in 1865.

40 Ileana Muñoz García offers an interesting discussion of this topic with regard to Costa Rica, in *Educación y régimen municipal en Costa Rica 1821–1882* (San José: EUCR, 2002).

41 Noelle Demyk, "Los territorios del Estado-Nación en América Central: Una problemática regional," Gudmundson Kristjanson, "Señores y campesinos en la formación de la Centroamérica Moderna: La tesis de Barrington Morre y la historia centroamericana," and Arturo Taracena Arriola, "Nación y república en Centroamérica (1821–1865)," in *Identidades nacionales y estado moderno en Centroamérica*, eds. Taracena Arriola and Jean Piel (San José: UCR-CEMCA-FLACSO, 1995), 13–62.

The First Period of the Central American Masonic Project: Under the Guidance of Father Francisco Calvo (1865–1876)

This was the period of the Central American Masonic project led by Catholic priest Francisco Calvo. It began with the foundation of the *Caridad* Lodge in the city of San José in 1865,[42] and ended with Calvo's renunciation of Freemasonry and the closure of all of the Central American lodges in 1876. Ten Masonic lodges were established in Costa Rica during these years, two in Guatemala,[43] and one in El Salvador,[44] all following the *Ancient and Accepted Scottish Rite*. They were sponsored by two grand lodges, the Gran Oriente y Supremo Consejo Neo-Granadino (*GOSCNG*) in Cartagena, Colombia[45] and the Gran Logia de Colón (*GLC*), based in Havana, Cuba,[46] until the foundation of the Gran Oriente y Supremo Consejo Centro Americano *(GOSCCA)* in San José, Costa Rica, in 1871. The Central American lodges also continually sought out the support and governance of the United *Grand Lodge* of England. After the *GOSCCA*

---

42 This lodge was sponsored by the *GOSCNG* in Cartagena, Colombia. Its charter arrived on June 28, 1865 and it was designated as Lodge Number 26. The lodge followed the guidance of reference books brought to Costa Rica from Peru by Spanish architect José Quirce Filguera. Later, in 1871, Freemasons in Central America began to use the *Manual de Masonería: El Tejador de los Ritos Antiguo, Escocés, Francés y de Adopción* by the Franco-Cuban writer Andrés Cassard. Quirce Filguera was initiated as a Freemason in 1861 in Peru, where he became acquainted with Francisco Calvo. AGLCR, *Registro Oficial Masónico del Gran Oriente Neogranadino* (Cartagena, Colombia) 28 (August 1, 1865): 257. ASCC33, *Registro Masónico del GOSCCA* (Guatemala City, 1889–1899), No.1, Folio 1. Obregón Loría, *José Quirce Filguera, fundador de la masonería en la República de Guatemala* (San José: Imprenta Tormo, 1951), 6–7. Obregón Loría and Bowden, *La masonería en Costa Rica* (San José: Trejos Hermanos, 1938), Vol. I, 5–14. Guzmán-Stein, "Andrés Cassard y su vida en Nueva York. Tres nuevas facetas de un masón polifacético," in *La Masonería Española: Represión y Exilios*, ed. Ferrer Benimeli (Zaragoza: CEHME, 2011), Vol. I, 509–544.

43 Martínez Esquivel, "Un estudio comparado del establecimiento de logias masónicas en Costa Rica y Guatemala (1865–1903)," *Número especial de Diálogos 9° Congreso de Historia Centroamericano* (2008 [accessed August 5, 2012]): available at: http://historia.fcs.ucr.ac.cr/articulos/2008/especial2008/articulos/07-regional/100.pdf.

44 Roberto Armando Valdés Valle, "Origen, miembros y primeras acciones de la masonería en El Salvador (1871–1872)," *REHMLAC* 1, No. 1 (May–November 2009 [accessed June 15, 2012]): available at: https://revistas.ucr.ac.cr/index.php/rehmlac/article/view/6861/6548.

45 The *GOSCNG* was founded on June 19, 1833. It was recognized in 1851 by the *Grand Orient de France*; in 1872 by The Supreme Council, Ancient and Accepted Scottish Rite, Northern Jurisdiction of the United States of America; and in 1875 by the First Universal Congress of the Confederation of Supreme Councils held in Lausanne, Switzerland. Today, this Grand Orient is known as the Supreme Council of the 33rd Degree for Colombia, and its website can be found at: *http://glcentralcolombia.org/supremo_consejo33.htm*. Gilberto Loaiza Cano, *Sociabilidad, política y religión en la definición de la nación (Colombia, 1820–1886)* (Bogota: Externado University of Colombia, 2011), 135–212.

46 Eduardo Torres Cuevas, "Masonerías en Cuba durante el siglo XIX," *REHMLAC* 3, No. 2 (December 2011–April 2012 [accessed May 3, 2012]): available at: https://revistas.ucr.ac.cr/index.php/rehmlac/article/view/6576/6267.

was formed, Costa Rica's Freemasons were no longer dependent on foreign grand lodges, and they assumed the authority (jurisdiction) to direct and manage all Masonic activity in Central America from San José. Calvo was appointed Grand Master.[47]

Modernity had gained a firmer foothold in Costa Rica, offering Freemasonry a more promising chance of success. However, whenever a dictator seized power, civil liberties were abolished and Masonic activity ground to a halt. In Guatemala and El Salvador, radical liberalism alternated with military authoritarianism, and so Freemasonry's advance was sporadic. As for Nicaragua and Honduras, both countries experienced dictatorial governments imposed after the failure of liberal impulses that were stifled by foreign intervention. As a result, Freemasonry only really began to develop toward the end of the nineteenth century, with the consolidation of the enclave economies of which these countries were a part.[48]

The next section of the paper will explore three aspects: the factors that contributed to the establishment of Freemasonry, the anti-Masonic response of the Catholic Church in Central America, and the political value of Freemasonry in the wake of the multiple coups d'état that took place in the region between 1870 and 1871.

Why Did Freemasonry Only Begin to Develop in Central America Around 1865?

This is an interesting question, because in all other parts of Latin America, some form of Masonic activity had been present since the transition to independence. The relatively late development of Freemasonry in Central America can be explained by the slow pace at which modernity rolled out over the region, which held back the onset of favorable contextual conditions for the commencement of a Masonic project until this moment. Even so, it would be another six years (1871) before a Central American Masonic lodge was established outside of Costa Rica (in El Salvador).[49] What was it about Costa Rica that allowed it to take the lead in the development of Freemasonry in Central America? The answer to this question can be distilled into five factors.

First, the growth and expansion of the University of Santo Tomás

---

47 Obregón Loría and George Bowden, *La Masonería en Costa Rica* (San José: Trejos Hermanos, 1938), Vol. II, 4.

48 James Mahoney, *The Legacies of Liberalism: Path Dependence and Political Regimes in Central America* (Baltimore: The John Hopkins University Press, 2001), 111–235.

49 Although we know that a Masonic lodge was set up in Guatemala City in 1870, sponsored by the *GLC*, it lasted only a few months and was not part of Calvo's project. In fact, all that has been determined about this lodge is that it was founded by a group of Spanish merchants, Eleázaro Asturias Catalán, Francisco C. Castañeda and Juan F. Rodríguez C, and that it was located at number 4, Callejón Manchen. Library of the *Grand Lodge of Cuba, Constitution of the Supreme Council of Colón and its Subordinate Bodies. Rito Escocés Antiguo y Aceptado* (Havana: Imprenta El Siglo XX, 1922), 22.

is significant, as throughout the 1860s[50] its rectors were all Freemasons who had been initiated abroad before 1865, during a time when a number of Costa Rican politicians and intellectuals had been forced to leave the country after the 1859 coup d'état.[51] Some later returned as initiated Freemasons, and this had a significant effect on the development of the Masonic movement, because they found in Freemasonry the civilizing discourse of a culture based on sociability and debate, a discourse that matched their aspirations for the University.[52] We must remember that the University of Santo Tomás was created in 1843 out of an appetite for all that was liberal and learned, and it served as a place where members of Costa Rica's intellectual and political elite could meet and interact. Some were Freemasons, initiated in foreign lodges prior to 1865 and actively involved in bringing Freemasonry to Central America.[53] In addition, the dynamics of university departments were such that members could become well-versed in the tenets of rationalism and the French philosophical tradition, promoting an erudite culture centered around sociability and debate.[54] This helped usher in the necessary intellectual climate for the establishment of Freemasonry in Costa Rica—an institution offering a way to fraternize with others in an environment that encouraged new ideas.

Second, there was, throughout these years, a developing national culture of associations with social dynamics based on elected membership.[55] The electoral practices of the Masonic lodg-

50 Obregón Loría, *Los rectores de la Universidad de Santo Tomás de Costa Rica* (San José: EUCR, 1955).

51 Carmen Fallas Santana, "La voluntad de la Nación y la regeneración política: Los pronunciamientos militares de 1859, 1868 y 1870 en Costa Rica," *Diálogos Revista Electrónica de Historia* 9, No. 2 (August 2008–February 2009 [consulted February 14, 2010]): available at: http://historia.fcs.ucr.ac.cr/articulos/2008/vol2/03carmenfallaspronunciamientos.pdf. Morales García, *Cultura oligárquica y nueva intelectualidad*, 72–76.

52 Years later, one of these returnees, Lorenzo Montúfar y Rivera, wrote: "... In Costa Rica there was an interesting circumstance that cast a great deal of light on religious, political, and social questions. Some of those individuals expelled from the country after the fall of Juan Rafael Mora made their way to various countries across the Americas, where they joined Masonic lodges of all the different rites, particularly the ancient and accepted Scottish rite. On their return to Costa Rica, they opened lodges in that country." Lorenzo Montúfar y Rivera, *Memorias autografiadas* (San José: Lil S.A., 1988), 239.

53 Archives of the Grand Lodge of Costa Rica (AGLCR), *Historic Records* (1865–1899). Luis Felipe González Flores, *Evolución de la instrucción pública en Costa Rica* (San José: ECR, 1978), 293–318 y 424–430. González Flores, *Historia de la influencia extranjera en el desenvolvimiento educacional y científico de Costa Rica* (San José: ECR, 1976). Paulino González Villalobos, *La Universidad de Santo Tomás* (San José: EUCR, 1989), 161–164. Miguel Guzmán-Stein, "Masones españoles en Costa Rica: el Krausismo y la Institución Libre de Enseñanza en la formación y desarrollo de la Democracia Liberal Costarricense," in *Masonería Española y América*, ed. Ferrer Benimeli (Zaragoza: CEHME, 1993), Vol. I, 449–470.

54 Obregón Loría, Abelardo Bonilla and Enrique Macaya, "Significación intelectual de la Universidad de Santo Tomás en la Costa Rica del siglo XIX," *Revista de Filosofía* 3, No. 9 (January–June 1961): 79–93.

55 Vargas González, "Procesos electorales y luchas de poder en Costa Rica," 122–130.

es were no different from those of other organizations, but were in fact perfectly consistent with what other groups were doing. They did not, then, stand out as exceptional for that time. Thus, the establishment of Freemasonry was perfectly in keeping with the prevailing climate of ideas, and with the kinds of social organization typical of the nineteenth century, especially in its latter third.[56]

With this new culture, there was a gradual shift toward greater social freedoms (the third factor) on the part of the new governments, while, at the same time, there were attempts to decentralize some of the political power held by the executive.[57] These changes occurred primarily during the second presidency of José María Castro Madriz (1866–1868), a Freemason. This administration, in fact, made significant moves to advance the cause of social liberty,[58] which laid the foundations for the modern public sphere in civil society and encouraged members of various political and intellectual networks to join an organization like the

Freemasons. Freemasonry, therefore, was able to establish itself as a space of ideological diversity at a very important moment in the expansion of the public sphere in Costa Rica. Among these new social liberties was freedom of association, and in this respect Freemasonry was not unusual for the time, but rather formed part of a tapestry of social organizations that displayed significant similarities in this period.[59]

Another social freedom worth considering is freedom of worship, which started to become institutionalized in Costa Rica from the middle of the nineteenth century.[60] As has been discussed, economic growth fueled by coffee exports drove up immigration, and many of the newcomers came from non-Catholic religious backgrounds. Freedom of worship was crucial for the Masonic movement, not because Freemasonry was itself a religion, but because its ecumenical character and rhetoric of religious tolerance meant that Central American Catholics now had the opportunity to socialize with people from all over the world and many

---

56 Morales García, *Cultura oligárquica y nueva intelectualidad*, 36–43.

57 David Díaz Arias, "Construcción de un estado moderno: política, estado e identidad nacional en Costa Rica," *Cuaderno de Historia de las Instituciones de Costa Rica* 18 (San José: EUCR, 2005), 34–44.

58 Cleto González Víquez, *Obras históricas* (San José: EUCR, 1973), 273. Francisco Montero Barrantes, *Compendio de Historia de Costa Rica* (San José: Librería Moderna de Antonio Font, 1896), 69

59 In relation to the advocacy of social freedoms in Costa Rica, *La Gaceta Oficial* published a propaganda piece in July 1865, entitled "Freedom of Association." This article, which appeared in issue number 325, could not be consulted as no copies could be traced. In the newspaper archives of the National Library I was informed that this is one of the issues that is missing from the library's collection. Cited in Bernardo Villalobos Vega, *La mesocracia en Costa Rica* (San José: ECR, 1986), 46. In fact, by this time Castro had already set up the "Club Nacional," founded on April 16 of that year (1865). Adolfo Blen, *El Periodismo en Costa Rica* (San José: ECR, 1983), 152.

60 Daniel Isaac Montero Segura, "La evolución de la tolerancia religiosa en Costa Rica durante los siglos XIX y XX" (Undergraduate Thesis in History, University of Costa Rica, 1978), 86–88.

different religious backgrounds. Freemasonry was therefore one of the first arenas in Central America to facilitate this kind of interaction. To illustrate, a glance at the social composition of the Masonic lodge reveals members from a range of religious backgrounds, including Catholics (around 80 percent),[61] Anglicans, Quakers, Evangelicals, Jews (both Sephardi and Ashkenazi), some of the earliest Deists, freethinkers, and rationalists, and possibly even some of Central America's first Atheists and Spiritualists.[62]

Furthermore, between 1865 and 1868 there were twenty-six different newspapers in publication,[63] and while none of these catered specifically to Masonic interests, as was the case elsewhere,[64] 14 percent (thirty-two out of 239) of Freemasons had some kind of connection to the press, whether they were directors, editors, or had simply published a poem.[65] Thus, the newspaper as a vehicle for fostering public debate, and the Masonic lodge as a space of free association, both of which provided a platform for free expression, were developing at a time when the public sphere was expanding. In other words, the establishment of Freemasonry was the product of a key moment in the advancement of various civil liberties in Costa Rican society.

This conjecture holds up to further analysis in that it allows us to identify an interesting circumstance in the Costa Rican political scene at that time, which had a positive effect on Freemasonry's development. During the period between 1865 and 1868, when the movement was becoming established, the members of the first Masonic lodge (*Caridad*) included the President of Costa Rica, the President of Congress, the President of the Supreme Court of Justice, one of two government ministers, between 14 and 42 percent of par-

61   Martínez Esquivel, "Composición socio-ocupacional de los masones del siglo XIX," *Diálogos Revista Electrónica de Historia* 8, No. 2 (August 2007–February 2008 [consulted January 11, 2013]): available at: http://historia.fcs.ucr.ac.cr/articulos/2007/vol2/6vol8n2martinez.pdf.

62   AGLCR, *Historic Records* (1865–1899). Archives of the Supreme Council of Central America of the 33rd Degree of Guatemala (ASCCG33), *Masonic Records of the GOSCCA* (Guatemala City, 1889–1899). Valdés Valle, "Masones, Liberales y Ultramontanos salvadoreños: Debate político y constitucional en algunas publicaciones impresas, durante la etapa final del proceso de secularización del Estado salvadoreño (1885–1886)" (Doctoral Dissertation in Ibero-American Philosophy, José Simeón Cañas Central American University, 2010 [accessed June 2, 2012]): available at: http://uca.edu.sv/filosofia/admin/files/1260825405.pdf. Martínez Esquivel, "Masones y Masonería en la Costa Rica de los Albores de la Modernidad (1865–1899)" (Master's Thesis in History, University of Costa Rica, 2012), 214–237.

63   Patricia Vega Jiménez, "El mundo impreso se consolida. Análisis de los periódicos costarricenses (1851–1870)," *Revista de Ciencias Sociales* 70 (1995): 85.

64   See, for example, Janet Iglesias Cruz and Javiher Gutiérrez Forte's article on the Cuban experience, "Las elecciones de 1908: los masones y sus logias en la política de los primeros años de la República Cubana," *200 años de Iberoamérica (1810–2010). Congreso Internacional* [accessed March 20, 2012]: http://halshs.archives-ouvertes.fr/docs/00/52/92/78/PDF/AT4_Gutierrez-Iglesias.pdf.

65   Valdés Valle, "Masones, Liberales y Ultramontanos salvadoreños," 25–33. Martínez Esquivel, "Masones y Masonería," 255–264.

liamentary representatives, three of six judges, the Rector of the University of Santo Tomás and the entire Government Council.[66]

As our fourth relevant factor, we must consider the number of foreign nationals who had arrived in Costa Rica. Immigrants from Spain, France, Germany, and Great Britain had a transformative effect on the social dynamics of the capital, San José. The 1864 census indicates that there were 207 Europeans living in the city.[67] This point is worth highlighting, because Europeans in Costa Rica followed their own diverse cultural practices, consumption patterns, forms of association, and religious beliefs, but if there was one thing that many of them had in common, it was the fact that they were active in the Masonic lodges. Freemasonry, therefore, served as a vehicle for social integration, sociability, and identity among foreign nationals, who played a crucial role in its evolution in Central America.

In fact, between the years 1865 and 1876, around 60 percent of all Freemasons in Central America were for-eign nationals.[68] Just like marriage or trading networks, the opportunity to mix freely with others that the lodges offered opened up another avenue for integrating into Costa Rican society. With regard to Freemasonry in Central America, in the first three years alone, 38 percent of members were European immigrants.[69] The large numbers of foreign nationals who had settled in Central America, among whom were Masons or, at the very least, individuals familiar with this kind of organization, therefore meant that the region offered fertile ground for the growth of the Masonic movement.

We might also add that when Central America's first Masonic lodge—Caridad—was formed, the twelve founding members comprised three Costa Ricans and nine foreign nationals: two Spaniards, two Frenchmen, two Germans, two Britons, and one Chilean. Of those nine, five were merchants and two teachers. All twelve founding members of this lodge are known to have become Freemasons prior to 1865.[70] Similarly, of the six founding members of El Salvador's first Masonic

---

66 AGLCR, *Historic Records* (1865–1899). Luis Dobles Segreda, "Memorias ministeriales," in *Índice bibliográfico de Costa Rica* (San José: Imprenta Lehmann, 1936), Vol. 5, 511–540. Obregón Loría, *El Poder Legislativo en Costa Rica. Segunda Edición Reformada* (San José: Impresión Comercial S.A., 1995), 314–404. Jorge Sáenz Carbonell y Mauricio Masís Pinto, *Historia de la Corte Suprema de Justicia de Costa Rica. 180 Aniversario 1826–2006* (San José: Editorama, 2006), 111–189. Martínez Esquivel, "Masones y su participación política en Costa Rica (1865–1899)," *Número especial de Diálogos 9° Congreso de Historia Centroamericano* (2008 [accessed August 5, 2012]): available at: http://historia.fcs.ucr.ac.cr/articulos/2008/especial2008/articulos/06-politica/76.pdf.

67 *General Census of the Republic of Costa Rica. November 27, 1864* (San José: Tipografía Nacional, 1868 [consulted March 6, 2012]): available at: http://ccp.ucr.ac.cr/bvp/censos/1864/1864c03-cr.pdf.

68 AGLCR, *Historic Records* (1865–1899). ASCC33, *Masonic Records of the GOSCCA* (Guatemala City, 1889–1899).

69 Martínez Esquivel, "Masones y Masonería," 178–188.

70 Martínez Esquivel, "Masones y Masonería," 125–126.

lodge (*Progreso*),[71] established in 1871, half were foreign nationals: one Spanish, one French (both merchants), and one Cuban.[72] In Guatemala's case, the first lodge (Hiram)[73] was founded in 1873 by twelve foreign nationals: six Spaniards, one German, one Frenchman, one Irishman, an Italian, a Mexican, and a Peruvian. All, incidentally, were merchants or businessmen.[74] We can therefore see that, from a very early stage of Masonic activity in Central America, the involvement of foreign nationals was of paramount importance.

The fifth and final factor was the ideological transformation that occurred within the Costa Rican Catholic Church in this period,[75] which produced a particular kind of priest and, consequently, a particular kind of parishioner, which in this author's opinion also aided the development of Freemasonry. Indeed, none of the Church's institutions at this time could be regarded

as ultraconservative and diametrically opposed to Freemasonry. The Costa Rican Church was in fact governed by a hierarchy of leaders who were strongly influenced by modern ideas, and who therefore agreed in many respects with the ideals and practices of the Masonic lodge. By the 1860s, members of the Church hierarchy also tended to be members of the political and intellectual elites. Among them was none other than the leader and most prominent figure in nineteenth-century Central American Freemasonry, the priest Francisco Calvo.

Similarly, we also find during this period a cluster of priests who were supportive of secular freedoms (such as freedom of thought, expression, and the press), and who were often more concerned with civil interests than those of the Church, or else who maintained close connections with politicians and intellectuals with liberal sympathies.[76] As well as Calvo, other priests were

---

71   This lodge was sponsored by the *GOSCCA* based in San José, Costa Rica. It was opened on September 30, 1871, as Lodge Number 5. Valdés Valle, "Origen, miembros y primeras acciones," 155–171.

72   Valdés Valle, "Masones, Liberales y Ultramontanos salvadoreños," 36.

73   Again, this lodge was sponsored by San José's *GOSCCA*. It was opened on June 17, 1873 and assigned the number 11. Martínez Esquivel, "Un estudio comparado," 2358–2382.

74   Obregón Loría, *José Quirce Filguera*, 12.

75   On this topic, Armas Asin argues that this transformation was part of a set of wider trends at work in Latin America, and that the Catholic Church was endeavoring to adapt and find its place within a society built upon modernity's ideals. We see a number of examples of this in Costa Rica at this time: the country's first political party was Catholic and there was also a Catholic press and a variety of Catholic clubs. The Church's veneration of the Los Angeles Virgin as the national symbol par excellence also dates back to this period. Armas Asin, "Radicalismo liberal," 1–16. Gil Zúñiga, *El culto a la Virgen de los Ángeles*, 71–108. Rodríguez Dobles, "Reconsiderando el Período Liberal: Mentalidad y Sociabilidad," 33–48. Esteban Sánchez Solano, "Los círculos y clubes católicos del Partido Unión Católica (1890-1894)," *Revista Estudios* 22 (2009 [accessed June 3, 2012]): available at: http://estudiosgenerales.ucr.ac.cr/estudios/no22/papers/isec3.html.

76   The relative weakness of the Church's institutions, which had few resources, a tendency to sidestep diocesan authority, and a secular clergy that was very much aligned with civil society, meant that the first few decades after independence were fairly uneventful in terms of relations between the

also initiated as Freemasons. Calvo also founded the first mutual societies for craftsmen, and many other priests joined these associations.[77] A great many members of the clergy held positions in the Constituent Assemblies and the Congresses of the Republic.[78] Most were not involved in Freemasonry at all, but their sympathy with similar political ideals, or their connections to those who espoused those ideals, Masons or otherwise, speaks to the fact that in certain circles within the Catholic Church in Costa Rica, progressive aspirations were not hard to find.

All of these features were conducive to the development of Freemasonry, in the sense that, in one way or another, they brought about a congenial socio-political climate that softened the impact of the papal sentence against the Masonic lodges on popular perception. It cannot be said that all of those within the Costa Rican Catholic Church proved supportive of Masonic activity,[79] as there was also an antiliberal wing among the clergy,[80] which in due course turned out to be anti-Masonry as well.

Church and the state. This facilitated the consolidation of the state and a coalescence of benign political values that were highly supportive of civil freedoms. The Diocese, then, was a late arrival on the political, ideological, and social scene, the contours of which had been determined some time before and in which religion had been almost entirely supplanted by an Enlightenment-inspired liberalism as the basis for national spiritual identity—albeit with a Christian grounding and praxis that were not incompatible with the nation-state project. Guzmán-Stein, "La 'Cuestión Confirma' y la represión ideológica: El debate entre el clero reaccionario, el clero liberal y masón y la autoridad vaticana en Costa Rica (1870–1880)" (paper delivered at the *First International Symposium on the History of Freemasonry in Latin America and the Caribbean*, Havana, December 5–8, 2007). Carmela Velázquez Bonilla, "La educación formal del clero secular en la Diócesis de Nicaragua y Costa Rica," *Número especial de Diálogos 9° Congreso de Historia Centroamericano* (2008 [accessed November 19, 2012]): available at: http://historia.fcs.ucr.ac.cr/articulos/2008/especial2008/articulos/03-Colonial/31.pdf.

77   Mario Oliva Medina, *Artesanos y obreros costarricenses 1880–1914* (San José: EUNED, 2006), 65–86.

78   Claudio Vargas Arias, *El Liberalismo, la Iglesia y el Estado en Costa Rica* (San José: Editorial Guayacán, 1990), 41–46.

79   In fact, the majority of Masonic lodges with anticlerical tendencies are rooted in the Latin tradition, including those in Mexico, Bogotá (Colombia), Uruguay, and Cuba. Freemasons in Cuba, for example, adopted the tripartite motto of the French revolution—"Liberty, Equality, Fraternity"—in preference to the three theological virtues of Christianity—"Faith, Hope, and Charity" (incidentally, these were also the names of the first three Central American lodges). Later, members in Republican Cuba switched to the motto of the Anglo-Saxon Masons, "Brotherly Love, Relief, and Truth." It is worth adding here that "Liberty, Equality, Fraternity" was not used by the Masonic movement until the time of the Third French Republic (1870–1940). Arturo Ardao, *Racionalismo y Liberalismo en el Uruguay* (Montevideo: Publicaciones de la Universidad de Montevideo, 1962). Dominique Soucy and Delphine Sappez, "Autonomismo y masonería en Cuba," *REHMLAC* 1, No. 1 (May–November 2010 [consulted May 15, 2010]): available at: https://revistas.ucr.ac.cr/index.php/rehmlac/article/view/6858/6545.

80   The tensions between liberalism and the Catholic Church derive from the former's encouragement of certain ideals, such as rationalism and absolute freedom of conscience, which could lead people to question the Revelation and the doctrines of the faith, and, ultimately, to abandon the

However, neither this group nor the papal sentence that remained in place for almost 150 years prevented a Catholic priest from bringing Freemasonry to Central America in 1865.

In conclusion, we cannot approach the rise of Freemasonry in Central America in the same way as we would study its development in Western Europe or the United States of America, because it emerged and evolved under very different contextual conditions. As has been indicated, the various studies of eighteenth-century European Freemasonry portray it as a key driving force behind a shift in the mindsets of intellectuals and politicians, given that speculative Freemasonry came into being and developed alongside the ideals associated with modernity. In Central America, the process was quite different, as Freemasonry was a consequence rather than a catalyst of a modernity that was still taking shape.[81]

The Anti-Masonic Response of the Catholic Church in Central America

Despite the fact that the form of Freemasonry being established in Central America was based on the Anglo-Saxon tradition, the region could not escape the specter of the conflicts associated with the Latin tradition, partly because of its Catholic identity and partly as a result of the gradual process of modernization that it was undergoing. In each country, the Catholic Church took action in response to this new organization, issuing pastoral letters, publishing circulars or newspaper articles, and preaching against Freemasonry from the pulpit. This elicited an almost-immediate retaliation from the Masons, who adopted similar tactics. The important thing to note about this conflict is the fact that the subject of Freemasonry was entering the public sphere just as it was beginning to crystalize. This is significant because the Masons' arguments helped inform the moral values of both the Church and modern Central American civil society.

The first clash between the Freemasons and the local Catholic Church took place between 1865 and 1867.[82]

Church. This friction was occurring against a backdrop of secularization, with a new civic culture taking root among the population as new ideas and social institutions grew in prominence—posing a threat to the Catholic Church's traditional monopoly on ideological matters. One of the new social structures promoting liberal ideals was Freemasonry. González Ortega, *Vida cotidiana en la Costa Rica del siglo XIX*, 26–67. Morales García, *Cultura oligárquica y nueva intelectualidad*, 36–53.

81 In contrast, in other countries, such as Mexico, Freemasonry was not able to thrive until after liberal socio-political reforms were enacted. Vázquez Semadeni, "Historiografía sobre la masonería en México. Breve revision," *REHMLAC* 2, No. 1 (May– November 2010 [accessed June 15, 2012]): available at: https://revistas.ucr.ac.cr/index.php/rehmlac/article/view/6608/6297

82 Guzmán-Stein, "Masonería, Iglesia y Estado: Las relaciones entre el Poder Civil y el Poder Eclesiástico y las formas asociativas en Costa Rica (1865–1875)," *REHMLAC* 1, No. 1 (May–November 2009 [accessed June 15, 2012]): available at: https://revistas.ucr.ac.cr/index.php/rehmlac/article/view/6859/6546

The key figures in the ensuing war of words were the Bishop of the Diocese of San José, Anselmo Llorente y Lafuente (1851–1871); the priests Francisco Calvo and Carlos María Ulloa, both Masons; Domingo Rivas Salvatierra, also a priest, and a rival of Calvo and Ulloa in the Church's internal power struggles; the Auxiliary Bishop of the Archdiocese of Guatemala, Manuel Francisco Barrutia y Crocker (1867–1874); the President of Costa Rica, Worshipful Master of the Caridad Lodge and "Grand Protector of the Masonic Order," José María Castro Madriz;[83] and the Rector of the University of San Tomás and Orator of the Caridad Lodge, Guatemalan lawyer Lorenzo Montúfar y Rivera. Here is how Montúfar described the beginning of this affair:

The first Bishop of Costa Rica, Anselmo Llorente y Lafuente, was incensed by this new development (the establishment of a Masonic lodge) and fired off a pastoral letter. I was the chosen target of this letter, because I happened to be the Orator of the Caridad Lodge, and so I was quite well known. I replied and thus entered into a feud with the Bishop, for which purpose I found my newspaper, El Quincenal Josefino, to be very useful. I do not know that our success could be called joyous, but the fact remains that since that time, Freemasonry has become established in Costa Rica.[84]

In reaction to these events, from 1866 Llorente y Lafuente ordered those priests who were members of the Freemasons to publish denials of their involvement. Ulloa subsequently declared that he did not belong to the Freemasons and Calvo claimed that he had never been a member of any institution at odds with the Catholic Church and its interests.[85] Ulloa never returned to the lodge.[86]

---

83 Castro was initiated into the lodge known as *Estrella del Torquemada* in Bogotá in 1864 or 1865, during his time as Minister Plenipotentiary of Costa Rica in Colombia. Gilberto Loaiza Cano suggests that this lodge may have formed part of a Masonic network operating at a regional level. He argues that, in international relations circles toward the end of the nineteenth century, being a Freemason smoothed the way for effective connections among liberals and modernizers, since political peers would sometimes be introduced for the first time in the fraternal environment of the lodge, before being thrown together in the meeting room. For example, when Castro was first initiated, other members of *Estrella del Torquemada* included the President of Colombia, Manuel Murillo Toro, and the Minister of Foreign Affairs, Teodoro Valenzuela. Loaiza Cano, *Manuel Ancízar y su época. Biografía de un político hispanoamericano del siglo XIX* (Medellín: Fondo Editorial Universidad EAFIT, 2004), 211–292. Guzmán-Stein, "Dr. José María Castro Madriz: Masón y liberal, diputado, embajador, ministro, Presidente de la República, Presidente del Congreso, Presidente de la Corte Suprema de Justicia," in *La masonería española en la época de Sagasta (1825–1903)*, ed. Ferrer Benimeli (Zaragoza: CEHME and Fundación Práxedes Mateo-Sagasta, 2006), 954–955.

84 Montúfar y Rivera, *Memorias autografiadas*, 240.

85 Historical Archives of the Metropolitan Archdiocese of San José (AHACMSJ), Historical Catalog (Box, Volume, Folios): 48, 136 and 168, 172–173.

86 In a public letter dated August 24, 1866, Ulloa had denied that he was a Freemason, and later, on

Llorente y Lafuente then consulted with the Metropolitan Archbishop of Guatemala, Francisco de Paula García Peláez (1845–1867), as to what action should be taken in response to the establishment of Freemasonry in Costa Rica. However, due to García's death, it was Barrutia who, worried about the developing situation, raised the matter with President Castro on March 15, 1867:

> I know that I am addressing a father who is devoted to the well-being of his children; a distinguished citizen with great love for his compatriots; a President, in short, who is not only a true Catholic himself but the President of a Catholic nation ...
>
> As I understand it, Your Excellency, it is now a wholly accomplished fact that Freemasonry has taken root in this country ...
>
> (On Freemasonry) Its morality is depraved, its religion ungodly; both are condemned by God as inimical to the well-being of the people. I do not believe, therefore, that it could please the Creator of the Universe, the only one who can bestow happiness and good fortune, to deliver these blessings through channels that He has disavowed ...

(Addressing the president) ... Your Catholicism and the love you profess for your people will impel you to give careful thought to this very serious question, and this reflection will surely afford you all the necessary energy and motivation to defend, as is fitting, the cause of God and the Republic.[87]

The President, displaying his strong affinity for the Masonic value system and despite regarding the organization as exclusionary, couched his response in terms of the defense of social freedoms, arguing to the Auxiliary Bishop that Freemasonry posed no threat to right-minded values:

> On my return from Bogotá in June 1865, I found that in January of the same year a Lodge had been instituted for the purposes of fellowship and charity, subject to certain rules devised to prevent access by those lacking the requisite virtues and faculties.
>
> The honest aims of the institution to which I refer, not to mention the benevolence of its actions thus far, which, as I am given to understand, do not interfere in any way with religion nor with politics, place it above

April 2, 1867, he issued a further public statement railing against the "public gossip" that had tarred him as a member of the Order. AHACMSJ, Historical Catalog (Box, Volume, Folios): 48, 1, 136; 48, 1, 140; 168, 172–173; and 205, 1, 304–305. Obregón Loría and Bowden, *La masonería en Costa Rica*, Vol. I, 16–20.

87   Federico Góngora Herrera, *Documentos de la Masonería Centroamericana (Antigua y Aceptada). Desde el año 1824–1933* (San José: Imprenta Española, 1937), 26–29.

all reproach ...[88]

Nonetheless, Barrutia urged Llorente y Lafuente to be cautious, prompting the latter to condemn Freemasonry through two pastoral letters in 1867.[89] This censure was characterized by a number of features: (i) it was prompted by the pressures that Llorente y Lafuente was under at the time, (ii) it was delivered in accordance with instructions issued by the Vatican, (iii) it responded to a global Catholic position of condemning Freemasonry, and (iv) it elicited no known official response from the Freemasons of Costa Rica.

This first confrontation between the Freemasons and the Catholic Church came to an end when Montúfar replied to the Bishop's pastoral letters, which had also taken aim at his newspaper (*El Quincenal Josefino*). Like Castro, Montúfar invoked social rights, but his response differed from that of the President in that he went beyond the conventional arguments in defense of Freemasonry to portray it as a new moral and spiritual alternative. At first glance, he seems to have drawn a close parallel between Freemasonry and Christianity, but, in keeping with the Deist discourse popular at the time, he paid more attention to metaphysical matters than to theology. In one extract, he argues that:

The Masonic moral code is set out in those succinct principles that are instilled in every initiated member, as laws that may never be broken: Respect for God, religion, and the law. Tolerance, love, and charity toward men. Hospitality, shelter, and protection for our brothers. To work to live, study to learn, and learn to teach. To treat others as we would wish to be treated. To do no harm to anybody that we would not wish upon ourselves. These Masonic principles do nothing more than reiterate the Ten Commandments; they are nothing more than a condensed version of the moral teachings of the Gospel. To condemn an organization that professes these principles, as laws that may never be broken, would be to condemn the supreme code that God revealed to Moses on Mount Sinai; it would be to condemn the Gospel.

At the Lodge, members are taught man's duties to God, to himself, and to his fellow men. This is what they are told: What is it that man owes God? He owes Him his existence, he owes Him his being, he owes Him his

---

88   ACMG, Correspondence Series, Docket 264, Box (August 1, 1867).

89   The first dated August 20, 1867, and the second October 12 of the same year. Furthermore, it is worth mentioning that these pastoral letters were signed by Ulloa in his capacity as Llorente y Lafuente's secretary. Ulloa was initiated as a Freemason at the Caridad Lodge on June 24, 1865. The documentary evidence relating to the Caridad Lodge is incomplete, and so we do not know when his membership ceased. What we do know is that, until his death, Ulloa continued to move in the same social circles as various active Freemasons. AHACMSJ, Historical Catalog (Box, Volume, Folios): 48, 1, 141–160.

soul—that soul that is none other than the breath of God, which will return to whence it came and which gives man dominion over all the animals of creation. Belief in God is the fundamental basis for all morality, as without this belief, disorder and crime would reign over the land. Lawbreaking, homicide, and murder would lead to the complete destruction of society.[90]

As we can see, Montúfar based his defense on a characterization of Freemasonry as an organization respectful of the established social order: God-Religion-State, which also happened to conform to the teachings of the Catholic Church at the time. Furthermore, he described the fundamental principles of Freemasonry by drawing on a set of Christian values that concurred with those of the Catholic Church—showing it to be compatible with the dominant religious discourse in terms of what was considered right and true within the socially-ingrained value system of nineteenth-century Latin America.[91]

Soon after this first run-in between the Masons and the Catholic Church came a new set of struggles, this time with the state. The crises that fol-lowed for the Freemasons were precipitated by internal discord over personal and political matters, as, for example, the politicians among their number switched sides and joined coups and counter-coups, only to be reconciled and band together in a new rebellion. Personal interests were pursued at the expense of any shared ideal, alliance, or membership, and that included Freemasonry.[92]

In 1868, the year after the affair of the pastoral letters, a coup d'état in Costa Rica pitted the politicians in the Order against one another, with some being part of the government and others leading the revolt. A precedent had already been set with the very first split in a Costa Rican lodge, after a group of Masons from Caridad, unhappy with the government led by Castro, also Worshipful Master of the Lodge, left to set up a new lodge. Ultimately, some of these dissenters would go on to be involved in the coup. The 1868 coup swept Jesús Jiménez Zamora back to power, and his second presidency brought restrictions on civil liberties, including freedom of association and freedom of expression. As a result, the Masonic lodges were shut down by the military.[93]

---

90   Góngora Herrera, *Mis últimos documentos de la Masonería Centroamericana Antigua y Aceptada. Años 1809–1939* (San José: GLCR, 1940), 215.

91   John Lynch, "La Iglesia Católica en América Latina, 1830–1930," in *Historia de América Latina: Cultura y Sociedad 1830–1930*, ed. Leslie Bethell, trans. Jordi Beltrán and Angels Sola (Barcelona: Crítica, 1992), 65–122.

92   Guzmán-Stein, "Masonería, Iglesia y Estado," 100–134. Valdés Valle, "Masones, Liberales y Ultramontanos salvadoreños," 24–98. Martínez Esquivel, "Masones y su participación política en Costa Rica," 1816–1848.

93   Obregón Loría, *Hechos militares y políticos* (Alajuela: Imprenta Nacional, 1981), 152–158. Obregón

Masonic activity resumed in Costa Rica after the coup d'état of April 27, 1870,[94] which led to the restoration of civil freedoms.[95] The perpetrators and the victims of the 1868 coup worked together to aid Freemasonry's recovery. Some of them had also been involved in the latest uprising, this time on the same side and sometimes working together. The rebels named doctor and Mason Bruno Carranza Ramírez temporary President of Costa Rica, but it was clear that the man who really held the power was General Tomás Guardia Gutiérrez,[96] who would be initiated as a Freemason in 1873. The majority of the new government were members of the Caridad Lodge.

With the restitution of Freemasonry in Costa Rica and the formation of the *GOSCCA,* Calvo's Masonic project began to extend across Central America. As had occurred in Costa Rica in 1870, in the following year (1871) coups d'état in El Salvador (April 12) and Guatemala (June 30) ushered in a new political era of civil liberties. Thus, an ideal set of conditions for the foundation of new Masonic lodges began to develop. Again, their arrival provoked an immediate reaction from local representatives of the Catholic Church.

One month after the first Masonic lodge opened in El Salvador, *La Verdad,* a Catholic newspaper, began to publish a twelve-part series entitled: "The Free-masons: What They Are, What They Do, What They Want."[97] Five months later, now into 1872, the Bishop of San Salvador, Tomás Miguel Pineda Saldaña (1848–1872), published the country's first anti-Masonic pastoral letter, warning the Salvadoran people that:

> ... There exists among us an enemy of the Church and the principles of our society, which, shrouded in the cloak and mask of virtue, seeks to lure in the unwary and imprison them as if in a tomb. Without realizing the abyss into which they are falling, they are tainted by the condemnation of the Catholic Church, sundered from her and inducted into the phalanx of her enemies and tormentors.[98]

Loría, "La segunda caída del Dr. Castro" (San José, 1968). Montúfar y Rivera, *Memorias autografiadas,* 244–251. González Víquez, *Obras históricas,* 128–139 and 197–223.

94 Obregón Loría, *Hechos militares y políticos,* 159–163. Molina Jiménez, "Espías visibles, sorpresas esperadas y tiros sin puntería. El golpe de Guardia de 1870," *Anuario de Estudios Centroamericanos* 20, no. 1 (1994): 143–168.

95 The 1871 Constitution even included an article, number 33, declaring that freedom of assembly existed: "For the purposes of conducting private business, or indeed to discuss political matters and scrutinize the public conduct of government officials."

96 Donna Lillian Cotton, "Costa Rica and the era of Tomás Guardia 1870–1882" (Ph.D. in History, George Washington University, 1972), 32–68.

97 Valdés Valle, "Masones, Liberales y Ultramontanos salvadoreños," 43.

98 Tomás Miguel Pineda y Saldaña, "Pastoral," *La Verdad* 44 (San Salvador, March 23, 1872), 1–3. Also on the subject of this pastoral letter, see: Francisco J. Ponte Domínguez, *Historia de la Masonería Salvadoreña* (Sonsonate: Imprenta Excélsior, 1962), 24 - 27. Valdés Valle, "Masones, Liberales y

One month later, Pineda's successor, the then Auxiliary Bishop José Luis Cárcamo y Rodríguez (1872–1885), published another pastoral letter, this time in the *Boletín Oficial*. In it he declared that, "It is on the basis of fact and not belief that we warn you that any books that aim to promote Freemasonry have been prohibited by His Holiness, Pope Pius XI, on pain of excommunication ..."[99]

However, the most interesting aspect of the eruption of the Freemasonry question into the Salvadoran public sphere, cast in a distinctly negative light, was the defensive response of the Masons themselves. With the probable involvement of the Vice President, Salvadoran lawyer Manuel Méndez, who was a member of the Progreso Lodge, there appeared in the *Boletín Oficial* an alleged reprimand from Pope Pius IX—the author of three papal bulls, two encyclical letters, one apostolic constitution and 145 local documents, all opposing Freemasonry[100]—admonishing the Catholic Church in

El Salvador for its condemnation of the movement:

> The Resident Minister of El Salvador in Rome, Márquez de Lorenza, informed the Ministry of Foreign Affairs on June 25 that on the same day, His Holiness Pope Pius IX had seen fit to admonish His Grace, the Bishop of this Diocese, for the abuse of authority committed against the Freemasons.[101]

In Guatemala's case, the first pastoral letter appeared five months after the first lodge opened,[102] written by the Governor of the Archbishopric of Guatemala, Francisco W. Taracena (1873–1874). This letter, like its predecessors in Costa Rica and El Salvador, warned of Freemasonry's offenses against religion, and blamed it for the legal reforms enacted by the Guatemalan government that diminished or removed ecclesiastic influence over various aspects of civic life.[103] Immediately,

Ultramontanos salvadoreños," 65–72.

99   "La pastoral del Ilustrísimo Señor Cárcamo," *Boletín Oficial* 49 (Friday April 19, 1872), 3.

100 Martínez Esquivel, "Masones y Masonería," 97–98.

101 "Noticia Oficial," *Boletín Oficial* 67 (Thursday 8 August, 1872), 1.

102 Published November 4, 1873.

103 H. J. Miller, *La Iglesia Católica y el Estado en Guatemala, 1871–1885* (Guatemala: Editorial Universitaria, 1975). José Manuel Fajardo Salinas, "La Iglesia Católica y el Estado en Guatemala desde el inicio de la Segunda Revolución Liberal hasta la Asamblea Nacional Constituyente de 1879 (1871–1879)" (Undergraduate Thesis in Theology, Francisco Marroquín University, Guatemala, 1999 [accessed September 4, 2012]): available at: http://www.tesis.ufm.edu.gt/59973/tesis.html. José Edgardo Cal Montoya, "La Iglesia de Guatemala ante la Reforma Liberal (1871–1878)," *Estudios* (San Carlos, Guatemala, 2000 [consulted November 13, 2012]): available at: http://ress. afehc-historia-centroamericana.org/_articles/portada_afehc_articulos3.pdf. Rebeca Calderón, "La Reforma Liberal de Justo Rufino Barrios—Una Evaluación" (Undergraduate Thesis in Social Science, Francisco Marroquín University, Guatemala, 2003), 79–157 [accessed September 4, 2012]): available at: http://www.tesis.ufm.edu.gt/pdf/3602.pdf.

the membership of the Hiram Lodge responded with a circular entitled "The Masonic Program," which included the wording of the "Masonic Code."[104] The text argued that the practice of some kind of religion was very important to Freemasons, but also allowed for the possibility of accepting Atheists. This not only contradicted the stipulations of *Anderson's Constitution*, but also the Masonic Constitutions in use in Central America at that time.[105] Moreover, their rebuttal denied that Freemasonry was a secret society and extended an invitation to those who might be interested in joining.

Another event worth noting, and which links the conflicts discussed above, was the expulsion of the Company of Jesus and the seizure of its assets by the Central American governments following the various coups d'état of 1870–1871. The first country to take this step was Guatemala, on August 12, 1871. On January 24 of the following year (1872), the Guatemalan government signed the "Arbizú-Samayoa" decree with El Salvador, which committed the latter to following the same policies that were being imposed in Guatemala, including those pertaining to the Jesuits. Consequently, on June 6, 1872, at the behest of Francisco Esteban Galindo, Undersecretary to the Ministry of Government and a member of the Progreso Lodge, the Jesuits were expelled from Salvadoran national territory, accused of being the intellectual authors of the anti-Masonic pastoral letters that had appeared the year before. The Jesuits tried to reach Honduras, but it seems that the armed conflict with Guatemala and El Salvador closed off this option. They then attempted to enter Costa Rica, but the Minister for Foreign Affairs, Public Instruction, Religion and Social Welfare, Caridad Lodge and *GOSCCA* member Lorenzo Montúfar took every necessary measure to keep them out. Eventually, the Jesuits arrived in Nicaragua, although they were later expelled from here too—in 1881, the foundation year of both the first Nicaraguan Masonic lodge (Progreso, in the city of Granada) and the Catholic Conservative Party.[106]

---

104 Fajardo Salinas, "La Iglesia Católica y el Estado en Guatemala," 37–40.

105 Valdés Valle, "Elementos para la discusión sobre masonería, política y secularización en la Centroamérica del siglo XIX," *REHMLAC* 2, No. 2 (December 2010–April 2011 [accessed August 15, 2011]): available at: https://revistas.ucr.ac.cr/index.php/rehmlac/article/view/6597/6288. Martínez Esquivel, "Masones y Masonería," 226–230.

106 Cardenal, *El poder eclesiástico en El Salvador*, 81–88. Valdés Valle, "Masones, Liberales y Ultramontanos salvadoreños," 48–49. Jorge Mario García Laguardia, *La Reforma Liberal en Guatemala. Vida Política y Orden Constitucional* (Mexico: Instituto de Investigaciones Jurídicas, 1980), 120–130. Fajardo Salinas, "La Iglesia Católica y el Estado en Guatemala," 110–116. Roberto Marín Guzmán, "El primer intento de entrada de los jesuitas a Costa Rica (1872) y el inicio de la controversia entre el Dr. Lorenzo Montúfar y P. León Tornero, S.I.," *Serie Cuadernos de Historia de la Cultura* 25 (San José: EUCR, 2011). Annie Lemistre, "Les Maçons du Nicaragua: Episodes d'une lutte pour la démocratie," *Chroniques d'Histoire Maçonnique* 37 (1986): 53–57. As yet there has been little study of "anti-Jesuitism" in Central America, or elsewhere in the Latin American sub-continent. Such work would, in my opinion, help build a fuller understanding of many of the self-proclaimed "liberal" groups that emerged in the nineteenth century and which never gave

Following the conflicts that arose between the Freemasons and the Catholic Church in Central America, throughout the remainder of the nineteenth century the term "Mason" was a constant feature in the political commentary of the press. Its ubiquity was enhanced after the enactment of legal and educational reforms, and, needless to say, at times when new political parties were forming.[107] Against this background, part of the lodge's social function was to provide a space for education, debate, and the dissemination of new ideas, and in this respect Freemasonry contributed to the broadening of the public sphere, where press coverage of the lodges played a role in the formation of political identities as well as the spread of values and principles associated with the new political system. Meanwhile, pastoral letters and anti-Masonic articles tended to reproduce documents originating in the Vatican and elsewhere. They propagated a series of disparaging epithets such as "Masonic Deism," "Masonic Satanism," "Masonic politics," (characterized as conspiratory, liberal, and anticlerical) and "Masonic Protestantism."[108]

Freemasonry and the Central American Coups D'État of 1870–1871

The coups d'état that took place in Central America in 1870 and 1871 gave rise to a (tentative) political and ideological movement rooted in a strongly secular liberalism. This time, political leaders, and the intellectual elite, sought to move towards reforms capable of stipulating the rules by which the state would interact with the Catholic Church. This was a necessary goal in light of the state's professedly secular stance in relation to both civil society and other power blocks like the clergy. The ensuing "liberal triumph" prompted each country to begin putting in place the political and legal institutions and directives required in order to build the new nation-states. The uprisings were accordingly portrayed by their instigators as potential catalysts for a new society based on democratic and En-

---

up their Catholicism. Traditionally, such groups have been perceived as anticlerical, but it appears that they may in fact have been merely "anti-Jesuit." Roberto di Stefano, "Liberalismo y religión en el siglo XIX hispanoamericano. Reflexiones a partir del caso argentine" (paper delivered at *Liberalism and Religion: Secularisation and the Public Sphere in the Americas*, London, April 18, 2012 [accessed May 7, 2012]): available at: http://sas-space.sas.ac.uk/4121/1/LIA%2C_Liberalismo_y_religi%C3%B3n%2C_DiStefano%2C_18.04.12.pdf.

107 Valdés Valle, "Elementos para la discusión sobre masonería," 66–84. Martínez Esquivel, "Masones y Masonería," 255–263.

108 Martínez Esquivel, "Masonic Societies of Ideas and their Social Representations in Costa Rica (1865–1899)," *CRFF Working Paper Series* 4 (2008): 1–21. Martínez Esquivel, "Documentos y discursos católicos antimasónicos en Costa Rica (1865–1899)," *REHMLAC* 1, no. 1 (May–November 2009 [accessed December 15, 2012]): available at: https://revistas.ucr.ac.cr/index.php/rehmlac/article/view/6860/6547. Sánchez Solano, "La identificación del desarticulador del mundo católico: el liberalismo, la masonería y el protestantismo en la prensa católica en Costa Rica (1880–1900)," *REHMLAC* 2, No. 2 (December 2010–April 2011 [accessed May 15, 2012): available at https://revistas.ucr.ac.cr/index.php/rehmlac/article/view/6595/6286

lightenment ideals.[109] However, these "liberal regimes," to use Max Weber's term,[110] were to morph into systems for patrimonial subjugation as their various leaders all ended up governing with a large dose of arbitrariness, making decisions on the basis of personal rather than pragmatic considerations and surrounding themselves with civil servants who were given financial incentives or other privileges in exchange for their cooperation.

Meanwhile, by the start of the 1870s, there was for the first time a Masonic presence in three different Central American countries. The social composition of the lodges continued to be dominated by foreign tradesmen connected with the coffee export industry that was booming in all three nations,[111] but this was also a moment in time when the number of politicians among their members reached a peak. Why was this happening?

In the context of the coups, politicians who were initiated members portrayed Freemasonry as a social and moral symbol of the liberal civil-society project that they were trying to bring forth. The fact that the Masons promoted civic patriotism in their constitutions and took a somewhat abstract approach to theological principles made it attractive to the typical politician of the time. Furthermore, Freemasonry held itself up as a school for humanistic and spiritual guidance, a center of knowledge, and a bastion of Enlightenment ideals such as rationality, solidarity, tolerance, and man's autonomy as a social actor. Masonic rhetoric also considered state sovereignty to be quite separate to the individual, holding human beings to be divine creations, with no differences between nations. This is perhaps what allowed Central American Freemasonry to be construed in political circles as a socially acceptable organization, beneficial to the furtherance of "progress."

Politics in Central America never fell completely under Masonic control, as this would have required the entire political elite to become initiated members. This did not happen, among other reasons because, historically, the region's political class has always been predominantly Catholic, as is still the case today. There has, moreover, been

---

109 Oficial, *Político-Religiosa. Discusión sobre los artículos 2° y 6° del decreto de elecciones, dictado por el Gobierno Provisorio, en lo que concierne al clero* (San José: Imprenta Nacional, 1870). Fallas Santana, "La voluntad de la Nación y la regeneración política," 54–76. Rodolfo Cardenal, *El poder eclesiástico en El Salvador 1871–1931* (San Salvador: UCA-CONCULTURA, 1980), 33–108. Taracena Arriola, "Liberalismo y Poder en Centroamérica (1870–1929)," in *Historia General de Centroamérica. Las Repúblicas Agroexportadoras, Vol. IV*, ed. Acuña Ortega (Madrid: FLACSO, 1993), 179–185. Cal Montoya, "La Iglesia de Guatemala ante la Reforma Liberal," 1–44.

110 Max Weber, *Política y Sociedad* (Mexico: FCE, 1981).

111 Cardoso, "América Central: la era liberal, c. 1870–1930," en *Historia de América Latina. 9. México, América Central y el Caribe, c. 1870–1930* (Barcelona: Crítica, 1992), 183–209. Mario Samper Kutschbach, "Café, trabajo y sociedad en Centroamérica (1870–1930). Una historia común y divergente," in *Historia General de Centroamérica. Las Repúblicas Agroexportadoras, Vol. IV*, 11–110. Valdés Valle, "Masones, Liberales y Ultramontanos salvadoreños," 63–64 and 96–99. Obregón Loría, *José Quirce Filguera*, 12–15. Martínez Esquivel, "Masones y Masonería," 165–188.

no prosopographic study of the entire nineteenth-century political elite in Central America and their social networks. If Freemasons in Central America were politically active, then, it was because some, but not all, were part of the ruling class. We should therefore regard political involvement as one of a great many vocational activities in which Freemasons took part as members of the dominant social group.

As such, the Masonic lodge became a highly valued social space for politicians during those years, as it allowed them to express their views on new ideas in an age when such open discussion was still a sensitive prospect. Freemasonry, as a result, became a symbol of everything that claimed to be liberal and enlightened, and, by joining, its members vouched for their belief in these ideals. It grew to be an arena for normal social interaction between individuals who regarded themselves in some sense as social guardians. In other words, participation in Masonic activity was portrayed as a pursuit for those who considered themselves distinguished, and it became one of the established criteria by which individuals could be selected from a small, politically active, and socially dominant pool, although the Masons did not have a monopoly on this process.

So, although some politicians

conferred upon Freemasonry a symbolic value in the context of their program for civil society (instantly bringing it into the political sphere), this does not imply that the Central American Freemasons were beginning to develop a political social agenda. Furthermore, the fact that Masonic lodges came to serve as spaces for expression and identity-building was not inevitable, given that many liberals were not Freemasons, and many Freemasons were not liberals. Clearly, the Masons did not constitute a majority by any means, nor were they the only social actors involved in liberal-leaning politics. A great many people were responsible for the changes that occurred at that time, and the Masons did not act as a monolithic block, but evidently were very often divided by political rivalries.

However, it *is* clear that some of the same people who were active in politics were also active Freemasons, which can be attributed to the fact that many of the same modern ideals popular at the time[112] could be found, *at least in their speeches and statutes*, in both the state project and the Masonic lodge.[113] It is also evident that, among the politicians who took an active role in promoting and implementing modernizing reforms,[114] there was one group that joined the Central American Freemasons after the liberal reforms of

---

112 Morales García, *Cultura oligárquica y nueva intelectualidad*, 36–43.

113 An interesting exercise might be to compare the political rhetoric of the time with the language used in Masonic statutes and other texts. An essay on this topic, focusing on Central America, appears in Valdés Valle, "Elementos para la discusión sobre masonería," 66–84. For further reading on the political vocabulary of this era, see Taracena Arriola, "Nación y república en Centroamérica (1821–1865)," 13–62.

114 Morales García, *Cultura oligárquica y nueva intelectualidad*, 36–79.

1870–1871 were declared, and many of them continued to occupy some of the most influential political positions in each country for quite some time.

Masonic activity recommenced in Costa Rica with the reinstatement of the Caridad Lodge in May 1870, which would lead to a new crop of politicians joining the Freemasons. The most senior positions in the new government, including the whole of the executive, the President of Congress, and the President of the Supreme Court of Justice, as well as the rector of the university, were filled by members of Caridad. From this point forward, these same figures introduced a whole series of structural reforms within Freemasonry, in parallel with the liberal political reforms they were pursuing simultaneously at the national level. To carry out these plans for the nation's future, a Constitutional Assembly was convened. 60 percent of its members were Freemasons.[115] It was called the "National Convention" in emulation of the assembly set up after the French Revolution, revealing the extent to which the politicians involved in the uprising of 1870 were inspired by French republican ideals. Indeed, it was with more than a hint of Jacobinism[116] that Bruno Carranza announced the beginning of a period of "radical reform"[117] as the outcome of the "revolution of April 27."[118] These reforms, however, did not yield the hoped-for results. Carranza quickly realized that as interim President he lacked muscle, and that the real power lay with Tomás Guardia Gutiérrez as General Commander of Arms. This situation drove Carranza to tender his resignation as President before the Constituent Assembly, which handed executive power to General Guardia in August 1870.[119]

Not long afterwards, substantial political differences between Tomás Guardia and the Assembly became apparent. Guardia eventually prevailed, and the Assembly was dissolved. This was a new setback for the plans for political reform, and many of the Freemasons on the political stage chose to make their exit, as the General, now President, ran his government as a dictator with absolute power for more than a year—stifling both the reforms that had been announced and any attempt to change the established order. Years later, Lorenzo Montúfar wrote that Guardia's political tactics against the constituent power were interpreted in some quarters as a backward step for the political modernization of the country.[120]

The hopes cherished by many politicians, Masons and otherwise, of seeing their civil-society project come to life at last, entered an unpredictable state of flux that persisted for the en-

---

115 Same sources as for note 65.

116 Morales García, *Cultura oligárquica y nueva intelectualidad*, 38–39.

117 Eugenio Rodríguez Vega, *El Pensamiento Liberal* (San José, ECR, 1979), 81.

118 Rodríguez Vega, *El Pensamiento Liberal*, 81.

119 Obregón Loría, *Hechos militares y políticos*, 163. Vargas González, "Procesos electorales y luchas de poder en Costa Rica," 157.

120 Montúfar y Rivera, *Memorias autobiográficas*, 271.

tire decade of the 1870s.[121] Some even felt that, under the weight of General Guardia's authoritarianism, the project was disintegrating before their eyes. Meanwhile, the Masonic project, due to a combination of contextual factors unique to Central America, Francisco Calvo's personal problems,[122] and a lack of leadership,[123] failed. First, dues went unpaid, and many "Masonic brothers" withdrew from the lodges. Later, the curtailments on freedom of expression and association imposed by General Guardia's government[124] took their toll. So, as Guardia continued to corral more and more power, most politicians who had been active Freemasons, including a number of government ministers between 1870 and 1876, distanced themselves from both the lodge and the president. Sixteen different individuals held ministerial positions during this time, eight of whom were Masons of the Caridad Lodge.[125]

Despite Guardia's volatility during his first year in office, there were some who chose to remain within the circle of power, awaiting the much-trumpeted Constitutional Reform. In the meantime, in a move that would seem to dash any such hope, the President reduced the number of land-owners who were eligible to vote. This was an obvious attempt to boost his chances of winning the next elections, to be held in 1872. In August 1871, however, news finally came of the decree to enact Costa Rica's new and long-awaited constitution.[126] Guardia inaugurated the Constituent Assembly in October, and just two months later, in December, the document was published.[127]

The drafting of the new constitution induced some of the politicians among the Freemasons to take up the baton again, eager to push forward with their civil-society project. Of the seventeen members of the Constituent Assembly, seven were Masons belonging to the Caridad Lodge and members of the Masonic assembly that produced the movement's first Central American constitution. Moreover, the leader of the Constituent Assembly had Guardia's trust: He was Manuel Antonio Bonilla Nava, President of Congress that year, and a relative of a number of Masons both in the Caridad Lodge and the Constituent Assembly.

Meanwhile, in El Salvador, following the coup against Francisco Dueñas (1863–1871) on April 12, 1871, power was seized by his former Minister of War, Marshal Santiago

---

121 Morales García, *Cultura oligárquica y nueva intelectualidad*, 36–53.

122 More details can be found in the Epilogue of this work.

123 As Obregón Loria and Bowden point out, the minute books containing records of the final years of lodge meetings have been lost, and so it is difficult to ascertain exactly what caused this schism. Obregón Loría and Bowden, *La Masonería en Costa Rica*, Vol. II, 48–49.

124 Cotton, "Costa Rica and the Era of Tomás Guardia," 32–68. Orlando Salazar Mora, *El Apogeo de la República Liberal en Costa Rica 1870-1914* (San José: EUCR, 1998), 22–43.

125 Martínez Esquivel, "Masones y Masonería," 298–300.

126 Salazar Mora, *El Apogeo de la República Liberal*, 73–93.

127 Obregón Quesada, *El proceso electoral y el Poder Ejecutivo en Costa Rica*, 180–191.

González Portillo (1871– 1876), a naturalized Salvadoran citizen born in Guatemala. A little over five months later, on September 30, the first lodge of Calvo's project was founded in San Salvador: Progreso. The Vice President of El Salvador, the President of the Supreme Court of Justice, the President of the 1871 Constituent Assembly, five government ministers, the Governor of San Salvador and the Chancellor of Costa Rica all immediately became members.[128]

González's government escalated the process of centralizing power and strengthening the Salvadoran state. Mechanisms for exerting control over the municipalities were honed and sharpened, and there was a strong push to secularize Salvadoran society and modernize the coffee industry. On May 13, 1871, González convened a Constituent Assembly led by José Larreynaga, soon to become a member of the Progreso Lodge. The new Constitution of the Republic of El Salvador was promulgated on 16 October, 1871, triggering a significant decline in the sphere of influence of the Catholic Church, as, for example, the state prescribed tolerance toward other Christian denominations. But González, keen to increase the length of presidential terms from two to four years, formed a new Constituent Assembly, which coincidentally met

for the first time on the anniversary of the foundation of the first Salvadoran lodge (September 30, 1872). The new constitution came into effect on November 9, 1872 and remained in place until February 16, 1880. It went even further than its predecessor in eroding the power of the Catholic Church in the public sphere, even omitting all mention of the word "God."

Subsequent developments included the legalization of divorce and civil marriage, the introduction of secular education, the abolition of religious orders and the Catholic press, the cancellation of the Concordat planned for August 8, 1873, and, by 1875, the closure of the National University's theology department. A number of new regulations were also to be imposed on the University's board of governors. All of this was taking place at the same time as a number of substantial economic changes that affected land tenure and property rights. Communal and cooperatively-owned lands held by indigenous communities were privatized, their culture portrayed by El Salvador's intellectual elite as an impediment to progress and modernity. It was not long before indigenous groups began to rebel. The strength of the army, too, was reinforced; laws against vagrancy were passed and resources invested in modernizing military infrastructure.[129]

---

128 Valdés Valle, "Masones, Liberales y Ultramontanos salvadoreños," 74. In all likelihood, the number of politicians who joined the Progreso Lodge was greater, but unfortunately the minute books are missing and so this figure cannot be determined with the same degree of accuracy possible in Costa Rica's case.

129 Cardoso and Pérez Brignoli, *Centroamérica y la economía occidental (1520–1930)*, 208–275. Cardenal, *El poder eclesiástico en El Salvador*, 33–130. Valdés Valle, "Masones, Liberales y Ultramontanos salvadoreños," 35. Carlos Gregorio López Bernal, "Las reformas liberales en

In neighboring Guatemala, a coup on June 30, 1871 had swept revolutionary fighter Miguel García Granados (1871–1873) to power on an "interim" basis, along with his right-hand man and military colleague Justo Rugino Barrios Auyón, who would later replace him as President (1873–1885) and also become an initiated Freemason. A series of sometimes contradictory legal reforms were set in motion, which reveal a tension between the drive to modernize the country and the inherent limitations of that process. Early policies were aimed at expanding the Guatemalan public sphere. García's government institutionalized freedom of the press, creating a new discursive space that served predominantly for debates over which reforms were necessary for the modernization of the country. At the same time, there were efforts here also to lessen the influence of the Catholic Church. Both ecclesiastic jurisdiction and the practice of tithing were abolished, and the new government encouraged the free exercise of religion. Any dissenters were exiled, as both Archbishop José Bernardo Piñol y Aycinena (1867–1881) and the entire Company of Jesus discovered. Moreover, one of García's first acts as president was to recognize the new Costa Rican government led by General Tomás Guardia. A wave of recurrent uprisings

against these measures began in 1871 and continued until 1873, when, under pressure from the patriotic councils, religious orders were expelled from the country.[130]

By March 15, 1873, freedom of conscience and, therefore, freedom of worship, had become mandated principles of the Guatemalan state. In the mission to build a modern civil society, Protestantism was regarded in Guatemala as an ally of liberalism, because it helped diversify the religious landscape as well as encouraging tolerance, ecumenism, and civil power. It also offered a practical religious grounding for the liberal civil-society project.[131] Protestantism, therefore, was attributed with the same practical value for the consolidation of the secular state as Freemasonry. This explains the "conversion" to Presbyterianism of one General Barrios, who would take control of the Guatemalan government on June 4, 1873 after assuming dictatorial power, and the tightening of his ties to the Masons. Indeed, just thirteen days after Barrios seized power (June 17), the first Masonic lodge of Calvo's project was established in Guatemala City. It was named Hiram, and at once attracted the membership of four ministers, one member of the Constituent Assembly, one member of the Government Council, a pro-

El Salvador y sus implicaciones en el poder municipal, 1871–1890," *Revista La Universidad* 1 (May–June 2008 [accessed May 15, 2012): available at:http://www.ues.edu.sv/sites/default/files/Revista_La_Universidad_1%20.pdf#page=73.

130 Fajardo Salinas, "La Iglesia Católica y el Estado en Guatemala," 82–146. Alfredo Guerra-Borges, *Guatemala, el largo camino a la modernidad: (su trayectoria, primera etapa, 1871–1944)* (Mexico City: IIEc, 1999), 34–70. Cal Montoya, "La Iglesia de Guatemala ante la Reforma Liberal," 1–44.

131 Arturo Piedra Solano, "Notas sobre la relación entre liberalismo, francmasonería y penetración protestante en Centroamérica," in *Protestantes, liberales y francmasones*, 119–131.

vincial political leader, two high-ranking military officers, and the German Consul General.[132]

Barrios proved more zealous than his predecessor, quickly secularizing the country's nunneries, closing the seminaries, and implementing a ban on the wearing of clerical or monastic robes in public. However, civil marriage had not yet been introduced in Guatemala, and this allowed a diverse range of religious practices to become institutionalized to a greater degree.[133] In terms of the economy, Barrios nationalized property held by religious and indigenous groups, it being fundamental to his vision of "order" and "progress" that land ownership should be subject to the rules of the market and a diversified commercial agricultural sector put in place. Although he spoke of the social integration of indigenous communities, Barrios conscripted them into forced labor, and so this "integration" appears to have taken the form of social dislocation and cultural leveling, creating a workforce that was subdued, dependent, and cheap.[134]

A Constituent Assembly was convened in 1875, with meetings beginning the following year. At this point,

the state also took over the civil registry and introduced free public education. With the constituent process just beginning, it was argued that civil liberties were impractical in Guatemala, and that it was therefore necessary to extend Barrios's dictatorial powers for a further four years. This measure was supported by the Minister of Foreign Affairs—a position now held by Supreme Court Judge, Rector of the University of San Carlos, member of the Hiram Lodge, and former key figure on the Costa Rican political scene, Lorenzo y Montúfar. Montúfar maintained that, because the country was still immersed in "darkness," the time had not yet come to map out an appropriate political system, and that a transitional dictatorship was therefore essential. The question was decided by a committee led by two members of the Hiram Lodge: Montúfar himself and Raymundo Arroyo. Later, in 1882, when Montúfar had fallen out with Barrios and returned to live in Costa Rica, he would have cause to regret this decision.[135] The new Constitution of Guatemala, the first of the Republic, was finally promulgated on December 11, 1879.[136]

As we have seen, the years 1870

---

132 The difficulty with this lodge is that its minute books have not been found, and so we can only identify those individuals who were initiated there and not all of its members. Obregón Loría and Bowden, *La Masonería en Costa Rica* (San José: Trejos Hermanos, 1940), Vol. III, 110–112. Fajardo Salinas, "La Iglesia Católica y el Estado en Guatemala," 82–146. Carlos Lavarreda, *El Reformador Justo Rufino Barrios. Centro América, Carrera, Belice, Chiapas, Soconusco y la Revolución de 1871* (Guatemala, s.a.), 44. Guerra-Borges, *Guatemala, el largo camino a la modernidad*, 34–70. Valdés Valle, "Elementos para la discusión sobre masonería," 66–84.

133 Cal Montoya, "La Iglesia de Guatemala ante la Reforma Liberal," 1–44.

134 Cardoso and Pérez Brignoli, *Centroamérica y la economía occidental (1520–1930)*, 208–275.

135 Obregón Loría and Bowden, *La Masonería en Costa Rica*, Vol. III, 110–112. García Laguardia, *La Reforma Liberal en Guatemala*, 154–159.

136 García Laguardia, *La Reforma Liberal en Guatemala*, 149–166.

and 1871 brought a series of socio-political upheavals to Central America, the fruit of mechanisms set in motion years before. In each case, a coup d'état was followed by the foundation of a Masonic lodge (met by anti-Masonic pastoral letters from the corresponding local bishop) and, later, the formation of a Constituent Assembly. In Costa Rica and El Salvador these events occurred almost immediately, whereas in Guatemala there was a delay of several years while certain essential civil liberties were established. Freemasons involved in drafting the new constitutions simply repeated the exercise, reapplying their understanding of the principles driving this national process inside the Masonic movement itself. Thus, they endeavored to modernize the Freemasons as well as the country, by introducing a series of reforms very similar to those being brought forward at the national level. This shows that the very same ideals associated with liberalism and the Enlightenment lay at the heart of two different projects, both linked to the expansion of civil society and the public sphere and both featuring the same protagonists.[137]

Specifically, the Masonic reforms consisted of the creation of a Central American Grand Lodge and the drafting of a Masonic constitution. In fact, the very next month after the coup d'état in Costa Rica (May), the Caridad Lodge was reopened, and the first National Assembly of Freemasons was convened in November 1870. The *GOSCCA* was in place by the end of January 1871, and in September of the same year, one month after General Guardia issued the decree for the promulgation of the new Costa Rican constitution, it announced the completion of Central America's first Masonic constitution and the foundation of the first lodge outside Costa Rica—Progreso in El Salvador.[138]

These developments in the evolution of the Central American Masonic project are striking because of three features that are also found in the political project that was then being announced: (i) they were led by public figures born in Central America;[139] (ii) the prevailing discourse supported the idea of Central American unity, and (iii) the underlying value system was republican in nature. The first observation is

---

137 A separate study is needed to fully explore these connections, including an analysis of the political and intellectual rhetoric of the time, the social influence of the various schools of thought that arrived with modernity, and the statutes and speeches of the various grand lodges created in Central America up until the early years of the twentieth century.

138 Obregón Loría, *Hechos militares y políticos*, 158–172. Obregón Loría and Bowden, *La masonería en Costa Rica*, Vol. II, 4–16.

139 Eight of the eleven. The three foreign nationals were Leonce Vars Dumartrai (French) and José Quirce Filguera and Francisco Javier Peralta Alvarado (both Spanish). AGLCR, *Historic Records*. Obregón Loría and Bowden, *La masonería en Costa Rica*. Guzmán-Stein, "Costa Rica, España y Cuba: Antecedentes, desarrollo e impacto del movimiento de independencia en la sociedad costarricense finisecular y la masonería," in *La Masonería Española y la crisis colonial del 98*, ed. Ferrer Benimeli (Barcelona: CEHME, 1999), Vol. II, 1041–1087. Herrera Balharry, *Los alemanes y el Estado cafetalero*, 110–112, 211– 213. Marín Araya, "Inmigrantes españoles," 142–144 and 264–267. Murchie, *Imported spices*, 143–147 and 223–331.

apparent when we look at the eleven dignitaries who were elected to lead the *GOSCCA*, all Masons of the 33rd Degree of the *Ancient and Accepted Scottish Rite* and all leading public figures in the region.[140] Most of those in the upper echelons of the *GOSCCA* were Costa Rican, as well as prominent local politicians. This demonstrates a desire to cast the Grand Orient in a national and socially prestigious light, despite the fact that the majority of Freemasons at that time were foreign nationals (56 percent).[141] It was, perhaps, part of an effort to legitimize the process in the eyes of local people.

The second striking feature, incidentally also observed by Roberto Armando Valdés Valle,[142] was the Masonic project's supportive stance towards Central American unity at this time, with Freemasons echoing the popular pro-union mood.[143] In his speech on the occasion of the inauguration of the *GOSCCA*, Guatemalan-born Lorenzo Montúfar declared that:

> If, in the eyes of many in the profane world, the political union of Central America is impossible, a utopia dreamed up by delirious minds, the Masonic union of Central America is now a reality, an accomplished fact. Today, new lodges are being created. Tomorrow, there will be more. The momentum has begun; the movement is swift and its strength formidable. The walls of intolerance, built up out of solid rock over three centuries, will fall to the power of the true light, just as the strong walls of Jericho fell in the presence of the Ark of the Covenant.[144]

Finally, the third aspect to note is the pro-republican nature of the Masonic project, which is understandable given that it was progressing in parallel

---

140 Martínez Esquivel, "Masones y Masonería," 303.

141 Same sources as note 110.

142 Valdés Valle, "Elementos para la discusión sobre masonería," 73. This could be attributable to the political desire to imbue the resurgent Masonic project with a symbolic value, at a time when democratic reforms were being announced. In this respect, it is important to remember that it was members of the Caridad Lodge who held most of the key positions in the Costa Rican government formed after "April 27, 1870."

143 Central American unity was in fact a recurring theme in presidential speeches in Costa Rica between the second half of the nineteenth century and the 1920s. Acuña Ortega, "Historia del vocabulario político en Costa Rica," in *Identidades nacionales y estado moderno en Centroamérica*, 67–68. Nevertheless, in the historiography of Costa Rica we find the argument that Central American unity was not an integral part of the world view of the country's liberals—see, for example, Cotton, "Costa Rica and the era of Tomás Guardia," 125–129. In light of what has been discussed, the present author certainly cannot agree with that interpretation.

144 AGLCR, *Balaustre presentado al GR∴ OR∴ Centro-Americano el día de su instalación, el 12 de febrero de 1871. Por el IL∴ H∴ Lorenzo Montúfar GR∴ 33.* (Single sheet). A reproduction of this document can be found in: Góngora Herrera, *Documentos históricos de la Masonería Centroamericana*, 65.

with the process of state modernization then underway in Central America.[145] Freemasonry in Central America, then, simply adapted to its environment. This conclusion further supports the argument that it developed as a consequence of the transition to modernity in Central America and, therefore, can be regarded as a socio-historical construct.

The Masonic constitution formulated by the *GOSCCA* introduced rules to promote the smooth progression of Freemasonry in Central America, as well as for resolving conflicts among Masons and lodges. It also set out the rights and duties of the individual in the Masonic cosmos, the established rituals, the eligibility criteria for members, both voting and qualifying, and the functions of the various Masonic offices. The constitution also governed the executive, legislative, and judicial powers.

Here we can see how Freemasons involved in the political scene echoed the dominant ideologies of their time (republicanism, secularism, liberalism, Central American unionism, etc.), aspiring to put them into practice both inside and outside the lodge. This demonstrates that the Masons were in fact a product of ideas that had become popular as a *consequence* of the process

of modernization unfolding across the region, rather than its cause.

Calvo's Renunciation and the End of His Masonic Project

Between 1870 and 1873, Central American Freemasonry progressed steadily and at a quickening pace,[146] despite continued attacks from the Catholic Church, mostly aimed at the movement's political ideology and at Francisco Calvo personally.[147] After 1873, a new phase of decline began that persisted until 1876 and culminated in the closure of all of the Central American lodges in 1878. This decline can be attributed to three root causes: (i) the political instability of the region (the three "democratic revolutions" having transfigured into dictatorships), (ii) Calvo's own personal problems, and (iii) the split that developed within Central American Freemasonry.[148]

The years between 1873 and 1876 were a period of political crisis and instability in Costa Rica. Tomás Guardia's government was marching towards authoritarianism and centralization, occupied with building up the military and pursuing economically costly projects that provoked heated dispute.[149]

145 Morales García, *Cultura oligárquica y nueva intelectualidad*, 36–79.

146 Martínez Esquivel, "Modernity and Freemasonry in 19th Century Central America."

147 Valdés Valle, "Masones, Liberales y Ultramontanos salvadoreños," 39–72. Guzmán-Stein, "Masonería, Iglesia y Estado," 100–134. Martínez Esquivel, "Conspiradores políticos y sectas misteriosas: Imaginarios sociales sobre la masonería en Costa Rica (1865–1899)," *Revista Estudios* 22 (2009 [accessed December 15, 2011]): available at: http://estudiosgenerales.ucr.ac.cr/estudios/no22/papers/isec1.html.

148 Obregón Loría and Bowden, *La masonería en Costa Rica*, Vol. II, 31–32.

149 Cotton, "Costa Rica and the era of Tomás Guardia," 32–68. Salazar Mora, *El Apogeo de la Repúbli-*

The situation meant that many of the country's Masons were focused on politics rather than on the preservation of Freemasonry, and a number of foreign-born members returned to their home countries.[150]

Other factors also came into play, such as the threats and invasion attempts coming from Barrios's government in Guatemala. The political atmosphere in Costa Rica was therefore tense, resulting in a Congress that produced the minimum possible amount of legislation and an executive power that used military might to entrench its authoritarian rule. These were all factors that caused the initiated members among the political class to be more concerned about safeguarding the system than a social organization like Freemasonry. At this moment in time, the struggle for political values and ideologies, whether individual or collective, took precedence over any Masonic interest, despite the fact that, often, many of the basic principles were the same. In 1874 and 1875, Costa Rica suffered five attempted coups, led, incidentally, by Freemasons. There were also border tensions with Colombia and Nicaragua, which were sufficiently acute to spark talk of war.[151]

To complicate matters further, during those years (1873–1876) Calvo was facing new problems with the Costa Rican Catholic Church. He had been suspended from his duties as a priest due to allegations of slander and defamation against Domingo Rivas Salvatierra, now Chapter Vicar of the Diocese of San José.[152] The allegation coincided with the conflict known as the *cuestión confirma*, which embroiled the civil and ecclesiastic courts as well as Calvo's Masonic brothers, the Supreme Court of Justice, the Ecclesiastic Council, the Metropolitan Archdiocese of Guatemala, and even the Vatican.[153]

The conflict between Calvo and the Church intensified after Rivas assumed his new role in Costa Rica, seized with the notion that the clergy should submit to his spiritual guidance, he being the country's sole custodian of the Catholic Church and the purity of its faith and rituals. With ambitions of becoming a Bishop, Rivas endeavored to follow every instruction from the Vatican to the letter, in order to paint himself as the ideal candidate for the bishopric. Not a single one of the papal sentences issued at that time by Pius IX, therefore, escaped his notice during his time as Chapter Vicar in Costa Rica, es-

ca Liberal en Costa Rica 1870–1914 (San José: EUCR, 1998), 29–30.

150 Montúfar Rivera, *Memorias autografiadas*, 315–322.

151 Obregón Loría, *Hechos militares y políticos*, 170–178.

152 Víctor Manuel Sanabria Martínez, *La primera vacante de la Diócesis de San José 1871–1880* (San José: ECR, 1973). The choice of Rivas Salvatierra is evidence that, for certain members of the political and intellectual elite Freemasonry was no more than a social marker after the 1870 coup, and that there was no "systematic conspiracy" of any kind. Indeed, after all the excitement over the anti-Masonic pastoral letters of 1867 and 1868, how could a Minister of Religion like Lorenzo y Montúfar agree to the nomination of Rivas as Chapter Vicar?

153 Guzmán-Stein: "La 'Cuestión Confirma' y la represión ideológica."

pecially if they helped him to undercut his potential rivals.[154]

Rivas began to fulminate against various ideas and practices, including: (i) liberalism, and Freemasonry as its accomplice; (ii) rationalism, which he condemned in a pastoral letter in 1875[155] as well as in the newspaper *La Razón* (no copies of this could be traced, and so we do not know whether Freemasons also featured in this rebuke); (iii) Krausism, which was taking the country by storm at that time, owing to the influence of the Fernández Ferraz brothers who were known Freemasons and in charge of the San Luis Gonzaga College in Cartago;[156] (iv) and finally Spiritualism, at a time when the works of Allan Kardec, pen name of French author Hippolyte Léon Rivail, were enjoying a wide circulation.[157]

Besides this affair, another event within the Masonic community in 1875 had an impact on its Central American activities. Two main candidates had come forward for the position of Grand Master of the *GOSCCA,* both of whom were Costa Rican.[158] Neither one gained enough votes to win the election, and so, in an attempt to reach a consensus, it was decided that Calvo should retain the title. This decision was not well received among the Order's various leaders, causing a deeper division. The eventual outcome was the closure of all of the Masonic lodges in Central America. In El Salvador, with Marshal González amassing more and more power, an approach emulated by his successor, future Freemason Rafael Zaldívar (1876–1885),[159] the lodge waned. A similar thing happened in Guatemala, despite the fact that the political environment there was, in theory, supportive of this kind of social organization because of the liberal reforms that were being pushed through.

Finally, July 1876 brought a crucial event that would shape the future of Freemasonry in Central America for many years to come: the renunciation of the man who had been at the forefront of the Masonic project for the last eleven years.[160] Historiographers

---

154 The other candidates for the bishopric were former Freemason Ulloa and Ramón Isidro Cabezas Alfaro, who was known for his liberal leanings. This is why Rivas's condemnatory rhetoric contained clear references, on one hand, to Ulloa and his earlier involvement with Freemasonry, and on the other hand to Calvo, who had close family and social ties to members of the country's political elite, and so was in a position to exert influence in the selection process. Moreover, Ulloa and Calvo were close friends, and both Calvo and Cabezas were friends of General Tomás Guardia. Sanabria Martínez, *La primera vacante*, 14.

155 AHACMSJ, Historical Catalog (Box, Volume, Folios): 168, 1, 67–68.

156 Guzmán-Stein, "Masones españoles en Costa Rica," 449–470.

157 Sanabria Martínez, *La primera vacante*, 199–208.

158 They were Andrés Sáenz Llorente, a doctor, and Manuel Antonio Bonilla Carrillo, a tradesman.

159 Valdés Valle, "La Masonería y el Gobierno de Rafael Zaldívar (1876–1885)," *Boletín AFEHC* 37 (2008 [accessed August 15, 2012]): available at: http://www.afehc-historia-centroamericana.org/index.php?action=fi_aff&id=1976.

160 AHACMSJ, Historical Catalog (Box, Volume, Folios): 99, 1, 328. Obregón Loría, *Presbítero Doctor Francisco Calvo*, 82–86.

of Central American Freemasonry are yet to find any sources that explain why Calvo resigned, and the present author is no exception. However, one possible theory is as follows: Calvo was mired in a bitter struggle with certain factions within the clergy, incited by Rivas, who had kept him suspended since 1873. Tensions had increased to the point that there was talk of a canonical process against him,[161] and so Calvo found himself at a crossroads, forced to decide between his faith and his membership of an organization that his faith condemned. Disillusioned by the decline of Masonic activity across the region due to wider socio-political events, he was left with a straightforward decision.[162]

Calvo's renunciation sent the Masons into a crisis that was deepened by the political situation. They responded by engaging in infighting over disparate political agendas, and as a result, the Masonic brotherhood once again ceased to exist outside the confines of the lodge. It is also possible that discord of this kind played a part in Calvo's decision in the first place, since whenever members were implicated in political wrangles, they tended to stay away from lodge meetings.

It is therefore conceivable that this apparent lack of interest pushed Calvo to turn his back on Freemasonry, or perhaps he saw his resignation as the only viable way to calm the situation. Irrespectively, this strategy, if made known, was unsuccessful, since many of the initiated members among the political and intellectual elites of Central America, and many others in their social circles, did not spend the next few years yearning for the regeneration of Freemasonry but instead drifted towards the literary and scientific societies, Krausist educational organizations, adult education schools, and social clubs. There they found the social and cultural capital, and the opportunity for political action, that they had once found in Freemasonry.

For a number of years afterwards there were no active Masonic lodges in Central America, due to continuous clashes between members over a variety of political and personal issues. With the closure of the Central Ameri-

---

161 Regarding a possible canonical process against Calvo, the priest Guiseppe Stappaini, a Vatican informant, went so far as to say: "I think I might be excused for saying something in relation to Dr. Calvo, since over there you know him as well as I do. He has been suspended from his duties and privileges, he is the founder and propagandist of the lodges now found in Costa Rica, and he refuses to give up his nefarious ideas and conduct. (ASV: A III America, Costa Rica N° 28, Fascícle N° 566, folio 115vto)" I am grateful to Professor Miguel Guzmán-Stein for supplying me with a copy of this source.

162 The refusal of the Central American Masons to allow him to continue as Grand Master of the *GOSCCA* may also have played on Calvo's mind. Why, though, did they reject the possibility that Calvo might carry on as the supreme leader of the Masonic Order in Central America? One possible explanation is his support for the 1876 coup d'état against Aniceto Esquivel Sáenz, which led to the suspension of Costa Rica's constitution until 1882. The uprising was a setback in the utopian quest to build a free society that was declared after the 1870 coup, and went against the basic principles of Freemasonry. It is possible, therefore, that Central America's Masons had lost "faith" in Calvo's leadership of the movement.

can lodges, those who wished to remain active in the region did so by joining the *GOSCCA,* a grand lodge which, incidentally, managed to survive without any project whatsoever. The never-ending social strife that had plagued Freemasonry from the moment that the first lodge was opened in Costa Rica is the clearest indication that the Masonic brotherhood was no match for personal interest.

Furthermore, the suspension of Costa Rican constitutional guarantees in effect since 1876 led to the exile of certain foreign nationals and native citizens who were political opponents of General Tomás Guardia, among them a number of prominent Freemasons.[163] On the other hand, there were also several influential Masonic leaders in the country who had close ties to the General.[164] In Guatemala, Barrios's government, spurred on by its Minister, Montúfar, refused to recognize the Costa Rican regime,[165] while in El Salvador the *Liga Antiguardista* was formed, organized by Masons exiled by Guardia.[166] And so it seems that the Masonic brotherhood was eclipsed by scheming and personal interest.

Another factor was the number of those with no involvement in the political scene, including some Freemasons, who simply opted to escape the socio-political situation in Costa Rica by emigrating. In addition, the new Apostolic Administrator in Costa Rica, Luis Burschetti, drew on articles of the Concordat to keep up the Church's condemnatory campaign against Freemasonry.[167] Some Costa Ricans did continue their involvement with Freemasonry elsewhere in Central America. Manuel Antonio Bonilla Carrillo even became the new Grand Master of the *GOSCCA* (1877–1887) in place of Calvo.[168]

We also need to consider the fact that the palpable new dynamic that had appeared in Costa Rican society as modernity took hold prompted the local Catholic Church to actuate its own courts, the *Tribunales de Justicia,* and to begin persecuting anything it regarded as irregular, criminal, or simply sinful. For example, twenty-one cases have been identified between 1874 and 1881 of individuals who were put to death by the ecclesiastic courts for being Masons. Most of them were immigrants who had attempted to marry Costa Rican women from staunchly Catholic families.[169] The majority of those who

---

163 Obregón Loría, *Hechos militares y políticos,* 195–198.

164 Sáenz Carbonell, *Los días del Presidente Lizano* (San José: EUNED, 1991), 9–13.

165 Obregón Loría, *Hechos militares y políticos,* 182–183.

166 Valdés Valle, "Masones, Liberales y Ultramontanos salvadoreños," 72–80.

167 Sanabria Martínez, *La primera vacante,* 167–188. Vargas Arias, *El Liberalismo, la Iglesia y el Estado,* 74–77. Guzmán-Stein, "La 'Cuestión Confirma' y la represión ideológica."

168 Obregón Loría and Bowden, *La masonería en Costa Rica,* Volume II, 33.

169 AHACMSJ, Historical Catalog (Box, Volume, Folios): 226, 2, 2–20, 21–37, 68–69; 240,185; 254, 295; 416, 342. The *tribunales* also heard cases involving charges of Protestantism, witchcraft, fornication, and the practice of Islam. As yet their activities have received little detailed study in Costa Rican scholarship.

renounced Freemasonry resumed their membership when Masonic activities recommenced in Costa Rica.[170]

The hiatus came to an end in 1880 with the intervention of *The Supreme Council of the 33rd Degree, Ancient and Accepted Scottish Rite, Southern Jurisdiction of the United States of America* (*The Supreme Council of the 33rd Degree*),[171] which opened a lodge in Guatemala City.[172]

* * *

The establishment of Freemasonry in Central America, then, came about as a consequence of the transition to modernity over the course of the nineteenth century. Freemasonry was one of a number of new forms of social organization that developed at that time, and it became one of many liberal practices within the purview of Central America's burgeoning middle-class culture. Furthermore, Central American Freemasonry was one of several significant factors in the shift toward a secular society, and in the popularization of new ideas such as Deism and Krausism.

The evolution of Masonic activity was characterized by: (i) a long succession of peaks and troughs linked to political crises, particularly when a non-constitutional government was in power; (ii) the self-interest and personal strategies of the Freemasons themselves, which often served as stumbling blocks to the Masonic project and slowed its progress; and (iii) the forceful anti-Masonic diatribes of the local Catholic Church.

Freemasonry's social dynamic (praxis) was part of the process whereby modernity percolated through Central American society. This dynamic had an impact on the lives of Freemasons in society, but it also exerted an influence over the modernization process itself. By the same token, the Masons did not form a closed or exclusive group in their participation in the public sphere and in civil society. As a social organization, Freemasonry acted as a key exponent of cultural modernity, in the sense that it was involved in promoting certain ideas that were regarded as novel, and in building up artistic, philosophical, scientific, and educational social networks. In other words, it contributed to the development of cultural institutions or, as people might have said at the time, of civilization.

The modernization of the Central American states was not driven by the Freemasons but was a sign of the times, in which Freemasonry found a niche. It was, firstly, one of the many

---

170 Sometime after these years of renunciations had passed, there was yet another attempted coup in January 1881 in which several former members of Masonic lodges in Costa Rica were implicated. The attempt was a resounding failure. Obregón Loría, *Hechos militares y políticos*, 199–201.

171 James D. Carter, *History of the Supreme Council, 33° (Mother Council of the World) Ancient and Accepted Scottish Rite of Freemasonry Southern Jurisdiction, U.S.A. 1861–1891* (Washington D.C.: Supreme Council 33°, 1967).

172 Obregón Loría and Bowden, *La Masonería en Costa Rica*, Volume II, 73–74.

consequences of this process, and secondly, a symbol of the new society that was emerging. We can say this because the same ideals that featured prominently in the aims of the nascent nation-states were also to be found in the system of norms and values that guided Central American Freemasonry as it developed over these years.

Rather than being the vanguard of political and ideological (and even proto-partisan) change, then, it would appear that the Freemasons were closely intertwined with other actors caught up in the political projects of the age (namely, state-building and the construction of the modern public sphere). In this context, politicians who were involved in Freemasonry often entered into conflicts, but they also collaborated with other actors to achieve their political goals.

Besides, the members who took part in the drive to modernize Central America constituted a very small group, since the majority of Freemasons were foreign nationals with no wider political involvement. It is therefore simply untenable to argue that the construction of the modern state was a "Masonic project." If this select group did play a part in this process, it was not primarily because they were Masons, but because they were members of the political and socio-economic elite who subscribed to modernity's ideals.

The Masonic project in Central America came to an end in 1899 with the foundation of the *Gran Logia de Costa Rica*, an institution that transformed Freemasonry in Costa Rica by giving it independence and a national impetus. In 1903, it was Guatemala's turn, then Nicaragua in 1907, El Salvador in 1912, and finally Honduras, in 1922. The advent of these grand lodges was part of a stage in the process of modernization (nation-building) that Costa Rica undertook from the final third of the nineteenth century to the beginning of the twentieth century. It was marked, among other events, by the appearance of new organizations and institutions with names featuring the words "national," "Costa Rican," "Guatemalan," "Nicaraguan," "Salvadoran," or "Honduran," or "of Costa Rica," "of Guatemala," "of Nicaragua," "of El Salvador," or "of Honduras."[173]

---

173 Palmer, "A Liberal Discipline: Inventing Nations in Guatemala and Costa Rica, 1870–1900" (Doctoral Dissertation in History, Columbia University, 1990).

Freemasonry, Control and Other Fraternal Loyalties: the Rescue of Porfirio Díaz by a Masonic Brother.[1]

Guillermo de los Reyes Heredia[2]

ABSTRACT

This article explores the role that Porfirio Díaz played in Freemasonry and his relationship with such an institution, analyzing one of the stories that proves that Díaz benefited from his Masonic affiliation before he was president of Mexico. This story tells how Díaz managed to smuggle himself into Mexico with the help of a brother Mason in 1876, after his brief exile in New Orleans aboard the steamship, "City of Havana." At first, it was widely believed that such a story was simply a legend, part of the folklore that surrounds Freemasonry. However, two witnesses, both Masons, who were in the same boat with Díaz, confirm the veracity of the tale that even William Deslow, the historian of American Freemasonry, cataloged as a, "not verified" incident. In addition, it studies how Díaz promoted the unification of the Scottish Rite lodges in an institution called The Symbolic Grand Diet. The primary reason why Díaz promoted such unification, as stated in this article was to carry out his plan of national reconciliation. Díaz knew he had to gain control of Freemasonry to avoid future confrontations and trouble. He didn't want anybody to interfere with his governmental policy of order and progress. Therefore, the dictator always made sure that neither masonry nor any other institution that had substantial influence in society were out of his control.

Keywords: *Freemasonry, Porfirio Díaz, Symbolic Grand Diet, Lodge La Parafite Union, Masonic brotherhood*

RESUMEN

En este artículo se explora el papel que jugó Porfirio Díaz dentro de la masonería y su relación con dicha institución. Se analiza una de las

---

1   This article was previously published in the review *REHMLAC*, Vol. 7, no. 2, December 2015-April 2016. We are grateful to the editorial committee of *REHMLAC* for having given us permission to publish this article in English.

2   Associate Professor, Department of Hispanic Studies, University of Houston, USA. Email: jgdelosr@central.uh.edu

historias que comprueban que Díaz logró ciertos beneficios gracias a su afiliación masónica desde antes que fuera presidente de México. Esta historia narra la manera en que Díaz logró entrar de contrabando a México con la ayuda de un hermano masón en 1876, después de su breve exilio en Nuevo Orleans a bordo del buque de vapor, "City of Havana". En un principio se pensaba que ésta era simplemente una leyenda más del folklore que envuelve a la masonería. Sin embargo, dos testimonios, ambos de masones que iban en el mismo barco ratifican la historia que incluso el mismo historiador de la masonería norteamericana, William Deslow, catalogaba como un incidente, "no verificado." Asimismo, se describe cómo Díaz promovió la unificación de las logias del rito escocés en una institución que se llamó La Gran Dieta Simbólica. La razón principal por la cual Díaz promovió tal unificación, como se afirma en este artículo, fue para llevar a cabo su plan de pacificación nacional. Díaz sabía que tenía que obtener el control de la masonería para evitar que ésta le causara problemas para lograr el orden y progreso que caracterizó a su gobierno. Por tal motivo, el dictador siempre vigiló que ni la masonería, ni cualquier otra institución que hubiera podido tener cierta influencia en la sociedad estuvieran fuera de su control.

Palabras clave: Masonería; Porfirio Díaz; Gran Dieta Simbólica; Logia Parafite; Union; fraternidad masónica

共济会、控制和兄弟般的忠诚：共济会兄弟对波费里奥·迪亚斯的营救

摘要

本文探索了 波费里奥·迪亚斯（Porfirio Díaz）在共济会中扮演的角色以及他和共济会之间的关系，分析了一个能证明迪亚斯在被选为墨西哥总统之前受到共济会帮助的故事。这个故事讲述了迪亚斯在新奥尔良市"哈瓦那市"（City of Havana）轮船上度过短期流放后，如何于1876年受到共济会兄弟帮助而成功将自己偷运到墨西哥。起初，人们都认为这仅仅是一个传说，一个有关共济会的民间传说。然而，当时和迪亚斯同在船上的两个目击者（都是共济会成员）都证实了该故事的真实性，尽管研究美国共济会的历史学家William Deslow将该故事列为"未证实"事件。此外，本文研究了迪亚斯如何在名为"The Symbolic Grand Diet"的机构中推动了苏格兰礼（Scottish Rite）共济会的统一。迪亚斯推动统一的主要原因是为了实施其民族和解（national reconciliation）计划。他知道自己不得不控制共济会才能避免未来的对抗和麻烦。他不想让任何人干预其政府的命令政策和进程。因此作为独裁者，他总是确保共济会或任何其他机构无法对社会产生实质性的影响。

关键词：共济会，波费里奥・迪亚斯，Symbolic Grand Diet，Lodge La Parafite Union，共济会兄弟会

Introduction

The presidency of Porfirio Díaz has been widely discussed within academic and political circles. Repression, excessive control of all political and social sectors, progress without development, *pax porfiriana*, the "pan o palo" (bread or stick) policy, Porfirian diplomacy, have all been central to analyses of the Mexican dictator. Little study has been carried out, however, into the role played by Díaz within the Freemasons and his relationship with this institution. In this paper, I therefore propose to analyze some aspects of the participation of Porfirio Díaz in Freemasonry, his relationship with the institution and the ways in which he used and controlled it to suit his political discourse and aims. In so doing, I will focus on one of the events that provides evidence of Díaz receiving certain advantages from his Masonic affiliation, even before he became President of Mexico. The event I am studying in this essay relates to the way in which Díaz managed to smuggle himself into Mexico on board the steamship *City of Havana* with the help of a brother Mason in 1876, following his brief exile to New Orleans. At first it was thought that this was simply one more folk tale involving the Freemasons. However, two testimonials—both from Masons who were aboard the same boat—verified the story that even the North American Freemasons' historian, William Deslow, categorized as an "unverified"[3] story.

I will also discuss some of the strategies used by Díaz to achieve unification of the lodges of the Ancient and Accepted Scottish Rite into one single institution that he named the "Gran Dieta Símbolica" or Grand Diet of Symbolical Masonry. I suggest that the main reason why Díaz promoted such a unification was more to gain control over the Freemasons more easily, keeping them as allies and in this way achieving his national peace plan. Díaz knew that he had to achieve control over the Masonic lodges to prevent them from disrupting his ambition to achieve the order and progress that characterized his government. Unifying the lodges was crucial

---

3   William R. Denslow, *10,000 Famous Freemasons* (Richmond, VA: Macoy Publishing & Masonic Supply Co., 1957), Vol. I, 313.

in order to avoid—at all costs—a continuation of the rivalries and struggles that were a feature of Masonic ranks during the nineteenth Century. For this reason, the dictator always ensured that neither the Masonry, nor any other institution that might have had influence on society, were outside his control.

Fact or Fiction—the Importance of Primary Sources

Behind the biographical and prosopographical studies of illustrious men and women who have been key to the history of their respective countries, there are always fantastical stories and legends about these great people. Such stories, based on a historical event or on a particular personality, are legion within historical studies of the Freemasons. As I argue in (*Herencias secretas: Masonería, política y sociedad en México* (Puebla: BUAP, 2009), Secret Inheritance: Freemasonry, Politics and Society in Mexico), there is an obsession with maintaining that leading nineteenth century politicians in Latin America belonged to the ranks of the Freemasons and that it was thanks to this that they achieved victory in whichever revolution they spearheaded. Many of these statements are made without foundation or scientific proof. For this reason, many students of Freemasonry have dedicated part of their efforts to clarifying these statements and knocking down arguments

based on fiction and foundational stories with no provable historical underpinning—both typically promoted by Masonic members or their detractors[4]. In fact, at the *Fourth International Symposium on the History of Latin American and Caribbean Freemasonry and Associative Movements: Associative Practices and Modernity, 18th to 21st Centuries*, that took place in San José, Costa Rica in November 2015, there were a variety of round tables and presentations at which both the importance of verifying primary sources, and of proving the facts, before venturing to state (without evidence) that such or such a person was a Freemason were widely discussed. It was stated that the responsibility of these researchers, and for anybody studying the topic, was to be cautious when drawing conclusions without adequate documentation and/ or primary sources to back them up. On the other hand, hyperbolical stories that enhance and glorify their national heroes, presidents or politicians also feature in the historical narratives of every nation. Many of these stories are packed with fictitious details manipulated to give these foundational narratives more impact, and appropriate for developing and promoting these "imagined communities," as they have been termed by Benedict Anderson.[5] They are essential for creating national sentiment and promoting nationalism. According to him, there are many examples of marvelous stories about national heroes both in

---

4   See, José Antonio Ferrer Benimeli, *Bibliografía de la masonería: introducción histórico-crítica*. (Madrid: Fundación Universitaria Española, 1977).

5   Benedict Anderson, *Imagined Communities: Reflections on the Origin and Spread of Nationalism*, (New York, Verso, 1983)

national historical folklore, as well as in Masonic folklore around the world.

In relation to Porfirio Díaz,[6] one of the most notable stories—and of particular interest to historians of Freemasonry—is the story of his rescue in June 1876 by a Masonic brother at the Barra de Tampico, before he became president. In fact, many researchers in the field believed this to be a fictitious story, since they had found no primary sources to corroborate it. Such a story was deemed to be a fictional narrative, just another of the many myths, legends and fantastical stories surrounding the Freemasons.[7] However, in the archives for the La Parfaite Union Lodge, part of the archive of the California Grand Lodge in San Francisco, there is a manuscript in which part of the abovementioned story is described, based on the viewpoint of Alexander K. Coney, purser of the ship *City of Havana*, on which

Porfirio Díaz travelled.[8] There is also a manuscript document by Don Manuel Gutiérrez Zamora that is in the possession of the family of Professor Renato Gutiérrez Zamora in the port city of Tampico, Tamaulipas, Mexico.[9] Gutiérrez Zamora was an eye witness who worked as a mail agent on board the steamship *City of Havana*, and in this manuscript—with a chronicler's pen— he recounts, in the most detailed possible way, the story of the rescue of Porfirio Díaz. It should be mentioned that the narration of the events by Gutiérrez Zamora is distinctly more detailed than the document of the La Parfaite Union Lodge, and is told in the first person, whilst the San Francisco document is in the third person, which means that they are the words of the speaker of that lodge about what happened, based on the events experienced by Coney, but not in his own words.[10]

6   The case of Porfirio Díaz is not exceptional, since there are other cases, as I mentioned in my article, "Freemasonry and Folklore in Mexican Presidentialism." *Journal of American Culture* Vol, 20.2, (Summer 1997): 61-69. Please also see, Guillermo de los Reyes, *Herencias secretas: Masonería, política y sociedad en México*. México, D.F.: Benemérita Universidad Autónoma de Puebla, 2009.

7   There is a mutlitide of these stories, some of which are verified and others which are of dubious origin: soldiers giving the Masonic sign as they are about to be scalped by Red Indians, sailors asking for help by hoisting a blue banner with the compass and square. See, e.g. Brian J. Bennett, "The First Australian Aboriginal Mason" *Newsletter* (Investigation Lodge CC, Ireland, 1992), s. p.

8   The manuscript in question is entitled: "A Master Mason's Word of Honor and a Brother who Refused Fifty Thousand Dollars for it, Alexander K. Coney, Preceding Remarks by the Speaker." Grand Lodge of California, Archive 17, s/f. It is important to note that this is a speech apparently given at a meeting at the Parfaite Union Lodge.

9   Testimony of Manuel Gutiérrez Zamora, "El salvamento de Don Porfirio Díaz frente a la barra de Tampico," manuscrito propiedad de la familia Gutiérrez Zamora. I had the opportunity to speak with the family in order to locate the original document, which was held by the family of Professor Renato Gutiérrez Zamora. For the purposes of this article, I have used a transcript of the same, published in, *Historia mexicana* 5, no. 1 [17] (Jul. Sept., 1955): 62-85

10   In my book *Herencias secretas* (See Chapter 3) I thought that it had been told by Coney, but on checking the document again when I was in San Francisco in August of 2015, I realized that while it appears that Coney had signed it, it was in fact a quote in quotation marks of a request made by Coney, and which the speaker wished to withdraw.

On the other hand, the aim of the Gutiérrez Zamora manuscript is to present a faithful and detailed chronicle of what happened on board the steamship *City of Havana* in 1876, whilst the purpose of the San Francisco document is to pay tribute to Coney, a tribute in which his various heroic Masonic actions are depicted through a description of how he helped his Masonic brother Porfirio Díaz, of whom he also speaks with respect, expressing admiration for his courage.[11] Both manuscripts confirm that Díaz received certain advantages from his affiliation with the Freemasons, and that, certainly in the period before his presidency, and at the start of his term of office, Díaz had a close relationship with the Freemasons. Similarly, both documents stress the composure, decisiveness and revolutionary spirit of Porfirio Díaz. Gutiérrez Zamora's story relates the way in which the fugitive managed to enter Mexico after his brief exile in New Orleans, on board an American steam boat and with the help of a number of Masonic brothers.[12] There are marked differences between the stories in terms of how Coney realized that Díaz needed his help, as I will discuss later. Nevertheless, as regards the manner in which Díaz received help from his Masonic brothers (both Mexican and American), and how he benefited from his affiliation with the Freema-

sons, both stories have all the elements needed to reach these conclusions. Later in this essay, I will discuss in detail the story of Díaz's rescue, which both confirms the support he received from the Freemasons and illustrates one more episode of the history of Mexico, until now little mentioned, about the return of Díaz after his exile in New Orleans. I will likewise discuss the differences and similarities between the primary sources that bear witness to the event.

Two Versions, One Aim: The Saving of Porfirio Díaz by a Masonic Brother

In 1876, Porfirio Díaz found himself on the run from the government of Sebastián Lerdo de Tejada (1872-1876) who was not very happy about the rebellions led by the hero of Tuxtepec against the reelection of President Lerdo. In fact, the government had offered a fifty-thousand-dollar bounty to any person who could bring them the head of Díaz, alive or dead. Because of this, as mentioned above, Díaz decided to flee to the United States, where he lived for a period of time in New Orleans, a city with strong Masonic links to Mexico. During his time in exile, Díaz looked for ways to return to his country without being noticed, in order to rejoin his allies, the revolutionaries

---

11 It is important to note that the San Francisco document relates to another incident linked to Coney and Dr. Herrera, who was the personal physician of Coney's father-in-law General Labastida. It recounts the petition for the exhumation of the body of Dr Herrera, the removal of his heart, and its return to Masonic lodges in order to carry out a Masonic funeral. At the time of his death, this honor had not been carried out, according to Coney.

12 In the San Francisco manuscript, mention was only made of the help that Coney gave to Díaz, but in the Tampico document, Coney is accompanied in the venture by Gutiérrez Zamora and other Masons.

of Tuxtepec, and to pursue his fight against re-elections.[13] To this end, the future dictator approached other political exiles, as he did Masonic brothers in need of help. The answer was favorable towards Díaz, since it left him indebted to his Masonic brothers for their support, which enabled him to return to Mexico to continue the struggle. According to the Grand Lodge of California document, a Masonic brother (whose name is not cited) put Díaz in contact with Alexander K. Coney, a member of the La Parfaite Union no. 17[14] Lodge in San Francisco, and purser of the steamship *City of Havana*, which was set to sail from New Orleans to a number of ports in Mexico, including Tampico, Tuxpan and, as final destination, the port of Veracruz. On this topic, the document *A Master Mason's Word of Honor* stated:

> [Díaz] couldn't endure the isolation of being a fugitive in disguise, and being a Freemason, it was natural for him to seek the Fraternities' aid, as a duck would take to the water—so he asked, and he received. He sought, he found—He knocked, and the honor of Freemasonry opened unto him. Placing his trust in God and in a good brother from New

Orleans, who would give him any assistance needed, when requested. He had not long to wait, for his trusted Brother knew what to do. He was well acquainted with Alexander K. Coney, a Brother mason and purser on the steamship "City of Havana" plying between New York, New Orleans, Havana and Mexican ports; and also knowing the steamer would soon arrive in his city, he made the necessary arrangements with Díaz, to meet him at the ship's landing and when it arrived <u>they met agreeable to appointment</u> [emphasis in the original]. Díaz was introduced to Brother Coney, the signal Flag of Distress was raised, which none but the purser could understand and grant, and then too under the most trying and peculiar circumstances. It also might involve him in great danger personally, and almost in a certainty cost the Brother in need, and assistance his life. When these two brethren met, it seemed as though they verily stood on the Five points of Fellowship. They consulted, agreed, and both pledged to each other their sacred word of honor "A Master Mason's Word" in

---

13   Porfirio Díaz came out against Juárez first, and Lerdo de Tejada next, because of their intention to stand for re-election. The ironic thing is that once Díaz managed to get into government he paid no heed to the "effective suffrage, not re-election." See Elisa Speckman Guerra, "El Porfiriato," in *Nueva historia mínima de México* (México D. F.: El Colegio de México 2011).

14   This contact might have been the so-called Dr. Jonnes, who indeed was the travel companion of Díaz on the boat, in accordance with Gutiérrez Zamora's story. The La Parfaite Union Lodge was established in 1851 and had many members from Mexico, Latin America and elsewhere. Its rites were different from other Californian lodges and they frequently received visitors from places as exotic as Tahiti.

safety or distress[15].

In this version of the story, the interest in emphasizing the Masonic connection between the protagonists is clear. Coney promised to help him, giving him "his sacred word of honor," the word of a Master Freemason, that he would not cheat him, and would do the impossible to save him. In consequence, in order to prevent Díaz from being found out, Coney registered him under a fake name, Dr Rodríguez de la Boza, and hid him away in a secret cabin on board the steamship. The document of the Grand Lodge of California gives no specific details about places, people, secondary situations, but merely devoted itself to emphasizing key elements that showed the word of honor being fulfilled, along with some details such as the ones I mentioned above. In contrast, Gutiérrez Zamora does present many details, such as the false name received by Díaz (his travel companion), at the time in which they saved him, among many other things. In this respect, he noted in his chronicle: "The night before we set sail, two individuals came on board with travel tickets for the port of Tuxpam. One was young, and wore spectacles, and was called Dr Jonnes (sic). The other was the Cuban homeopathic doctor Dr Rodríguez de la Boza, according to Dr Jonnes. I must say that Rodríguez de la Boza never appeared in the lounge at mealtimes and outside of those times I didn't see him

around either."[16] Gutiérrez Zamora was very suspicious of these passengers, of the supposed Cuban doctor because he was never seen in public, and of Dr Jonnes because, "I don't know what motive this man might have to say he has never lived in the Republic of Mexico, since he speaks Spanish quite well, and, although he is very shy, he knows some Mexican idioms."[17]

Thanks to Gutiérrez Zamora's story, we have some important details at our disposal, such as the names of the two characters and certain key facts, such as the events in Tampico. On the third day, they reached Tampico, and *The City of Havana* anchored up alongside the "Independencia," a Mexican steam gunboat, and the national brigantine-schooner, "Constante," belonging to Captain Ramírez. Gutiérrez Zamora states that this was maybe the main reason why Porfirio Díaz wanted to get off the boat as soon as they arrived in Tampico:

A short time later the other barges came up close to the American steamship, and the following came on board: a Lieutenant Colonel Arroyo, short, stocky and pock-marked, an old man named Ruiz, who appeared kind, thin, olive-skinned and with an intelligent look, and several other subordinate officers ... But among them was a captain, tall, bald and of intelligent appearance, with decent manners, and who spoke

15 "A Master Mason's Word," 2.
16 "El salvamento," 62.
17 "El salvamento," 63.

with refinement and was very civil. ... Practically all the officers had come aboard, and some or all of the soldiers' wives and a great number of the soldiers themselves. ... Lunchtime came and I had the pleasure of meeting Colonel Arroyo. ... We began to talk about the country's politics and how likely it was that the Tuztepec Plan, amended in Palo Blanco, would succeed. Since the chief of these forces was surely a government man, I neither freely expressed my own opinions, nor came out in favor of the government, but instead I praised the organization of the army under Colonel General Ignacio Mejía, and allowed myself to be led by his opinion, in order not to start off a political tussle aboard the steamship *City of Havana* with the chief of the federal forces. [18]

At the time, Gutiérrez Zamora did not know of the presence of Díaz on board the boat. Alexander Coney and the so-called Dr Jonnes [sic] were the only ones who knew it. It was only after the meal and after socializing with the people on the boat that Gutiérrez Zamora recounted in detail the intention of Díaz to leave the boat so as to avoid being found out, and because they were close to Barra de Tampico.

I was heading towards my cabin on the port side ... when I heard something falling, and everyone ran to starboard to find out what was going on. ... Out of curiosity, I ran there as well. Imagine my surprise when I saw, swimming right there in the Gulf of Mexico, a man, who in all truth was doing it rather well. I approached Captain Philips, who was still in the same place, and said to him:

—What's happening, Captain?

—I don't know, I think it's that mad doctor having a swim; he came out of his cabin, went down the stairs leading to the WC, and, running naked, he climbed over the port side railing and dove head first into the water.

—Well, it's vital that we get him out again because he might get eaten by a shark ...

In those critical moments, as we lowered the dinghy, Dr Jonnes [sic] held my arm with a nervous strength, and said to me in English:

—For God's sake, Zamora, don't put the boat to water, because the man who is swimming away is General Díaz.

A bucket of cold water couldn't have had as much effect on me at that moment than those short but fast words from Jonnes. With the pole in my hands, I approached Philips and said to him:

—Captain, the man who is in the

---

water is General Díaz. We absolutely must save him.

With very English phlegm, he answered:

—It's the only way, because if we delay five more minutes the sharks will account for him.

The time it took for the boat to reach the swimmer was truly nervewracking, because as soon as he saw the craft approaching, he did his best to speed up. His intention, and this is how it looked, was to reach the bow of the brigantine Constante and to take shelter on it, or else, sheltered from view by it, to reach the coast out of sight of those watching from the steamship. [19]

According to Gutiérrez Zamora, Díaz's plan was to flee the ship in order not to be found out. However, as stated in his manuscript, it would have been very dangerous to swim the nearly three nautical miles to the shore on account of the fury of the sea at that time, as well as the tide. Furthermore, it seemed that Díaz had been sick and this had made him delirious. Once the little boat had got near to Díaz, who tried to avoid being pulled from the sea—since he thought that once they had caught him they would hand him over to the authorities—they managed to pull him into the boat and made sure that he would not throw himself back into

the sea. Gutiérrez Zamora mentioned that, as the boat came near, he wanted to cover him with a "blue coat that he had ready and had thrown in the boat to cover him up," but the coat fell into the water.

The eye witness telling the story commented that, as a last-ditch attempt, and "without asking permission, nor using any polite phrase, I grabbed a bed sheet and a bed cover at random and, as we returned to moor up at the ship, I said to Bovais [the second in command who had pulled Díaz from the water]: —"Cover him up really well, up to this head."[20] Bovais followed the instructions and when they reached the boat Díaz "mumbled a few incoherent words because he was wrapped up in the blanket, and couldn't be understood properly. ... The first words I said to him, as he climbed on board, were: "Keep quiet, they haven't recognized you ..." As you'd expect, everybody wanted to see what was going on. ... I said to them: "Sirs, only the doctors may come this way, and I beseech those that are not doctors to withdraw because this man is quite ill.[21] At that moment, Gutiérrez Zamora joins the group of Freemasons who were helping Porfirio Díaz and does everything in his power to avoid him being recognized. Along with Alexander Coney, they start to make plans to get Díaz off the boat at one of the next few stops. Immediately after having rescued him, Dr Jonnes tells Gutiérrez Zamora that Díaz wants to speak to him, as un-

---

19 "El salvamento," 67
20 "El salvamento," 68.
21 "El salvamento," 69.

derlined by the narrator of the story:

> When I entered the cabin ... he was in his bunk, very pale, and still shivering. I own that for my part I was very afraid, but not for myself. What would the government of Mr. Lerdo do to me if they could prove that I was mixed up in this business? Strip me of my entirely subordinate job and fate as a mail agent, as happened later when they took it away by telegram, giving it to a Mr. Jurado ... very good friends with General Marcos Carrillo, military commander of the Veracruz military compound. ... If I was afraid at those times, it was for the person of the leader of the revolution, because if they had caught him, and maybe shot him, the Tuxtepec Plan would have been dashed for sure. ... My mother, my brother Ignacio and all my family were involved in the revolution. ... In the end, all that effort would be in vain if General Díaz died. And this was my great fear: for a disaster to happen at a solemn moment."[22]

The writing of Gutiérrez Zamora demonstrates his respect and sympathy for Díaz, as well as his eagerness to help him. There is no doubt that the narrator of the story wants Díaz to pursue his struggle for the Mexican people, and, as mentioned in the story, that he would personally have helped him to avoid revealing his identity, or would have planned another way to help him escape, such as the one previously proposed via Colonel Torres. As an alternative, he promised Díaz "that he would speak to the purser Coney—who was a very good friend of mine—as a Masonic brother and that this would stand him in good stead."[23] At this point a potential discrepancy occurs, since, according to Gutiérrez Zamora, Coney didn't know that Díaz was on board. However, in the San Francisco document, the opposite was the case. They were, in fact, recorded as knowing each other. My theory is that Coney, having given his word of honor to Porfirio Díaz to keep the secret, was not going to reveal it until he was safe. Independently of whether or not my theory is proven, what I wish to emphasize, for the purpose of this paper, is how the Masonic brotherhood was used and how this was a key factor in the event which saved Díaz from the forces of Lerdo and other enemies. It should be mentioned that Gutiérrez Zamora gives a lot of credit to Coney, noting that "from that moment on, Doctor Alexander K. Coney took the lead and worked hard, extremely hard, to try to save General Porfirio Díaz."[24] Gutiérrez Zamora recounts that there was an occasion when Coney told Díaz that they could transfer to an American warship that was passing close by and that he had taken steps to help him, but Díaz flatly refused, saying "I do not wish to owe the United States anything

22 "El salvamento," 69-70.

23 "El salvamento," 71.

24 "El salvamento," 72.

at all. But to particular friends, from this country or another, that is another thing." [25]

As the *City of Havana* set sail from Veracruz, it made a stop in the night to unload. Coney and Gutiérrez Zamora decided that this was a suitable opportunity for Díaz to leave the boat, particularly because there was a rumor about, and it was thought that they already knew that Díaz was on the boat. Several people joined in the venture to save Díaz, including General Juan de la L. Enriquez, Joaquín Alpuchem Manuel Caldelas, Abraham Aguirre and Joaquín Cruz, among others. They dressed Díaz in the clothes commonly worn by boatmen in Veracruz port, and transferred him to the Alpuche launch.

After loading, the launch cast off from the steamship and set course for Veracruz Port. ... Don Juan Enríquez observed, through binoculars, every movement coming from the house of Don Manuel Levi, facing the port. He looked like a general afraid of losing a battle. ... When they were a certain distance from the fort, they used the launch dinghy to bring General Díaz to shore. Upon setting foot on dry land, he threw wide his arms and legs and exclaimed lustily: "Thank God that I have been lucky." He

walked a few steps, in conversation with Mr. Marañon, and reached the spot where the guide with the horses stood. Marañon gave him some money, a pistol, some ammunition, and took his leave. General Díaz mounted his horse and set off on the road to Boca del Río. A letter sent on to him from Santa María reached him in La Matosa, the place where the defenders of the Tuxtepec Plan met up. [26]

This is how the escape of Porfirio Díaz was successful. Months later Díaz became President of Mexico and returned the favors to all those who helped him in this venture. [27]

The Brotherly Reward

When Díaz came to power, he issued an invitation to his Masonic brother Alexander Coney to come to the National Palace. The latter was pleased to accept, and journeyed to the City of Mexico, where he was escorted to the National Palace to be reunited with Díaz. The San Francisco document is the only one that describes this visit. As soon as he arrived, Coney "was ushered through the lines of the officers with drawn swords at "<u>present swords</u>" [emphasis in the original] and then for the first time met

---

25 "El salvamento," 76.

26 "El salvamento," 84-85.

27 Archive 17: Grand Lodge of California, San Francisco. "A Master Mason's Word of Honor and a Brother who Refused Fifty Thousand Dollars for it, Alexander K. Coney, Preceding Remarks by the Speaker." Please also see the description by William R. Denslow on this incident in *10,000 Famous Freemasons*, 313.

(after what had previously transpired) Díaz as President of Mexico and Alexander K. Coney, Purser on the "<u>City of Havana</u>" [emphasis in the original].[28] After the appropriate greetings, Díaz announced "I have here the man who saved my life, making it possible for me to become President of our beloved country." [29]

As a gesture of thanks, Díaz gave Coney a check for fifty thousand dollars, the same amount as the bounty on his head. Coney was very grateful for this gesture, and returned the check very respectfully, saying that he had sworn to help him "as the word of honor of a Brother Master Freemason," and for this reason could not accept the money. President Díaz understood that, in this case, offering money was not appropriate, and offered him instead the post of General Consul for Mexico in Paris, France. Coney was pleased with such a gesture of gratitude and accepted. Later, Coney was naturalized as Mexican and became Mexican Consul in Paris, and later, Mexican Consul in San Francis-

co." [30] It should also be noted that Coney benefited from the brotherhood of the Freemasons, which is a crucial element of fraternity in Masonic ranks and is discussed in *Herencias Secretas* in the section entitled "Freemasonry as a school of government." [31]

The prior history in his two presentations shows that Masonic affiliation helped Porfirio Díaz to enter Mexico without being captured by his enemies. Given what is described in the two documents, this was not an easy undertaking, but it achieved its main aim and none of those involved had any negative repercussions, especially thanks in particular to the fact that Díaz managed to get into power. Similarly, it proves that the principles of Masonic brotherhood (despite what may happen due to political rivalry) can have an influence on individuals, which in some cases extends into the political sphere. Maybe this event contributed to Díaz supporting the Freemasons, and, in spite of his personal interests, he neither alienated nor destroyed it. On the

---

28 Denslow, *Famous Freemasons*, 5.

29 Denslow, *Famous Freemasons*, 5.

30 As I said above, before finding it in the archives of the Grand Lodge of California in San Francisco, I did not know whether or not this was just another of many legends about the Masonry. A variation of this story is also referenced in the Meyer and Sherman book: "There is someone among us whom we hope will soon occupy the Oriental Chair of that Lodge—the protector and saviour of a Great Masonic Brother who was a fugitive with a price of 50 thousand dollars on his head. He who was once a fugitive, pursued and hunted to the very brink of death, is now at the head of all the genuine Masonry of this country and was set free thanks to his aid—our most well-loved and illustrious brother PORFIRIO DÍAZ, 33°, Great Master Mason and President of the Mexican Republic. The brother who protected him in his time of greatest desperation is the illustrious brother ALEXANDER K. CONEY, 32°, Prince of the Royal Secret of La Parfaite Union Lodge, No. 17, and General Consul of Mexico in San Francisco... *"Haut le Calice! À la hauteur du front. Vive la Loge La Parfaite Union! À moi pour la batterie! Acclamation!"* Michael Meyer and William Sherman, *The Course of Mexican History* (New York: Oxford University Press, 1987), 140.

31 De los Reyes, *Herencias*, capítulo IV.

other hand, it may be noted that, even though the two versions are presented with different registers, styles and languages, they have a common denominator: the brotherhood of Masons. In fact, the San Francisco document had a clear and slightly hyperbolic aim of showing that Masonic values gave him the strength and fortitude to escape and become President of Mexico, maintaining that "[Díaz] was not yet where he could call his life his own, but Masonry had taught him that 'Time, Patience, and Perseverance would accomplish all things.'"[32] Furthermore, in the same manuscript, Porfirio Díaz was presented as an "illustrious Mason." The audience for this message were the members of the La Parfaite Union Lodge and maybe other lodges and grand lodges that had received such a communication, but it was not destined for the general public. The purpose of Manuel Gutiérrez Zamora's manuscript was to be a chronicle, to leave behind for posteriority a written account of one of the key episodes in the life of Porfirio Díaz, because if he had not helped him to escape, then maybe his fate would have been quite other. Gutiérrez Zamora wishes to leave nothing out and to speak only the truth about what happened. Despite this, he does not stray from the Masonic theme, identifying, as he does, Díaz, Coney, Phillips—the captain of the ship—and himself as Brother Masons.[33] He recalls various conversations between himself and Captain Phillips, writing that "He asked if Coney was a Mason. I answered

that he was, that very few months before I had been at his lodge, when he was awarded the third degree." Another time, when talking to Captain Phillips about Porfirio Díaz, he records himself as saying: "Maybe they will speak to you about this. You are my friend and know my opinions. Furthermore, you know that he is a brother in danger." Very seriously and drily Phillips answered me: 'I know my duties as a brother, and please allow me to say that I don't wish anybody to teach them to me.'"[34] Clearly, there was a group of key people that belonged to the Freemasons. There is no room for doubt, given the way these stories are presented, that it was thanks to Masonic links and these brotherly support networks that he managed to save himself and, in that same year, 1876, would become President of Mexico, exercising power for more than thirty years.

The Compass and Set Square in the Hands of the Dictator

In the previous section, I outlined an event in which Díaz received help from his Masonic brothers, to the extent that many of them risked their lives to keep their Freemasons' word of honor. However, what was the involvement of Porfirio Díaz within the Masons before he ascended to the presidential throne? Before coming to power, Díaz received a great deal of support from the Masons in his role as member of Fraternal Lodge no. 1, as is proven

32 "A Master Mason ... ," 4.

33 "El salvamento," 71.

34 "El salvamento," 73-74.

in a letter sent by Ignacio Pombo to Porfirio Díaz on February 12, 1869, in which he stated:

> The columns of this [illegible ...] ∴ Fraternal Lodge ∴ No 1, were raised that since the month of November 186[illegible ...] ∴ V ∴ had been fallen due to the political events that had taken over the country (as I wrote), recording that for your great [illegible] ∴ you are a [illegible] Member ∴ of this [illegible] Lodge.[35]

This last statement is evidenced by Porfirio Díaz himself in a letter sent on March 27, 1869 to Ignacio Pombo, in which he responds to him personally: [36]

> Very Y∴ and ven ∴ H∴
>
> I have the honor of acknowledging receipt of your [illegible ...] ∴ dated February 12 1869 [...] with the cordial gratitude for the medal included with which you honor me.
>
> By this [illegible ...] ∴ I receive with satisfaction the information that on August 22 1868 ∴ V ∴ the columns were raised of this Resp ∴ Fraternal Lodge No 1 of which I have the honor of being

an active member.

> Please receive I ∴ H ∴ and the [...] of peace and fraternal greetings O ∴ S∴ C ∴ L ∴ S ∴ Y ∴ B ∴ O ∴S ∴ C ∴[37]

This is only one example of the active participation of Porfirio Díaz within the Mexican Masonic ranks. He was always mindful, as I maintain in this paper, of the importance of having them as allies in order to achieve his political aims. It may also be ventured that maybe the Masonic lodges were, for Díaz, the place where he prepared politically, which he combined with the military training he had gained on the battle field. As a member of the Masonic Brotherhood, he received substantial privileges, since he was admired as a famous general who was victorious in various battles. He was called the *hero of April 2*. His stature only grew later, when he took on the role of President of the Republic. It is relevant to mention that it is a great Masonic tradition (although it is neither mentioned in their statutes, nor their books) to invite to their ranks illustrious men who might enhance the profile of the brotherhood. In consequence, Porfirio Díaz never let the place the Masons gave him to go to waste, and at times he used them for his own benefits. The Freemasons

---

35 Porfirio Díaz, *Archivo del general Porfirio Díaz, memorias y documentos; prólogo y notas de Alberto María Carreño*. VII, (México D. F.: Editorial "Elede," 1947), 218.

36 Díaz, *Archivo del general Porfirio Díaz,* 219.

37 It is important to mention that in the above-mentioned letter sent by Y Pombo to Díaz, he informs Díaz that he would be awarded a medal as a sign of membership of the Great Fraternal Lodge No. 1 of Veracruz. *Archivo Porfirio Díaz*, Alberto Ma. Carreño, Tomo VII, 218-219. *Archivo Porfirio Díaz*, Alberto Ma. Carreño, Tomo VII, 218-219.

were seen by Díaz as one of the means through which he could reach the presidency. He also hoped to recruit many followers from within these societies. This was evidenced by a letter written to Porfirio Díaz by Luis Pombo on August 13, 1870:

> My dear Sir and good friend:
>
> The precipitousness of my departure for the capital precluded my coming by and taking my leave of you as I wished to. But I asked my brother to present my compliments to you, and to transmit to you the reason why I had not come to bid you goodbye.
>
> Thanks to your good intentions in establishing in this city a National Mexican Rite, after I arrived I proposed to the G. L. that they permit you to set up a workshop, and my proposal was unanimously accepted. Today they have sent me the letter of authorization, which I am not sending to you in the original, since that is in Bristol, and it would deteriorate too much in any case. However, I can, meanwhile, send you an authorized copy of the letter, with which it will be possible to undertake the works of the liturgies of the first, second and third degrees, which are the ones that are covered at present.
>
> Soon I will send permits and other things that are missing.
>
> Before I finish this letter, I will congratulate you because you have been lucky to establish the Freemasons in our state, and open up the doors of light with the torch of reason, as more than once you have brought freedom with your sword from tyranny and foreign yoke.
>
> Luis Pombo. Please see in what way I may be useful to you
>
> Your attentive friend and I affirm that [illegible B.S.M. ...]
>
> Luis Pombo[38]

The exchange between Díaz and Luis Pombo reaffirms the relationship that Díaz had at that time with the Masons. There is clear interest from his brother Masons in involving the Freemasons with a leading war hero and future leader. On the other hand, Díaz gave them a place in his political agenda, in order to keep them on his side, and he achieved greater fame, popularity and support from the Freemasons who helped him to recruit followers from within Masonic ranks. It should be borne in mind that at this time Díaz had the Juaristas and the Lerdistas against him. It has not been proven that Díaz introduced Freemasonry into any state. What Pombo is alluding to is that Porfirio Díaz contributed to the creation of several lodges. On the other hand, his eyes were firmly fixed on the future and he saw some members of the Freemasons as ideal people to work with him

---

38   *Archivo del General Porfirio Díaz*, Book IX, 9-10.

on his presidential reelection. Similarly, he was conscious of the fact that leaders were nurtured and prepared within Masonic ranks. These leaders had to be identified in order to invite them to take part in his government. Díaz had to keep them close to him and be able to control them. Luis Zalce y Rodríguez comments that "It was later said that amid such fraternizing tendencies and productive activity could be divined the hand of the illustrious Brother General Porfirio Díaz, President of the Republic, and personal friend of the Pombo family."[39]

Porfirio Díaz in Power: "Order and Progress" in the Masonic Ranks

At the time in which Porfirio Díaz came to power in 1876, beating other rival camps, his aim was to bring peace to the country, and thence be able to achieve economic progress and ease of governance for Mexico. Months after getting into power, Díaz declared: "I have here the noble and huge task that belongs to you all: to re-establish the supreme authority of the Constitution, to re-assert peace, and to use your influence to protect all legitimate interests in developing the natural resources of the country."[40] In these short lines, Díaz summarized his strategy, his so-called *pax porfiriana*, the policy of conciliation that he promoted

to establish himself in power and that some time later would transform him into a dictator.

During the period in which Porfirio Díaz was in power, he worked towards the unification of all the Masonic lodges of the Scottish Rite. The main reason Díaz promoted this unification was to bring about his plan of national unification of various sectors and institutions. However, what strategies did he use? What influence did this have on his *pax porfiriana*? In this section, I argue that, despite having become a dictator, Díaz did not entirely break away from the liberal principles that had been imposed by Benito Juárez and Mechor Ocampo, amongst others, and which the Freemasons fiercely defended. What he did was adapt these principles for his own benefit and convenience in order to gain total control of the country and to bring it peace. For this reason, his conciliation policy was extremely successful, and the Masons could not escape it. Nor, of course, could they evade his control.

Díaz knew that one important strategy was to gain control over the Masons, especially those belonging to the Scottish Rite. In the time of Juárez, some Masonic lodges and their members had had considerable influence in political decision-making. Díaz viewed such influence warily and for this reason decided to create a policy of con-

---

39   Luis Zalce Rodríguez, *Apuntes para la historia de la masoneria en México: de mis lecturas y mis recuerdos* (México D. F.: Talleres Tipográficos de la Penitenciaría del Distrito Federal, 1950), 322.

40   François-Xavier **Guerra**, *México: del antiguo régimen a la revolución. Tomo I.* (México D. F.: Fondo de Cultura Económica, 1991), 214.

ciliation that would strive, at all cost, to avoid any such tendencies, which could have had a potentially destabilizing effect on his government. For this reason, Díaz always kept a close eye to ensure that neither the Freemasons, not any other institution (such as the Catholic Church) could gain political ground without his permission or supervision. For this reason, Díaz's strategy was to keep them all under his control, be it directly or indirectly.

The Porfirian strategy towards the Freemasons can be clearly seen in correspondence sent to international lodges, especially to Masonic lodges in Washington, DC and in Paris, France. In these communications, a formal and cordial relationship can be detected between Díaz and his Masonic brothers abroad in achieving certain recognition for the lodges of Mexico. It was important to Díaz not only to contribute indirectly to the Mexican Masonic lodges, but also to demonstrate that in Mexico there was a conciliation policy in place, as well as order and progress. Even though Díaz was not very active within the Freemasons once he was in power, he did indeed use his affiliation as a strategy at the begin-

ning of his government.[41]

Among the aims of the personality politics[42] developed by Díaz from 1876 to 1911 was to achieve total control over all institutions. For his policy of conciliation, also known as "pan o palo" (bread or stick) it was vital to identify all groups and individuals that might potentially turn against the government, or represent a political counterweight. General Díaz understood this right from the start of his government, when he had to seek out economic resources in order to rout his two rivals, Lerdo and Iglesias, reasserting himself in power and retaining possession of the capital.[43]

There are various factors that enabled Porfirio Díaz to gain control of the Masonic lodges belonging to the Scottish Rite. The fact that Díaz was not directly involved in Masonic activities (unlike Juárez, in Díaz's case it was the Masons who sought him out to join them, and they who asked him to participate in the Masonic ranks) granted him a major advantage, since there would be, consequently, no close links, nor the need (on Díaz's part) to feel any regret at not fulfilling his Masonic obli-

---

41   Correspondence with the Grand Orient of France 1876-1900. Emilio G. Cantón, Secretary General. Archive of the Grand Orient of France in Paris.

42   Roderic Ai Camp suggests that consideration should also be given to the cult of his own personality and leadership promoted by Díaz. Camp also speaks of the tradition of personality politics use by Mexican leaders from Porfirio Díaz to Lázaro Cárdenas. The latter was the one who instutional-ized the Presidency of Mexico; which is to say that it does not matter who is president, what is important is the title, and therefore the head of the executive is automatically the most important political authority in the country. In the case of Porfirio Díaz, and the cult of the personality that he developed, it was not important whether he was president or not (as was the case from 1880 to 1884 when Manuel González Aldama was president), he always retained power. See Roderic Ai Camp, *Intelectuales y política en México* (Oxford: Oxford University Press, 1996), 32-40.

43   See Antonio Lara Téllez, "Compadrazgo Político en el Porfiriato" (Undergraduate Thesis in International Relations, Universidad de las Américas-Puebla, 1998).

gations. If one observed the illustrious Masonic titles and degrees conferred on Díaz as Grand Master and Deputy Grand Master (it should be mentioned also that in later documents he appears as Honorary Grand Master), one might conclude that he was very involved in the organization. Nevertheless, Díaz's correspondence with lodges in France and in Washington shows that it was mainly the Masonic brothers who wanted him to participate, his involvement being to the benefit and prestige of the Freemasons.

As Zalce y Rodríguez states, and as the abovementioned letters attest, Díaz was involved both in the National Mexican Rite and in the Scottish Rite. [44] Historian of the Freemasons Luis Zalce y Rodríguez states that Díaz was initiated into the National Mexican Rite and later transferred to the Scottish Rite. His status as member on paper helped him to gain control over the lodges, even as they sought his approval and good will. On this point the Mexican historian Luis González y González states:

> Díaz's strong personality also contributed to the fact that the Scottish Masons in some way accepted the leadership of General Díaz ... the achievements and triumphs achieved by Díaz since 1855 (when he became political leader of Ixtlán) bore witness to the fact that he was a tireless

man, self-possessed, adept at the use of the stick and the bread, self-sufficient, cold, diplomatic, globe-trotting and far-sighted. It is for these features that Díaz was cited as the leader of the "machete" generation, to which he and the group who gathered around him belonged. [45]

González y González refers to the personality of Díaz and to his clear and firm political strategies, both of which brought him political success and gave him control over all institutions, among which were to be found the Freemasons. Likewise, another factor that had an influence on Díaz's success with the "Scottish" Rite was that, from the beginning, and despite their differences, he understood the popularity and reputation of Juárez. In light of this, he always gave him a particular place of importance, using him as a symbol and at the same time aspiring to his reputation, and appeared to want to continue the great work of the so-called "Benemerito de las Americas." [46] Since Juárez had been a leading Mason, and was viewed by the Masons as a leading liberal, this meant that it was important that people believed he would follow his path. Díaz also felt it was important to include some members of the Scottish Rite in his cabinet so that he could control them more closely, enabling him to exercise an in-

---

44   Zalce Rodríguez, *Apuntes para la historia de la masoneria en México*, 295.

45   See Luis González y González, *La ronda de las generaciones* (México D.F.: Clío, 1997), 37.

46   Perry Laurens B. *Juárez y Díaz: Continuidad y ruptura en la política mexicana* (México D. F.: Era, 1996), 293.

stitutionalized hold over them.[47]

One significant element was the policy of conciliation with the Catholic Church which Díaz developed during his government. Such a policy did not fit in with what Juárez had achieved, but Díaz was wary at the beginning and later was far more inflexible, for which he was openly attacked by members of the Freemasons. This was a political strategy designed to prevent any group from gaining absolute power. Jean Pierre Bastian comments the "This rise of the Catholics brought about increasing polarization of subsections of the population, in which there were radical minorities, Protestants, Masons and spiritualists."[48] However, Díaz was conscious that the Masons could claw back the power and influence they had had at one time within Mexican politics, and in order to avoid this happening, he agreed to centralize the Freemasons under his control, contributing to the creation of a Masonic institution named "The Grand Diet of Symbolical Masonry."

The near-indiscriminate establishment of rites, and the dissidence and independence of some lodges led to the creation of the Grand Diet of the Symbolical Scottish Rite in 1890. Towards the end of 1889, the Masonic newsletter (an official organ of the Symbolical Grand Diet) stated that the Grand Orient of Mexico, wishing to unite all the Masonic elements of the Republic, would celebrate treaties with the Supreme Council of the 33rd Degree at his Grand Lodge of the Valley of Mexico No. 1, and that, in virtue of these, the Grand Orient was disbanded, and the Grand Diet of the Symbolical Masonry of the United States of Mexico would be founded, for the exclusive use of the degrees of Apprentice, Journeyman and Master Mason. On February 15, 1890, it was solemnly established and the Venerable Brother Porfirio Díaz, President of the Republic of Mexico, was elected as Grand Master.[49] It should be clarified, as previously mentioned, that despite being named Grand Master, he was not an active Mason, and that, more than anything, his role was honorific, and later honorary. This relationship of convenience was very important, on the one hand giving Díaz control over the Masons, and the support of its members, and on the other hand benefiting the Masons, who favored and appreciated the acknowledgement that Díaz granted them, since their mere closeness with him opened doors and gave them a certain prestige.[50]

---

47 "Once he came to power, he (Díaz), adopted a conciliation policy, freeing himself of men such as Tagle and Benítez, and making space for former Lerdistas such as Manuel Romero Rubio y Felipe Berriozábal." *Juárez y Díaz: Continuidad y ruptura en la política mexicana*, 273.

48 Jean Pierre Bastian, *Protestantes, liberales y francmasones. Sociedades de ideas y modernidad en América Latina, siglo XIX* (México D. F.: FCE, 1990), 148.

49 Félix Navarrete, *La masonería en la historia y en las leyes de Méjico* (México D. F.: Editorial Jus, 1962), 120.

50 For a more in-depth discussion on the Grand Diet of Symbolical Masonry, see, Paul Rich y Guillermo de los Reyes, "Policy Making and the Control of the Nongovernmental Sector: Porfirio Díaz and the Grand Diet," *Review of Policy Research* 22, no. 5 (2005): 721-725.

Conclusion

Díaz involved himself with the Freemasons as a way of gaining support for his *pax porfiriana*. The dictator was conscious of the importance that the Masons gave to the fraternal links and mutual support. On the other hand, given the tensions between the Freemasons and the Catholic Church, and with the aim of avoiding a resurgence of conflict, he managed to convince the Masons that by being part of the Freemasons he would ensure the secular interests of the state. It should also be mentioned that Díaz's policy was successful, since there was neither crisis nor major tensions between the Freemasons and the Church, as had happened decades earlier, or as would happen again during the 1920s. Díaz was a pragmatist who gave opportunities to every group, but always kept control.

The Freemasons, as discussed previously, were one of the institutions used by General Díaz to extend his power, and thereby keep all sectors of society under control. A detailed observation of what was happening among the Masonic ranks reveals that Díaz's plan to unify the Masons had two political advantages. Díaz, as Zalce y Rodríguez points out, "presented a liberal appearance. . . in order to 'get to know' better those who claimed to be 'his new friends' and to observe those who were unhappy more closely, he gathered them in places in which the least prudent would reveal their most intimate feelings, and let off steam in a safe way."[51]

The relationship that developed between the Freemasons and Porfirio Díaz was a positive one. The saving of his life by his Masonic brothers aboard the steamship *City of Havana* was a pivotal moment in Díaz's political life, since, thanks to the brotherhood and solidarity of his Masonic brothers, Díaz was able to pursue his political ambitions. This dynamic became crystallized in the strategy that he later used to further his *pax porfiriana*. Evidence suggests that the Masons were used as tools for most of his rule. As he became a dictator, Díaz grew less convinced of the loyalty of his Masonic brothers, despite the positive experience he had had when he was saved at Tampico and Veracruz. The Masons were essentially recruited by Díaz as part of his powerbase in order to keep them close, and avoid any kind of dissention. The Freemasons would provide the assurance that Díaz was a liberal (even though he was not), despite the fact that to many he seemed pragmatic and conservative. In any event, Díaz did not see the Masonry as a weapon against Catholicism as his predecessors had done. It was important to Díaz that the Freemasons were his allies in bringing about a peaceful, ordered and progressive government, in which he played the part of lead architect of the Republic of Mexico.

---

51   Zalce Rodríguez, *Apuntes para la historia de la masoneria en México*, 321.

Primary Sources

"A Master Mason's Word of Honor and a Brother who Refused Fifty Thousand Dollars for it, Alexander K. Coney, Preceding Remarks by the Speaker." Grand Lodge of California, Archive 17, s/f.

Correspondence with the Grand Orient of France 1876 to 1900. Emilio G. Cantón, Secretary General. Archive of Grand Orient of France in Paris.

Díaz, Porfirio. *Archivo del general Porfirio Díaz, memorias y documentos. Prologue and Notes by Alberto María Carreño.* Mexico D.F.: Editorial "Elede," 1947.

"El salvamento de Don Porfirio Díaz frente a la barra de Tampico," Testimony of Manuel Gutiérrez Zamora, property of the Gutiérrez Zamora family. See: Manuel Gutiérrez Zamora, *Historia mexicana* 5, no. 1 [17] (jul. sept., 1955): 62-85.

Bibliography

Anderson, Benedict. *Imagined Communities: Reflections on the Origin and Spread of Nationalism.* New York: Verso, 1983.

Aubert, Roger. *The Church in the Industrial Age.* Londres: Burns & Oates, 1981.

Bastian, Jean Pierre. *Protestantes, liberales y francmasones. Sociedades de ideas y modernidad en América Latina, siglo XIX.* México D. F.: FCE, 1990.

Bennett, Brian J. "The First Australian Aboriginal Mason." *Newsletter.* Investigation Lodge CC, Ireland, 1992, s. p.

Coil, Henry Wilson. *Coil's Masonic Encyclopedia.* Edited by William Moseley Brown. Richmond, VA: Macoy Publishing & Masonic Supply Company, Macoy Publishing & Masonic Supply Company, 1961.

Camp, Roderic A. *Los intelectuales y el estado en el México del siglo XX.* Oxford: Oxford University Press, 1996.

De los Reyes, Guillermo. "Freemasonry and Folklore in Mexican Presidentialism." *Journal of American Culture* 20, no. 2 (1997): 61-69.

De los Reyes, Guillermo. *Herencias secretas: Masonería, política y sociedad en México.* México D.F.: Benemérita Universidad Autónoma de Puebla, 2009.

Denslow, William R. *10,000 famous Freemasons.* Richmond, VA: Macoy Pub. and Masonic Supply, 1957.

Díaz, Porfirio. *Archivo del general Porfirio Díaz, memorias y documentos. Prologue and Notes by Alberto María Carreño.* Mexico D. F.: Editorial Elede, 1947.

Ferrer Benimeli, José Antonio. *Bibliografía de la masonería: introducción histórico-crítica.* Madrid: Fundación Universitaria Española, 1977.

Flores Zavala, Marco Antonio. "Los

ciclos de la masonería Mexicana." En *La Masonería en Madrid y en España del siglo XVIII al XXI*. Coordinated by José Antonio Ferrer Benimeli. Zaragoza: CEHME, 2004.

González y González, Luis. *La ronda de las generaciones*. México D. F.: Clío, 1997.

Guerra, François-Xavier. *México: del antiguo régimen a la revolución. Tomo I*. México D. F.: Fondo de Cultura Económica, 1991.

Gutiérrez Zamora, Manuel. "El salvamento de Don Porfirio Díaz frente a la barra de Tampico." *Historia mexicana* 15, no. 17 (1955): 62-85.

Lara Téllez, Antonio. "Compadrazgo político en el porfiriato." Undergraduate Thesis in International Relations, Universidad de las Américas-Puebla, 1998.

López, Herculano. *Cartas Pastorales*. Morelia: Imp. de San Ignacio, 1887.

Meyer, Michael y Sherman William. *The Course of Mexican History*. New York: Oxford University Press, 1987.

Knight, Alan. *The Mexican Revolution: Porfirians, Liberals, and Peasants*. Lincoln: University of Nebraska Press, 1986 [1990].

Navarrete, Félix. *La masonería en la historia y en las leyes de Méjico*. México D. F.: Editorial Jus, 1962.

Perry, Laurens B. *Juárez y Díaz: continuidad y ruptura en la política mexicana*. México D. F.: Era, 1996.

Rich, Paul y Guillermo de los Reyes. "Policy Making and the Control of the Nongovernmental Sector: Porfirio Díaz and the Grand Diet." *Review of Policy Research* 22, no. 5 (2005): 721-725.

Smart, Ninian. "Lands of Hope and Glory." *The Times Higher Education Supplement*. February 2, 1990.

Speckman Guerra, Elisa. "El Porfiriato." En *Nueva historia mínima de México*. México D. F.: El Colegio de México, 2011.

Zalce y Rodríguez, Luis J. *Apuntes para la historia de la masonería en México (de mis lecturas y mis recuerdos)*. Mexico D. F.: [Talleres Tipográficos de la Penitenciaría del Distrito Federal], 1950.

www.ingramcontent.com/pod-product-compliance
Lightning Source LLC
Chambersburg PA
CBHW081357270326
41930CB00015B/3328